A SECOND
BROWSER'S DICTIONARY

Other Books by John Ciardi

A Browser's Dictionary

You Read to Me, I'll Read to You

The Man Who Sang the Sillies

A SECOND

Browser's Dictionary AND

NATIVE'S GUIDE TO THE UNKNOWN

AMERICAN LANGUAGE

JOHN CIARDI

HARPER & ROW, PUBLISHERS, New York
Cambridge, Philadelphia, San Francisco, London
Mexico City, São Paulo, Sydney
1817

FIRST EDITION

Designer: Sidney Feinberg

Library of Congress Cataloging in Publication Data

Ciardi, John, 1916–
    A second browser's dictionary, and native's guide to
the unknown American language.

    1. English language—Etymology—Popular works.
2. English language—Terms and phrases. I. Title.
PE1574.C56 1983   422'.03   82–48658
ISBN 0–06–015125–0

83 84 85 86 87 10 9 8 7 6 5 4 3 2 1

For Constance Erskine,
  our beloved Aunt Connie,
    in whom our native tongue is safe.
      For the valor of her smiling.
        With love from all her Ciardi family.

SIGNS AND ABBREVIATIONS USED
IN THIS DICTIONARY

Signs used in this book

?   In doubt.

*   When placed before a root word, indicates that it cannot be traced beyond the form given.

=   Equals.

<   From.

→   To, yields, yield, leads to, lead to.

'   Indicates a vowel in an unattested form. Thus the stem *forfi-* may be more securely rendered as *f'rf'-* indicating "unspecified vowel."

/   Indicates a consonant shift, as g/h signifies "shift from g to *h.*" Similarly, p/f, b/v, d/t, th/t, etc.

Roman numerals indicate centuries. "XVII" should be read "the seventeenth century." To avoid confusion, the first through the fifth centuries and the tenth are written out. All dates are A.D. unless otherwise noted.

General abbreviations

approx.	Approximately.
colloq.	Colloquially. Colloquialism.
dial.	Dialect.
dict.	Dictionary.
dim.	Diminutive.
esp.	Especially.
etymol.	Etymology. Etymological.
exclam.	Exclamation. Exclamatory.

ext.	(Sense) extension (from one meaning of the word to another).
influ.	Influence. Influences. Influenced.
lit.	Literally.
myth.	Mythology.
neg.	Negative.
obs.	Obsolete.
part.	Participle
perh.	Perhaps.
plu.	Plural.
p.p.	Past participle.
prep.	Preposition.
prob.	Probably.
pron.	Pronounced.
redupl.	Reduplicated from (as *heebie-jeebies*).
ref.	Reference. Refers to.
sing.	Singular.
sthrn.	Southern American regional.
ult.	Ultimately. Ultimate.
usu.	Usually.
wstrn.	Western American regional.

Abbreviations of languages often cited

Am.	American English.
Brit.	British English.
Du.	Dutch.
Eng.	Modern English (since c. XVI).
Fr.	French.
Ger.	German.
Gk.	Greek.
Gmnc.	Common Germanic. Intermediate between Indo-European and the German, Scandinavian, and Dutch languages, as well as Scottish and English.
IE	Indo-European.
It.	Italian.
L.	Latin.
MD	Middle Dutch.
ME	Middle English.
MHG	Middle High German.
MLG	Middle Low German.
OD	Old Dutch.

OE	Old English.
OF	Old French.
OHG	Old High German.
OLG	Old Low German.
ON	Old Norse.
Port.	Portuguese.
Sc.	Scottish.
Sp.	Spanish.

Works frequently cited

AHD	*American Heritage Dictionary.*
Brewer	E. Cobham Brewer, *Dictionary of Phrase and Fable.*
EDD	*English Dialect Dictionary.*
Grose	Captain Francis Grose, *A Classical Dictionary of the Vulgar Tongue.*
Johnson	Samuel Johnson, *Dictionary of the English Language.*
MMM	Mitford M. Mathews, *A Dictionary of Americanisms on Historical Principles.*
NT	*New Testament.*
NWD	*New World Dictionary.*
ODEE	*Oxford Dictionary of English Etymology.* Edited by C. T. Onions (pronounced *On-ee-on*).
OED	*Oxford English Dictionary.*
OT	*Old Testament.*
P. *Origins*	Eric Partridge, *Origins, A Short Etymological Dictionary of Modern English.*
P. *Slang*	Eric Partridge, *A Dictionary of Slang and Unconventional English.*
Sc. *Dict.*	*Jamieson's Dictionary of the Scottish Language.*
Weekley	Ernest Weekley, *An Etymological Dictionary of Modern English.*

I owe a particular and grateful thanks to the original AHD, whose appendix on Indo-European Roots has enormously simplified the hunt. The most recent edition is a step backward.

FOREWORD

Some have claimed that we are damaged angels; others, that we are improved apes. If we began as angels, the damage is obvious. If we began as apes, or as cousins to the ape, the improvement is not readily visible from, let us say, the towers of a concentration camp. Angels or apes, we are the species that uses language, and that use is enough to set us apart from all other creatures. We behave as we do, largely because language makes such behavior possible, and because it suggests behavior to us. As we begin to know how language works, we begin to know something about how this species works.

No one knows how language started, or when. English is one of the Indo-European family of languages. For about two centuries now, brilliant scholars have studied this family of languages, and have been able to extract a body of word roots labeled Proto-Indo-European. That language was in use about eight thousand years ago, but its richness makes it clear that language itself was in much earlier use.

Whenever and however language came into use, it grew at a constantly accelerating pace. As soon as our ancestors had two words, it became possible to combine them into a third, to combine those three into more, and to combine that more into still more. I have seen the estimate that fifteen thousand words amount to a working vocabulary. It must have taken our earliest ancestors millennia to acquire fifteen thousand words. Today, if we count fad slang, new technical terms, and natural growth brought about by social changes, we generate something like fifteen thousand words at least every five or ten years.

But let a simple example serve. The Indo-European root *ni-*, variantly *ne-*, means "down," and with a standard suffix we still preserve that sense in *nether*. The root *sed-*, seat, to sit, similarly survives in *sedan* and *sedentary*.

(As a necessary note on language, beware of surface resemblances. *Sedition* and *sedulous* would appear to be based on this *sed-* root, but they are not. The first element of *sedition* is *se-*, self, and also a common reflexive pronoun. The second element is from Latin *ire*, to go; past participle *ito,* gone; and as a substantive *itio,* an act of going. *Se-itio* is, at root, "the act of going [apart] unto oneself." The first two vowels, however, are hard to pronounce one after the other, and so our language ancestors slipped in a *d* as phonetic slipstreaming, producing what looks like the root *sed-*. *Sedulous* has the same reflexive first element, the *d* being from Latin *dolo,* pain, and so once again what seems to be the root *sed-*, but isn't. *Se-dolo* means, at root, "to take pains unto oneself.")

So back to *ni-* and *sed-*. Once our language ancestors had those two stems, they were able to combine them into the new stem *nizd'-,* sit down (place); and by an ancient language convention the word was understood to be specific to birds, i.e., "place where the bird sits," or "nest." So Latin *nidus,* Italian *nido,* and French *nide.* The French form also passed into British gamekeepers' talk as *nide* (it rhymes with *side*), a hatch of birds, as pheasants ("as many as hatch from one nest"). There is also the rarely heard but standard verb *to nidify.* At ultimate root that might be argued to mean "to sit down," but among ornithologists it means "to build a nest." You might, with etymological reason, say "The legislature is nidifying," but the chances are you will not be understood, for idiom is not a logic but a systematic illogic to which we become conditioned.

The foregoing details the evolution of Indo-European *nizd'-* into Latin, through it to Italian and French, and through French to English. The same stem, modified to *nest'-,* also passed into prewritten Germanic, and the northern branch of our language ancestors noticed, as the southern branch did not, that where the bird sits it drips, and that after the rites of spring, in summer heat, the nest becomes a bespattered and stinking thing. They expressed this observation by a suffix the nature of which we can guess from Old Dutch *nestich,* and Old English *nestig,* like a nest, nest-like. Old English *g,* especially terminal *g,* regularly changed to *y* in later English *(hunig → honey).* And so with a slight vowel modification our word *nasty,* a still functioning label for a beshat and stinking thing.

Not all words can be traced so precisely. Sometimes the clues simply do not turn up. For years I have tried to run down the origin of *the whole nine yards.* I am not even sure I know what this idiom means. I think the sense is "all of it" and that the implication is (or was) "total loss." Can a three-masted square-rigger be said to have nine yards? If it is wrecked, does the captain lose the whole nine yards? Such guesses must be put aside until the clue is found. *Honcho* is relatively recent slang meaning "the man, the main man, the one who takes charge." The form suggests a Spanish or Mexican-Spanish origin, but after long searching I have rejected that suggestion. Such fragments of evidence as I have turned up point to an origin in the G.I. slang of the Korean War. At a guess, it is a G.I. corruption of some Korean (or Japanese) word. But what word, meaning what? Yiddish *schlemiel* is a corruption of the Biblical name Shelumiel. Shelumiel was a powerful war leader who is mentioned four times in the Book of Numbers, always honorably. How did the name of the Jewish war leader become the Yiddish word for a dolt? On that point, I haven't even a guess.

Guessing, however, is not etymology. Guesses, alas, are what one lives to regret. I let myself be tempted earlier into guessing about the origin of *chippie*, prostitute. If I managed to get some of it right, I nevertheless managed to get all of it wrong. I did finally locate the right origin as explained in the Supplement at the back of this book. In that Supplement, I have tried to make such amends as I could for going astray. May I mention in my defense, especially as an obsessive reader of dictionaries, that I have yet to find one that does not stray into seemingly logical but random guesses? Dictionaries not only take guesses, but label them. Any explanation following the notations "prob." or "probably" is a guess.

One respected dictionary (and I am among those who respect it) tells me that *butterscotch* is a butter-colored candy so called because it was first made in Scotland. I cannot see how the editor could know it was first made in Scotland. And if so, how about *hopscotch?* Was that first played in Scotland? And how about *scotching a rumor?* None of these terms arise from Scotland, but rather from Old French *escocher*, to cut. Butterscotch is cut (scored) into squares. A hopscotch diagram is cut (scratched) into the dirt (or it was before sidewalks and chalk). To scotch a rumor is to cut it down.

Nothing is easier than to let oneself be misled. Let the reader ask himself what image he visualizes at the root of *to flog a dead horse*, and then turn to *horse* in the entries that follow. I suspect that most readers will then have an image to revise.

Sometimes the problem is to recognize an idiom when it occurs. *Forlorn hope* would appear to be a simple adjective-noun combination. I was surprised, as I believe the reader will be (surprised and delighted), to discover it is from a Dutch military term, *verloren hoep*, suicide squad (a band of soldiers—and a hoop is in one sense, of course, a band —ordered to such duty that there is practically no chance to survive).

Or see *damn: not worth a damn.* That, too, would seem to be a natural, even an inevitable formation, yet it began as *not worth a weed*.

The one thing that marks a living language is constant change. *Upshot* was once, and very specifically, the last shot in an archery competition. It was the, so to speak, "last time up shot." We still use *upshot* to mean "an immediate consequence," as in: "the upshot of their discussion was a bloody nose." That is not the same thing as an *aftermath*. An *aftermath* is, at root, "a second mowing (as of hay)." It follows on, but much later. "The aftermath of that bloody nose was a long-smoldering resentment."

An upshot is also the opposite of a debut. English yeomen were once required by law to take regular archery practice on local fields commonly called the Artillery Grounds. They were also required, as their sons reached a certain age, to instruct them in archery. In the beginning, *debut* referred to the butts of the archery range. A debut was a lad's first appearance on the archery range. Simply enough, then, it also came to mean the opening shot of an archery contest. A *debutante* may still be said to be a girl who takes her first shot at potting a desirable husband, though unless she brings off a long shot, the upshot may have a diminished aftermath.

And consider *buxom*. Today we apply the word only to girls and women, and the reference is to an ample bust. How, then, are we to understand Langland in *Piers Plowman* when he writes: "And buxom to the law"? *Buxom* (the word appears in at least six Middle English variants) derives from Old English *bogan*, to bow to, with the extended senses "to be servile, to be obedient to," which is what Langland meant. Words slide about. Buxom came to mean all those qualities an Old English lordling wanted in his servants and workers, especially the bodily strength that would permit them to drudge on tirelessly and in servile obedience. Not until the seventeenth century (and who knows how?) did the sense "ample physical endowment" become specific to milkmaids and to their busts.

Once these changes have occurred, it is possible, in most instances, to trace them. Only a fool would attempt to predict such changes. The one rule I have been able to evolve is: *Language does what it does because it does it.* The corollary may be: *And it goes best when one knows what it has done.*

What is a *dormouse?* One might guess that it is a house mouse, an (in)door mouse as opposed to a field mouse. That sounds reasonable— which is to say it is almost certainly etymologically wrong. Ask, rather, why Lewis Carroll had it fall asleep at the Mad Hatter's tea party. The answer is because he knew it was not a mouse at all but a small nocturnal squirrel with an especially long period of hibernation, for which the French gave it the folk name *il dormeuse,* the sleepy one. Carroll probably also knew that when these creatures have fattened up just before their long hibernation, they are esteemed as a delicacy by

French gourmets. He certainly knew that the French do not eat mice.

See *pyramid.* The Arabic name is *pi-mar.* But Latin *pyramis,* later French *pyramide,* is from Greek *puramis,* wheat cake. One has to guess that *puramis* was a Greek soldiers' joke, as if to call the pyramids "Egyptian wheat cakes." Even as soldiers' humor, however, the joke seems farfetched. I was, in fact, prepared to go to press on a bed of question marks, when I learned from David Schroeder of Boulder, Colo., that the rock used in constructing the pyramids contained fossils of large one-celled animals *(nummulites)* that left disk-shaped shells, often more than an inch in diameter. I am not prepared to discuss Greek wheat cakes, but I am satisfied that these disk-shaped fossils explain what would otherwise seem to be a pointless joke. Etymology is where one finds it.

But the ludicrous is also part of idiom. We say he grew rich by *pyramiding his investments.* If logic is the measure, that can only mean that he began with a broad base and worked and worked until everything diminished to the vanishing point. To mean what we mean when we speak of pyramiding, we have to turn things upside down and stick the apex in the sand—a notably unstable position, and one that can only lead to a crash.

Yet in practice, we seem to find it easy to ignore the fact that we turn pyramids upside down. As we ignore the ridiculous redundancy of *time clock.* What else is a clock for? (Perhaps a nontiming alarm clock for those who don't want to get up in the first place?) People who use time clocks are called *clock punchers. Punch clock* would certainly have been a less ludicrous idiom—though not less ludicrous than piling up assets in upside-down pyramids. To do so is to get things all *assbackwards.* But why do we say that instead of *assfrontwards* when we mean "all turned around"? Ass backwards does remain the normal order of things. As does *head over heels.* Isn't that the normal position? If we mean all topsy-turvy, would it not make better sense to say *heels over head?*

It would if logic were the essential measure of idiom. But idiom is a special sort of coding. It may better be thought to be a systematic illogic. The natives of each body of idiom acquire the key to the code, and the code established, illogic seems not to interfere with communication.

I became an obsessive etymologist when I realized, after forty years of trying to write in the American language, that I simply did not know enough about my own tongue. So far, I have compiled my findings into two volumes, of which this is the second. If I am left time, I hope to compile at least a third, and perhaps a fourth. If I have had no serious purpose, I have piddled away more than ten years. Yet I have no serious claims I care to assert. I may have been doing nothing more than beachcombing to see what shells I might turn up. When the shells were ordinary or badly broken, I have tossed them aside. The inner directive has been simply, "Hey, look at this one!—and this one!—and this one!" This beach is covered with specimens too good to leave ungathered. Nor have I any ambition to be a conchologist, and to give up collecting in order to classify what I have collected. The longer I beachcomb, the more I sense what the sea is doing and has been doing inside itself. But the collection is for its own sake.

How else could I have learned that *fornication* is from an Indo-European root meaning "hot, heat," and that it became associated with oven, as in Italian *forno.* Latin *fornicatio* labeled brickwork arches, like those of old ovens, and like the cellar supports of large public buildings. Fornication is, in fact, a surviving term in architecture. In time, the poor of Rome found mean, dark quarters in such cellarworks, and there the cheapest whores had their cribs. Publius Vulgus once went down to the fornications to find them, and stayed there to fornicate. I am glad to have turned up that information, as I am to pass it on. It is just as well to check on our ancestors while we sit around trying to decide whether we are much damaged angels or questionably improved apes.

Consider *liquid,* the word we use for one of the three common forms of matter. It derives from Latin *liquere,* to be liquid, to liquefy. But beyond the Latin is the compound Indo-European stem *leik-wo-,* to go away. At root, a liquid is that form of matter that goes away!

The word, I submit, is a natural poem. One written by the language itself. The base image is probably of flowing water. But there are other ways for a liquid to go away—consonant ambiguities, as in a poem. It may go away by seepage, or by evaporation, or in the way bourbon disappears from my bottle; and welcome to these resonances.

Then, with a simple *de-* prefix and a nasal infix, *-n-, liquere* became Latin *delinquere,* which is the base of English *delinquent.* And as the second stanza of this fossil poem, is not a delinquent also one who goes away (from normal expectations and social standards)? Give the language a chance to be all of itself, and it turns out to be surprisingly— even dazzlingly—much more.

My son, a guitarist with a rock group, did not think highly of another musician. "That dude," he said, "is out of his furrow." As far as I could see, none of his friends worked in what I could think of as a straight line, but I ignored that point. "You," I told him, "have just reinvented a Latin etymology!" He was not as excited as I was, I must confess, but I still think of it as a discovery. "Out of one's furrow" is the exact root sense of English *delirious,* which is from Latin *delirare,* to rant and rave, but which is at root from *lira,* furrow, prefixed *de-,* out of. A delirious person loops his plow all over the field instead of working a straight furrow. "To rant and rave," is the extended sense of the word. "To plow erratically" is the root sense.

When a writer has both senses available to him, a word can be made to fall into place like a chime. Richard Wilbur has a fine small poem called "Seed Leaves." In it he describes a vegetable shoot so new it lacks specification. It could be a blade of grass coming, or a bush, or a tree. There is yet no way of knowing. The poem closes with the statement that it then:

> Takes aim at all the sky
> And starts to ramify.

Ramify, in this context, is a gem word. Its extended sense is "to become more complex." But the word is from Latin *ramus,* branch, the root sense being "to add more branches." By playing the root sense against the extended sense, the poet has renewed the life of the word. Milton, describing a regal Oriental procession of elephants decked out with howdahs, writes "elephants endorsed with towers." He reminds us that *endorse,* through all its extended senses, is at root "on the back."

We use *dilapidated* to mean "in a run-down condition," but if all we know is the extended sense, we lose specification. The root is Latin *lapis,* stone, whence Latin *dilapidare,* to throw or to shed stones. It would probably be confusing, by now, to label as *dilapidated* a ring from which the gem has fallen. It would be accurate to speak so, but who would understand? It would be root accurate, and not confusing, to say that the Colosseum (or any stone ruin) is dilapidated. But can there be a dilapidated frame house? or a dilapidated jalopy?

How far is it permissible to go in ignoring root senses? Suppose that a rich Egyptian bought a newspaper and wrote stirring editorials in favor of social improvements, and that an American newspaperman called him "a crusading Egyptian editor." Most of our press would accept such phrasing, but what does it do to the word *crusade,* and where were the Egyptians during the crusades? Go ahead and say it that way, if you insist, but I reserve my right to snicker at your phrasing. I think, as a matter of fact, that when you ask what I am snickering about, I will refuse to explain. You may have before you a fine career as a comedian, and why spoil your prospects by bringing your language into focus?

Latin *focus* meant "hearth." No, not fireplace: Roman houses did not have fireplaces with chimneys, but fire pits that burned under an opening in the roof. We use *focus* to mean "point of convergence." That follows: in ancient Rome the *focus* was the place where the family came together, a different sort of convergence, but a convergence. In Italian, however, *focus* became *fuoco,* fire. Both derivations are logical enough, but equal logic has led to widely different conclusions.

I think of such turnings as the gist of language, as the sort of thing I most want to know about our words and idioms. And I must add that I do not commonly find such information in our standard dictionaries. By reading many dictionaries side by side, I can sometimes glimpse the whole word process from its root, through its various shifts, to its present usage. But one must also consult dictionaries of foreign languages, reference books, histories, and the language notes of many scholars past and present.

Because the standard dictionaries seek to be complete, their space is precious, and most words and idioms must be treated in a sort of shorthand. Because I have no hope of dealing with every word in common use, and because I am in no hurry, I am free to browse, and to take time for a fuller discussion of the words and idioms here listed.

I even have time to amuse myself with spook etymologies. A spook etymology is one made up after the fact by ingenious people who would rather invent an origin than trace it. The language is beset by spooks and I have at times noted their inventions as fair wonders.

Everyone seems to know that *posh* is acronymically derived from *p*ort *o*ut *s*tarboard *h*ome, the reference being to the ideal stateroom location when making the passage to India through the Suez Canal. The fact that the word was nearly three centuries old in English by the time some brilliant spook dreamed this acronym seldom makes it into the footnote. *Posh* in Romany means "half." British rogues sometimes worked with the Gypsies, and in seventeenth-century thieves' cant *posh* came to mean "money," because British thieves picked it up in such contexts as *posh houri,* half penny, and *posh kooruna,* half crown. So the word remained until the beginning of the nineteenth century, when it passed into more general slang and into common colloquial with the altered sense "swank," the shift being from "money" to "the good things money can buy."

It would seem to follow that a word in use in the early seventeenth century cannot be assigned a late-nineteenth-century origin. (See *gringo* in *Browser's* I for a similar case.) Yet such is the power of spooks upon us, that once we have given our faith to their inventions, no persuasion of evidence can readily turn us. Not long since, I mentioned *posh* in the course of a lecture. The talk over, a distinguished gentleman, and the editor of one of my favorite dictionaries, introduced himself. It was a pleasure to meet him. As it was a surprise to hear him defend his faith in ectoplasmic etymology. Almost his first words were: "I still think there is something to be said for 'port out starboard home.' " He may be right. There is no evidence for it, and what evidence there is works against it, but our faith in spooks is not only beyond evidence but safe from it.

Consider *ass in a sling*. The common spook etymology explains what that means. A jackass, the spooks explain, cannot balance on three legs while being shod. The fact that a jackass is as sure-footed as a goat seems not to matter. To hold the animal for shoeing, therefore, American smiths rigged large slings. No writer of the past ever mentioned seeing such a sling in a smithy, and no one has ever found traces of one, but spooks ignore such details. What they want you to understand is that a farmer who has his ass in a sling is in a bad way because he cannot get his plowing done, not, at least, until the blacksmith has finished the job.

As etymologies go, this one ranks as a counterfeit platinum penny. It is false on the face of it but worth more than true money. Or almost so. I know I would not have missed it. It is a pleasure to deal with such generous counterfeiters. And yet the true word mint of our species is even more generous. This book is from my pleasure—as I hope it may become yours—in the lavishness of our language and its sources.

A SECOND
BROWSER'S DICTIONARY

abominate   To detest. To loathe. [XIV. < OF *abominable* < L. *abominari;* which is *ab-*, away from; with *ōmin-*, omen; hence with root sense: "to turn away from a thing of ill omen."]

   HISTORIC. In some Medieval L. and OF sources, the root was rendered *abhom-*, as if "away from mankind," i.e., "(revoltingly) inhuman." Owen Barfield, *History in English Words*, attributes this error to XVI: "Sometimes . . . these Elizabethan dons made learned howlers, as in the now abandoned spelling *abhominable.*" But ODEE dates this alternative English spelling from XIV, which allows the Elizabethan dons 200 years of English precedent, as well as the Medieval L. and OF rationale for their "howler."

absurd   Ridiculous beyond all reason. [L. *absurdus*, beyond reason. < *surdus*, deaf (also, disorderly); by ext., not to be communicated with; hence, not reachable by reason. A bull of Pope Paul IV, 1555, begins: *"Cum nimis absurdum,"* which may be rendered: "Among great (no little) disorder."]

abyss   1. Inconceivably deep place. 2. Any profound declivity. *abysmal* 1. Of inconceivable or immeasurable depth. 2. *Colloq.* Utterly depressing. *We had an abysmal time* = we did not enjoy it, only more so. *abyssal* Labels ultimate sea depths and earth profundities to the magmatic core. [< Gk. *bussos*, bottom; with neg. prefix *a-*, *abussos*, bottomless; in the fixed form *abussos limnē*, bottomless lake. The Greeks saw the cosmos as partly formed matter bounded by particular chaos whose formlessness constantly threatened creation. That chaos of unformed particles was their *abussos limnē*. Christian writers in Late L., shifting the metaphor to their own views, contracted the Gk. label to *abissus, abyssus,* and used it to label the pit of hell.]

1

accrue [IE *ker-* (which see), to grow. Zero-grade form *kr-* → L. *crescere,* to grow; *accrescere,* to increase. P.p. *accretus,* increased → OF *accroistre,* p.p. *acreu;* whence ME *accruen,* to accrue, to increase.] 1. To increase a sum of money by periodic addition, as of interest payments. 2. *Ext.* To acquire greater reputation, status, advantage, through work done in one's career.

addle *v.* 1. *Of food. Rare.* To become spoiled. To cause to become spoiled. 2. *Ext.* To lose, or to cause to lose, one's wits. (But more commonly functioning with an adjectival force in such standard compounds as ***addlebrained/addleheaded/addlepated*** [The intermediate root sense, though in error, is "urine." So an *addlehead* is, in one sense, a piss head, though at ultimate Gk. root, "a rotten-egg head." < Gk. *ōon,* egg, *ourion,* wind; whence *ōon ourion,* lit. "wind egg," but applied to a fertilized egg that fails to hatch—by which time it is not exactly full of wind but will, when cracked, yield the blood-flecked mess of a dead embryo and, likely, a sulfurous whiff that can reach out to spoil the air.

By a translator's error the Gk. form was rendered in Latin as *ovum urinae,* urine egg, rotten egg. Then some later scribe rendered *urinae* as ME *adel, adelèd egg,* piss egg. An addled etymology.]

adjective 1. *Part of speech.* A word or phrase that modifies a noun. *Never send an adjective on a noun's errand.* 2. *Law, but rare.* A procedural point apart from the substantive argument. (As if *adjunct.*) [At root: "thing thrown." < L. *jactare,* to throw, p.p. *jectus,* thrown; prefixed *ad-,* to, at, hence "thrown at." Cognate with *agio,* commission charged by dealers in exchanging one currency for another; at root: "(fee) thrown into (the transaction)." And also *ghetto,* but for that evolution, never before properly traced in English, see Vol. I.]

aftermath A somewhat delayed consequence or result, especially a bad one. [Root sense: "second mowing." < *After;* with OE *maeth,* a mowing, a swath. Hence, at root, a second mowing of hay. And since in most of Britain the growing season is short, the second mowing is likely to be inferior to the first, whence the root implication: "lesser (bad) result." As distinct from an *upshot* (which see), an aftermath is an eventual rather than an immediate result. *The aftermath (but not the upshot) of the drought was ruin for thou-*

sands of farmers. The upshot (but not the aftermath) of their discussion was a bloody nose.]

agley Awry. [Sc. In Am. only in the now standard phrase from Robert Burns: "The best-laid schemes o' mice an' men/Gang aft agley."]

agony 1. Physical or mental anguish. 2. *Ext.* The death throes. *the final agony. agony on the cross.* [IE *ag-*, to impel, to drive. → Gk. *agein*, to lead. (The sense association is "to direct," but "to lead" is the action opposite "to drive.") In L. *agere* (another sense shift), to act, to perform, to do; p.p. *actus*, done (ACT).

Gk. *agein* → *agon*, (with the early sense) legislative assembly ("body that leads? body that drives?"). Then, as a horse's mouth description of Greek politics, the later sense became "competition, contest, struggle," and by association with athletes straining every muscle to outdo one another, the sense became "utmost straining," whence the now current Eng. sense.]

agony column The personal notices in a newspaper's classified advertisements. [So called because made up of anguished personal messages, e.g.: "John—I promise not to beat you again. The babies cry for you. So do I. Please forgive and return home. Judith." *P. Slang* says such notices first appeared in the London *Times*, 1870, and this name for them had become common by 1880. In Am. usage, soon thereafter.]

al fresco [It., in the fresh air; out of doors.] The sense may be most accurately rendered as "just out of doors." Ref. is to an outdoor meal, a lawn party, an outdoor performance in a courtyard or other open-air stage; but the presence of some nearby structure is implicit. One does not hike or go mountain climbing or sail across the ocean al fresco, but in the great out of doors (far from houses or other edifices).

alibi [L. *alibi*, elsewhere < *alius*, other; *ubī*, where.] 1. *Law.* Proof of innocence in a criminal case by establishing that one was somewhere else at the time of the crime. 2. *In loose ext.* Any excuse. [An alibi is in one sense an excuse, but a specific one. This ext. to any excuse blurs a useful distinction.]

Alibi Ike A weasely character who can always find excuses for what he did wrong. [Am. XIX. No one has been able to identify a specific Ike, and the name was prob. chosen for sound values, because the initial long *I* of Ike repeats the terminal long *i* of alibi.]

alimony   Maintenance money paid to a former spouse. [The root sense is "food money," but as a synecdoche it serves for "all living expenses." *Ali-* < L. *alere,* to nourish (ALIMENTATION); with *-mony,* condition of. In XVII a living allowance paid by a husband to a wife from whom he had separated. With divorce now firmly established by law, and with the new sexual equality, some few ex-wives are paying alimony to their shed husbands. (Is there a male version of Zsa Zsa Gabor in the social offing?)]

alive   1. Not dead. 2. Animated. *Look alive, you swabs.* 3. In existence at a given time. *the fastest man alive. alive to* Sensitive to. Responsive. *alive with* Aswarm with. Teeming. [OE nominative *līf,* life; dative, *on līfë* (the *f* between two vowels rendered as if *v*). The *on,* as if *at,* persisted into ME but was gradually replaced by the prefix *a-: on līfë* → *alive;* ME *on slepe* → *asleep.* Ult. < IE *leip-* with the sequence of meanings: 1. fat, grease; 2. sticky stuff, to stick; 3. continued adherence (as greasy stuff clings and persists; whence: 4. life ("what clings and persists"). Via Gmnc. with p/f to the OE form.]

allegory   A narrative in which the characters, situations, and properties, though more or less specified as themselves on one level, are, on another, personifications of ideas and states of being. [At root: "other-speak." < Gk. *allēgoria,* allegory; at literal root: *allo,* combining form of *allos,* other; *agoreuein,* to speak in public, to orate (lit. to address the *egora,* legislative assembly).]

aloof   Distant. Holding oneself apart from. Hence, haughty, though this sense is a late extension. [Du. nautical, *te loef,* to windward. Eng. nautical *luff,* to turn into the wind. Earlier, now obs., *loof, to loof.* Prefixed *a-,* to, toward. Earlier *on loof,* the "on" serving for *a-,* as in obs. *fall on sleep,* for *fall asleep.* A ship of a fleet sailing with the wind was said to be *on loof* when it turned into the wind and drew away. *Aloof* had become obsolete by early XIX, when it was revived by Coleridge.]

also-ran   1. *Horse racing.* A horse that did not finish in the first three places. 2. *Ext.* Any loser in any context. [From the daily published racing results, which list the win, place, and show horses, and then, under the head "Also ran," the horses that finished "out of the money."]

ambrosia   [Root sense: "not for mortals," or variantly: "(food) of the immortals." < Gk. *mbrotos*, mortal; with neg. prefix *a-* → *ambrotos*, not mortal, hence, immortal. The *b* is an unexplained, prob. Hellenic accretion. Otherwise cognate with L. *mortis*, of death (MORTAL). Ult. < IE *mer-*, death, to die.] 1. *Greek myth.* The food of the gods. It is said to confer immortality, but see note below. 2. Any food so delicious as to be thought fit for the gods. 3. A symbol of the infinitely desirable. So the poeticism *the ambrosia of her lips.* (But please don't bite them, immortal Ambrose.) 4. *In the gawdy overreaches of the Am. cookbook.* A dessert with many variations, but at hashed essence, made of chopped fruit and marshmallows doused with a sweet syrup and sprinkled with shredded coconut. It is generally more in favor with grandmothers than with the gods.

HISTORIC. *Ambrosia* is the food of the gods, as *nectar* (which see) is their drink. Both are said to confer immortality, but Greek mythology is vague on this point, the gods being already immortal by virtue of their ichor (< Gk. *ikhōr*, of unknown origin), what they have in place of blood.

There are, however, various legends of food or drink that can make human beings immortal. The fisherman Glaucus laid his catch on a mythic sort of seaweed and found that his fish did not die. Curious, he ate some of the stuff and felt himself become immortal.

The legends are further confused by the many demigods said to be born of one mortal and one immortal parent. Aeneas was said to be born of Aphrodite by his mortal father, Anchises. *Tantalus* (which see) was sired by Zeus on a variously ascribed earth maiden. I can find no record that Aphrodite ever invited her son to a home-cooked dinner, but Tantalus and various other demigods were given access to Olympus and to the table of the gods, and it must have been on these half-immortals that ambrosia and nectar conferred immortality, though perhaps it also sustained and strengthened it in the already immortal gods.

ampersand   The symbol (&) for "and." [A *gazinta* word, as in "2 gazinta 4 twice, 2 gazinta 6 three times." The alphabet was, in XVIII custom, presented as 26 letters followed by "&." The formula recited by abecedarians was *A per se A* and so on to *Zed per se Zed,* and concluding *And per se And,* the last being run together as *andpersand* → *anpersand* → *ampersand.*]

andiron   A metal firedog. Commonly *andirons* because used in pairs, but the sing. has its function. *She modified her earlier view of marriage by braining her husband with an andiron.* (May imply that she did not utterly reject marriage, for in that case she might better have used both andirons.) [Origin in dispute. The etymon is certainly OF *andier,* andiron, prob. < Frankish-Gaulish **anderon,* young bull; because these irons were traditionally decorated with bull's horns or the head of a bull. And perhaps such decoration was fixed in early French tradition, though museum specimens of early andirons are decorated with all sorts of animal motifs, and also with other devices.]

angels: on the side of the angels   Now describes one who works for the good in any context. *I have had my disagreements with Norman Cousins, but he still keeps turning up on the side of the angels.* [But at root, with the sense: "opposed to the theory of evolution," as if in answer to the question: "Is man a damaged angel or an improved ape?" In 1864 Benjamin Disraeli spoke to churchmen who had met to discuss and denounce Darwin's theory of the origin of species. Ever the politician, he played for the church vote, saying: "The question is this: is man an ape or an angel? I . . . am on the side of the angels."]

anvil   1. The steel (earlier iron) block on which a blacksmith hammers and shapes hot metal. 2. *Medicine.* The central one of the three bones of the inner ear; its shape said to resemble that of an anvil. Also called **incus.** [Root sense: "thing beaten on." First element, *an-,* is a variant form of "on." Second element, *vil,* is ult. < IE *pel-,* to beat (as a draft animal is beaten to urge it forward) (COMPEL, IMPEL). With p/f in Gmnc. → OE *anfilt, ME anvelt,* anvil.]

NOTE. The rarer form is *incus,* a Latin form, and like *anvil,* a simple description of function. L. *incusus,* anvil < prefix *in-,* on, with *cusus,* p.p. of *cudere,* to strike. Ult. < IE *kau-,* to strike, to beat. And cf. the numismatic term *incuse,* a stamped coin. Otherwise *incus* has passed exclusively into medical use in Am.

aphesis   (By way of explaining some of the language notes in this volume.) The common language process by which the initial part of a word is dropped. Usu. defined as the dropping of an unaccented initial vowel. (*possum < opossum; squire < esquire.*) But Cockney *air < hair* is aphetic, as is *odsbodkins* (sometimes erroneously *oddsbodkins < Godsbodkins,* and so, too, *copter < helicop-*

ter. [< Gk. *heinai,* to send; prefixed *ap(o)-,* away, away from → Gk. *aphesis,* the act of sending away, of letting a thing go.]

appreciate [< L. *pretium,* price; prefixed *ad-,* to; → L. *appretiare,* to appraise ("to go to the matter of the price").] 1. *In common Am. usage.* To value and be grateful for. *I appreciate your kindness* = at root: "I set a high price on your kindness." 2. (With same literal root sense) To esteem. And so the common sports cheer: *Two, four, six, eight. Who do we appreciate? Our team! Our team! Rah! Rah! Rah!* 3. *Financial.* To increase in value. *Real estate can be depreciated for tax purposes, while its value appreciates.* ("If only that were true of husbands," said Judith, reaching for the red ink.)

artillery Now means long-range guns, but earlier applied to any device for launching a projectile, as a bow, crossbow, sling, or catapult. [The form of the word is from OF *artillerie,* which with an intrusive *r* (as Bostonians still say, "I sawr it") is < *atillier,* to arm, to fortify < L. *aptare,* to make suitable arrangements (APT). But the intrusive *r* once established, the altered form must have suggested L. *art- (ars, artis),* art, here with the sense surviving in "arts and crafts," the technical skills whereby man draws his means from nature. And cf. *martial arts.*]

HISTORIC. In the Middle Ages, and into XVI, by which time gunpowder had become established as the essential means of war, English yeomen were required by law to practice their archery or artillerie. *Artillery Lane* in London is so called because so many fletchers and bowyers, the artisans of archery, were there concentrated. *Artillery Lane* was near the ancient wall of the city, just beyond which was the *Artillery Ground,* a large field in which archers practiced and competed. In the King James Bible, I Samuel 20:40, "artillery" is used for "bows and arrows."]

Aryan [Sanskrit *aryā,* noble (adj.), nobleman, but with effective sense: "one of our (superior) tribe, one of our chosen sort."] A member of the language group that spoke Proto-Indo-European c. 6000 B.C. or a bit later. Hence, one of our language ancestors. [Max Muller, XIX German philologist-etymologist, was the first to use Aryan in this sense. The verbal witch doctors of Hitler's race theories seized on the root sense "ethnically superior sort" and asserted the "true Aryan" to be the Nordic superman. Muller and the Nazi theorists could both summon etymological arguments for their interpretations of the word, but with the Nazi madness at an end, it is well to restore the word to Muller's sense of it, because it is a useful language label.]

HISTORIC. The languages of Europe are all of Aryan (Indo-European) origin, with three exceptions: Finno-Ugric is an intrusive Uralic tongue substantially traceable to Mongol invaders and their allied tribes. Maltese has visible elements of Italian and Arabic but seems to have evolved from lost common Mediterranean elements, once the language of the sea traders. Basque remains untraced and unexplained, an idiom fluent in itself, related to nothing around it.

ash   The residue of combustion, most commonly but not exclusively of wood or coal. [IE *as-*, to burn, an ember. Prob. suffixed *-k-* in Gmnc. → OE *aesce, asce* (in which *c* is pronounced as if *k* but, before the front vowels *e* and *i*, alters to the sound *sh*, as in:) ME *asshe*, ash.]

ashcan 1. In the era of the coal-burning home furnace, the ubiquitous refuse container of heavy galvanized iron equipped with a lid and two handles. [Because, in winter, used to contain the ashes hauled from the furnace, and necessarily of metal because the ashes might contain live coals.] 2. *Since WWI.* Depth charges. [They roughly resemble the old home ashcan.] 3. A popular but dangerous firecracker that replaced the earlier "two-inch salute." Ashcans are commonly covered with silver paper and they are cylindrical. [But since they appeared after the domestic ashcan had passed from the scene, they must have been named after the depth charge.]

Ashcan School A group of American painters loosely organized in NYC in 1908 and surviving, with various alterations in style, into the Depression years. They had a social comment to make and favored drably itemized street scenes that included rows of ashcans. [But the name is from the derisive reviews of early XX art critics, and later happily embraced by the group.]

Sackcloth and ashes Symbols of bereavement, sorrow, penitence. [Because the Jews, in bereavement or self-abasement, dressed in sackcloth, put ashes on their heads, and squatted in lamentation.]

Ash Wednesday The first day of Lent (seventh Wednesday before Easter). [So called because Roman Catholics go to church on this day and a priest smears ashes on their foreheads as a sign of penance and lamentation. The ritual is obviously akin to the earlier Jewish sackcloth and ashes.]

asset   1. An item of value in one's possession. 2. A talent or trait that enhances one's worth. [The sing. *asset* did not evolve till XIX. Previously, and since ME, *assets* had been a singular, though often treated as a plural because of its terminal *s* (as *pease, pea, peas*). < OF *asetz, asez* (which is modern Fr. *assez,* enough); cognate with It. *assai,* a lot, plenty. All as if < L. *ad satis,* enough to state, satisfy, serve a purpose; but not attested until OF *aver asetz,* a legalism meaning "to have enough (to satisfy claims)." (Among your assets, may you ever *avez asetz* to satisfy claims against you, *e assai più.*)]

ass in a sling: have one's ass in a sling   To be in a bad way. [Sthrn. regional for sweet style's sake, but now widely diffused. To have an arm in a sling is to be partially incapacitated (one still has the other arm for hoisting the moonshine jug). In exuberant fancy, then, to have a sling so large that it goes clear around the ass is to be entirely slung up to one's own shoulder. *Jim Whitehead, down Arkansas way, knew a feller had his ass in a sling so tight, his feet couldn't reach the ground.*]

HISTORIC. A persistent spook etymology (which see) has it that *ass* here is donkey. It asserts that donkeys cannot stand on three feet to be shod. (Not true.) American blacksmiths, therefore, rigged slings for asses. (No trace of one has ever been turned up in any smithy.) To have one's ass in a sling, this spookery explains, is to be in trouble, because one cannot work one's land. (But give the smith a few minutes and you can ride your ass home and get to work.)

Spook etymologists are shameless in their elaborations of false facts, yet as etymologies go, this one is a counterfeit platinum penny, false on the face of it, but in pure chicane, worth more than the genuine article.

astern   *Nautical.* Behind the ship or boat but not on it. [Toward the after part of the ship but not overboard is expressed by *abaft.* A whale may breach *astern.* Were it to breach *abaft* it would have to come up through the hull and deck aft of the startled observer, who is, I will hope, a strong swimmer. Nautical English is precise in observing this distinction, yet etymologically, *astern* is < ON *stjoren,* steering oar, OE *stēoran,* to steer, both forms specific to what *abaft* now means, i.e., "toward the stern." I have not been able to find when this distinction in despite of etymology became established.]

astute 1. Keenly perceptive and sound in judgment, esp. in practical matters. 2. *Ext.* Shrewd. Crafty. [L. *astutus,* perceptive, capable < *astus,* craft, trade, skilled occupation. Intermediate root sense: "in the manner of a skilled craftsman." Ult. < IE *wes-,* being; and by association, settled community ("place of being"). *Astute* is root-related to *wassail* (which see).

The IE root, suffixed *-t-* → *(w)es-tu-* → Gk. *astu,* town, city; whence the L. forms above. The sense sequence, from being → city/town as one's place of being → skilled craftsman of a city, is a specimen sense evolution by association.]

-athon An illiterate but established suffix signifying protracted intense action. So *danceathon, sellathon, talkathon.* [< *marathon* (race) taken as if *mar* meant to run, and *athon* meant at great length. Gk. *marathon* labels the wild fennel that covers the plain of Marathon (which see).]

atom 1. *Physics.* A complex once believed to be the irreducible unit of matter. 2. *Ext.* The least amount. *He hasn't an atom of mercy in his soul.* [Root sense: "indivisible unit (of matter)." < Gk. *temnein,* to cut, to divide; p.p. stem *tom-* with neg. prefix *a-* → *atomos,* that which cannot be cut/divided. Earlier *atomy,* smallest unit of matter. *As You Like It,* III. ii: "It is as easy to count atomies as to resolve the propositions of a lover." Also, tiny creature. *Romeo and Juliet,* I. iv: "Drawn with a team of little atomies/Athwart men's noses as they lie asleep."] **atomic** 1. *Physics.* Pertaining to noun sense. 2. *By association with power and horror of atomic bomb.* Superpowerful. *Ali delivered an atomic right to the chin.* **Atomic Age** The achieved but portentous era of atomic energy as a nearly limitless source of energy, and of the atomic bomb as an ominous possibility of human annihilation. And note that theatrical agents have already taken to dubbing energetic and sexy female performers as *Atomic Bomb* and *Atomic Blonde.*

auction [IE *aug-,* to increase, to multiply (AUGMENT). → L. *augere,* same senses. P.p. *auctus,* and so the substantive *auctio:* 1. An increase. 2. An auction. Sense 1 now expressed in Eng. by *augmentation;* sense 2, by *auction* (in which the prices augment as the action proceeds.)]

auction bridge A form of bridge in which overtricks count toward game. In contract bridge (variant ploys aside) one bids the hand up to full expectation. In auction bridge one tries to become declarer with the least possible bid.

on the auction block 1. Up for sale at auction. 2. *Ext.* Bankrupt, with all one's property up for sale to satisfy debts. [The *block* is lit. the usu. wooden plate on which the auctioneer strikes his gavel. The figure, therefore, is a synecdoche, the plate representing the entire transaction.] *knock down at auction* To strike the gavel, completing the sale to the highest bidder. *put on the block/put up at auction/auction off* 1. To sell an item at auction. 2. To liquidate an estate at auction.

Dutch auction A reverse form of auction in which the price starts high and is reduced by increments, the item or lot going to the first bidder.

And see *inch of candle auction.*

auger A tool for boring. Sometimes (as in "Ballad of the Lowland Sea") *brace and auger,* drill and bit, but an auger is at root a large gimlet, the handle being permanently affixed to the metal borer. [Earlier *nauger,* but nonced (see *noncing,* Vol. I) from *a nauger* to *an auger.* < OE *nafogar,* a tool for boring a hole in the hub of a wheel. Ult. < IE *nobh'-,* navel. By metathesis, and with *n* syncopated to *m* before *b* → *ombh'-* → L. *umbilicus;* and though *nafogar* and *umbilicus* seem to bear no resemblance to one another, they remain related in the common sense "perforation in the center of."]

avast *Nautical.* A command meaning: *Halt! Stop! Hold it right there! Don't move!* [Slightly altered form of Du. *hou' vast,* elided form of *houd vast,* hold fast. In effect: "Stay right where you are."]

average 1. *Mathematics.* The result obtained by adding all the numerical elements in a series and then dividing by the number of elements. (In statistics, *median* is generally preferred, i.e., that point in a series above which and below which there occur the same number of elements; for if 200 people in Coaltown earn $6,000 a year, and one earns $3,000,000, the average income is more than $20,000, whereas the median income remains at the more representative $6,000 level.) 2. *In common loose ext.* Normal. So-so. Not good, not bad. C for the course. 3. *Marine law.* Damage to a cargo and to a ship, plus towing and salvage charges if the ship requires salvage.

law of averages 1. In mathematics, as formulated by Jacob Bernoulli, Swiss mathematician (1654–1705): "When the number of trials *n* of an event of probability *p* is increased indefinitely, the probability of any assigned deviation from the expected value of *np* approaches zero." 2. *In common usage.* The never defined but intuitively expected rate at which things recur.

[A double evolution. OE *eafor,* draft horse, nag; *aferian,* to supply draft horses for the supply train of a military expedition. ME *aver,* a draft horse; *average,* under the feudal system, the number of draft horses a landholder was expected to supply at the need of his liege lord. That expectation was, of course, based on his land-holding, i.e., on what he had, i.e., on his (Fr.) *avoir.* So Fr. *average* refers to both draft animals and to one's *avoir,* as determining one's "average" obligation to a liege.

In Arabic, *awār* was the loss of goods in shipping, or damage sustained; plu. *awārīya,* damaged goods. Since many backers commonly bought shares in a cargo, *awār* was deducted from each according to his "average" investment. In Old It., then, *avaria,* cargo loss or damage in transit.

Both senses of these stems come together in Fr. *average,* the common element being "proportionate assessment."]

awkward 1. Clumsy. 2. *Since XVI.* Unwieldy. 3. XVII. Embarrassing. *an awkward situation.* 4. *XVIII.* Unpleasant. *an awkward error.* [At root: turned backward, "in the direction of the wrong direction." Early evolution obscure. Perhaps ult. < ON *öfugr,* backward. The consonant shift f → v → w is standard, whence one may hypothesize *öfugr* → *owugr,* and with a g/k → *ow'k'r* → Eng. *awk-,* backward; with *-ward,* toward; hence, "backtoward," or in Am. slang, bassackwards.]

    awkward squad 1. *Armed services.* A squad of recruits notably inept at close-order drill. 2. *Armed services and extended to general usage.* Any group of bunglers.

bachelor 1. A man who has not married. 2. A scholar who has completed undergraduate courses and received a baccalaureate degree, signifying that he is qualified to be a candidate for a higher degree. 3. *Chivalry.* A squire who serves a knight as attendant, groom, and man at arms, and who is a candidate for knighthood. [In ME *bachelor-at-armes,* a young knight serving a further apprenticeship under an experienced knight. At root: L. **baccalaria* (prob. akin to *vacca,* cow), a herd of cows; *baccalarius,* a cowherd. In OF *bachelor,* squire of a knight.

    bachelor quarters/bachelor apartment The living quarters of unmarried men.

    bachelor girl [Once common but frowned on by Women's Lib.] A marriageable woman who has chosen to remain single, usu. to pursue a career, and to exercise her options in the manner of male bachelors. Grandmother might have called her an old maid or a shameless hussy, but she seeks to be an independent being who has chosen her own life-style.

back formation (By way of explaining some of the language notes in this book.) The alteration of a word by dropping one or more rear syllables. So *laze* < *lazy.* But also *zoo* < *zoological garden,* in which six of the seven original syllables have been dropped from the "back" of the word, the one surviving (and slightly modified) syllable doing the work of all.

bacon *Now.* The cured fat meat from the back and sides of a pig. *But earlier, in loose generalization.* Any part of the pig. [The earlier generalization is apart from the root sense. < Gmnc. *bak-,* back → OF (via Frankish) *bacun, bakun* → ME *bakoun, bacon.*]

    bring home the bacon 1. (Still surviving country sport at fairs and festivals.) To catch, and thereby win, a greased pig. 2. To

13

succeed. To triumph. To bring home the prize. 3. To provide food. To be the family breadwinner.

save one's bacon To avoid a disastrous loss. (See historic note below.)

> "What frightens you thus, my good son?" says the priest,
> "You murdered, are sorry, and have been confest."
> "O father, my sorrow will scarce save my bacon,
> For 'tis not that I murdered, but that I was taken."
> —Prior (1664–1721)

[The expression is proverbial, a ref. to the small farmer who raised a pig or two to slaughter, cure, and store as winter meat. The loss of this meat to rogues, dogs, wild animals, or spoilage was a family disaster, the prudent man taking every precaution to *save his bacon*.]

HISTORIC. *Bacon* has had special associations in the history of Britain's rigid class structure. English has avoided the use of *peasant,* and in common use into XVI *bacon-eater* labeled what might otherwise be called a small landowner peasant, or a tenant farmer, as above, one who could raise a pig or two to cure for winter meat. The gentry ate game and choice cuts of beef, mutton, etc., leaving the entrails and butt ends for servants. Farm hands and the lowest classes ate mush—when they could get it, even a touch of fat being a luxury.

The most memorable enshrinement of bacon as the basic food of the landed or tenant lower class is the story of the *Dunmow flitch,* whence the Brit. idiom *eat Dunmow bacon,* to live in marital bliss.

The idiom is based on an institution either founded or revived by Robert Fitzwalter, one of the barons of Magna Carta. He willed a flitch of bacon in perpetuity, to be awarded to any married person or couple who would travel to the priory of Little Dunmow and there, kneeling on designated stones before the prior and his monks, swear that in at least a year and a day of marriage there had been no discord nor the least wish to be unmarried, but only mutual love and joy.

Both Chaucer and Langland mention the Dunmow flitch or Dunmow gammon, but no record of awards was kept until 1445. In 1772 the award lapsed, to be revived later at Great Dunmow, but only as a tourist attraction for selling bacon and eggs or ham sandwiches.

Brewer, *Dictionary of Phrase and Fable,* as a testimonial to the

British institution of matrimony, offers a record that shows eight awards between 1445 and 1772. (Eight claimants in over 300 years is at least a tribute to British honesty.)

Brewer also gives the following doggerel form of the oath required of claimants:

> You will swear by the custom of our confession,
> That you have never made any nuptial transgression
> Since you were married man and wife,
> By household brawls or contentious strife;
> Or since the parish clerk said *Amen,*
> Wished yourselves unmarried again;
> Or in a twelvemonth and a day,
> Repented not in thought any way.
> If to these terms, without all fear,
> Of your own accord you will freely swear,
> A gammon of bacon you shall receive,
> And bear it hence with our good leave.
> For this is our custom at Dunmow well known—
> The sport is ours, but the bacon your own.

bad   [The early etymology is obscure but the visible root image is "homosexual." So OE *bǣddel,* commonly rendered "hermaphrodite"; and *baedling,* commonly rendered "sodomite." As the sexual connotation receded from the word, the root senses, "evil, misbehavior," remained in force. ME *badde,* adj., signified "aberrant, shameful, to be scorned." Now used in many many senses, some of which are:] *adj.* 1. Not good. (*a*) In behavior. *Lizzie is best when she's bad.* (*b*) In function. *bad health.* (*c*) In intention. *Bad ideas run through my head / When I see Lizzie out with Ed.* (*d*) In performance. *John Barrymore played a bad Hamlet.* (*e*) Spoiled, rotten. *a bad apple.* (*f*) Immoral. *It used to be good to be bad with Lizzie.* (*g*) Severe, grievous. *a bad wound.* (*h*) Defaulted. *bad debts.* (*i*) Counterfeit. *bad money.* (*j*) Causing distress. *bad news.* (*k*) Unpleasant, disgusting. *bad breath.* (*l*) Not valid. *Ed's land title turned out to be bad.* (And many more.) 2. *Slang.* (*a*) Good. *Lizzie was big, bad, and beautiful.* [In this sense from Black English, in which powerful assertion, even in evil, became the virtue opposed to being an Uncle Tom, hence much to be approved.] (*b*) Powerful. *I had it bad for Lizzie.* —*n.* Evil. Wickedness. *Lizzie took the good and the bad and made them into one.*

Having compiled a long list of idioms based on *bad*, I have concluded that they are all self-evident.

bagel   A hard-shell doughnut of plain yeast dough, made by forming into a ring, scalding briefly, and then baking. [Root sense: "Finger ring." (Some finger!) Akin to OE *beugen*, finger ring, but *beugen* passed out of Eng. use, the root surviving in OHG *boug*, ult. < IE *bheug-*, a swelling, swollen, but with earlier associated senses: "bent, curved, circular." The stem was reintroduced into Eng. via Yiddish *beygel*, a bagel < MHG *bouc*, ring, bracelet.]

bail   *n.* A bond, either in cash or as a lien on property, for the release of a person under arrest, as a pledge that he or she will appear for trial, failing which the bond is forfeited. ***go bail for/go one's bail*** To post such a bond. —*v.* ***bail out*** 1. To secure a detained person's release on bond. 2. *Ext.* To come to one's aid in any sort of difficulty, esp. a financial one. [Root sense: "water carrier." So L. **bajulus*, lit. "water carrier," but with developed effective sense: "person in charge of." I can find no explanation of this sense development, but it survives (BAILIFF, BAILIWICK). In Vulgar L. *baila*, nurse, nanny, guardian of a child. OF *bail*, custodian, guardian. ME *baille*, custody, area of authority. And the posting of bail is in effect the act of picking up and taking charge of the arrested person as guardian, promising stated delivery of his person on pain of forfeiture.]

baiting   Animal baiting [< ON *beita*, to hunt with dogs] was a favorite sport of old England. Bear baiting was the most common practice, waning in XVIII, and outlawed in 1835 by act of Parliament as a cruel sport. (As cockfighting has been made illegal in U.S.) The bears were bred for baiting and were commonly tethered either by the neck or by one leg when the dogs were set on them in an arena called a *bear garden*. Spectators generally bet on the number of hounds the bear would kill before it was itself killed. The word "Bear" in the name of a pub invariably meant that the place had a bear garden; *Bear and Bull* meant that bulls were also baited there. One bear baiting attended by Queen Elizabeth I put up thirteen bears for the sport. (The count of hounds set upon them, and the number killed, are not given.)

backbite Prob. originated in bear baiting as the act of dogs that attacked from behind sooner than face the bear's teeth and front claws.

Bull baiting was also common, bulldogs having been especially bred for the work. At one time, a bull about to be slaughtered had, by law, to be baited, commonly at a post before the lord mayor's house. (Was there some once current belief that such baiting improved the flavor of the beef? Cf. Charles Lamb's "Dissertation on Roast Pig," in which he argues ironically the merits of beating pigs about to be slaughtered as a way of making the flesh more tender by bruising it.) In bull baiting, however, only one dog was used. And so the now archaic Brit. saying: *one dog, one bull,* meaning "fair play."

Badger baiting [origin of *the badger game)* was also considered sport, but was limited by the number of badgers that could be available at a given time. The badger was usu. placed in a pit about the size of a trash can and bets were placed on the number of dogs it would kill before it was ripped to pieces.

And there was also pony baiting, often with a monkey strapped to the pony's back.

Balaam's ass   A dumb creature more attuned to heaven than was its master, hence, though vaguely, a symbol of natural piety. Mohammed selects it as one of the ten individual dumb creatures permitted into heaven. (See note to *bees: telling the bees.*)

HISTORIC. Balak, king of the Moabites, summoned Balaam, a priest-magician, to curse the army of the Israelites. Balaam prayed to the Lord and was ordered to withhold his curse. The story, drawn from various ancient sources, becomes a bit confused, but the gist of it is that when Balaam's way was blocked by an angel, the ass saw it before Balaam did, and knelt in adoration, while Balaam, still blind to the holy presence, beat it to make it get up. So Numbers 22: 28–31:

And the Lord opened the mouth of the ass, and she said unto Balaam, What have I done unto thee, that thou hast smitten me these three times?

And Balaam said unto the ass, Because thou hast mocked me: I would there were a sword in mine hand, for now would I kill thee.

And the ass said unto Balaam, Am not I thine ass, upon which thou hast ridden ever since I was thine unto this day? was I ever wont to do so unto thee? And he said, Nay.

Then the Lord opened the eyes of Balaam, and he saw the angel . . .

Balkanize   To break up a potentially powerful state or alliance into many relatively powerless, bickering units. [As the Great Powers divided the Balkan states in early XX, removing the threat those states might have posed as a unified force. I had thought this idiom was fading from use, along with the memory of the events that gave rise to it, but found it again in Arn and Charlene Tibbetts, *What's Happening to American English?* (Scribner, 1979): "We could hope for a return to the silences of the past and to better edited prose to read. But in the meantime, we are being linguistically Balkanized."]

ban/banal/banns   [All are ult. < IE *bha-,* to speak (which may be echoic of the "speaking" of a sheep, though the echoic origin may only be speculated and not asserted). By a regular shift of the voiced stop bh/f in Latin, as demonstrated by Grimm's Law, → *fari,* to speak. So from present part. *fans,* speaking → L. *infans,* infant ("not yet speaking"). So *fatum,* fate, may be, at root: "what the gods speak/decree"; though here the stem may be IE *bhat-,* to strike (BATTER), and so, at root: "what the gods hit us with" (FATE).

The stem *bha-,* suffixed *-n-* in Gmnc., functions in all related languages with the sense "official utterance, decree"; and so OE *bannan,* to proclaim, to decree.]

ban Earlier, an official proclamation. But now, an official prohibition. [The folk mind, forever set to find no good in official decree, naturally equated royal utterance with prohibition rather than permission.]

banal Too commonplace to be of interest. Hackneyed. Trite. [In feudal usage, *banal rights,* the decreed, absolute rights of a lord to his estate (which was often the size of a county or more). Within this territory, all mills, ovens, animal pens, storage buildings, and other facilities belonged to the feudal lord, who decreed that his underlings use them and who set the terms for their use. These banal rights prescribed and routinized all events of the agricultural year. With the passing of the feudal system, *banal* came to mean commonplace, routine; and then, by ext., humdrum, commonplace, uninspired; and so, trite, hackneyed.]

banns The repeated (hence always plu.) announcement of intention to marry. Traditionally announced in church for at least three Sundays before the ceremony. [In one sense, "repeated official announcement." But part of the traditional wedding ceremony calls on anyone who has reason to say why the ceremony should not be completed "to speak or forever after hold his peace." The banns offer a preliminary announcement of intention, and opportunity for any who have just cause to speak their objection.]

banister   Stair rail assembly. [The form is by an n/l dissimilation of *baluster,* and until early XIX was viewed by some purists as a corruption. But the two words are not identical in meaning. *Baluster* (still surviving) is < Gk. **balaustion,* wild pomegranate, because the supporting shafts of a stair rail were once commonly carved with stylized representations of a wild pomegranate blossom. *Banister,* though originally a corruption, provided a useful name for the whole assembly of handrails and vertical supports. (The surname *Banister* or *Bannister,* however, has nothing to do with stair rails, but is a similar n/l dissimilation of Fr. *balestier,* crossbowman.]

barber's pole   Many barbers still post a flat sign with alternate red and white stripes painted diagonally, and some sport a small white pole painted with a spiraling red stripe. In the past, the barber's pole was a more elaborate and more imposing pole, with a rounded gilt top. From c. 1900 to c. 1940, such poles were commonly illuminated and made to revolve electrically.

    The pole symbolizes the medieval tradition in which doctors scorned surgery and left the cutting to barbers, though the main barber's work was in bloodletting (phlebotomizing), a common treatment for most medical disorders, the idea being to restore the balance of the bodily humors, even in the treatment of anemia. The red and white stripes represent the blood and the bandages used by the barber, the bandages serving primarily to "raise" the vein. The gilt dome represented the basin into which the blood dripped.

baron of beef   A double sirloin roast. [So called because it is a "lordly" cut. Ultimately based on a spook etymology of *sirloin* as *Sir Loin,* a cut of meat so choice that the king is supposed to have drawn his sword and dubbed it a knight baron. Even E. Cobham Brewer, in his authoritative and perdurable *Dictionary of Phrase and Fable,* accepted this spook etymology, ascribing the dubbing to Henry VIII. Others have repeated the tale, ascribing it to various other kings.

    Sirloin is < Fr. *sur,* above; OF *loigne,* loin → *surloigne,* (cut of beef from) above the loin. In XV Eng., *surloyn.* By XVIII (Fielding, *Tom Jones*) the form is *baronet of beef.* (There is also a baron of lamb or mutton, but it is usu. called a standing rib roast.)

    As an example of the eccentricity of English, *surloyn* became *sirloin,* while *sirname* (sir name, the second name of a knight) became *surname,* the first vowel in each case reversing its field.]

basement   A toilet. [Am. Primarily city usage. A gift from the American school system, whose XIX schools were commonly two (sometimes three) stories high, with toilet facilities in the basement. In school usage, *go to the basement* = go to the toilet.]

HISTORIC. Within my own time in the school system, pupils had to request permission to "go to the basement" and were required to raise one finger for permission to urinate, two for permission to defecate. Teacher, presumably, could use this highly personal information to gauge how much time was required for the visit, but any pupil who merely wanted a little time off could signal dump instead of wee-wee, and how was teacher to know?

Brought home from school, *basement* became a generalized term for toilet, with some curious consequences. Most big-city ethnic slums were five-story, cold-water walk-ups, built in XIX, usu. around a central courtyard containing backhouses for direct use or for dumping chamber pots. (In Italo-American patois, the Italianized form *baccauso* still survives for *toilet*.)

These tenements were originally built with an air shaft running from bottom to top. C. 1900 it became customary to seal off half of this shaft and install a pull-chain toilet for common use by all families living on a given story. So it was that even a fifth-floor toilet was called a basement; and so it was that the below-street-level section of such tenements was never called the basement but only the cellar.

This usage is probably passing, but it does still survive, especially in ethnic slums.

bead   1. A small, ornamental bauble of wood, glass, or metal (now also of plastics), perforated for threading. 2. *Ext.* A droplet of moisture more or less resembling such a bauble. 3. *Ext. in various trades.* Bubbles of air or of carbon dioxide in a liquid, as in beer or champagne. 4. *Ext. by resemblance.* The small round ball mounted on a pin as the sight of a shotgun. So *draw a bead* To take aim. *beady-eyed* Having small, brightly highlighted eyes, usu. close-set. [At root: "prayer." < IE *bhedh-*, to bow down, to beg, to supplicate. Via Gmnc. → OE *bed*, prayer. Attested only in *gebed*, prayer (collectively). So in earlier Eng.:] *bedesman/beadsman* The Occidental form of the Oriental prayer wheel. A pious, usu. old man, commonly a minor friar retained by a great family to pray for the good of the house in the family chapel. The beadsman in Keats's "Eve of St. Agnes" was such a one. Also earlier *bedehouse/beadhouse* Prayer house. A hostel for the sick, aged, and destitute, who were tended at the expense of a great man, and were required to pay for their soup and bread by praying for their sponsor and his house. (At a time when indulgences were commonly for sale, there seemed to be nothing incongruous in purchasing grace through mercenary prayer.) *beadle* A pious, prayerful, minor church official and custodian. (The approximate equivalent of a Jewish *shammash.*)

The Venerable Bede St. Bede, c. 673–735. English priest pronounced a Doctor of the Church in 1899 by Pope Leo XIII. His feast day is March 27. [*Bede* cannot be a last name, for surnames did not come into British use until XI–XII, and then only slowly, and at first only for the aristocracy. Nor has *Bede* any precedent as a given name. The form was simply *Brother Bede,* brother prayer, a pious name assumed upon taking holy vows.]

tell one's beads To recite part of the rosary. Earlier, also, *bid a bede,* to pray a prayer. And note that *do one's bidding* earlier meant to do as one had been beseeched to; not, as now, to do as commanded. (See also *bidding prayer.*)

HISTORIC. The Rosary (so named for the Virgin's traditional crown of roses) comprises fifteen series of ten beads (decades), each consisting of ten *Ave Marias* preceded by a *Paternoster* and concluding with a *Gloria Patri.* The perforated counters for the *Paternoster* and the *Gloria* are traditionally larger than those for the *Ave Marias.* The usual recitation at one time is five decades, one third of the whole rosary, called a chaplet.

Thus the original sense of *bede/bead* shifted to mean the perforated bauble on a string used for keeping count of decades of prayer. And so, as above, *draw a bead,* to take aim. And so it is that when an expert marksman draws a bead on you, you haven't a prayer.

Beelzebub   The devil. [Prob. with the original sense: "false God." The first known form is in II Kings 1:11: "Baalzebub, the god of Ekron." *Baal* had some function as a generic term for a false god/ idol worshipped by non-Jews. *Zebub* may derive from a Semitic (prob. echoic) root meaning "flies"; whence the possible root sense: "God of the flies." (But ???) In the Greek Bible the form is given as *Beelzebub,* the second element of which may be < Hebrew *zebub,* dung. In which case the whole name would mean at root: "God of the dung." Either rendering would aptly express the Jews' scorn of false gods, but neither rendering is fully attested.]

bees: telling the bees   It was customary in many cultures to go to the beehive(s) and announce to the bees any birth or death in the family. It was believed that if one failed to do so, the bees would swarm away. "Telling the Bees," by John Greenleaf Whittier, is a poem based on telling the bees of a death in the family.

HISTORIC. In many cultures the bee was associated with the soul from earliest times. Mohammed allowed ten holy animals into heaven as individuals: 1. Jonah's whale; 2. Solomon's ant; 3. Abraham's ram; 4. The lapwing of Balkis (the Arabic name of the Queen of Sheba); 5. The camel of Saleh the prophet; 6. Balaam's ass; 7. The ox of Moses; 8. Kratim, the faithful dog of the Seven Sleepers; 9. His own faithful ass; 10. Noah's dove. All these individual creatures had been variously God-touched, hence were "saints" among creatures. But the bee is admitted to heaven generically to add sweetness to the flowering gardens of paradise.

The legend of the sacred bee is immemorial, a natural expression of humankind's pleasure in these mysterious creatures of sweetness, industry, and total loyalty to the hive. Dante, at the height of his *Paradiso,* describes the souls of the elect, tier on tier, like petals of a Mystic Rose, with God above it as the Sun, and at the same time as an anagogical hive. From God the Hive swarms of angels, like radiant bees, forever descend to the nectar of the rose, and forever return to God, bearing to him the sweetness of all human virtue and bliss.

Additionally, the protolegend may have derived from the early discovery of bees in amber, a natural jewelwork that must have seemed a powerful talisman to primitive man.

benedict   1. A man assumed to be a confirmed bachelor who turns up as a new husband. 2. *Loose ext.* A newly married man. (But the term should be reserved for sense 1. A man newly entered upon his fourth marriage is not a benedict, i.e., an apostate bachelor, but rather a compulsive conjunctive.) [After Benedick, the protagonist of Shakespeare's *Much Ado About Nothing.* But there is precedent in Fr. Benêt, variant of *Benedict.* I have never been able to locate a copy of Cotsgrave's rare *French and English Dictionary,* 1611, but Ernest Weekley, *Romance,* cites from it: "*Benêt,* A simple, plaine, doltish fellow; a noddy peake, a ninny hammer, a pea goose, a coxe, a silly companion." Ah, to be the owner of such a book!]

bidding prayer   In Roman Catholic Britain, and continuing in Anglican Catholic ritual, prayer(s) requested from the congregation for the ill, for the suffering, for some national purpose, or for the repose of the souls of the dead. In the last instance such prayer would be for the advancement to heaven of souls in purgatory. Such prayers were never for the damned, for the souls in hell, having been excluded by God, were beyond the assistance of prayer. The request for such prayers has been a traditional part of the Roman Catholic Mass, but the term *bidding prayer* has only recently become a stated part of the new R.C. liturgy. [Here *bid,* cognate with Ger. *bitte,* please, used to mean "to entreat, to plead for." < OE *biddan a bed(e),* to entreat prayer. (See *bead.*) But OE *biddan* became confused with *bēodan,* to bid, to command. So *bidding prayer* may be argued to be "prayer commanded from the pulpit," though the more accurate sense is "prayer entreated from the congregation."]

bidet   A *Sitzbad.* An abbreviated bath about the size of an elongated toilet bowl, fitted with hot and cold water taps, and usu. with an upward spray. One sits asquat and astraddle it for a quick crotch-wash. Rare in U.S. Common in Europe and esp. in France. Most American G.I.s first met them in French whorehouses as the Normandy invasion advanced from D-Day to bidet. [Gothic *bid,* small, also applied to a burro so small the rider had to ride with legs drawn up to avoid dragging. The *bidet* was named whimsically after that odd squatting stance.]

bit   [IE *beidh-,* split, to split. And by what must have been an early and natural association, "thing split off from" and hence "small particle." In Gmnc. with the further sense shift to "morsel" (thing bitten off). → OE *bitan,* to bite. (Which, unless one bites off more than one can chew, also implies "morsel/small thing.")] 1. A small thing / amount. 2. Mouthpiece of a bridle. ["thing bitten."] 3. A drilling tool. ["thing that bites."] 4. *Brit.* A small coin. *thrupenny bit. Also in Am.* An eighth of a dollar. (See *bits,* Vol. I.)

    do one's bit To do one's (modest) best to help. (Common in WWI, by way of overly modest disclaimer, for "to do military service," a coy euphemism when that service involved rotting and dying in the trenches of the forever ungrateful French.) *bit part Theatrical.* A small role. A minor role. [But distinct from a *walk-on,* which is a brief, usu. single appearance, as of a delivery person with a package.] *bit by bit* Little by little. *a bit of* 1. A small amount. 2. *Primarily Brit.* A damned sight too much of. *Well, that was a bit of brassy insolence, I must say.*

take the bit between one's teeth 1. *Horsemanship.* The act of a horse that clamps its teeth on the bit so that the rider cannot signal by small tugs against the lips. In effect: To bolt, resisting all direction by the rider. So: 2. To run away. To bolt. And so: 3. *Ext.* In any context, to throw off all external controls and to insist on one's own course. Hence: 4. To rebel.

bite [See *bit.*] *v.* 1. To grip, cut, chew, or break off with the teeth. 2. *By association.* To do so with a tool. 3. To eat into. To corrode. (Said most commonly of rust, but also *frostbite.*) 4. To swallow bait, as a fish. Whence: 5. To be gullible. —*n.* 1. A small amount of food. A snack. *a bite of lunch.* 2. *Dentistry.* The way in which upper and lower teeth meet. 3. Distinctive strength and flavor. *This bourbon has a bite to it.* 4. Mechanical grip. *These tires have a great bite on a wet road.* —*adj.* **biting** 1. Sharp. Acrid. 2. Stinging. *a biting remark.*

backbiter One who speaks ill of a person whose back is turned, or who is, in effect, absent. [As a vicious cur sneaks up to bite from behind.] See *baiting.* **bite the dust** To die. To suffer a disastrous fall. [A stereotype of cowboys-and-Indians stories, "and another Indian bit the dust," but yet a fossil poem, the image being of a fall from a horse face-first, as if "biting" the dust.] *bite for* To be gullible. [Take the bait as a fish does.] *bite one's lip* To show chagrin, remorse, anger.

bite one's thumb at To show contempt. [Obs. in Eng. A Mediterranean gesture of contempt made by placing the tip of the thumb against the inside of the front teeth and flicking it forward as if spitting out something foul, the effective sense being "That for you." The act of biting one's thumb is part of the early business of Shakespeare's *Romeo and Juliet,* I. i.

bite off more than one can chew To be greedy, overambitious. [A fossil poem, though now stereotyped. The image is of stuffing one's mouth so full one cannot chew. As a curious natural attestation, it is possible to trap a chipmunk (but please don't do it) by putting seeds in a milk bottle. Having filled both its cheeks, the chipmunk cannot get through the opening, and adamantly refuses to spit out any of the seeds. It has bitten off more than it can eschew.] *put the bite on Slang.* To borrow money from. (Implies not just borrowing, but worrying someone, like a persistent and snapping cur, until the loan is forced out of him.)

hard-bitten Obdurate. Tough. [Emotionally inured by past exposure (bites).] *once bitten, twice shy Proverbial.* Now wary because of past harms suffered. [If the dog bites you once, he caught you off guard. If he bites you a second time, you should have been on guard.]

bizarre   *adj.* Startlingly unexpected. Outlandish. Grotesque. [One of the few English words ultimately traceable to the Basque language, in which *bizar* means beard. Did Basque warriors sport especially striking beards? I do not know, but they must have impressed their neighbors with a certain awesome hairiness, for Sp. *bizarro* came to mean "warlike, martially awesome, knightly"; and the same word in It., "strange and awesome, ominous, menacing, fierce." Whence Fr. *bizarre*, which dropped the senses "warlike, menacing" and stressed "outlandish."]

blacklist   [Prob. < *to blackball*, to vote against. In Brit. club society, one blackball (vote against) was traditionally enough to exclude.] *n.* A list of persons to be shunned or proscribed in one way or another. —*v.* To place a person's name on such a list.

   HISTORIC. Section 2 of the British Licensing Act of 1902 authorized the preparation of a list of habitual drunkards in various cities and areas, and the distribution of that *blacklist* to liquor dealers, with a prohibition of liquor sales to people on the list.

   In a city the size of London, a drunkard could walk away from his home grounds to a pub that would not recognize him, but c. 1900 the British poor were not given to travel, and in country places, a local blacklist would cover all the pubs a neighborhood sot might get to.

   Sometime before 1902, however, American mine owners and manufacturers, along with their Pinkertons and private goons, were preparing and distributing blacklists of workers who were not to be hired. Employers justified such lists as a way of getting rid of "troublemakers" (for which read "union organizers and sympathizers"), but no reason was required for blacklisting a man, and once so listed, he was unemployable, at least within a given industry and geographical area.

blimp   1. A lighter-than-air airship with attached motors but lacking a rigid frame, its rotund shape and fins resulting from inflation of its treated canvas skin. [< British Army designation, Type *B*, *limp*, to distinguish it from the once formidable dirigible, with its rigid frame.] 2. *Ext.* An obese person.

   Colonel Blimp A complacently dogmatic, fat, and fatheaded, elderly British clubman, usu. retired from service in Injah, and full of antiquated assertions. [A caricature of the upper-class British tory, conceived and popularized as a figure of self-important stupidity by David Low, cartoonist for the London *Evening Standard.*]

blizzard   A heavy, sustained snowstorm with strong, below-freezing winds. ("Cold" snow is powdery and easily blown in great, ever-shifting drifts by strong winds. The characteristics of a blizzard are cold, massive drifts, near-zero visibility, and such strong winds that the snow seems not to fall but to be blown laterally. This blinding lateral driftage can continue for days after snow has stopped falling.) [Am. coined, prob. in Penna. Dutch to describe the great snowstorm that struck the eastern U.S., Mar. 11–14, 1888. Based on Ger. *blitzen,* to strike hard; *Blitz,* a sharp, hard blow, lightning. (*Blitz* was made familiar to English-speaking people by Hitler's *Blitzkrieg,* lightning war; and by *the Blitz,* the devastating air raids on London by the German Luftwaffe, these raids conceived as a lightning-fast way of forcing Britain to a quick surrender.) So *Blitz,* with pejorative suffix *-ard* (see Vol. I.) → *blizzard.*]

blue murder   A scream of terror or of extreme rage. In Brit. **blue murders.** In Am. commonly in such a phrase as *screaming bloody blue murder.* [No murder is implied. The idiom is from an inventive mistranslation of the Fr. exclam. of vexation or alarm, *morbleu!* a minced oath altered from *mort de dieu!,* God's death!]

boatswain   Or (as pronounced) *bos'n* A petty officer in the navy or merchant marine. [ME *swayne, swain,* a country youth. Prob. into Eng. under IX–X Dane Law < ON *sveinn,* boy, son, servant, one who tends herds. (Cf. *Sven,* common Norse male given name.) Ult. < IE *seu-,* third person (in a household). If third person other than the parents → son; if other than the master and mistress → servant.

A boatswain, therefore, is at root the captain's servant or son as the boat tender. "Boat" here for "ship," earliest ships being themselves open boats.]

book   1. A bound volume of pages. 2. A subsection of a long writing in poetry or prose. [< IE *bhago-,* beech tree. Via Gmnc. in some such skeletal form as *b'g'-* or *b'k'-* → OE *bōk,* document; ME *bok(e),* book. The etymological connection of *beech* and *book* is firmly established, but difficult to explain.

book 27

Runic writing reached the Teutons sometime in III A.D., along trade routes running northwesterly from Asia Minor. I cannot believe that beech bark was used for scrolls of runic writing, which was, at least at first, incised. Beech is a hard wood with a smooth grain and splits easily, but I doubt that tablets of beech were split off with wedges, trimmed, sanded smooth, and used for runic carvings. In any case, I can find no record of any surviving specimen of such scrolls nor of fine, small tablets in any museum. There are, however, many surviving examples of runes incised in stone or on wooden staves (and later on shields, cups, and other metal objects). Beech is an ideal wood for runic staves and tablets, and the *beech–book* association prob. began with runic carvings on beechwood staves.]

the book Any book of regulations and specifications. *go by the book* To proceed exactly according to regulations and specifications. *book him* [*Book*, here, for "police register."] To enter his name in the record of persons arrested and charged with a criminal offense. *throw the book at him* To charge him with every possible offense against regulations or the penal code. *bring to book* To charge a suspect and require him to answer to charges against him.

book learning Theoretical academic knowledge. (Used only by persons who lack it, and who use the term as a defensive pejorative, implying that their practical experience is a better thing than an advanced education.) *bookkeeper* One who keeps the ledgers. [Word fanciers, puzzlers, and riddlers cite this word as the only one in English with a triple series of double letters. (Or have the computers come up with another?)] *bookmaker* 1. A manufacturer of books. 2. More commonly *bookie* One who posts odds and accepts bets. *make book on* 1. To act as a bookie. (Though in this sense more commonly *make book*). 2. To bet on confidently. *You can make book on that* = it is a sure thing. 3. *Ext. to any context.* To be able to rest assured. [Is the assumption that bookies always win?]

close the book(s) on 1. To make the last accounting entry in abandoning a financial enterprise. 2. To write off an account receivable as uncollectible. 3. *Generalized ext.* Close out. Have done with. *in one's book* In one's opinion. [The root idea is of a bookie setting the odds according to his evaluation of things.] *in one's black book* In disfavor. [Various stories are told of persons proscribed in various registers, but I can find no specific black book that can be asserted to be the prototype.] *know someone like a book* To know someone in minutest detail. (But why is it always the illiterate who claim to know me like a book?) *one for the book* A notable act, thing, event. [Worth recording in the book of world records.] *he wrote the book on it* He knows everything about it. [As if he had written the book of regulations and specifications that others must turn to when in doubt.]

borscht Now, a beet soup. In U.S. a standard delicacy of Jewish cooking, transfigured to a gourmet classic by the addition of sour cream and chopped chives, dill, parsley. [But earlier, turnip soup; the root, slightly altered in Yiddish, being Russian *borsch,* cow turnip. By association with Jewish cookery, I had thought the substitution of beets for turnips to be an act of Jewish civilization, and the addition of sour cream to be an act of Jewish genius; but I must yield to Anton Chekhov, noting in passing that Russian Jews were permitted few opportunities for gourmet cooking.

In Chekhov's story "The Siren's Song," 1887, translated by Ralph E. Matlau, a Russian gourmand, rhapsodizing on ideal menus, speaks of *beet borsch,* and ascribes it to the Ukrainians: ". . . a nice little Ukrainian beet borsch with nice little bits of ham and nice sausages. It's served with sour cream and fresh snipped parsley and dill." The ham and sausages would exclude this Ukrainian soup from the diet of Russian Jews, and I will assert that the removal of these meat chunks from American kosher cooking has purified the borscht we know.]

boudoir What a woman calls her bedroom when she is feeling dramatic. [Root sense: "pouting quarters." So Fr. *boudoir* < *bouder,* to pout. Because the lady, when miffed, retired there. In great houses the husband had his private quarters and the wife hers. When the mood was right they called on one another. When the truth was out and flying, they withdrew and locked their doors. The lady's boudoir commonly consisted of a sitting room, bedroom, dressing room, and bath-toilet. When in full pout, she had her meals served there.]

boulevard A wide, usu. tree-lined and landscaped thoroughfare inside a city. [The untraced root is Gmnc., resulting in Ger. *Bollwerk,* at lit. root, bulwark, but in effect, city wall. Whence MD *bulwere;* OF *boloart, belouart.* Because boulevards were first built along the course of ancient city walls, which were torn down when the city outgrew them. City walls, it must be remembered, were usu. massively thick, often with shops and houses built into them, commonly with a roadway on top (reached by stairs) and in some cases with churches. Sometimes as the city grew, new walls were built around the first ones and some distance beyond them, the old walls often being cannibalized for stones. Vienna has a broad circular boulevard around the center of town, built on the site of its demolished early wall.]

HISTORIC. In the U.S. in the early days of the automobile, city planners deliberately planned winding landscaped drives (now often traffic nightmares) for "motoring pleasure." There were no city walls to establish the course, but early American builders of motor highways looked to European boulevards as partial models. As part of the early American concept of "motoring pleasure," commercial traffic was banned from boulevards, and the ban still commonly persists on American boulevards.

Alley (< Fr. *aller*, to go) is, by a language convention, a short, narrow passageway (a "go-away") and in Am. implies "in the city," though in Brit. usage, sometimes synonymous with *lane. Avenue* (< Fr. *avenir*, to arrive) is, at root, a more or less imposing, wide approach to the heart of the city. Park Avenue in New York was originally designed as such a stately approach to the heart of the city, ending in the towering gateway of Grand Central Terminal. The original Ecole des Beaux Arts concept was to line the avenue with sumptuous five-story houses dominated by the great mass of Grand Central; though much of the avenue is now lined by billboard skyscrapers, each seemingly striving to out-dazzle the others.

bowels   (Plu. except in compounds.) 1. The intestines. 2. *Figurative.* The seat of deepest feelings. *bowels of compassion.* 3. Deep inner part. *gnome-guarded treasures from the bowels of the earth.* [A complex evolution by association. < L. *botulus,* sausage, dim. form *botellus,* little sausage; OF *buele,* ME *bouel,* bowel. Bowels do, of course, resemble sausage links. But there is a further association in the fact that until recent times (before the introduction of synthetics) animal intestines were used as sausage casings.]

   bowels of compassion The deepest seat of human tenderness and sympathy. [As if there were some organ of compassion in the bowels, conceived as the core of deepest feeling. In a similar assumption, the Greeks, seeking to explain the fact that women did not control their emotions as men did, attributed their emotional outbursts to some specifically female organ, and believed they had found it in the uterus, which is Gk. *hystera,* whence both *hysterectomy* and *hysteria.*]

   bowel movement A defecation. [Clinically justified because defecation is caused by the undulant peristaltic motion of the intestines. In general use, however, the form is an effort to avoid the shock word "shit."] Also ***movement*** *Good morning, nurse. Did you have a movement?* Also ***b.m.*** Bowel movement. [Now common in nursery prattle as a latter-day replacement of *caca* and *poo-poo.*]

HISTORIC. *Bowels* and *botulism* have a common etymological source, and are also connected by association. Botulism is a form of food poisoning caused by the toxic wastes of the bacillus *Clostridium botulinum* infecting such preserved meats as sausages. If the intestines used for casings were not thoroughly washed out, even a bit of remaining fecal matter could introduce the bacilli into the food.

Botulism is New Latin, i.e., from Latin but unknown to the Romans. *Clostridium botulinum* is XIX scientific mishmash, combining L. *botulinum* with Latinized Gk. *clostridium* < Gk. *klōstēr*, spindle, with *ideon*, shape, form (IDEA). Hence "spindle-shaped sausage bacterium." *Bacillus* is, at root, "rod, walking stick," because bacilli occur as short, straight, sticklike units commonly linked together—like sausages, or like small rods or walking sticks.

bozo   *Am.* 1. A guy who doesn't amount to much. An ordinary, dime-a-dozen stiff. Whence: 2. *Circus.* A traditional name for a clown, commonly billed as *Bozo the Clown.* [< Sp. *bozo,* the down that forms on the cheeks of a boy before he reaches shaving age. Hence, a boy; hence, less than a man; hence, an inferior being. This identical sense was expressed in earlier Eng. by *beardless youth,* which in fond contexts could mean "boy," but was commonly used pejoratively to assert the dignity of elders as compared to the status of the unformed young.]

braille   A form of writing and printing for the blind in which the alphabet, numerals, and punctuation signs consist of a series of variously arranged embossments that a trained hand can identify by touch. [Invented by Louis Braille, 1809–1852, French musician and educator, who was blind from birth.]

NOTE. A persistent legend has it that a Napoleonic officer (never identified) first conceived the idea of embossed messages and commands so that the officer receiving them could read in the dark, with no need to use a lantern, which might reveal his position to the enemy. The legend is an obvious spook etymology. It takes trained and sensitive fingers to read an embossed message palpably. Nor is there any record of headquarters clerks trained to em-boss such messages. As a French general remarked of the charge of the Light Brigade, *"C'est magnifique, mais c'est ne pas la guerre."* The blind read braille only after careful study, for which they are motivated by the sad fact of having no other choice.

brand new   Just made. [At root: "hot off the fire, hot off the forge," originally with ref. to a newly forged sword, whence, in chivalric macho, the sword itself. So Tennyson, deliberately using archaic English: "the brand, Excalibur," i.e., the sword, Excalibur. Shakespeare expressed it as "fire new." < OE *brand,* burning branch, burning log, and esp. a branch burning at one end, a torch. Whence:] *firebrand* A troublemaker. A hothead who marches with a torch and sets fire to things as a way of voting. And so *brand/ branding iron* An identifying sign ineradicably burned into an animal; the hot iron used to make this sign. *brand name* The identifying label of the maker, as if burned ineradicably into his product.

Brazil   The South American country established by the Portuguese in XVI. [*Brasil, brasilwood, brazilwood,* with cognate variants in many European languages, were in use by XII to label a red wood from which a dye was extracted. As the Portuguese developed their colony in South America, they found a huge supply of red dye wood closely similar to that known earlier in Europe, and the country derived its name by association with this popular article of commerce. The word we now render as *Brazil* is of unknown origin.]

bread   [IE *bhrew-* (BREW), to bubble (as a ferment), to rise (as bread dough). Via Gmnc. with suffix *-d-* → OE *brēod, brēad,* bread. Also, food.] 1. Flour variously mixed with a liquid and kneaded, usu. with a leavening agent, and baked. 2. Food in general. So **break bread** To eat. And so **give us this day our daily bread** Give us this day our daily food. 3. Basic sustenance. *to earn one's bread in the sweat of one's brow.* 4. *Slang.* Money. [The wherewithal of life. This usage, first in Black English and then in Mod slang, has been recently revived. It was in use in mid XVIII Brit. slang *out of bread,* out of work, i.e., without wherewithal.]

   bread basket The belly. *bread and butter* Basic subsistence. *to earn one's bread and butter. bread-and-butter adj.* Of basic subsistence ("thing done just to get along"). *He took a series of bread-and-butter jobs and hated them. bread line* A line formed by the indigent to get a dole of free food. *on the bread line* Indigent.

breadwinner The family member who, so to speak, "brings home the bacon."

HISTORIC. Man's earliest bread must have been unleavened, a mixture of ground grains and water similar to johnnycake and tamales. The double sense of IE *bhreu-*, above, indicates that leavened bread was in use by about the fifth millennium B.C.. i.e., in early Indo-European. Yet the evidence is that leavened bread was uncommon in Europe, or at least in northern Europe, into XIX. I have a damaged copy (bibliographical data missing) of *Origins and Meanings of Popular Phrases and Names* by Basil Hargrave. Hargrave reports, unfortunately without giving a source, and with some evasive phrasing, as "it is reported": "The making of bread into loaves, instead of flat cakes, seems to have come into Europe comparatively recently. Even in the beginning of the 17th century loaf bread was almost unknown in many parts of the continent and it is reported that in 1812, when an English captain had ordered loaves to the value of one pound sterling in Gothenburg, the baker stipulated for payment in advance, on the ground that he would be unable to sell the loaves in the case they were left on his hands."

bread cast upon the waters In common usage, an act of spiritual investment that will be returned manyfold. But more accurately, to strip oneself of all earthly possessions, knowing that they are vanities and that only by so stripping oneself can one achieve spiritual perfection. [Ecclesiastes 11:1: "Cast thy bread upon the waters, for thou shall find it after many days." The idea of forsaking the things of this world in order to achieve spiritual perfection is common to many religions, but let it be said that the Bible commonly achieves better metaphors than this one; for even if one does get back what one cast away, what good is soggy bread? And how is one to find it after many days? Perhaps the metaphor will become glowingly clear among the revelations of Heaven.]

breaker 1. A long rolling wave that breaks on the shore or in crossing a reef. 2. *In the days of sailing ships.* A small water cask, more commonly for use in lifeboats than aboard ship. [Sense 2 < Sp. *barreca* (also *barrica, barril*), barrel. Sense 1 may be < *to break*, agentially "thing that breaks," but if so, heavily influenced by sense 2, being in ext. "thing that rolls (like a barrel)." One side of this necessarily ambiguous rendering emphasizes the breaking of such waves; the other, their rolling.]

briar/brier   Any of several thorny plants resembling both a bush and a vine, typically, the wild rose. [OE *braer, brēr,* is distinct from yet etymologically akin to OF *bruyère,* heather. The similarity of the forms has led to the common wrong assumption that briar pipes are made from the root of the *briar* or *brier.* They are made from the root of the *bruyère,* white heather *(Erica arborea).*]

bridal   [At root: "bride's ale," with ref. to the festive quaffing of ale and pledging of toasts to the bride at the reception after the wedding. OE *brydealu,* lit. bride-ale, was specific to the reception, not to the wedding.] *n.* The wedding ceremony from the bride's point of view. (A wife may refer to her wedding or to her bridal; a husband, only to his wedding. —*adj.* Of the bride.

    bridal path The aisle of the church. [Whimsical. A pun on *bridle path.*]

    bridal shop Originally a shop that specialized in gift-wrapping purported maidenheads in wedding gowns. Now, commonly, one that supplies gowns and accessories for all the female members of the wedding party, from flower bearer(s) to maids of honor to mothers of the wedding pair.

    HISTORIC. The traditional wedding drink was mead (honey wine), but it was expensive, and it would appear that except among the wealthy, only the bride and groom drank it. (See *honeymoon,* Vol. I.) The root sense of *bridal* certainly suggests that the guests at the early British wedding celebrated with tankards of ale, not with goblets of mead.

bridegroom   1. The marital male from the day of his wedding until he has more or less adjusted to it. (*Bride* and *groom* are commonly used in referring to the couple for the first two or three months of their marriage. *Newlyweds* is in common use for the first year. Cf. *spouse.*) [A folk-altered term, commonly taken as if "the bride's servant, attendant." But the OE form was *brydguma,* in which *guma,* man, is cognate with L. *homo,* g/h being a common shift. Ult. < IE *ghom-,* earth, soil, humus, with reference to the Biblical clay from which God is said to have formed Adam; and also with the earthly sense: "earth creature, inhabitant of the earth."]

brown-nose   An ass-kisser. *to brown-nose* To seek favor with one's superior(s) by ass-kissing. [Vulgar exuberance. Because this sort of *sycophant* (see Vol. I), in kissing ass to win favor, is said to acquire a spot of local color. Widely used by G.I.s in WWII, but may have been in use before the war.]

bucket shop   A dishonest brokerage house that speculates for its own gain with money received from customers. Necessarily fly-by-night operations, bucket shops simply closed up when their frauds could no longer be covered up. But no problem: they simply opened in another setting. Bucket shops have been put out of business, or presumably put out of business, by the Securities and Exchange Commission. In America c. 1875, a bucket shop was a cheap bar, often in a cellar, that sold most of its beer by the bucket (growler), to be taken out.

In 1882 the Chicago Board of Trade (now the Commodities Market) ruled that it would not accept grain futures trades in less than 500-bushel lots, with equivalent minimums for futures in other commodities. To handle small, odd-lot speculators, curb markets developed around the Board of Trade, and were taken to be the equivalent of bucket shop beer dives as opposed to ornate and affluent saloons. These odd-lot curb brokers were not necessarily dishonest, but it was easy for them to sharp their customers, and honesty rarely triumphs over dishonesty made easy. When sharpers opened small unregulated brokerage houses with pure intent to defraud, the label *bucket shop* was transferred to them.

Intermediately, a bucket was enough fractional orders to make up a trading lot on the Board of Trade, and brokers, some of them at least half honest, worked on the curb to put buckets together.

budge   *Slang.* A woman's bosom, esp. the brassiere encasing it and conceived as a sack or pouch for storage and safekeeping of small objects. *She slipped (stuffed) the double sawbuck into her budge* = She put the $20 bill into the Cleavage National Bank. [< Early ME *bugee*, pouch. < It. *bolgia*, sack, purse, ditch (BULGE, BUDGET). XIV *budge*, the lambskin bands that trimmed an academic gown (and caused a chest bulge where the two bands met and overlapped).]

But *budge*, to stir, to move, is < OF *bougier* < L. *bollire*, to boil, the connective sense being "agitated motion."

bump   [Echoic. "Things that go bump in the night." Of a class with *thud, wham, thump.*] *v.* To strike against. To collide. —*n.* 1. A bodily swelling caused by a blow or by colliding with a hard object. 2. Any rounded protrusion. A heap. 3. *Further ext.* A piled plenty.

[ODEE cites, 1566, "bumping bignes" (but gives no source).] *be bumped WWII.* To lose one's seat, esp. on a plane, to someone with a higher priority. *bump into* 1. To collide. 2. To encounter by chance. *bump off Criminal slang.* To murder gangland style. *bumps and grinds In girlie shows, esp. in burlesque.* An erotic dance routine. A grind is a circular pelvic motion; a bump, a sudden pelvic thrust forward.

bumper 1. A metal strip at the front and rear of an automobile, as an always inadequate (because stupidly designed) anticollision device. 2. A drinking vessel filled to the brim, and over. Earlier *bumperkin,* with *kin* as a fond diminutive. Also, Brit. only, *bumper glass.* [A spook etymology refers this form to the Fr. toast *au bon Père,* to the Pope. And carousers are readily capable of toasting the Pope while raising the devil. But "bumping bignes" (see *bump,* sense 3) remains the source, as in:] *bumper crop* An especially abundant (heaped) harvest.

bumpkin A mannerless, mentally scant person. *country bumpkin* A yokel. (I have never come upon *city bumpkin,* but that would be a yokel with pavement under his feet.) *bumptious adj.* Rude, crude, and distastefully forward. [The sense has certainly been influenced by the similar, though unrelated, forms *bump* ("heap" and also "not smooth".) and *bumpkin,* but the word is derived from XVI Du. *boomkin,* little tree, with the effective senses: "stunted, not properly developed, not worth much." It. uses *scemo,* scant, not complete, and by ext., fool, nitwit. And cf. common Am. slang: "He's not all there."]

burglar A thief who breaks and enters. [At root: "town thief." (As if there were no burglars in the country!) L. *borgus,* (walled) city. (See *bhergh-,* Vol. I.) Late L. *burgus;* and also *burgator* (with variant *burgulator*), town thief. In Norman Fr., once the legal language of England, *burgler. Bhergh-* in IE meant "high"; but came to mean "high walls defending a city," and so "wall." A burglar, implicitly, is one who enters "through walls."] *v.* 1. **burglarize.** 2. *Colloq.* **burgle.**

bush: beat about the bush To hem and haw. To avoid direct action. [The idiom is partially obscured by *beat the bushes,* to scour an area exhaustively, to campaign for every possible vote, originally the action of game beaters, who formed a line abreast at close intervals, flushing and driving forward all game. The present idiom is from XVII *go about the bush,* said of a hound that pursues game but veers around obstacles when to do so might mean to let the game get away. Attested only with ref. to hounds, but the same might as readily be said of beaters who avoid a copse for fear there might be a potentially dangerous boar, bear, or stag in it. It is on such an avoidance of the direct thrust that the modern idiom is based.]

business *Theater.* A discrete piece of stage action. *fifth business* Also *Fifth Business. Archaic.* 1. A secondary but essential supporting role. 2. The actor or actress who plays it. [Robertson Davies, to explain his title, *Fifth Business,* a best-selling novel in 1970, offers a definition from Tho. Overskou, *Den Danske Skueplads:* "Those roles which, being neither those of Hero or Heroine, Confidant nor Villain, but which were nonetheless essential to bring about the Recognition or *dénouement,* were called the Fifth Business in drama and opera companies organized according to the old style; the player who acted these parts was often referred to as Fifth Business." I am not certain of the old style here referred to, but according to the definition as given, I would take Laertes to be the Fifth Business in *Hamlet.* He is more referred to than visible in the main action of the play, yet his last-act dueling scene with Hamlet resolves the plot, bringing the whole drama to its chaotic resolution.]

butterfly The common and lovely insect. [Not as various dictionaries (including, quite incredibly, the valuable NWD) assert, because first applied to yellow (butter-colored) species, but because Old English folklore had it that these insects sucked milk and newly churned butter. So OE *buttorfleoge,* fly (drawn to) butter. Butterflies do suck flower nectar. Two qualified entomologists tell me they doubt a butterfly could suck a substance as cohesive as butter, but that they might be attracted to it. The Old English belief derives from the Germanic, in which it emerges more specifically as *Schmetterling,* cream-licker. The common assertion that *butterfly* is a metathesized form of *flutter-by* is whimsical.

The L. *papilio* is a redupl. form of IE *pel-,* to flutter, to swim, to fly. It survives in the botanical adjective *papilionaceous,* shaped like a butterfly. Also in Fr. *papillon.* And the same IE stem with p/f in Gmnc. → OE variant *fifealde,* butterfly. European languages have generally coined distinctive names for this creature: It. *far-*

falla, Sp. *mariposa,* Portuguese *borboleta,* Rumanian *fluture,* and Fr., as above, *papillon.*]

   social butterfly One who flutters from one social do to another. *butterfly bolt* A bolt with a spring-loaded nut. When inserted into a wall cavity through a drilled hole, the nut spreads its "wings." Used esp. through plaster or plaster board, the spread bolt serving as a clamp.

buttery   *In Brit.* 1. A pantry. Part of the domain of the butler. 2. *Earlier but with some survival.* A wine cellar. In charge of the butler (bottler). *In Am.* Survives only as an assertively chic, if not gay, name for a restaurant. [Any association with butter is by folk distortion. The root sense is "wine cellar"; the root word, *butt,* a cask.]

buttinski   One who insistently intrudes in the affairs of others. [< *butt in,* to intrude, to pry into the affairs of other, the act of being nosy. Modified, c. 1880, by Jewish immigrants or their children, by the addition of *-ski,* common Polish surname ending. Also, a bit later, perh. c. 1900, *Mr. Buttinski,* an archly ironic title of respect. *A little help I could use; a Mr. Nosy Buttinski I got no need for.* Mr. Buttinski's Brit. slang cousin is the well-known Nosey Parker.]

by and large   On the whole. In general. [< Nautical English in the days of sailing ships. The act of sailing a ship with sails close hauled (trimmed flat) and close to the wind. *Full and by* meant to sail as close to the wind as possible. Since an inexperienced helmsman might in such circumstances be *taken aback* (have the sails blown back against the masts), the related order was *by and large,* which meant to sail a few points off the wind, a less desirable course but a safer one. Hence in lubberly usage: "without totally accurate specification." Or so this lubber understands it, by and large.]

C

cab A taxi. [< *cabriolet,* a light public carriage. < Old It. *caprio,* wild goat; because these carriages were lightly bouncy and ran easily.]

HISTORIC. First introduced in London as a public vehicle on April 23, 1823, its fares set at one-third those of the standard hackney coach (and 'ow's a cabby to make a bloody living at tuppence to the tanner?). As part of the public blather, it was said to be in honor of His Majesty's birthday, the then resident majesty being the Hanoverian George IV. *Cabriolet* was shortened almost at once to *cab.* (This *cab* is not to be confused with the *cab* of a truck, crane, steam shovel, in which context *cab* means "control room" and is from *cabin.*)

cabal 1. A conspiratorial, implicitly evil group. 2. The secret plots and plans of such a group. [Hebrew *quabbālāh* → L. *cabala,* received doctrine. *Cabala* Bible-like books of rabbinical theosophism based on Scriptural interpretations so abstruse as to seem to be the decodings of mystic cryptanalysts. It was from these writings that *cabal* acquired the implication "arcane secrets," and from the fact that many churchmen denounced cabalistic doctrine that the word acquired the implication "darkly evil."]

HISTORIC. Under Charles II of England (reigned 1660–1685), the king's cabinet consisted of the five powerful ministers *C*lifford, *A*rlington, *B*uckingham, *A*shley, *L*auderdale, and the closed-door deliberations of these power brokers was jokingly said to be the origin (or at least the ultimate exemplum) of a *cabal.* There have been worse political jokes, but in etymology, after-the-fact-derivations do not count.

cadge To get by begging, cunning, wheedling. [Origin uncertain, but ME has **cacchen,* to catch, to snare (CATCH).]

NOTE. In falconry, a *cadge* (prob. a variant of *cage*) was a portable roost on which three or four hooded falcons were carried to the hunt, and the hunt servant who carried it was called the *cadger*.

The falcon is an endangered species, but a few doughty enthusiasts still hunt with falcons. By what seems to be a Falconers' Club rule, any falconer seems eager to explain that to *cadge tips* is, at root, to carry the cadge so solicitously that the noble falconer will toss the cadger a coin.

This spook etymology is ingenious, but as unlikely as it is unattested. Falconry was a lordly sport served by a trained retinue. There was no reason to reward the cadger more than the other hunt servants. The sense does not concur, for to *cadge* implies cunning and there was no particular cunning in the work of the hunt cadger. Nor were nobles in the habit of tipping servants for doing no more than was expected of them. In riding after deer, for example, the reward of the hunt servants was a dinner of meat pie made from the guts of the kill, while the lords sat to great roasts of venison. (See *humble pie*, Vol. I.)

caitiff   *n. In chivalric tales.* A vile coward. —*adj.* Cowardly. Base. *a caitiff knight.* [L. *captivus* (adj. & n.), captive. Hence, slave (as slavery was the common fate of captured soldiers). Via OF → ME *caitif*, prisoner, slave, base person, miserable wretch. And cf. the It. cognate *cattivo*, adj., bad; n., evil person.]

HISTORIC. Though archaic, the word is familiar to anyone who has read past English literature. It also summarizes a centuries-long view of soldiers who allowed themselves to be captured, and thereby enslaved. Today one may feel some compassion for prisoners of war. The older view was that such human refuse should have had the soldierly guts to die in battle, or to commit suicide in the Roman tradition—a Japanese version of which was strongly in force in WWII.

Irish warriors, when all was lost, traditionally chose death. Since most battles were fought on beaches, the defeated, still clutching sword and shield, swam out to sea to drown; and such is the reference in Hamlet's well-known, but commonly misunderstood, lines: "Or to take arms against a sea of troubles,/And, by opposing, end them."

calculus   A branch of mathematics formulated by Archimedes in crude form, but left undeveloped until XVIII. A student of mathematics gets (or used to get) to simple calculus at the end of high school or the beginning of college. It is not, therefore, a highly advanced form of mathematics, but I am too ignorant to attempt a definition or even to understand the definitions offered by my betters. [Root sense: "pebble" (with ref. to counting stones such as those used in an abacus) (CALCULATION). < L. *calculus,* little stone. < *calx, calcis,* limestone (CALCIFICATION).]

calendar   1. A tabulation of the year(s) by day, date, week, and month. 2. A dated book marked with the time and place of appointments. *I have no time for it on my calendar.* And so **court calendar** A schedule of cases to be heard. [The association with L. *kalenda,* the first day of each month, is obvious. Less well known is the derivation of *calenda, kalenda* < *calare,* to call (out), to announce. Because in Roman custom the first day of each month was proclaimed through the streets by town criers.

  And this might sufficiently explain the term. But L. *calendarium* was an account book kept by moneylenders, interest and payments being due (called) on the first of each month. Whence **call a loan** To announce (as if by the town crier) that payment is due on penalty of forfeit of pledged goods. And so, too: **call a case to court** To set the date for a hearing (according to the calling of the kalends, or calends).] And see *Greek calends.*

callous   Unfeeling. Insensitive. [< L. **callus, *callum,* hardened skin. In Am. *callus,* but the Brit. spelling is *callous.* A natural metaphor, the insensitivity of hardened skin being transferred to emotional insensitivity.]

calm   *adj.* Serene. At ease. —*v.* To soothe. To induce tranquillity. — *n.* 1. The condition of being relaxed, unagitated. 2. *Weather.* A windless period. **the calm before a storm** 1. Primarily a nautical observation, that a calm, windless period forebodes a storm (and to be sure, the wind has always, eventually, picked up again after a calm). 2. A foreboding time of calm in any context (with the natural pessimism of the folk mind, the feeling that really good times cannot last long, but can only forebode bad times ahead—which also seems to be true, given time enough). **becalmed** *Nautical.* The condition of a sailing ship when there is no wind. [An extraordinary evolution from "to burn" to "heat of the day" to "rest (siesta) taken in the heat of the day" to "tranquillity so induced." Ult. < IE *keu-, kau-,* to burn (CAUSTIC). In Late L., suffixed -*m*- → *cauma,* the heat of the day ("time when the sun burns hottest"). And so Old It. *calma* with a sense shift from "burning time of day" to "rest then taken." In OF and ME *calme,* with the burning root sense lost and the senses "at rest, tranquil" established. "But oh, what a burning calm we had / That afternoon in Millie's pad!" *Retrospetto,* Giovanni Nostalgico.

cancel   *v.* 1. To strike a word or a passage from a text by drawing a line or lines through it. 2. To draw or imprint a line or lines on the face of a postage stamp to prevent its reuse. 3. *Ext.* To eliminate, delete, call off a stated performance, appointment, reservation, or order for goods. [As if drawing lines across it.] 4. To offset. *(a)* *Mathematics.* To strike out equal values on either side of an equation. *(b)* To counterbalance one thing by its equal opposite. Commonly ***cancel out.*** *Joe votes Republican, his wife votes Democratic, and their politics, like their sex life, cancels out to nothing.* [Root image: "superimposed grid." < L. *cancer,* lattice; dim. form *cancellus,* little lattice, screen, grille. In Medieval L. the latticed screen behind which a court functionary had his desk. It. *cancello,* screen, wicket. And Eng. *chancel,* the grille or lattice between the choir and the nave (CHANCELLOR).]

cannibal   1. A man-eating human being. 2. *Ext.* Any animal that eats its own kind. ***cannibalize*** 1. To eat the flesh of one's own kind. [But in this sense rare.] 2. *In WWII and since.* To repair machinery, esp. airplanes, tanks, and trucks, by taking parts from similar machines that have been damaged beyond repair. [First used by Columbus in the form *Canibalis,* which may be explainable as a variant of *Carib* or *Caribes* with a common r/n dissimilation; but as part of Columbus's hemispheric error, he believed he had reached India, the land of the Grand Khan of Tartary, and on the shores presumably ruled by that khan, Columbus prob. took *Canibalis* to mean "people of the khan." It seems certain that Carib people were to some extent cannibals, and that the Aztecs ate human flesh as their main source of protein, Aztec priests sacrificing captives at the top of steep pyramids, reserving choice cuts for their own use and then rolling the bodies down the steep sides of the pyramid to the people waiting below, in what must have been an extraordinary church fair.]

canopy   [At root: "mosquito netting (above and around a bed)." So Gk. *kōnōpium* < *kōnōps,* mosquito. These non-native Greek forms are < *Canopus* ("Mosquitotown?"), an ancient Egyptian city from which the Greeks learned the use of mosquito netting. Whence a wide range of senses has developed, all stressing the flat upper panel above a canopied bed, and tending to suppress the vertical side netting.] 1. A flat cloth covering above a bed. 2. An ornamental cloth spread above a throne, or carried on poles above a personage in procession. 3. The sky. *the canopy of heaven.* 4. Overhanging foliage. *a canopy of leaves.* 5. A usu. laterally curved ornamental canvas affixed to metal poles running from curb to entrance of restaurants, private clubs, apartment houses, and various public buildings. 6. *Architecture.* A more or less flat roof with a prominent projection beyond the building. 7. *Aviation.* *(a)* The plastic bubble over the cockpit of a fighter plane or light aircraft. *(b)* The spread cloth of a parachute in descent.

And in modified form *canapé* [Fr. loan word.] A cracker or small shaped slice of bread or toast covered with any of an endless range of spreads and served as an appetizer.

cantankerous   *adj.* 1. *Now.* Testy. Contentious. Curmudgeony. 2. *Earlier but obs.* Given to brawling. (The sense shift has been from physical violence to moody snappishness.) [ME *contekour,* a brawler. < Norman Fr., prob. of lost Scandinavian origin, *contek,* a quarrel, a brawl.] Also in Am. *cantanker* A fit of testiness.

caper   *n.* 1. A frisky leap. A merry antic. 2. A madcap escapade. 3. *Criminal slang.* A criminal escapade. —*v.* To gambol, more or less like a goat. [IE *kapro-,* billy goat. → L. *caper,* It. *capra,* a goat. It. *capriolo,* wild goat; *capriola,* the antic bounding of a wild goat; *capriccio,* an antic whimsy, a whimsical music (CAPRICE). (Is sometimes parsed as *capo,* head; *riccio,* hedgehog, hence "shaggy headed," with effective sense "whimsical." But ???)]

carat   1. A measure of weight of gemstones. 2. A measure of the fineness of gold, 24 carat indicating pure gold. [A trade word. < Arabic *gīrāt,* weight of four grains. But derived from Gk. *kéras,* horn → *kération.* 1. A little horn. 2. Seed of the locust tree (because it is shaped, if only fancifully, like a little horn). 3. A small weight as measured by locust seeds. (*Grain* and *seed* are, in this sense, the same thing.)]

HISTORIC. From a time before recorded history man must have used small seeds as weights. The principle must have been simple: The weight of individual seeds might vary minutely, but if 10, 20, 50, or more small seeds were established as the weight, the variations would average out, and something like a true and constant standard (with allowances made for natural chicanery in lightening or weighting the seeds) would be available for weighing out precious goods. In any case, these "seed" standards of weight were formalized in early historic times.

cardigan   A long-sleeved, button-front sweater with a plain (not fold-back) collar. [After the seventh earl of Cardigan (1797–1868), who popularized this sort of sweater by making it his standard country wear.]

cardinal   1. A prince of the Roman Catholic Church and member of the Sacred College, which elects the Pope from its own members and serves as his chief advisory body. [Ult. < L. *cardō,* hinge ("that upon which things turn"). *cardinalis,* important. In Medieval L. *cardinalis* signified any cleric with a fixed assignment to a given church ("attached to it as a door is attached to a structure by its hinges"). Not till XII did *cardinalis* become specific to the members (then 70) of the Sacred College. Eng. *cardinal,* first used in XIII with ref. to the **cardinal virtues** justice, fortitude, temperance, prudence; so called because the good life "hinges" upon them.] 2. The crested North American finch, whose males have bright red plumage. [By association with the red cap and robes of an ecclesiastical cardinal.] 3. *Color.* Also *cardinal red.* A dark scarlet.

   cardinal number Mathematics. Zero and the counting numbers one, two, three to infinity, conceived as aggregate entities or magnitudes; as opposed to the ordinals, first, second, third, etc., which indicate placement in a series. [< L. *cardinalis,* important; the implicit assumption, seemingly, being that quantity or magnitude is more important than mere placement in a series.]

care   [IE *gar-,* to cry out, to lament. With g/k in Gmnc. → OE *caru,* sorrow, penury, drudgery. And so *life of care,* a life of sorrowful drudgery and penury. (Which is to say, the life of the world's poor.) The progression of meanings in Eng. has been from OE *caru,* the toilsome griefs of poverty → XIV *care,* responsibility for / in charge of. *The orphan was placed in her charge and care:* as in It. *a cura di,* in the charge of (one who pays painstaking attention, as the collater and purifier of a text). And so to XVI, attentive to, kindly and painstaking impulse, affection for. The original sense is no longer primary, but survives in such constructions as "her children have been a care to her."] 1. Affectionate impulse. *He cares for her.* 2. Charge of. *The estate was put in his care.* 3. Attention to, watchfulness. *Take care; the roads are icy.* (And corresponding verbs.)

Dame Care A folk personification of toilsome penury. **careless**
1. *Archaic.* Not burdened by OE *caru.* 2. Heedless. Unattentive.
Sloppy. **caretaker** A custodian of property. **careworn** Afflicted by
many burdens, griefs, toils. **not have a care in the world** To be
blithe, unworried, unburdened. **care and feeding of** A fixed phrase.
Originally with ref. to child nurture and animal husbandry, but
now widely generalized. *Wernher von Braun has spent his life on
the care and feeding of rockets.*

CARE package   Relief supplies sent to the poor of underdeveloped
countries. [CARE purportedly an acronym derived from *C*ooperative for *A*merican *R*elief *E*verywhere, but obviously, as is now
common practice, the acronym came first and the cumbersome
name of the charitable organization was fitted to it. As a personalized public relations touch, *package* to suggest delivery to an individual, though in more efficient fact, relief food and supplies are
delivered in bulk and distributed to individuals by resident agents
of the cooperative.] 2. *Whimsical.* Any of the packages of goodies
my wife sends to our rich son in college, as distinct from the checks
I send to keep him rich, and me indigent.

career   [At root: "a racecourse"; variantly: "a pounding charge of
horses." In XVI with the senses: race / race course / course of
action. Ult. < IE *kers-,* to run (COURSE). → L. *carrus,* chariot. But
in It. *corso,* OF *charrière,* Fr. *carrière,* racecourse.] *n.* 1. The total
or partial course of one's life work. [Metaphoric. As if "the race one
runs in this life." *His career in crime was interrupted by hanging.*] 2. A wild rush of horses. [Rare. More commonly as a verb. *The
frightened herd broke through the fence and careered through the
corn field.*]

   career girl A professional woman as distinct from a wife-
housekeeper. [In male chauvinist context, a woman competing in
the business world with males, who until recently tended to regard
her as a freakish intruder. But variantly, an actress, artist, or musician is said to work at her career. (Does a compulsive career girl
pursue a planned course, or does she charge about like wild
horses?)]

carp   To complain incessantly of petty grievances. To pick endlessly
at small faults. [IE *ger-,* to croak like a raven or a stork. Since these
birds tend to call gratingly over and over, the frequentative sense

is implicit in the root. Via Gmnc. with g/k and suffixed prob. -*p*-
→ ON *karpa*, to boast and brag incessantly. Into ME under the
Danish occupation (IX–X) as *carpen*, to converse, in which the root
sense, "to crow and croak," seems to have been temporarily suppressed, though since restored. The sense progression *to croak, to
brag, to converse, to complain* (always implying repeated action) is
a bit puzzling, but certainly not beyond the limits of language.]

caterer   *Now.* One who supplies and serves prepared meals for ban-
quets and large parties. A caterer delivers his food to an appointed
address, usu. a private house. He differs in this from a restaurateur,
who serves at a fixed place of business, and also in that he serves
essentially the same food to all guests. *Earlier.* One who supplied
whatever one wished. So, in present sense: *cater* To provide a food
service. But in surviving earlier sense: *cater to* 1. To indulge. To
provide for any wish. Whence: 2. To defer to. To attend upon
solicitously, obsequiously. [< L. *acceptāre*, to accept. OF *acater*, to
buy ("to accept at the stated price"), in Fr. *achater*. OF *acatour*,
purchasing agent for an estate or a monastery. Also, a buyer. → ME
catour, a supplier. But this form soon replaced in ME by (now obs.)
maunciple, manciple, for which modern Eng. uses "purchasing
agent."]

caterpillar   The larval stage of various insects, esp. of the butterfly and
the moth. [At root: "hairy cat," and usu. glossed < L. *catta*, cat;
with *pilosa*, hairy. But *cattapilosa* does not occur in Latin. Perhaps
a folk metaphor of vernacular Latin. In Medieval L., *catyrpel* → OF
chatepelose → ME *catirpel*. XVI *caterpiller*, with the doubled *l*,
must have come about by association with *pillage* because these
larvae despoil leaves. A common Ger. dialect form is *Teufelskatz*,
devil's cat, prob. for the same reason, but also because it seems to
be an "unnatural" creature in its "magical" power of metamorpho-
sis into a winged adult. In his *Dictionary*, Samuel Johnson first gave
the form as *caterpillar*, with the *a* in the last syllable.]

   caterpillar tread The endless track tread of military tanks and
of some farm and earth-moving machinery, conceived as resembling the many-footed motion of the caterpillar.

   Caterpillar Club A fanciful association of all who have made a
parachute jump. [Primarily Brit. and now archaic in Am. Because
in early aviation parachutes were made of silk, the silk being ultimately a product of caterpillars. Now that parachutes are of syn-

thetic fibers, it is still idiom in making a parachute jump to "hit the silk."]

caucus   *Politics.* An off-the-record meeting of party leaders to discuss issues, strategy, and slates of candidates. [Am. XVIII. Passed into Brit. c. 1878 and made specific to a meeting of party leaders who organized slates for elections. Most dictionaries still dispute the origin of the term, but I submit the following historic account to be conclusive.]

HISTORIC. Misleadingly Latin in appearance, the word came into common use in XVIII Boston as the name of a social and political group called the Caucus Club. An entry of Feb. 1763 in the diary of John Adams reads: "the caucus club meets, at certain times, in the garret of Tom Dawes, the adjutant of the Boston regiment." NWD seeks to derive the word from MHG *kaukos,* drinking cup, but the line of transmission is nebulous, and though "garret" as used by Adams probably meant "top-floor apartment," it is not likely that Tom Dawes could have provided mugs and liquor, pub style, for the more than twenty members mentioned below.

Gordon's *History of the American Revolution,* 1788, as cited in Bartlett's *Dictionary of Americanisms,* 1877, discusses the word as "not of novel invention. More than fifty years ago [i.e., before 1738], Mr. Samuel Adams's father, and twenty others, one or two from the north end of town, where all ship's business is carried on, used to meet, make a caucus, and lay their plans."

Bartlett, misinterpreting this passage, assumed wrongly that the Caucus Club met to discuss shipping matters, and invented, on this assumption, the spook etymology of *caucus* as a corruption of *caulkers.*

His citation is nevertheless evidential, for it places the word in early XVIII use, which puts it within reasonable range (more reasonable in those days of much slower language diffusion) of Captain John Smith of Virginia, who recorded c. 1625 an Indian word which he rendered *caw-cawessough,* giving its meaning as "adviser." Place (the American colonies), date, and sense concurring, the Amerind origin seems to me to be indisputable.

cavort   To prance, caper, frolic. *When Daddy goes to a convention, Mommy always says he is probably cavorting with floozies.* [Unattested, but prob. < *curvet,* an equestrian figure in which the horse leaps forward and kicks out its hind legs just before the front legs touch down. < It. *corvetta,* little curving leap; dim. form of *curva,* curve. < L. *curvus,* curved.]

chap   (Primarily Brit., but within the recognition vocabulary of Am., and in limited use.) A fellow. Esp. a congenial good fellow; and always with this favorable sense in Brit. *old chap.* [By back formation < *chapman,* a street peddler; the sense "congenial" implicit in the fact that chapmen had to be outgoing and affable as part of their sales pitch. Since XVI a chapman has been a street vender of pamphlets and broadsides, but in OE *cēapman,* a retailer at street markets and fairs. (See *cheap,* Vol. I.)

    chapbook 1. A pamphlet of poems, ballads, a topical essay, a religious tract. [What chapmen used to peddle in the streets.] 2. *In Am. literary use.* A pamphlet. A small literary magazine.

chauffeur   [Root sense: "stoker." A French agential form of *chauffer,* to warm. Ult. < IE *kel-,* warm → L. *calēre,* to be warm (CALORIE) → OF *chaufer,* to make warm. By early association with steam automobiles, in which the driver had to stoke the boiler to keep up steam.] *n.* 1. One who drives a private motor vehicle for pay. 2. One licensed to operate a public vehicle for hire. —*v.* To drive someone else here and there. [Originally in sense 1, but in colloq. extension, simply to give a ride to. *John will chauffeur you to the airport.* (But no stoking en route, please.) A loan word in transition. In Am. commonly pronounced *shō´-f'r,* a naturalized form, but some still pronounce it as if French, *shō-fûr´.*]

cheat   [Root sense: "to fall," but the origins of the word can be understood only in the context of the history of British graft. Based on IE *kad-,* to fall (CADENCE) → L. *cadere,* to fall, *excadere,* to fall out (of), whence in the Legal (Norman) Fr. of Britain following the conquest, *eschete,* with specific ref. to entailed feudal estates that reverted (fell) to the crown in the absence of legal heirs. The slightly later English form was *escheat.* For many centuries legal agents called *escheators* were responsible for keeping track of such estates and of making inventories of them for the crown. (But how complete need an inventory be? and if a prize bull wanders off into the escheator's estate, or if a few jewels, or a purse of gold, happens to fall into the escheator's pockets, who is to know?) So our word in memory of these grafting agents.] *n.* 1. A deception for gain. A swindle. 2. One who uses such means for gain. 3. A false lover. One who professes honorable intentions but has none. —*v.* 1. To use such means. 2. To betray a beloved, usu. by offering fair proposals to two or more ladies at the same time.

cheat the hangman Often in Am. *cheat the electric chair* 1. To escape a (deserved) death sentence. (Said of a felon who escapes detection and so is not punished, or of one who breaks out of prison before the sentence can be carried out. And also:) 2. To commit suicide before the executioner can do his bit.

check six *Naval pilots' voice code.* 1. An in-flight warning from one pilot to another. Short form of: Look at six o'clock, i.e., look behind you. Implies that there is an enemy fighter there. [A pilot's bearings are indicated as if he were on a clock dial, with the nose of the plane at twelve, the tail at six, and intermediate bearings at intervals of the numbers on a clock face.] 2. In the inevitable boy-boyishness of being on the town, calls a buddy's attention to an attractive girl behind him—or if not exactly behind him, worth checking out on its own merits. As guess only, I doubt that this idiom will pass into general usage, but let it be cited here, once, on its way to oblivion.]

chestnut [< Gk. **kastanea.* → L. *castanea,* It. *castagna,* OF *chastaigne,* Fr. *châtaigne,* chestnut. ME *chesten, chesten nut.*] 1. The tree, the fruit. In Mediterranean Europe it is so important a staple of peasants, who roast it fresh or dry it for storage, that in Italy it is called *pane di montagna,* mountain bread. 2. Also *old chestnut* A stale joke, story, theatrical routine. [A neat analogy. Chestnuts are easily dried and stored, and they keep well, but the flavor of stored (old) chestnuts is never as rich as that of roasted fresh nuts.] 3. The color of the chestnut. Most commonly applied to the coats of horses. 4. A horse of this color.

pull one's chestnuts out of the fire To save the day. [To end up with delicious roast chestnuts instead of a charred mess.] *horse chestnut* A handsome shade tree with large leaves, magnificent many-tiered blossoms, and bearing large, shiny, but inedible nuts in a spiny burr. [Some suggest that the tree is so called because a paste of the leaves and nut pulp was a common folk poultice for horses; and perh. so, but *horse* is a common combining form to label a coarse or inferior variant of plants, as *horse mint, horse nettle, horse radish.* Here, inferior because the nuts are not edible.] *horse chestnuts!* Exclam. of indignant rejection or incredulity. [Am. A minced form of *horse shit.* Horse droppings can be roughly chestnut in color and can resemble the ball made by two chestnuts within a burr.]

chic   *n.* Stylish but subdued elegance. The condition of being unasser-
tively soigné. —*adj.* Smartly stylish. *The essence of chic is to appear
to be elegant without premeditation. The commercialism of chic is
to make that art expensive.* [Once applied to male fops but now
specific to women. May it remain so; chic men are to shuck. <
MHG *shick,* deftness, skill. Perh. influ. by MHG *schicken,* appearance. Fr. *chic* combines these two senses. Also applied to behavior.
*I tried but failed to explain to Bruce Fennessey that it is not chic
to eat peas with a knife unless it is first dipped in honey to keep
them from rolling off.*]

chord   In traditional musical terms, a combination of at least three
harmonious tones sounded together. *cord* A length of string.
[There are various extended and technical senses of both these
terms, all derived intermediately from Gk. *chordē,* a length of
dried intestine (catgut). *Chord* derives from the fact that catgut was
used for stringed instruments; *cord,* from the fact that stretched
catgut looks like a string. Ult. < IE *gher-,* entrails (GORE), the Gk.
form undergoing a g/k. And so L. *chorda,* same sense. The *h* of the
L. form disappeared in OF *corde,* but was reintroduced into the
English musical term. This etymology is disputed and fair reason
may be given for the derivation from *concordance,* at root: "condition of being of (one) heart." And that may do for the musical term,
but *cord* is then left dangling, as it is not if the two senses of Gk.
chordē are taken as the base.]

Christmas comes but once a year   Common catch phrase exhorting
the indifferent to be merry and the merry to be giddy. "Christmas
comes but once a year./Make it merry while it's here." [In *Five
Hundred Pointes of Good Husbandry* the XVI rhymester Thomas
Tupper wrote: "At Christmas play and make good cheer/For
Christmas comes but once a year." Even then the phrase was used
as if it had a sort of proverbial status. (Perhaps the point of good
husbandry is that one Christmas a year is as much as any psyche can
stand.)]

cider   Apple juice. If unfermented, *cider* or *sweet cider.* If fermented
to about the alcoholic content of wine, it is called *hard cider.* The
term also applies to the juice of other fruits, but must then be
qualified by the name of that fruit, as *cherry cider. Apple cider*
occurs, but is redundant. [< Hebrew *shekar,* strong drink. Into Gk.
as *sikera.* OF. *cisdre,* ME *sydir, cidre,* with the primary sense

"strong drink" and secondarily "apple squeezings." In the King James Bible, Luke 1:15 reads: "He shall drink neither wine nor strong drink." Wycliffe's Middle English translation reads: "He schal not drink wyn and sydir."]

cleave There are two words here, one meaning to rend (CLEAVER, CLEAVAGE, CLEFT PALATE); the other, to adhere to ("If I do not remember thee, let my tongue cleave to the roof of my mouth."— Psalms 87:6). It is an accident that these two words of opposite senses have acquired the same form in English.

1. *cleave, cleaving, cleaved, clove, cleft, cloven* To split. [IE *gleubh-*, to split. With g/k in Gmnc. in some such skeletal form as *kl'b-*, whence, with common b/f → OE *cleofan*, and with f/v → ME *cleven, clave, cloven*, the OE *f* surviving in the p.p. *cleft*. The sense has remained the same from the beginning.]

2. *cleave, cleaving, cleaved* And also with the archaic p.p. forms *clove, clave*. To adhere. [IE *gel-*, to compact into a mass, to wad together. Zero-grade form *gl-*, with g/k in Gmnc. and suffixed *-b-* to hypothetical form *kelb-*, and with common b/f → OE *cleofan*, ME *cleven*, to adhere to.]

club 1. A group that meets more or less regularly for some common purpose or special interest, usu. recreational. 2. The place of assigned meeting. *I'll see you at the club.* In Am. commonly *clubhouse*. [ME *clubbe*, billet, prob. < ON *klubba* (same sense), by transmission under IX–X Dane Law. Some seek to derive the term < Ger. *Gelübde*, vow (as if in accepting the club rules), but the dating favors *klubba-clubbe*, as above.]

HISTORIC. The gentlemen's club is a specialized convention of the British caste system, now threatened by inflation and high taxes. One of the laments of upper-middle-class Britons is that they cannot afford to join the club(s) of their fathers. The tradition began with the frequent association of select groups in a favorite pub, the group in time taking over a special room. One of the earliest and best known was informally established c. 1600 at the Mermaid Tavern on Friday Street in London, with Sir Walter Raleigh, Shakespeare, and other literary figures as members. As the British upper middle class prospered, elaborate houses with a full staff of retainers became a home away from home for self-selecting groups of gentlemen.

The natively English character of this institution is attested by the fact that the languages of mainland Europe lack a word for it and use English *club* on loan. So It. *boxing club, tennis club, il club del alpinismo.* And so Fr. *club sportif.*

coal　1. *Present primary sense.* The carbonized organic matter dug by miners. 2. *But earlier, and with first reference to wood.* An ember. [Ult. < IE *geu-lo-*, an ember (GLOW). Via Gmnc. with g/k → OE *col*, a live coal, a glowing ember. And so, too, an ember of peat. Coal, sense 1, did not come into general use as a fuel until XIX.]

　　rake/haul/drag over the coals To berate. To reprimand severely. In slang, to chew out, to blister one's butt. [So today, but earlier a common form of torture, in which the chosen wretch was variously exposed to a bed of hot embers, or grilled over them. The pious legend of St. Lawrence reports that he was so grilled, and being well done on one side, said to the king who had organized the roast: "Thou hast cooked the one side, tyrant; now turn the other and eat"—

　　　　　A level of discourse, I submit,
　　　　　Never heard from a cookout pit.]

Cock-a-nee-nee　(See *cockamamie*, Vol. I.) Trade name of a hard molasses penny candy (to be sucked rather than chewed, though in time it softened in the mouth) popular in NYC in late XIX–early XX. It served to influ. *cockamamie* in the sense: "thing of no consequence." [< New England and upstate NY dialect *cockany*, residual maple syrup that forms into hard lumps and is sucked like hard candy.]

cold duck　A carbonated wine foisted upon Americans (who else would drink it?) by winery ad agencies as a way of getting rid of inferior champagne by mixing it with inferior sparkling burgundy. [Dating c. 1960. The origin of the name is not securely attested, but I lean toward the suggestion of Katherine S. Testar, writing in *Verbatim*, Autumn 1980. German bus boys, she points out, commonly pour into a reserve bucket all the drink left in glasses and bottles. After clearing away for the night, they then drink this salvage at a party of their own called the *Kalte Ende*, the cold end (of the party). In passing into Am., *Ente*, duck, was substituted for *Ende*, and so, mistranscribed from the slop bucket, cold duck.]

　　HISTORIC. Slop-bucket punch must be an ancient scullery custom, and a widespread one. Among the lovable bums of Steinbeck's *Cannery Row* is a bartender who empties all glasses and bottles into such a bucket, his pals later dipping with him for their regular late-night festivity. To the thirsty, all is drink.

cold shoulder   A disdainful sidewise glance along one's shoulder. *give (someone) the cold shoulder* To disdain. To rebuff. [But these are transfer senses. *Shoulder* was originally not one's own shoulder, but a shoulder roast. Shoulder roasts are generally inferior to round roasts. At the tables of the mighty, shoulder roasts were served to inferiors (those who sat below the salt). When such a one had outstayed his welcome, dinner consisted of a few cold (leftover) slices from the inferior shoulder roast. The rules of hospitality were rigid, but a serving of cold shoulder delivered a message. The French, as an added hint to freeloading poor relatives, served such inferiors a practically undrinkable wine called *chasse cousin*, lit. "cousin chaser (away)."

collar   [IE *kwel-* with the general sense: "moving around, about." Variant *kwol-*, the neck ("that on which the head moves around"). Variantly *k(w)ol-* → L. *collum*, neck, *collāre*, necklace. Norman Fr. and ME *coler*, collar necklace.] *n.* 1. The part of a garment that goes around the neck. 2. A band, usu. of leather, fastened around the neck of an animal—or slave (see *boy*, Vol. I)—for securing, tethering, and, c. XI, for harnessing a draft horse. —*v. Police & criminal slang.* To arrest. Also *put a/the collar on.*

    up in the collar Working hard. [Like a horse straining against its collar to pull a plow or a load.] "You run a newspaper and you got to be up in the collar." —A. B. Guthrie, Jr., *The Last Valley*, 1974.

    horse collar 1. A neck harness. (See below.) 2. *Slang.* A derisive dismissal. [A minced form of *horse shit!*] 3. Nothing. [The horse collar conceived as the letter *O* for zero.] 4. No luck or bad luck. *All we got was the horse collar.* [Prob. a whimsical play on "we got it in the neck."]

    HISTORIC. The horse collar, like stirrups, came late. Both appeared c. XI, and they amounted to an enormous technological advance. Stirrups, by allowing mounted men to stand and to reach out far to either side, made for vastly more efficient killing. The collar, by placing the strain on the horse's muscular neck and shoulders, doubled or tripled the work one could get from a draft horse, such animals having been earlier harnessed with a leather strap across the chest, which constrained the heart and limited the horse to a relatively short day's work. These two devices, together with the horseshoe, which was developed two or three centuries earlier, transformed the horse into a creature the ancients could not have imagined.

collation   1. A meal. [A bringing together of the elements required for a meal. So It. *colazione,* a meal; *prima colazione,* breakfast. < L. *collatione,* a collection of writings on a single theme < *collatus,* brought together. OF *collacion* added the sense "discourse" (an orally delivered treatise). From these roots:] 2. Dummy of a projected book (a first bringing together). 3. *In duplicating reports by photocopier.* The arrangement of the pages in exact order to make all copies identical. 4. The close comparison of various editions of a work in order to establish a text closest to the author's intent. 5. The close comparison of all documents in a case to eliminate inconsistencies.

HISTORIC. The shift from these specialized senses to a generalized term for a meal (which, to be sure, must also be "brought together") was probably by association with monastic practice. Monks of various orders gathered after vespers to hear a reading from a *collatione,* commonly of meditations, or of the lives of the saints. An evening meal was then served, skimpy or abundant according to the rules of the order, and the reading was discussed over the meal. By association, then, the meal took on the label of the reading. Cf. *symposium,* at root: "with wine-pouring," the traditional after-dinner discussion of Greek men over their slave-attended wine cups.

collie   The dog, of which there are many strains, most commonly, but not exclusively, the brown-and-white, long-haired, bushy-tailed large dog with a short-haired, sharply pointed snout. Bred originally in Scotland in XVII as a medium-sized shepherd's dog, commonly black, or black with white splashes. [Whence the name, as if *coal-ie* < OE *col,* a live ember, but in this sense as if charred coal, always bearing in mind that coal as it is known to the United Mine Workers union did not come into common use until c. 1835–1840.]

companion   1. A crony, a comrade, a messmate, and a buddy. 2. One who for pay or affection lives with and attends upon an enfeebled person. [At root (same as messmate): "person with whom one shares bread." The word is based on the ancient, sacred significance of "breaking bread together." < L. *com-,* with; *panis,* bread. But the

form is from Medieval L. *companiōnem* (accusative of *companiō*).
Cf. **company** At root: a group that shares food.

companionway   *Nautical.* A stairway or ladder from a deck to the
cabins below. [The association is still with bread/food, but by a
separate evolution. < It. nautical *camera della campagna*, store-
room, provision room, for the journey. *Campagna*, here, is based
on *campo*, open field, but earlier applied also to the open sea.
Companionway, by association, is the passage that leads to that
seagoing larder.]

conceit   1. An exaggerated sense of one's own worth. *If I could buy
Congressman Richard Ichord at market value and sell him at his
own evaluation, I could pay off the national debt from pocket
money.* 2. A conception. An act of the imagination. *a pretty conceit.*
[< L. *concipere*, to take unto oneself. Late L. p.p., *conceptus*, taken
to oneself (as an idea). It. *concetto*, concept, esp. as an artist conceives a work he is about to undertake. *Concetta*, a common Italian
feminine given name, and dear to me because it was my late
mother's.]

    metaphysical conceit A metaphoric extension as if the poet had
forgotten the X of his basic "X is like Y" and had proceeded to treat
Y as if it were the literal X. So John Donne:

> Oh, do not die, for I shall hate
> All women so when thou art gone,
> That thee I shall not venerate,
> Remembering thou wast one.

A pretty conceit that may perhaps be paraphrased: "Oh, do not die,
for the total worth of womankind will be so reduced by your death
that I shall grow to think little of you when I remember that you
were one of those (so reduced) creatures."

Congo Square   A once powerfully operative term in American Negro
history. I am indebted to Robert F. Thompson, master of Timothy
Dwight College, Yale, for a reference to George Cable's *Grandis-
simos*, a late-XIX novel of life in New Orleans in the very early XIX.
Cable refers to Congo Square in New Orleans, where, on Sundays,
Negroes, Amerinds, and some white athletes met to play a wild ball
game called *raquette*, perhaps a form of lacrosse.

    A large playing field would not likely be in the center of down-
town New Orleans. (See *The Big Apple*, under *apple*, Vol. I.) Congo

Square was also the scene of dancing, chanting, and funky music. Cable writes: "old men and women chanted a song that appeared to me to be purely African in its many vowelled syllabification. . . . I asked several old women to recite [the words] to me but they only laughed and shook their heads. In their patois they told me— 'no use, you could never understand it. *C'est le Congo.' "*

I once helped Sidney Bechet prepare his autobiography, *Treat It Gentle.* For him, Congo Square was an open place in the plantation slave quarters where Negroes met on Sunday to sing and dance to the accompaniment of crude homemade instruments. Congo Square was the place of funky music, originally a combination of spirituals and African stomp-and-chant. Drums were not used. The white masters forbade them in fear of a general slave uprising signaled by drum talk.

For percussion, therefore, the slaves stomped, blew into jugs, clapped, and beat on their own bodies. Imported into New Orleans in late XIX and furnished with the standard jazz instruments, funky emerged as Dixieland c. 1900, and so to the full flowering of jazz as the one truly indigenous American art form.

connive   1. To abet a wrongful act by shutting one's eyes to it, by giving it tacit approval, or by giving it covert assistance. *connive with* To conspire. To plan a wrongful act in secret with another or with others. *connivance* The act of conniving. [Root sense: "to shut one's eyes to," lit. "to lean on one's eyelids." IE *kneighwh-*, to rest one's weight upon, but with particular ref. to the eyelids, whence the effective sense "to shut one's eyes to." → L. *cōnīvēre,* to indulge someone, to approve.]

cookie pusher   *U.S. State Department.* A most junior member of a diplomatic corps. [Whimsical. As if his or her total duties consisted of passing trays of cookies at diplomatic receptions. Cf. *gofer.*]

copasetic   *Slang.* All in order. All O.K. Everything is fine. [Origin in doubt, and all standard dicts. gloss as *origin unknown,* but much is known and should be noted. First attested 1919 by OED as an Americanism. A normal lag from first use to attestation suggests an origin c. 1890–1900, and OED should prob. have glossed it as Black English. Bill ("Bojangles") Robinson (1878–1949), popular Negro comedian and prob. the best tap dancer of his time, made copasetic his personal catchword.

The form and the meaning are inseparable from Hebrew *kol ba seder,* all in order. Leslie Fiedler, newly returned from a trip to Israel, told me that he heard the Hebrew phrase everywhere in Jerusalem.

So far everything is copasetic, but what is the possible line of transmission from Hebrew to Black English of the 1890's? Am. slang is replete with terms of Yiddish origin, but except for Biblical references (e.g., *shekel, schlemiel*), I can find none from Hebrew. I am left to suppose there was a Jewish shopkeeper or pawnbroker of the 1890's, prob. in the South, who dealt with Negroes, and who had a few tags of Hebrew which he repeated over and over. I must suppose further that his Negro customers picked up the cadence of *kol ba seder* and altered it to *copasetic,* a fine lilting way of saying everything is fine and dandy.

My ghostly storekeeper is, of course, a speculation, and speculation is not etymology, but let this much at least be noted before glossing this robust Am. idiom "origin unknown."]

coquette A flirtatious woman. [The word has undergone a sex-change operation. < Fr. *coq,* rooster; suffixed *-et,* little → *coquet,* little rooster, but used to label a strutting male fop. Whence *coqueter,* to flirt ("to strut in rut"). But into XVII Eng. with the feminine dim. suffix *-ette,* and then and since, in both Fr. and Eng., specific to women.]

corporation 1. A legal entity with stated officers and usu. a board of directors. At law it is treated in many ways as if it were a person. [< L. *corpus,* body, the physical body of a human being. But also *the corpus of an author's work,* the entire body of his work.] 2. *Informal.* A body. One's body. [Bartlett Jere Whiting, *American Proverbs and Proverbial Phrases,* attests this Am. usage as early as 1809: "A fellow who has not so much sense in his whole *corporation* as your son has in his little finger."] 3. *Slang.* A pot belly. *You seem to have developed quite a corporation, Mr. Arbuckle.* 4. *Slang.* The entire thing. [As above, the whole *corpus.*]

cosset To pamper. To treat as a pet. To make much of. To coddle. "We cosseted the four remaining elms."—"Goodbye Mighty Elms," by Barbara W. Freedman, *N.Y. Times,* Aug. 9, 1980. [Earlier, as a noun, a pet lamb. The one that followed Mary to school was a cosset. The form of the word is < OE *cotsaeta,* cottage dweller. (*Cottage,* here, for "humble, thatched, dirt-floored home for the rural poor.") In the Domesday Book (early XI) the form is given as *coscet, cozet,* cottage; but in widespread dial. *cosset,* a pet lamb.]

HISTORIC. It was once common custom to take a lamb from field or fold and to raise it in the cottage (its endless stippling at least partially absorbed by the dirt floor). In the poverty of early farm dwellers, livestock was not to waste. The beast would eventually be slaughtered, but for a time it could be a winsome pet, adopted perhaps because it was sickly and needed particular attention, perhaps as a pet for the children, perhaps because its mother had died or strayed, perhaps as whimsy. In any case, the custom was widespread, such lambs being called in Ger. *Hauslamm,* house lamb; and in It. *casiccio,* little (dear) house thing.

cottage [IE *ku-,* a covering, to cover. (Via Gmnc., with k/h and suffixed *-t-* → HAT, "covering for the head.") Akin to *cote,* rude animal shelter. Hence, a humble abode for the impoverished farm worker, usu. (in early Britain) thatched and with a dirt floor.] *In Am.* 1. A more or less rustic small house. A vacation home. [But some seaside cottages, as at Newport, R.I., are notably expansive and expensive.] 2. A romantically idealized little house, as a love nest for newlyweds. *rose-covered cottage.*

    cottager In Brit. 1. A landless farm worker. 2. One of the rural poor. British land was long since sealed in private ownership. The colonies, where land was plentiful and often free (at least if one moved west), offered no parallel to British poverty. The abundant (or once abundant) woodlands of the New World gave rise to the dirt-floored log cabin as the equivalent of the cottage, and Am. *cottage* tended to acquire literary and romantic connotations. ***cottage industry*** Piecework done at home for low wages. *The assembly and sale of Saturday Night Specials has become a Harlem cottage industry.* (But it pays a bit better than early British home weaving, as in *Silas Marner.*) ***cottage cheese*** (Earlier Brit. also had *Dutch cheese.*) Unaged cheese made from the strained curds of milk.

cotton to Be apt for. Take a liking to. *I don't cotton to it:* 1. I am not apt for it. 2. I don't like it. [Attested XVI. Now obs. in Brit. but survives in Am. regional, one of many such terms of Elizabethan Eng. brought to the colonies by settlers, and surviving in their isolation long after passing from Brit. use. In XVI, *this gear cottons well,* in which *gear* = loom, and *cottons well* = weaves cotton with a fine texture and nap. Then, by ext., said of anything that works well, or is apt to the task in hand. Whence the senses "approved of/liked."]

counterfeit   A sham, imitation. Implies (now) intent to defraud or deceive. [*Counter,* here, as in *counterpart,* with root sense: "responsive to" *(to counter a blow). Feit* modified from L. *factum,* thing made. Hence, at root: "thing made in response to." So Hamlet: "The counterfeit presentment of two brothers," with the neutral sense "the portraits (responsive to nature) of two brothers." But in XVI the present pejorative sense "sham" was already emerging by association with forged coins, signatures, and documents.]

country   [Based on L. *contra,* against, across from, facing one. Medieval L. *contrata,* tract of land (what one finds facing him, and by ext., surrounding him). Old It. *encontrare,* to meet (ENCOUNTER). The main senses given are in the chronological order of their use in Eng.] 1. One's native land. [XIII.] 2. Land of a people. Region under a single rule. [XIV. The simple sense ext. is from "our native land" to "their native land."] 3. Outlying district. [XVI. Includes the senses: 1. Heath. Wilderness. 2. Cultivated rural district.

Most idiomatic forms are self-evident, as *country club, country cousin, country folk, countryman,* etc. But two are worth noting:

country mile A long distance. *Stan Musial hit the ball a country mile.* [Am. Whimsical. As if a mile were longer in the country than in the city. The intent is perhaps evident in *I could see a country mile* (the view not blocked by city construction). Yet once above tree level: *From the top of the skyscraper I could see a country mile —or about fifty of them, in all directions.*

God's country What all natives, especially of backwoods, open spaces, and mountains, call their region self-vauntingly. God, to the best of my knowledge, has not commented, but He must be used to having everyone speak for Him.

cow   [As bull is < IE *bhel-,* swollen, a ref. to male tumescence, so IE *gwou-, kwou-,* cow, ox, is ult. < IE *ku-,* rounded, hollow thing, a vaginal reference, bull being to cow as lance to cup. The form is Gmnc. As with the names of all domestic animals, Eng. retains the OE rather than the OF forms. The Normans left the Saxon serfs to work with the livestock, letting them name the beasts in their own way. Their meat, however, was served in a French manor house and given Fr. names. So English cows produced *beef* (Fr. *boeuf*);

sheep, *mutton* (Fr. *mouton*); pigs, pork (Fr. *porc*); hens, *poultry* (Fr. *poule*).]

cowcatcher A visor-shaped steel grille placed in front of a locomotive just above track level, used to deflect obstacles on the right of way. [Am. XIX. Partly whimsical, but cows were a common obstacle on early tracks, and trains of the early transcontinental roads (before fenced range) were often stopped by herds of cattle, and also of buffalo.]

cow college A small backwoods college. [Not to be confused with aggie school, the agricultural college of a university; rarely an independent college of agriculture.] **cowlick** An unruly tuft of hair that resists all efforts to groom it. [Folk whimsy. As if that tuft had been licked by a cow.]

cowslip The common wild flower. In North America, the marsh marigold, also called *shooting star,* because its petals turn backward. In Britain, the European primrose. [At root: "cowflop flower," because it grows in pastures, commonly by a nutritious cowflop. OE *cuslyppe* < *cu,* cow; *slyppe,* what slips out of it. Ult. < IE *sleubh-,* slime. As anyone may say in crossing a pasture, "Where the cowslips, there slip I."]

holy cow Common Am. mild exclam. of surprise, vexation. (See historic note below.)

sacred cow A person above question, criticism, reproach, or hindrance.

HISTORIC. As a survival of primitive totemism, many animals and plants are held sacred by various cultures. Hindus hold sacred certain plants, monkeys, snakes, and—most prominently—cows and bulls. The sacred cow is free to wander unhindered through crops and street markets and to eat and trample without interference. It cannot, of course, be eaten, and that in a land of starvation poverty.

In Florence in the Middle Ages there was founded a monastery of St. Anthony the Hermit, and the *pigs of St. Anthony* were similarly allowed to roam and to gorge unhindered. In religious art St. Anthony is commonly depicted with a pig at his feet, the pig representing the devil, who kept tempting him with obscene visions. I can find no explanation of how the holy devil-pigs became sacred cows. Except on days of fasting, the Florentines had no taboo against eating pork. In any case, the Florentines have long since abandoned this pious nonsense, the monastery swineherds can damned well feed their own stock, and pigs are no longer welcome in the garden or the street market.

coward Though apparently from *cowherd* with the sense "a low, servile peasant," the term is at root: "a tail-tucked person, one forever ready to tuck tail and run." < Fr. *coue,* tail; with pejorative suffix *-ard,* as in *bastard, drunkard, stinkard.*

coxcomb An inane fop. A vain, overdressed, empty-headed strut-about. [< *cock's comb,* the red, serrated crest of a rooster. Its edges do, remotely, suggest a comb. And so earlier, a court jester's floppy cap topped with a red felt cock's comb. Whence *coxcomb* or *cox* for the jester himself. With XVII variants *coax, cokes.* (In Am. securely within the recognition vocabulary of the literate, but less commonly used than in Brit.)]

cranberry 1. A North American shrub related to various European species. 2. The berry of this shrub, used for jellies, juice, and as a relish, esp. with roast turkey. [At root: "crane berry," Low Ger. *kraanbere* < *kraan,* crane; *bere,* berry. So called because the flower of this plant has petals that grow backward from a distinctive stamen conceived to resemble the bill of a crane.]

crapper A toilet. [Origin unknown. (By back formation < *crapulent?*) P. *Slang* cites *"crap, a defecation: low coll; mid 18th century."* OED *Supplement,* Vol. I, cites earliest verb form, *"to crap, to defecate,"* as 1846.

Wallechinsky and Wallace in their popular but shoddily researched *The People's Almanac* refer *crapper* to Sir Thomas Crapper, said to have been knighted for inventing the Crapper Valve-less Water Waste Preventer in 1882, thus preserving London's water supply from serious depletion by freely running toilet drains. W & W go on to say that the British valveless toilets, with Crapper's name said to be fixed on the bowls, were much admired by U.S. doughboys in WWI and that *crapper* for toilet then passed into Am. use.

On the side of W & W, all Am. citations are post WWI, and the word is not in Brit. use, or only rarely, perh. as an Americanism. Yet the mid XVIII noun form and the mid XIX verb form substantially predate Thomas Crapper's time in the john.]

credenza A sideboard or buffet table. In the original form the base was a chest of drawers. [It. *credenza,* credence, confidence in. So called because food and wine about to be served were placed first on a side table to be sampled by the butler/food taster. If he showed no symptoms of poisoning, the food was, so to speak, given credence.]

HISTORIC. Political poisoning was one of the immemorial arts. (See Housman's *Epilogue.*) In Renaissance Italy the art was so common and so refined that it was not called murder *(omicidio)* but an assisted death *(una morte assistata).* The butler/food taster/wine steward placed samples of the food and wine on a *salver* (which see) for tasting, and either died or went on to serve dinner.

crestfallen Dejected. In emotional withdrawal. The opposite of aggressive or perky. [The image is from cockfighting. Said of a gamecock that has had the worst of it and draws back, its crest no longer bristling, but adroop, and the defeated bird ready to turn and run; or it has already fled.]

crypt-/crypto- Also *cryp-/crypha-.* Suffix or prefix meaning "hidden," but in many different contexts. [Ult. < IE *krau-,* to hide, hidden. Suffixed, prob., in Hellenic → Gk. *kruptein,* to hide.]
 crypt A burial chamber, esp. one in the cellarworks of a church. ["place for hiding the corpse."] *Apocrypha* The 14 books of the Septuagint, related to Scripture but not universally accepted as such. Protestantism generally rejects these books. The Roman Catholic Church accepts 11 of them as authentic Scripture. [Prefixed *apo-,* away from; hence with the root sense: "out of hiding," hence "revealed." (Unsupported but now traditional assertion has it that in the third century, 70 (or 72) scholars gathered on the island of Pharos and translated these books from Hebrew into Greek in 70 or 72 days. Hence *Septuagint* < L. *septuagintā,* seventy.] *apocryphal* 1. Of the *Apocrypha.* (In this sense, commonly capitalized.) 2. [Because of centuries of theological dispute, there developed the sense progression:] Unauthenticated → not genuine → counterfeit, spurious.
 cryptic Secret. Mysterious. Enigmatic. Concealed. *cryptography* The writing and study of codes and ciphers. [The second element < Gk. *graphein,* to write. Hence with root sense: "secret writing."] *cryptanalysis* The breaking down of codes and ciphers.
 crypto-communist [Lit. "hidden communist."] A party member who for one reason or another conceals his affiliation in order to "bore from within."
 And in many specialized scientific and technical compounds, a few of which are:
 Psychology. cryptesthesia Ability to feel or perceive by hidden

(unknown) means, as in ESP. [Second element < Gk. *aestethos,* of feeling, perception.] *Biology.* **cryptic coloration** Protective coloration. Natural camouflage. *Botany.* **cryptogam** A plant that reproduces by means of minute, sometimes microscopic ("hidden") spores. [Second element < Gk. *gametē,* wife, *gametēs,* husband, both of which tend to reproduce in private ("hidden") places.] *Geology.* **cryptoclastic** Adj. applied to sedimentary rock made up of microscopic particles. [Lit. "of hidden parts, elements." Second word element < Gk. *klastos,* broken, here with ref. to the elements into which a compound may be broken.] *Medicine.* **cryptogenic** *Said of a disease.* Of unknown ("hidden") origin.]

cuss   A guy. Esp. in *tough cuss,* a hard-to-handle guy. [Am. XIX. A convergent evolution. In earlier *he's a cuss of a fellow,* the sense is "he's a curse of a fellow." But mainly by back formation from *customer,* one who must be dealt with, the term common on western frontier, with precedent in Brit. XIX *rum customer,* a queer person to be dealt with. *Rum* here (see *rum go,* Vol. I) from *rom,* another back formation, from Romney, i.e., Gypsy, i.e., queer, outlandish, thing to be wary of.]

D

dairy   [At root: "where the milkmaids work." ME *daie*, milkmaid. <
OE *daege, dege*, kitchen maid, she who kneads (bread). See *lord*,
and in Vol. I, *lady*. The OE *daege, dege*, worked flour dough with
her fingers; the ME *daie* milked cows with a quite similar hand
motion; the *-ry* signifies "having to do with." Cf. Fr. *chinoiserie* <
chinois, Chinese; *-erie*, having to do with; a term applied in XVIII
to decoration in (more or less) the Chinese style.] 1. A farm that
produces milk for sale or for processing into cheese or butter. (As
distinct from a small farm that has a milk cow for family use.) 2. A
place where milk and milk products are stored and processed. 3.
Milk products.

   meat and dairy The two sorts of food that are not to be mixed
in a kosher kitchen, nor to be prepared in the same utensils, nor
served, even separately, in the same dishes, nor eaten with the
same utensils. The kosher division of these foods is based on the
ancient Jewish command: "Thou shalt not cook the kid in the milk
of its mother."

damn: not worth a damn   Worthless. [At root: "not worth a weed." An
oddly folk-modified form. Langland, *Piers Plowman* (XIV), has
"noghte worth a kerse," not worth a weed. In XV *kerse* was metathesized to *cress*, now specific to various mustard weeds including
watercress, but in XV applicable to any weed. As metathesized *cress*
came into common use by the young, many XV elders must have
clung to the earlier form *kerse*, which the young must have received
as "curse," and since *damn* is a curse → *not worth a damn*, now
commonly taken to mean "not worth damning to hell," but this
sense, now a long-established error, is after the etymological fact.
(Cf. *sea cook: son of a sea cook*, Vol. I; *sea cook* being an alteration of
Algonquinian *sēkonk*, skunk, a term known to the elders of the new
settlements, but not to the young, who modified it to the nearest
familiar pattern by an etymological gestalt.)]

dander: get one's dander up   To become irate. [The standard Am. dicts. commonly gloss this idiom as "origin unknown," but to do so is merely evasive, the word being attested 1795 in use in the West Indies to label the yeast used in fermenting molasses for rum-making, and also to label the resultant ferment. By metaphoric association, then, the sense shift from "ferment" → "mental agitation." What is unknown is the Carib or Afro-Carib source from which West Indies *dander* evolved. (Not to be confused with *dandruff*, which is < ON *hrufa*, ME *roufe*, scab, crud; with the untraced element *dand*—tooth?)]

danger   Peril. A source of peril. [IE *deme-*, household, area of authority (DOMAIN, DAME, MADAME). → L. *dominus*, lord and master of a house. In Medieval L. *domnus*, which was altered in OF to *dangier*, danger, *daungereuz*, unbending, having magisterial power, not yielding to entreaty. Hence by a natural connection in the folk mind, the sense shift from "authority" to "trouble, danger," for the peasant has never expected to come before the law except to be found guilty. And so in Frenchified English from Chaucer to Spenser, "that she is dangereuse" signified in the tradition of courtly love that the lady is unyielding to entreaty (whereby the poor swain must die of love). She is *la belle dame sans merci*, a sort of siren who dooms men in luring them. In XIII signified: "subject to punishment"; in Chaucer (XIV) with the modern sense: "likely to cause injury."]

dangling participle   *Grammar.* A participial construction not immediately followed by its subject (the subject or the participle being left to dangle in disconnection). *Being well, the task gave me no difficulty.* Implies that the task was well, when the intent is, clearly, that the subject was well. Should read: *Being well, I had no trouble with the task.* Or better: *I was well enough to handle the task with no difficulty.*

Sometimes the effects of the dangling participle can be ludicrous. *Turning the corner, the ocean came into view.* (It's a tidal wave!) *Piloting a plane, the scenery is often wildly beautiful.* (Can the plane stay airborne with all that scenery at the controls?) *Reaching the top of the ladder, the damage to the roof was immediately visible.* (Obviously; part of it had blown away to light on the top of the ladder.) I conclude that pointing out this much, dangling participles should stay out of airplanes.

dead reckoning   *Nautical (and now aeronautical).* Navigation by clock and compass. Radio, loran, and other devices have changed the game. In days of sail, old skippers had various means of estimating speed through the water and driftage caused by ocean currents (see *Gulf Stream*), but storms could upset all calculation, and only a shore sighting or accurate celestial observation could reliably fix a ship's position. [Prob., though unattested, because a position so computed was marked on charts with the notation "ded. (i.e., deduced) reckoning," with *ded.* → *dead* in oral ref. I shall continue to seek a firm attestation and I shall be grateful for the help of any salty reader who can point me to one. For the time being, I can only submit that *ded.* is exactly conformable to the sense and to the general forms of notation on navigators' charts.]

  NOTE. The AHD, in my opinion the best desk dictionary available, yet has occasional lapses. (As a special howler, it glosses *blatherskite* as "BLATHER + SKATE [fish]"—and so at last, mother, we have a talking fish! Sorry, but see *shit* for a correct etymology.) AHD clearly fails again in glossing *dead reckoning:* "From DEAD (probably 'complete,' 'exact,' because it is the closest estimate possible)." *Dead reckoning* may be the closest estimate possible under the worst possible navigational conditions, but it is the least complete and least accurate form of navigation.

debacle   1. A ruinous shattering that causes an utter rout. *Waterloo turned into Napoleon's debacle.* 2. Any failure so ruinously bizarre as to seem comical. A fiasco. (Some dicts. give a third sense, "the breaking up of ice in the river," and this can be etymologically justified, but is it in Am. idiom to say, "Shall we go to the river and watch the debacle?") [< Fr. *débâcler,* to break < L. *baculus,* rod, staff. Root sense: "to shatter with one's rod, walking stick." < IE *bak,* stick, rod. (And so *bacillus,* because *bacilli* occur in chains of rod-shaped single cells.) An oddly extended figure, as if an army could be shattered with a stick. I am left to suppose, though I cannot attest, that the extension is by association with *scepter,* the "rod" of royal power. Let in a little metaphor and anything can happen.]

debut   [The term is from archery. At root: "first shot at the target." Also: "first appearance on the archery range." < Fr. *de-,* of; OF *but,* butt, target. In medieval England yeomen were required by law to practice shooting the longbow, and "artillery grounds" (see *artillery*) were maintained just outside many towns and cities. A large one was maintained for centuries outside the walls of London. A debut, therefore, could be the first appearance of a tyro archer on the artillery grounds, or a first shot in a tournament. (See *up-shot.*)] 1. A first appearance, esp. one in a new context. *Gil Gallagher made his debut as a spear carrier in* Aïda. (*So-and-so will debut tonight* is common and offensive Am. usage, the forms of the present and past tense being especially unmanageable. Cf. the common, and equally offensive, *will première* for *will make his/her première appearance.*) 2. To appear formally in society for the first time. (Said of a *debutante.*)

   debutante Also commonly *deb* The daughter of a family with traditional social pretensions in the year of her "coming out," usu. at eighteen, usu. at a ball as lavish as the family cannot quite afford. The original Am. notion was that she thereupon had her own place in the social register. The *debut* is in effect a family announcement that the girl is sexually serviceable under cover of matrimony, and who will have her, please? [Tourist legend has it that the Amish announce the same availability of a marriageable daughter by painting the front gate blue, but scholars of Amish life tell me that the blue gate is not a common custom, and that it is in any case an unnecessary announcement within the small and tightly knit Amish communities.]

decant   To pour wine from a bottle into a glass; or into a *decanter,* taking pains not to disturb the sediment at the bottom of the bottle. [< IE *kantho-*, corner, edge. With th/t → It. *canto*, as in *a canto di*, at the side of. L. *canthus, cantus,* iron rim around a wheel. Late L. *decan(t)are,* to decant (the sense shift was from "rim of a wheel" to "lip of a bottle." So Fr. *de cant,* on its side; *mettre de cant,* to place a thing on its side (as an opened wine bottle in a serving basket).]

decimate   [L. *decem,* ten; *decimare,* to take (and kill) one in ten; p.p. *decimatus,* reduced by a tenth.] 1. To reduce a population or a military force by a tenth. [In the Roman legions, organized on a basic ten-man squad, mutiny and cowardice in battle were punished by forcing each squad to select one man by lot and to kill him.] 2. *In common but illiterate usage.* To destroy a large part of a population, or even to wipe it out completely. *Smallpox totally decimated many Indian tribes.* (See *shambles,* Vol. I, for a word similarly subjected to illiterate abuse.)]

   HISTORIC. Military analysts have had various theories about

what percentage of losses will destroy the fighting ability of a military force. None has remotely suggested that decimation was a critical loss, and the Romans, by their practice, found the loss of one in ten acceptable as a disciplinary measure, obviously in the belief that 900 survivors so disciplined would fight as efficiently as an unpunished 1,000.

demise   An evasive word signifying a death. *Thomas Jefferson, upon his demise, lost interest in the Republic.* [And this sense is now firmly established in undertakers' English. At root < L. *mittere,* to send; with *de-,* out of. Whence *demission,* a putting aside, as the transfer of an estate by sale or testament, the passing on of an office by resignation or death. Cf. It. *fare le sue dimissioni,* to make one's demissions, in effect, to resign an office, to leave an employment by giving notice, to give notice that one is planning to leave.] *to demise Law.* To convey a title, office, or estate by legal means. *Hotshot Harry demised eighteen big ones at dice last night.*

demon   1. A fiend. 2. A corruptive power personified as the work of a fiend. *the demon rum.* 3. One who has an unusual power or ability. *speed demon. John Doe is a demon for anonymity.* [IE *dai-, da-,* to divide, to set apart, with unexplained suffix *mo-* (perhaps with some sense of "labor" or "special exertion") → *dai-mo-* → Gk. *daimon,* being set apart by special powers, good or bad. (In primitive belief, surviving into Greek myth, all living things had a *daimon* or indwelling spirit and so did such natural features as large rocks, pools, mountains, caves. Any of these had its own special power for good or evil.) Gk. *demos,* the people, is from the same root, prob. with the sense: "a distinct and powerful body set aside from all others, i.e., barbarian foreigners."

HISTORIC. The sense "being with special powers" still survives, but in general the *daimon* of the Greeks, for good or ill, became the devil-fiend of the early Christians. The Jews had long regarded the "false gods" of their neighbors as demonic, while granting them distinct but limited powers, which were only for evil. The Old Testament often appears to be a contest in which such false gods oppose the true God and are defeated. By XIV Dante believed that the spirits of the Greeks were true manifestations of the eternal (i.e., his) God, but squintingly observed and misinterpreted because the Greeks lacked the revelation of Christ, the word of Scripture, and the guidance of the "true" church. (Seek as you will, son of man, those who come after will explain you away.)

denizen   1. An inhabitant. *denizens of the deep* Fish and other marine life. 2. One who frequents a given place. *the denizens of the local pool halls.* 2. *Brit. only.* An alien who has been naturalized or given limited privileges as a British subject. 3. *Ecology.* A life form, esp. a plant, that has become established in an ecosystem to which it is not native. (And among tin-eared literalists, alas, also as a verb, as in *The New World potato has been denized* [!!] *in most of Europe.*) [< Anglo-Norman, the legal language established in Britain by the Norman conquerors, *deinz la cite,* within the city, with the effective sense: "native to the city." (*Deinz,* in, within, is the forerunner of Fr. *dans.* A non-native was designated *fors* (in Fr. *hors*) *la cite* (FOREIGN). *Deinz* is ult. < L. *de intus,* from within. The word might naturally have evolved *deinzen* or *denzen* but acquired the inserted *i,* prob. by association with *citizen.*]

HISTORIC. Ernest Weekley, *The Romance of Words,* cites the Anglo-Norman *Liber Albus,* circa XII, to show the meticulous provisions that applied to *deinzeyn* and *forrein.* (*Carfeux* is an intersection of two streets, lit. "a four-fork" < L. *quadrifurca.*):

> Item, qe nulle pulletere *deinzen* n'estoise a Carfeux del Ledenhalle deins mesoun ne dehors, ove conilles, volatilie, n'autre pulletrie pur vendre . . . issint qe les *forreins* pulleters, ove lour pulletrie estoisent par eux mesmes, et vendent lour pulletrie sur le cornere de Ledenhalle, sanz ceo qe ascuns pulletere *deinzein* [sic] viegne ou medle en vent ou en achate ove eux, ne netre eux.

> Also, that no denizen seller of poultry shall stand at the Carfax of Leadenhall, either in a house or out of doors, with rabbits, fowls, or other poultry for sale . . . and that the foreign poulterers, with their poultry, shall stand by themselves, and sell their poultry at the corner of Leadenhall, without any denizen poulterer approaching or meddling in the sale or purchase with them, or among them.

dessert   [Root sense: "clear the table." < P.p. of Fr. *deservir,* which is *servir,* to serve (a meal), prefixed *de(s)-* to indicate opposite action. Because the table is cleared before dessert is served.]

HISTORIC. The commonest American desserts are pies, pastries, sherbet or ice cream, and puddings. All require considerable amounts of sugar, and sugar was not generally available in Europe until XVIII. What we call "dessert" was customary in earlier Europe, but sweets are relatively recent.

detective   An investigator of crimes. If a policeman, usu. a plain-clothesman. But also *private detective (private investigator, P.I., private eye)*. [At root: "one who strips (others) bare." IE *(s)teg-*, a covering, to cover. → L. *togere*, to cover, to dress (TOGA, INTEGU-MENT); *dētegere*, to uncover, to strip; p.p. *detectus*, uncovered, stripped. Hence with intermediate root sense: "toga stripper (and so to the naked truth)."]

deus ex machina   *Literary criticism*. The resolution of a tangled plot by the abrupt interjection of an implausible element whose possi-bility has not been established in the preceding action. (A fantastic event may resolve an action established to be fantasy; it cannot be accepted as the resolution of an action established to be realistic.) [Gk. *theos ek mēkhanēs*, god from the machine. The ref. is to the convention of Greek drama by which gods were lowered to the stage by a pulley system, returning to Olympus by the same device. If a god or goddess was an established part of the mythic action, there could be no objection to such Olympian descents and ascents. But if a god suddenly appeared for no reason, and without prepara-tion in the preceding action for such an appearance, such interven-tion could not be received as credible.]

devil: speak of the devil (and he will appear)   *Exclam*. Used when one who has been mentioned in a conversation suddenly turns up in the flesh. [Proverbial. The equivalent Fr. form is *Parlez du loup, et vous verrez sa queue:* speak of the wolf and you will see its tail. The substitution of wolf for devil is because Fr. *loup*, pron. *loo*, rhymes with *queue* (pron. *koo*). But:]
    HISTORIC. This word formula, now used more or less lightly, is nevertheless a survival of primitive ritual, name magic, and the summoning of demons and other spirits by pronouncing their names. At deep root, therefore, to speak of the devil (to pronounce his true name) was to force him to appear. For primitive man believed that one's true secret name was an essential part of one's being, and that to speak that name gave the speaker a power over the person named. The child's story of *Rumpelstiltskin* is a late pure survival of these ancient beliefs.

diabolic   Demonic. Infernal. Devilish. [Often—to give the devil his due—implies "fiendishly clever." < Gk. *diabolos* < *bolos*, thrower, agential form of *bollein*, to throw; with *dia-*, across. (Cf. *discobolos*, discus thrower.) What the diabolic spirit throws, across what distance, and to what destination, are matters best left to the theological imagination.]

dicker *n. & v.* To haggle. To make a business or political deal. Or the act of so doing. [NWD asserts the form to be of American origin, but certainly that assertion must yield to ME *dycer,* to dicker, with cognates in Ger., Du., and Danish. Ult. < L. *decuria,* a trade lot of ten units, based on L. *decem,* ten. Originally with ref. to small dealers who haggled over lots of ten hides, bales, amphorae, in hot curbside wrangles. Dealers in whole cargoes must have had sharp bargaining sessions, but held them over wine in more or less private rooms. The root sense, therefore, is street haggling, but the word has been softened in English, now implying delicate negotiation rather than hot, fish-market haggling.]

dickey *At point of origin, with many variations since, esp. in women's wear.* A biblike shirt front with an attached or attachable collar, worn by men under a suit coat to give the appearance of a shirt. Popular in XIX and early XX. I have seen a turn-of-the-century mail order catalogue (not Sears, Roebuck) that offered union suits with button-on dickeys and starched cuffs; slip on a coat and you're dressed for company. [Origin in doubt. Some refer the term to Ger. *decken,* to hide (a dickey hiding the absence of a shirt). But ???]

diet A deliberative assembly of high church officials from all the many districts and countries served by the church. [At root: "(council arrived at after a journey of) many days." < L. *diēs,* day. Medieval L. *diēta,* a day's work or travel. Hence, assembly to which church officials come from afar. And see *synod.*]

digest [Root sense: "to separate into basic elements." L. *digerere,* to separate; p.p. *digestus* < *gerere,* to bear, to carry on (*bellum gerere,* to wage war); prefixed *di-,* apart. Late L. *digesta,* a collection of writings.] *v.* (Accent on second syllable.) 1. To break down and absorb food. 2. To understand. [To grasp and absorb the elements of idea, thing, situation.] 3. To condense and abridge, as a piece of writing, by sorting out and summarizing the essential elements. — *n.* (Accent on first syllable.) 1. The result of sense 3. 2. As in Late L. *digesta,* a collection of writings, esp. of short pieces. [But in Am. a *digest* firmly connotes noun sense 1.]

dilemma   [Not, as commonly understood, a "two-horned" proposition in logic. *Lemma* (plu. *lemmata, lemmas*) is a rare but standard Eng. word, meaning: 1. A glossed word. *All the entries in this book are lemmata.* 2. A subject or proposition or argument set forth in the title of a treatise. 3. *Logic.* A subordinate premise supporting a major one. Prefixed *di-*, Gk. two, double → *dilemma.* Ult. < IE *(s)lagw-*, to seize, to grasp; with a shift, prob. in Hellenic, from *gw* to *b*, and with nasal infix *-m-* → Gk. stem *lamb'-*, whence *lambenein*, to seize, to grasp; past perfect *eilēmmai*, in which *lemma* becomes visible, the substantive having the root sense: "thing (proposition) grasped."] 1. *Logic.* A choice of two propositions, either of which will lead to defeat of an argument. (As in the standard trickster's question: "Have you stopped beating your wife yet?"—yes implying that you have been a wife-beater; no, that you still are.) 2. *In more common usage.* A choice between two equal evils. (The root sense permits a choice between two equal goods, and one might say, "Both candidates are so superbly qualified that we are left in a dilemma"; but in general, and as always in the folk mind, evil has triumphed.) 3. *In loose ext.* A bad situation. (In illiterate usage: "The energy shortage leaves us in a terrifying dilemma.")

    on the horns of a dilemma Caught in a choice between equal evils. [As if impaled on both horns of a bull. It is this, by now, fixed phrase that has led to the common assumption that *dilemma* is, at root, "two-horned." And this assumption was already implicit in the OED's citation from T. Wilson's *Logike,* 1551: "Dilemma, otherwise . . . called a horned argument, is when the reason consisteth of repugnant members, so that whatsoever you graunt, you fall into the snare."]

    USAGE NOTE. *Dilemma* labels a choice between two equal evils. *Quandary* (origin unknown) is what a dilemma becomes when there are more than two choices, all of them bad.

dirt   [IE *drit-*, excrement, to excrete. (Eng. *shit, q.v.,* is from a root meaning "to cut, to divide," with root sense: "stuff divided from the body"—a curious evolution to what *drit-* meant in the first place.)

    With shift of the voiced stop dh-/f in Latin, as established by Grimm's Law → modified skeletal stem *f'r-* → L. *forire*, to defecate. The original stem unchanged in Gmnc. → OE *dritan*, to defecate; *drit*, shit, unclean thing. Then by metathesis → ME *dirt*, unclean thing; with later additional sense: "earth, soil, the dirt under one's feet." Today, in the senses "miner's pay dirt" and "farm soil," no sense of "unclean" adheres, but note that good farm soil has traditionally been enriched by manure. (Eastern Amerinds often placed a small fish in the ground near a planted seed of maize, and the fish, of course, soon became an "unclean and stinking" but richly nutrient thing.)] 1. Any unclean thing. 2. Soil. Earth. 3. Anything common (as the dirt under one's feet) or contemptible (as filth). Note that *he treats her like the dirt under his feet*, or *he treats her like dirt*, implies both senses. 4. Gossip. [The moral "lowdown" on who's doing what and with whom.]

dirt road Unpaved road. **dirt floor** An interior floor of packed earth. [The traditional flooring of the huts of the poor, and in Am. log cabins well into XIX.] **dirt farmer** A small farmer who sweats a living from the soil. [Am. Dating uncertain but prob. XIX. A curious idiom in that all but hydroponic farming is ult. "dirt" farming, but the language convention has chosen this form as distinct from such other forms as rancher, planter (plantation owner), and gentleman farmer. The idiom is prob. from the post–Civil War westward expansion, in which dirt farmers (sodbusters) moved in on the cattle barons.]

dirt cheap Costing almost nothing. [As if one could buy a thing with a handful of soil scraped from the ground. Occurs in both Brit. and Am.]

pay dirt *Placer mining (as distinct from hard-rock mining).* 1. A vein rich in ore. 2. Soil and small gravel from which ore, esp. gold, can be panned, washed, or sluiced. 2. *Generalized ext.* A source of wealth. *She finally hit pay dirt when she married a sugar daddy.*

do one dirt To do one a shitty trick.

hit the dirt Military command or warning on hearing an artillery shell whistle, or under hot small-arms fire, or later under aerial bombardment or strafing.

dirty   *adj.* 1. Soiled. 2. Morally unclean. *dirty talk, dirty joke.* 3. Muddied. *dirty river.* [But now, polluted.] 4. Expresses contempt, dishonor. "That dirty little coward / Who shot Mr. Howard / And lay Jesse James in his grave." —*"Ballad of Jesse James."* 5. Dangerous. Unethical. *a dirty business.* 6. Unsporting. *a dirty player.* 7. Criminal. *There's dirty work afoot.* 8. Indicating disapproval. *a dirty look.* 9. *Originally nautical but generalized.* Foul. Not good. *dirty weather.* 10. *Am. jazz.* Rasping, growling, moaning, or gutbucket, as in Dixieland. *low-down and dirty.* —*v.* To soil. —*n.* (Does not occur in Am. but in one of the depravities of Cockney.) A sex act. *'E's doing the dirty with 'er.*

not wash one's dirty linen in public See *linen,* Vol. I.

down and dirty A standard poker player's formula on dealing a card face down, as, e.g., the last card of seven-card stud.

dirty pool 1. *Lit.* Cheater's pool. 2. *Ext. to any context.* Any dishonest or unfair stratagem. [A curious idiom. Unless one is physically cowed by an opponent, pool is all aboveboard, and a watchful player can call an opponent who moves the cue ball or manipulates any of the object balls. In this case the primary sense seems to be in the extension rather than in the literal sense. (The most obvious way to cheat at pool is by "playing the wire," i.e., by moving over more counters than one has scored, but only a dolt would fail to check the count.)]

dirty shame A fixed formula expressing disapproval of a harmful act and sympathy for the injured party.

disease   1. An illness, esp. one that is more or less serious, usu. chronic and progressive, and often infectious. (A broken bone is not a disease but an injury. Indigestion caused by overeating is not a disease but an indisposition.) 2. *Metaphoric ext.* Condition threatening well-being. *Avarice is a social disease.* [At root akin to L. *esse,* to be. Intermediately, "not at ease" (not in a good condition of being). So OF *disaise,* ME *disese.* 1. Illness. 2. Not at ease (not in good being). Since which the sense *malaise* has receded, and the medical sense has taken over.]

disgruntled   In a bad humor. Peevish. Surly. [Based on *grunt* by way of the obs. frequentative *gruntle,* to grunt (complain) repeatedly; and doubled by the prefix *dis-,* twice; hence, at root: "double gruntled." [The antonym might reasonably be taken to be *ungruntled,* no longer gruntling and complaining, but the form has never become idiom. Similarly, we might have had the verb *to disgruntle,* with the sense: "to put an end to (his) gruntling." But again, the idiom never came into use. These matters are not determined by reason but by the language convention's doing what it doesn't know it is doing until it has done it.]

ditto   Abbreviated *do.* Or indicated by the sign: ". 1. The same again. 2. *Colloq.* I agree. I think I will, too. *A. I need a stiff drink. B. Ditto.* [It. *detto.* North It. *ditto.* P.p. of L. *dicare,* to dictate, to pronounce solemnly. (Variant of *dire,* to say.) Ult. < IE *dik-,* to pronounce solemnly, as in religious ritual or at law. Akin to DIGIT, INDICATOR ("that which points out").] *ditto machine* A mimeograph.

D.O.A. *Police and hospital records. D*ead *o*n *a*rrival.

document   *n.* (Accent on first syllable.) 1. An official information or legal paper sufficient to serve as evidence or identification. 2. *Ext.* A weighty and full written account. *Darling, this isn't a shopping list; it's a document. —v.* (Accent—waveringly—on final syllable.) To support or establish a claim or case by written evidence, analysis, and citation from various sources. *documentary evidence.* [A many-sided evolution < IE *dek-*, to take, to accept, to make acceptable (DECENT). Variant *dok-* → L. *docēre*, to teach ("to set forth what is acceptable and proper") (DOCENT). So L. *documentum,* a lesson; but also, an example, an admonishment (DOCILE, DOCTRINE, DOCTOR). In It. and Sp. *documento,* an official paper, a letter of identity, a passport.]

    documentary Movies & TV. An assertedly factual survey of a usu. squalid situation. The film-maker's version of social truth, though when mind seeks to function through a lens, camera angles tend to count for more than judicial analysis. When the medium itself is a lie, truth is a bastard.

    documents 1. Official reports. 2. Official papers (of identity). *He was detained at the border as a person without documents.* (In the ult. root sense: he was not acceptable.)

    undocumented 1. Not supported by (official) evidence. 2. Lacking papers of identity, as, for instance, a passport.

dogcart   A small two-wheeled gig drawn by a single horse and accommodating two persons seated back to back. [Spook etymology has it that hunters once used such carts to carry their dogs to the hunt, but the dogcart was badly designed for this purpose, and the form is a corruption of Fr. *dos-à-dos,* a back-to-back seating arrangement common in XVII French gigs, and also in once popular sofas. The evolution was < *dos-a-dos* (cart) → *dogcart* because *doscart* fits poorly on the English tongue. (The square dance call *dosie-doe*— and local variants—instructs the dancers to dance back-to-back. It is an XVIII Am. corruption of this same Fr. *dos-à-dos.*)]

dog watch   *Nautical.* A two-hour (half) watch from 4 to 6 P.M. It offsets the regular (four-hour) watches by two hours in each twenty-four, in time distributing day watches and night watches evenly. [Origin in doubt. Sometimes explained as a corruption of unattested *dodge watch* (watch that causes duty hours to "dodge" around the clock), and where nothing is known, this speculation cannot be ruled out. *Dodge,* to elude, did not come into standard Eng. until XVII, but had a long prehistory in various Brit. dialects, with various senses. Nautical Eng. is, at root, a dialect, and *dodge* is plausible as a dialect-to-dialect transmission. Yet, on no evidence but my own ear, I suggest that *dodge watch* would more naturally have corrupted to *Dutch watch;* and I will venture that *docked watch* (also unattested) is a more likely source.

As a substantive, *dock* has many, though obscure, Gmnc. precedents. (See *doxy.*) It is attested in XIV by both Chaucer and Wycliffe. *Dock,* to curtail, did not come into standard Eng. until XVI (if there was, in fact, a "standard English" at that time), but it, too, was in earlier dialect usage.

These speculations, I submit, are better than no comment at all, but they yet remain simply speculations on limited evidence.]

dogwood   The common name of the small, early-flowering tree. [Earlier also *dogberry* and *dogberry wood,* with ref. to the glossy red berry-like fruit the tree bears in late summer and early fall, so profusely as to seem to be a second blooming. *Dog* is a simple corruption of OE *dagge,* spit, skewer, because the wood of the European dogwood, being hard and smooth-grained, was commonly used for spitting meat. The whole family of related shrubs and trees is *Cornacaea,* horns (because the seeds were conceived to be shaped like horns). The fifteen genera are widespread in temperate zones. *Cornus florida* is indigenous to eastern U.S., occurring abundantly as far north as Boston, and also along the southern Maine coast. It is also common on the Canadian shore of Lake Erie, whose waters moderate the temperature there. A related species occurs on the northwest U.S. coast, and under the moderating influence of the Japanese Current, grows so abundantly in coastal Canada that it has been named the provincial flower of British Columbia.]

dolce far niente   Sweet idleness. [It. sweet do nothing (time). A loan term, and as such retains the Italian pronunciation.] *Our summer on the island was a dolce far niente.*

domestic science   In the robotic and self-inflating language of the schools of education, this, along with **home economics,** labels any course in the fundamentals of home management for women who aspire to "Occupation: Housewife." ["Home-making" might be an unpretentious and intellectually modest term, but "science" and "economics" are more pretentious, and who needs pretentiousness more than the incompetent? Cf. *political science* for *political studies*. (What is less scientific than politics?)]

Donnybrook   1. A violent free-for-all with no particular sides, every man flailing away at drunken random. 2. *Loose ext.* Any violent or merely loud altercation. *We happened to arrive just as the Fennesseys were having their after-dinner Donnybrook.* [After Donnybrook, a section of Dublin. In 1204 it was granted royal permission to hold an annual two-week fair. Legend has it that revelers sloshed endless amounts of whiskey and took to cracking one another's skulls with their shillelaghs out of sheer exuberance. For most of its history, however, the revels were more boisterous than murderous. The legend grew on beer and exaggeration. The introduction of New World corn, potatoes, and cane made hard liquor common, but not until mid to late XVIII. The general availability of hard liquor did increase the violence. It was probably (?) at this time that the fair was reduced from two weeks to one.

Permission to hold a fair was a coveted economic boon, and its sponsors must have fought to preserve it, but by 1835 everyone seems to have had enough and the fair was abolished.]

doodle   *v.* To jot, sketch, or scribble aimlessly. (*In Brit.* To wander aimlessly, to putter.) —*n.* Any jotting, sketch, or scribble so made. [At root: "to toodle a bagpipe." < Ger. *dudeln,* to play the bagpipe. < *Dudelsack,* bagpipe; lit. tootlebag. Despite likely objections from the proud Scots, the Germans thought of tootling the dudelsack as an aimless sort of puttering.]

doodlebug A whimsical nonesuch. [A whatchamacallit connecting the dingbat to either the right or left coefficient of a gimcrack's doohickey when the moon is full, and otherwise either visible or invisible, whichever is first.]

doodly-squat   Nothing at all. *I don't care doodly-squat.* [A minced form of *I don't give a shit.* < *do-do,* nursery talk for *poo-poo;* with *squat.* And cf. *poppycock* (Vol. I), at root: "baby shit," but so minced and modified as to pass the genteelest scrutiny. Also *shoot,* a simple variant of *shit,* yet common enough in the speech of genteel ladies.]

doom   [Ult. < IE *dhe'-,* to fix in place, to set in order. (Whence the earlier sense in which *doom* was used for *fate,* i.e., "that which is preset in place.") Via Gmnc. with suffix *-d-* or *-t-* → OE *daēd,* deed ("thing decreed"). IE variant *dho-,* suffixed *-m-* in Gmnc. → OE *dōm,* judgment at law. (The OE form survives in *domesday,* variant spelling of *doomsday.*)] 1. A bad end (earlier implied that it was fated from the start, or at least decreed by the influence of the stars). 2. Ruin. 3. Judgment Day. *trump of doom.* (Preserves the sense: "decreed at law.")

HISTORIC. The word is, at root, neutral. What is "preset in place" could be for the good. A "decree at law" could be favorable, and is even likely to be, for one of the litigants. Even *Doomsday* will be a day of glory for the admittedly outnumbered virtuous. But once again the folk mind has associated all pronouncement and indication from on high, whether from God or king's law, with dreaded evil. So *ominous* from *omen,* any sign from heaven, good or bad. Similarly *portentous* from *portent.* So, too, *forebode,* dark foreseeing, but earlier merely advance news (as delivered by an OE *boda,* messenger, herald). And also *on the carpet,* at root: "under official review" (good or bad), but now with the firmly set sense: "in trouble." Humankind is willing to hope for the best, and has long supported a powerful priesthood to tend and advance its hope, but all etymological evidence is that the folk mind foresees only trouble from the decrees of God or emperor, its one most native wish being to escape the notice of all high authority. (If only IRS were totally unaware of us!)

doubt   *n. & v.* Uncertainty of belief. To view as uncertain. [Ult. < IE *dwo-,* two → L. *dubitare,* to doubt ("to go two ways at once"). In ME, *dout.* The *b* was inserted by XVI scholars as if to show the Latin ancestry, but in a typically British adjudication, the inserted letter was left unpronounced. So, too, ME *det, dette* → XVI *debt.*]

　　beyond the shadow of a doubt With whole certainty. In legal formula, the jury must so find for a guilty verdict, failing which the defendant must be presumed to be innocent.

　　give one the benefit of the doubt As in preceding, to exonerate one who may be guilty but against whom no conclusive case can be made.

doxy　(Rare in Am., but known to all who read earlier British novels.) A whore. [Since XVI. In earlier thieves' cant, the female companion of a vagrant, rogue, or thief. Of obscure but pervasive Gmnc.

origin with the likely root sense: "round bunch of cut stuff." ODEE cites Frisian *dok*, ball of twine; (M)LG *dokke*, bundle of straw. OHG *dokke*, doll (prob. straw doll). Prob. into Eng. < obs. Du. *docke*, bundle, (straw) doll, with the root senses: 1. bundle (perhaps term of endearment; cf. Am. slang "bundle of bliss"). 2. Straw doll (bundle of cheap stuff).

drat Exclam. of vexation. Earlier *drat ye.* Now commonly *drat it/ oh, drat it.* [A minced oath. Prob. *God rot ye!* → *'od rot ye* → *oh drat.* But this sequence, though likely, is unattested. ODEE, however, cites XIX *odrat*, glossing *rat* as an affected pronunciation of *rot.* Rawther!]

drawn and quartered 1. A medieval form of execution in which a high felon had his arms and legs roped to four horses who were driven in different directions until they tore him apart as a public spectacle. 2. In early England, the butchering of a high felon's body after hanging; usu. into four quarters and the head, the pieces often impaled on iron or wooden posts as a dire warning. (In most cases, at a time when even minor theft was a hanging offense, the noose was adjudged to be sufficient. Had all the victims of Tyburn's gallows been drawn and quartered, London would likely have run out of stakes, and it certainly would have become a seat of pestilence. It was long common, however, for the hangman to disembowel major felons after hanging them.)

dropsy A pathological accumulation of water (lymph) in tissues and body cavities. *dropsical* 1. Suffering from a dropsy. 2. Lethargic, morose. (This sense partly from the old medical theory of the humors, but certainly influ. by a misreading of *drop* for *droop[y].*) [Now rare, and generally replaced in medical use by *edema.* ME *dropesie*, by aphesis from OF *ydropesie* < Gk. *hydōr*, water (HYDRANT, HYDROPHOBIA). It is likely that in ME the OF form was taken as if *ye dropsie*, the dropsy.]

drumhead court-martial *Military.* A court-martial convened in the field to hear charges arising from misconduct in battle or in wartime maneuvers. [Because the court once commonly convened around a drumhead pressed into service as a field-expedient table. The most common charges being cowardice in battle, desertion in the face of the enemy, disobedience in battle, and related capital offenses, the drumhead court-martial was commonly a brief formality preliminary to execution.]

dry sack   Dry sherry. [A root redundancy in that *sack*, earlier *seck*, is a corruption of Fr. *sec*, dry; or possibly of the Ger. equivalent *sekt*. The intent was to distinguish dry from cream sherry, as Falstaff does in *2 Henry IV*, IV. iii, when he calls for "sherris-sack." By association *sack* also became a generic term for sherry, but always implying dry.]

HISTORIC. *Dry Sack* is now a trade name for an excellent dry sherry, and such is the power of words that the maker has gone to the trouble of placing each bottle in a small burlap-like sack with a drawstring. *Sherry* is < Xeres, Jerez, in Spain, which is the original center of sherry production. *Xeres* is a corruption of the original Roman name for the city there established as *Caesarea*, city of Caesar. One could, with good etymological authority, ask the bartender for a "dry dry Caesar," but what would he then set on the bar?

DSB   A doctorate from a school of education. [For "Doctor of Sand Box," by way of sneering at the boondoggling academic standards of our schools of education. Also *DBW*, Doctor of Basket Weaving. Both forms are jibes at the tendency of such schools to teach method without content.]

duck's ass   Also *d.a.* A haircut in which the hair of the nape is tapered to a point in the inverted image of a duck's tail feathers. [Am. 1950's (and imitated in Britain). This was the fad haircut of the heavily pomaded young of that period, always on the recurring adolescent premise that one achieves splendid individuality by dressing and acting exactly as does everyone else in the sacredly inane peer group. In the 1950's the main items of uniform were the duck's ass and a leather jacket. The hair was worn full, heavily pomaded, and given a "wave" by a lateral and slightly backward thrust of a comb. An inevitable part of the uniform was a pocket comb, and the frequently repeated gesture of touching up the hair in public was a peer ritual.]

dukes   Fists. ***put up one's dukes*** To square off for a fistfight. [< Early XIX Brit. rhyming slang in which *Duke of Yorks* = fingers for forks. Hence, by association, five clenched fingers = one duke. The evolution seems to be a bit farfetched, but rhyming slang was a cant.

Its purpose was to communicate with an in-group, not to explain its inner windings to an outsider.]

d.v.   God willing. [A common short form of L. *deo volente,* God willing. *The stock market, d.v., will go up—but when?]*

eager   1. *Now.* Marked by keen desire. 2. *Earlier.* Sharp. Biting. Acute. "It is a nipping and an eager air." —*Hamlet.* [Root sense: "acute." IE *ak-*, sharp → L. *acer*, sharp; OF *aigre.*]

    eager beaver (One of the most successful G.I. coinages of WWII.) A derisive term for an overzealous G.I. or officer; one who is forever "bucking for promotion." [An approx. redupl. based on *beaver*, a symbolically busy beast. And given busyness as the norm of this beast, what then could be the condition of an overeager one, and what forest could be safe from its chomping?]

eagre   A small tidal wave caused by a high tide forced into a funnel-shaped inlet, the constriction of the passage causing the water to pile high. Also called a *tidal bore.* [IE *akwa-*, water. With k/h → Gmnc. *ahwa-, ehwa*, and with elision of the *hw* → OE *ēa*, water. With unexplained suffix *-g-* → *ēager, ēger*, tidal flood. So OE *iēg-land, igland*, island ("place upon the water").

    The synonym, *bore*, is ult. < IE *bher-*, to bear (as a burden or children), and from the latter sense, "swollen," whence *bore*, lit. "swollen water."]

earl   *Brit.* A title of nobility below *duke* and *marquis* and above *viscount* and *baron*. [The source fades into obscure Gmnc. pointed to by OE *ēorl*, war chief; and by Icelandic *jarl* (also *ēarl*).]

    HISTORIC. Having survived the Frenchification of English after the Norman Conquest, *earl* is the only British title of nobility of Gmnc. origin. (*King* and *queen* are Gmnc. in origin, but they are titles of royalty as distinct from those of the nobility.) William the Conqueror sought to call the hereditary earls of Britain *counts.* [Fr. *comte* < *comté*, area ruled by a count (COUNTY).] Despite the royal wish, English rejected *count*, but after the conquest an earl's wife was called a *countess.* Earlier, her title had been *lady, the lady, milady.*

earn   1. To accrue wages/fees for services rendered. 2. To merit, to acquire through effort. *Al Stein has fairly earned my considered contempt.* 3. To accrue a return on an investment or bank deposit. *Earned interest is unearned income.* [Root sense: "to harvest." IE *esen-*, harvest, to harvest. Via Gmnc. to Ger. *essen*, to eat (DELICATESSEN). With the form altered in Gmnc. → OE *earnian*, to harvest; and by ext., to acquire by labor. (This root sense located, note how it functions in the Biblical admonition to earn one's bread in the sweat of the brow—if one means *zu essen.*)]

earwig   The folk name of various beetle-like *Dermaptera* with prominent abdominal extensions that form a well-defined pincer-like "tail." [OE *ēorwicga*, ME *erwigge*, with root sense: "dweller in the ear," effective sense: "ear borer." < *ēor*, ear; *wic*, place of residence. OE *wic* survives in many place names, as *Moorwick*, at root: "house on the moors."]

HISTORIC. British folklore has concocted horror stories about this creature's habit of boring into the human ear to infest the head and to cause agonies that drive people insane and are finally fatal. All such tales are based on mistaking "vegetable ear" (as an ear of grain) for "human ear." Whatever buzzes in the head of folklore, it is into vegetable ears that this overdramatized creature bores.

ebb   *v.* To sink away. To recede. —*n.* A low point. *at an ebb.* —*adj.* Of a low point. *ebb tide.* Also *ebbing the last of his ebbing resources.* [IE *ap-, apo-*, away from, off. → Gk. *apo*, with same senses. So *apogee*, the point in an orbit farthest from the orbited body. Same IE stem with *a* dropped, and suffixed → L. *post*, after. This much-traveled stem with p/b and suffixed -*n*- in Gmnc. → Ger. *Abend*, evening ("time after day"). And in a variant of this evolution → OE *ebba*, low tide ("time after high water" / "time when the sea has gone away").]

economy   1. The prudent management of funds and resources. [< Gk. *oikonomos*, steward of estate, household. First element, from *oikos*, house, is akin to OE *wic*, place of residence, common in place names, as *Fenwick*, house in the fen. See *bailiwick*, under *bail*, Vol. I. Variantly, see *earwig*. Second element is Gk. *nomos*, law, regulation, systematization.] 2. *Colloq. ext.* A saving. *Three for the price of two is a real economy.* 3. (Among many other exts. best left to experts, who seldom seem to know what they are talking about.) The total resources of a nation in interplay with what is left of its financial and productive resources after taxation. *the national economy.* And so **Reaganomics** Everything President Reagan really does not know about the national economy, and which we shall all probably have to learn the hard way.

ecstasy   Intense emotion, as: 1. Joy. *the ecstasy of triumph.* 2. Rapture. *the ecstasy of the religious experience.* 3. Frenzy. *an ecstasy of rage, of fear.* [Root sense: "out of oneself." < Gk. *stasis,* standing, normal condition of being; prefixed *ex-,* out of.]

   HISTORIC. The sense of the Greek word is based on the immemorial daemonological belief that one's spirit can leap free of one's body in an excess of emotion, and this belief survived far beyond the classical Greeks. In XIV, Dante expressed the same belief in describing his rapturous ascent to Paradise (*Paradiso,* I. 73–75: *last created part,* the soul; *O Love that rulest Heaven,* God):

> Whether I rose in only the last created
>   part of my being, O Love that rulest Heaven,
>   Thou knowest, by whose lamp I was translated.

Dante is saying that he does not know whether he rose to Heaven in the flesh, or only in the soul which was called from his body in the ecstasy of contemplating the ascent.

edifice complex   An obsessive drive to build more and more buildings as proof that an enterprise is prospering and improving. [C. 1947. A collegiate pun based on *Oedipus complex.* ("Up against the wall, mother; up against all those walls.") Originally specific to colleges and universities, traditionally conservative institutions that underwent all but reckless expansion in response to the swollen enrollments of returning WWII veterans on the G.I. Bill. That expansion changed the nature of American college education, seldom for the better, for having committed themselves to an ever-expanding plant, our colleges were forced into the "numbers game" of recruiting more and more students, qualified or not, to use the plant.]

edify   1. To improve (someone else) spiritually and morally. In effect, to raise him to one's own glorious level of belief. 2. *Ext.* To raise one's spirits. *I found it edifying to return from Washington, D.C., to the United States of America.* [But earlier with the sense: "to build." So *Piers Plowman* (XIV): "I shall overturne this temple, and adoun throw it,/And in thre daies after *edifie* it new." But at ult. root sense: "to burn." < IE *aidh-,* heat, to burn. Whence L. *aestas,* summer (the hot season); whence It. *estate,* Fr. *été.* Whence also L. *aedes,* house (place where the hearth fire burns). And so L. *aedificare,* to build a house; and by ext., to build (EDIFICE). Sense 1, above, is by association with the improvement of the spirit, real or imagined, resulting from attendance in God's house, the church.]

egg/egg on (Earlier, now obs. *edge on*) To spur. To prod. [Root sense: "to urge on by poking with a sharp instrument." Ult. < IE *ak-,* sharp (ACUTE). With k/g in Gmnc. → OE *eggian* ME *eggen,* to prick.]

egg on one's face, be left with To be left speechless, nonplussed. To be taken aback. To be embarrassed. [Dating? I cannot find the idiom in Brit. and am left to conclude, on imperfect evidence, that it is Am. only and prob. late XIX. It seems clear, however, that the root image is of an actor or orator pelted with garbage and rotten eggs and so driven offstage.]

egg suction The country art of poking a fine hole in one end of a raw egg, a slightly larger one in the other, and then sucking out the contents, leaving the shell all but intact. [Robert Frost memorialized this ancient country practice. He mentions whimsically the nonstop prayer wheel of Asia, each turn of which adds a prayer to the mountain of the owner's merit, and scoffs at the idea that the Asians lack a sense of industrialized output. He concludes: "Teach those Asians mass production? / Teach your grandmother egg suction." The earliest attested usage may be in "Petites Conversations" by Jonathan Swift, 1667–1745: "Go teach your grannum to suck eggs," a ridiculous suggestion, for she long since knew all about it. The same sort of ridicule is suggestion by the Yiddish proverb, *"Ihr will ein alten Taten tauchen Kindermachen":* He would teach an old daddy how to make (beget) children.]

egregious *adj.* Outstandingly bad. [< L. *ex-, e-,* out of; *grex,* herd, flock. Ult. < IE *ger-,* together, a gathering. So at root: "standing apart from the herd," and in the English language convention, "outstandingly bad." Perhaps because proper herd animals should remain with the herd, whereby only the bad ones stray. Yet the Italians, with millennia of herd tending behind them, use *egregio,* outstanding one, as an honorific, and as a common letter-opening salutation. The root sense is open to either sense evolution; it is the language convention that decides.]

elixir   [< Arabic *al iksir,* the (philosopher's) stone. Long sought in earnest by alchemists, and peddled by cheats, it was said to transmute base metals to gold. Powdered and diffused in various liquids, commonly in alcohol, it was said, at first (c. 1000 A.D.), to confer immortality; but as the death rate continued unaltered, it was peddled as a panacea.] 1. *Pharmacy* A medicinal infusion in alcohol.

HISTORIC. Once a common pharmaceutical term, abuse by quacks has led reputable pharmacists to avoid it. Many elixirs have been more noted for their alcoholic content than for their medicinal virtues. Various "female tonics" were popular with genteel temperance ladies, and served during Prohibition as their afternoon pick-me-up, in effect an afternoon (perish the thought) cocktail. As a young man, Stuart Holbrook worked on lumber drives down the rivers of Maine. He told me once that when a crew was camped near a town, it pooled its money and sent someone into town for a case of Lydia Pinkham's Female Tonic to get drunk on.

2. A cure-all, a panacea.

HISTORIC. Before the enactment of Pure Food and Drug laws in the 1890's, there was no regulation (except for poison, of course) of the ingredients in such stuff as Dr. Homero's Indian Snake Oil Elixir. Most such quack medicine was loaded with laudanum, which is an infusion of opium in alcohol. The medicine man was no supersalesman, yet he commonly had little trouble selling his elixirs to XIX ladies for a dollar a bottle. They saved their butter and egg money and came flocking to buy from five to ten bottles at a time, and at a time when a dollar was a substantial piece of money. The ladies, alas, were at least mildly addicted. They knew their "female tonic" made them feel good. Doesn't every junkie feel good when he takes a shot? Some of these quack elixirs contained cocaine or morphine, or any combination of cocaine, morphine, or laudanum. Morphine was the only painkiller known to medicine, and many Civil War amputees became morphine addicts. Great-grandmother was often an addict without knowing it.

eminent   Outstanding by virtue of personal merit (earlier, also by birth). [< L. *ēminēns,* present part. of *ēminere,* to stand out, to jut, to project. Ult. < IE *men-,* to jut, to project, to overshadow (MENACE). The ult. root sense permits "outstanding and ominous," but the language convention has settled an honorific sense on all Eng. derivatives of *ēminēns.* (And see *egregious.*)]

eminence 1. The condition of being meritoriously outstanding. 2. *Capitalized.* The form of address to a Roman Catholic cardinal, or of reference to him. *Thank you, Your Eminence. His Eminence is arriving.* 3. *A surviving neutral sense.* A hill. An elevation. ["A jut of land." Milton, *Paradise Lost,* wrote of Satan on a "bad eminence," with the double connotation: (1) that he was seated on a hill in hell; and (2) that he was eminently evil. Milton was a Latinist. I know of no other instance in Eng. of *eminence* used with a connotation of evil.]

empty set   Variantly ***null set** Mathematics, logic.* A set having no members, as the set of all pregnant men, of all rectangular arcs, of all mosquitoes twelve feet high. [Not in common use, but bursting with metaphoric possibility, if at some violence to the strict sense. I can think of many organized groups that are an empty set of which there are no human members: all kibitzers, for one example.]

NOTE. The mathematical symbol resembles the Danish letter Ø, though it is at root a canceled zero, as road signs now use a red slash through a symbol to indicate "no/negative," as Ư means "No U-turn."

enthusiasm   1. Excited interest. Eagerness. Zeal. 2. Anything that excites avid interest. *Fast cars are his one enthusiasm.* [In XVIII, excess in dress, manner, intellectual discourse, i.e., any departure from the frozen norms of the Age of Reason. Earlier, religious rapture; and this is the root sense: "God-inspired, inspirited." < Gk. *theos,* God, prefixed *en-,* in → *entheos,* later *enthous,* ingodded, seized and made ecstatic by the spirit of God within. Whence *enthousiasmos,* religious rapture.]

entrechat   *Ballet.* A vertical leap during which the dancer crosses his legs or taps his heels. The higher the leap, the more such leg movements the dancer can work in. [The form is Fr. and misleadingly suggests the nonsense: "between / among the cat." But the Fr. is a corruption of It. *capriola intrecciata,* intricate goat caper < *capriola,* goat caper; with *intrecciata,* woven, braided. The Eng. cognate is *intricate.*]

Epsom salts   A powerful laxative, once in common use. [A hydrated form of magnesium sulfate, so called because first obtained by inspissating the waters of a mineral spring at Epsom in Surrey. Epsom Downs, the nearby racetrack, site of the annual derby, offers an alternative way of cleaning out Britons.]

escapade A more or less abandoned fling, from the consequences of which one narrowly escapes. [At root: "by slipping out of one's cape just at the point of being nabbed by the watch or by the bumbailiff." ME *escapen*, Norman Fr. *escaper.* < L. *cappa*, cape, cloak; with *ex-*, out of. Generally implies high jinks rather than criminal evil, but rogues and thieves were once capable of criminal escapades. In time *escapade* became associated with *adventure.*]

esquire/squire [At root: "shield bearer (in service to a knight)." (See *bachelor.*) ME *esquir, esquier* < OF *esquier, escuier* < Late L. *scūtārius*, shield bearer, L. *scutum*, shield. Ult. < IE *sker-, skei-*, to cut.]

In Am. usage: *n.* 1. A generalized title of respect. In written form, *Esquire* or *Esq.* In verbal address, *Squire. Jonathan Roe, Esq.* 2. In colonial use, with the form *squire.* A prominent landholder or substantial citizen (the two tended to coincide). In one quaint survival, Jack Sharkey, heavyweight boxing champion 1932–1933, the then most prominent citizen of Brighton, Mass., was dubbed by the Boston papers *The Squire of Chestnut Hill.* 3. In some states *squire* (with the sense "prominent citizen") is the official title of a minor magistrate. 4. When the title *esquire* fell into general disuse in the U.S. it was taken up by attorneys. (They tend to conceive of themselves as prominent citizens.) Today *Attorney* and *Attorney at Law* are more common, but *Esquire, Esq.*, persist. —*v.* To escort. Esp., in whatever is left of the tradition of gallantry, to escort a lady with appropriate flourishes. *Squire a lady around town* is to escort and attend upon her more or less as a squire once tended his knight.

In long-stratified British tradition, however, *esquire* is a formal title and applicable only to certain persons of what might be called the sub-peerage. Edwin Radford, *Unusual Words,* gives a summary from the Richmond *Herald* (undated) compiled by C. H. Athill, Esq. Those legally entitled to the designation in Britain are: "The sons of Peers, Baronets, and Knights; the eldest sons of the younger sons of Peers and the eldest sons in perpetuity; the Kings of Arms and Heralds of Arms; officers of the Navy and Army of the rank of Captain and upwards [*]; Sheriffs, J.P.'s while they are in commission, Sergeants-at-Law, King's Counsel, Companions of Knighthood, certain officers of the Royal Household, Deputy Lieutenants, Commissioners of the Court of Bankruptcy, Masters of the Supreme Court, and those whom the King in any Commission styles Esquires." Had C. H. Athill, Esq., commanded a clearer prose, his guide might have been more useful.

*Can he be accurate in equating army and navy captains? A naval captain is the equivalent of a colonel, which is three grades higher than an army captain.

etc./et cetera   [L. "and other things." *Cetera* is the neuter nominative plu. of *ceterus,* the part that remains.]
NOTE. Some purists take the position that *etc.* is properly used only with reference to things, and that where "other persons" is meant, the form should be *et alii* (abbreviated *et al.*), and others. The distinction is valid when based on Latin precedent, but *cetera* is ult. < IE *ke-,* widely diffused as a third-person and reflexive pronoun, as in Fr. *ce, ces.* Via Gmnc. with k/h, it is the base of OE *he,* he, her, him (HE).

etymology   The study of the origin and development of words and idioms. [< Gk. *etymon,* neuter of the adj. *etymos,* true; with suffix *-ology* < Gk. *logos,* word, but as suffix, with the sense "study of."]
etymon The earliest known form of a word.
HISTORIC. Greek *etymon,* lit. "true," had the effective sense: "the true word" / "the true name." "True name" is an idea whose implications go back to earliest black magic.

Magicians and sorcerers summoned spirits and fiends by uttering their "true names." (And we still say, "Now there's a name to conjure with.") Old Central European belief held that a werewolf would return to human form if summoned by its "true name." In the fairy tale, Rumpelstiltskin is powerless once his "true name" is known. In many primitive societies, newborn males are given a "calling name" for convenience, but also a "true name" known only to the witch doctor and the parents, or to the witch doctor and the father. It was not even revealed to the son until he performed his manhood ritual (the equivalent of confirmation). It was guarded because any conjurer who discovered the "true name" could use it to put a hex on the bearer. In some Far Eastern religions, monks compile a list called "the billion names of God," believing that when the "true name" is pronounced and recorded, God will die, Creation will end, and a new phase of being begin.

It was against this background that Greek philosophers examined the nature of words. Did they arise from nature, or were they a social convention? The Stoics taught that words were inherent in nature, and that if the original meaning could be found, one could grasp what the gods intended when they fixed a given name/label to a given thing. This view makes no allowance for the fact that other languages use other labels for the same thing, nor does it take note of the dramatic sense shifts, and even reversals of meaning, the words undergo in time. What the Stoics knew securely is that language is from the depths of some racial unconscious and that words have much to do with the ways in which we perceive and react.

eunuch A castrated boy or man. Variantly, though only by association, one whose testicles never developed. (And cf. *gelding,* of ON origin, a castrated domestic animal; now esp. a horse.) [ME *eunuke,* via L. *eunuchus* < Gk. *eunokhos,* at root: "one who guards the bed," a clear reference to harem eunuchs. The Gk. form is < *eunē,* bed; with *ekhein,* to hold, to possess, but with associated sense: "to guard." Ult. < IE *(s)egh-,* to hold; with g/k → Gk. *ekhein.* Variantly *(s)ogh,* which with same g/k and prefixed *epi-,* in, on → Gk. *epokhē,* a pause ("a holding of time") (EPOCH). And if only to illustrate the plasticity of word roots, *segh-,* via Gmnc., is clearly visible in Ger. *Sieg,* victory ("a holding/possession of the enemy and the field after battle").

HISTORIC. *Eunuch* came into XI–XII English as a result of the Crusades. Before the Crusades, England was in near-total ignorance of Arabian customs. *Eunuch* slowly supplanted *gelding,* which became specific to animals, though one will yet be understood in calling a man a capon or a gelding. Wycliffe uses *gelding* for *eunuch* in XIV. N. Bailey's 1764 *Dictionary* defines *eunuch* as "a gelded man," but defines *to geld* as "to cut out the Stones of a Male Animal." (I wonder what other sort of animal Bailey thought geldable.)

eureka Exclam. of exultant discovery. [Gk. *heurēka,* I have found it! The initial aspirate is indicated in Greek by a mark resembling an apostrophe—*'eurēka*—and here ignored in transcription.]

HISTORIC. King Hiero of Syracuse is said to have given a goldsmith a weight of gold with which to make a crown. Suspecting the man of keeping some of the gold for himself and of making up the weight with silver or some lesser alloy, the king called on Archimedes to verify the purity of the finished crown.

The principle is that if a lighter alloy was used, the crown must have been enlarged to make up the weight of the withheld gold. This principle is said to have occurred to Archimedes when he was in his bath, and noted that his body displaced a set amount of water. If pure gold displaced X amount of water, alloyed gold of the same weight must displace more than X. Archimedes is said to have leaped dripping from his bath and to have run naked through the streets, shouting, *"Eureka!* I have found it!" i.e., the right principle for determining the purity of the crown. By submerging the crown in a brimful vessel of water and weighing the amount of water displaced, as opposed to the weight of water displaced by the original weight of gold, Archimedes proved that the goldsmith had alloyed the crown.

Eureka! is the motto of the state of California, interpreted as: 1. I have found it! (the beautiful place). 2. The exultant cry of the forty-niners on striking gold. (And why not with both senses functioning?)

eve [Short form of *evening,* which is ult. < IE *apo-,* away from. With p/f in Gmnc. → OE *ǣfen,* ME *evening,* with prob. root sense: "that part of day away from (after) the sun," hence either "sunset" or "time from sunset to midnight."] 1. *Usu. capitalized.* The evening before a holiday or saint's day. *Eve of St. Agnes. Christmas Eve.* 2. *Ext.* The time just before any significant event. *the eve of war.* 3. Archaic and poetic for "evening."

HISTORIC. The early Christians, like the Jews, reckoned the day from sunset to sunset. "The Eve of the Feast of St. Paul" now signifies the evening before St. Paul's Day. In earlier usage it signified the beginning of the Feast of St. Paul.

ewer A large water pitcher with a wide lip. [< L. *aqua,* water; *aquarius,* of water. Some unattested Medieval L. form, perhaps *aquaria,* lit. "water thing," is suggested by the OF form *aiguière.* The Norman Fr. variant was *eviere,* whence with a common v/w → ME *ewere, ewer,* first attested in XIV.]

HISTORIC. Before internal plumbing, the common bedroom lavatory consisted of a ewer, a large wash basin, and a floor receptacle into which used wash water could be poured. (Or the water was often thrown out the window.) These utensils were often made of decorated stoneware in matching sets. I have stayed in Vermont country inns that still supply such sets on the dresser or on a separate table, and not simply as antiquarian touches but as serviceable utensils. Many such sets were offered for sale in turn-of-the-century Sears, Roebuck catalogues.

execute [IE *sekw-,* to follow, following (SEQUEL) → L. *sequi,* to follow; prefixed *ex-,* out of, here as an intensive; whence *exequi,* to follow (carry out orders) to the end. P.p. *executus,* done (carried to conclusion).] 1. To carry out orders. 2. *Capital punishment.* To put to death. (To carry out orders to do the blighter in.) *executive* One who manages things (carrying them step by step to, one hopes, a successful end). *executor* Manager of the affairs of a deceased person, or of an established trust (who follows out estate or fund purposes). *executioner* Person who carries out a legal order to kill. *gangland executioner* One who kills on orders from the crime boss.

expletive deleted   In place of a curse. *If you want my opinion, you can stick your adjectival shmuck up your expletive deleted nose.*

HISTORIC. Richard M. Nixon, it seems, had a foul mouth when talking to his intimates. The transcripts of his White House tapes abound with the term "expletive deleted" whenever our commander in chief turned a word or phrase not properly in the voice of the silent majority.

Will the phrase pass into Am. idiom? It has already done so to some extent. If I am asked my opinion of a given politician and I say he is an expletive deleted son-of-a-bitch, I will certainly be understood. Will it remain in idiom? Who knows?

explode   1. To detonate. 2. *Ext.* To refute an allegation as if by blowing it apart. *His rebuttal exploded the charges brought against him.* [But at root, from Roman theater: "to drive an actor offstage by jeering and derisive clapping." And this is the sense of L. *explaudere* < *ex-,* out; with *plaudere,* to applaud.]

HISTORIC. The Latin root sense, with XVI exts. to reject, to refute, and XVII, to discredit, remained in force until XVIII, when there developed the sense: to detonate gunpowder. Except for volcanic eruptions, and perhaps the blowing up of still fermenting amphorae of wine, the ancients had no instances of detonation. The now primary detonative sense might have developed by late XIV with the first military use of gunpowder, but was delayed until XVIII. Even then for a while the essential sense of *explode* was "to drive (the enemy) away," rather than "to blow (him) up." The sudden eruption of an audience into derisive applause is a lovely natural metaphor, and it is still idiom to say, "The house exploded with applause," or by ext., "He exploded with rage."

express   [L. *ex-,* out of; *primere,* to squeeze, to press; lit. "to squeeze out," but the language convention has turned these roots to widely different senses.]

v. To speak. To utter. To let one's views be known. ["to squeeze out of oneself."] 2. *Am.* To send by the most rapid means. *If you express this package it will be in Omaha tomorrow morning. —adj.* Rapid. *express (train).* A highballing train that makes few or no stops. [In It., *rapido.*] Also as *n. midnight express.* [Train that squeezes great speed out of itself.]

    expression 1. An utterance. 2. A familiar or characteristic form of speaking. *Begorra is an old Irish expression.* 3. An aspect. An appearance. *He wore a gloomy expression.*

    Expressionism A XIX (and since) trend, originally in French painting. Expressionist painters abandoned photo-realism in order to express (squeeze out of their inner being) what they felt about their subject.

extravagant   *adj.* 1. Given to spending beyond reasonable limits. 2. Given to immoderate behavior, opinions. *extravagant praises.* [At root: "to wander beyond (reasonable limits)." < L. *extrāvagārī,* to wander beyond (limits). < *extra,* beyond; *vagārī,* to wander without goal or purpose, to vagabond (VAGARY).]

eyeball to eyeball   In face-to-face, implicitly hostile confrontation. Hence, in hard, blunt negotiation. [Federalese, c. 1960.]

    NOTE. The basic metaphor and the identical sense is expressed in Italian by *a quatrocchi,* lit. at four-eyes, i.e., staring hard at one another in close confrontation. Eng. *eye to eye* is almost the same metaphoric form, but tends to imply straightforward honesty or agreement rather than harsh confrontation. Fr. *tête-à-tête* implies only intimacy, whereas the same form in Eng. **head to head** implies violent confrontation, at root based on the image of goats butting one another, hence, of people, with the sense: slugfest. Also expressed by **nose to nose** said of boxers who stand **toe to toe** with their heads together, punching and taking punches with intent to outbatter one another. These are all related metaphors, variously expressing gentle intimacy or violent confrontation, as the language convention decides.

eyetooth   An upper canine tooth. And by later association, a lower. [So called because the nerves of the uppers, as toothache has given many to know, pass close to the eye. The first OED citation is from 1580. In MHG *augenzahn,* lit. eyetooth (for same reason). But the Eng. is prob. < Du. *oogtand,* eyetooth. The late XVI was a time of Dutch preeminence in Europe, and a spate of Du. words and idioms passed into Eng. at that time. Whiting, *American Proverbs,* cites: 1770, "have his eyeteeth," to be mature; and 1782, "a sensible young man and upon my word (according to the vulgar saying) he seems *to have all his eyeteeth about him.*" The double citation, and the ref. to "the vulgar saying" suggest that "eyetooth, eyeteeth" came early to the Am. colonies and remained in common use. (The term "vulgar saying" means only that the form was not used in formal rhetoric among the colonials.)]

cut one's eyeteeth To mature. Hence, to gain experience. [From the fact that canines develop after the first baby teeth.]

up to one's eyeteeth in Deeply involved. Nearly engulfed in. [Variantly *up to one's eyes / ears in.*]

give one's eyeteeth for To yearn for. [Cf. *I'd give my right arm for.* (I'd give both arms for a chance to pitch for the Yankees.)]

facsimile 1. *Theoretically.* An exact copy. 2. *But in practice.* A more or less accurate reproduction. *facsimile edition* A photo-offset reproduction of a rare book. [< L. *fac simile,* do the same. *Counterfeit* < L. *contra,* against; *fecit,* he made; hence with root sense: "thing made against (from) an original," could be argued to have essentially the same root sense as *facsimile,* but the English language convention has reserved to *facsimile* the sense: "accurate copy (made with no intent to deceive)," and to *counterfeit* the sense: "spurious imitation made with dishonest intent." And see *counterfeit,* which did not acquire its sense of "sham" until late XVI.]

faction A dissident and contentious minority. *factionalism* More or less violent partisanship. [OF *faction,* such a group < L. *factio* (< *facere,* to make, to do), was "a concerted action" and also "a team of charioteers."]

HISTORIC. In the early tradition, chariot racing teams (*factii*) consisted of four men who wore as their racing colors green, red, blue, and white. These colors may have represented spring, summer, fall, and winter. Domitian (emperor 81–96 A.D.) added purple (imperial) and yellow (gold) factions, thus raising the traditional number of entries per race from four to six. The Corso, a main avenue of Rome leading to the Forum, was a traditional raceway for chariots, but races often occurred within oval stadia, the negotiation of the turns being an often lethal hazard.

Chariot racing was a commonly bloody sport involving murderous extensions of the axles to chew the wheel spokes of rivals and cause a deadly spill. The one rule was to win at all costs.

Under Justinian, emperor of the Eastern Empire, 527–565 A.D., a wrangle between the green faction and the emperor's favored blues set off a five-day riot that is said to have taken 30,000 lives and almost to have toppled the empire in civil war. The pejorative

94

sense of *faction, factionalism,* is prob. a surviving memory of this and similar bloody incidents, for it is not etymologically implicit, the root sense being simply: "concerted group action." Had the charioteers and their screaming fans not been bloody-minded, it might today have been possible to say (as it most certainly is not): "the Red Cross faction at the disaster scene."

fairy ring   1. *In Am., more in fancy than in folklore.* A circle of fungi within which fairies are said to dance at night. 2. *In Brit. (the earlier sense).* A circle of grass notably greener and glossier than that around it. It is said to be so brightened by the dancing of the fairies. [A fairy ring starts with a single, usu. large, fungus growing in a grassy place. The decay of the fungus inhibits the growth of new fungi on the spot it covers, but enriches the grass. New fungi sprout just outside the circle of decay, repeating the cycle and spreading the circle wider. When, in time, the nutrients of the first fungus, and of those closest to it, have been entirely consumed, the rim of the circle will still show a band of especially green and glossy grass. In this bit of minor folk whimsy, Am. has focused on the fungi, and Brit. on the grass.]

famine   1. A severe and widespread shortage of food caused by failed or destroyed harvests. 2. *Ext.* Any prolonged dearth. *the intellectual famine of the American school system.* **famished** Starved. Ravenously hungry. *famish* To starve. [L. **fames,* hunger. We now distinguish between *famine* and *hunger,* but through ME the Latin root sense obtained. Wycliffe's translation of the Bible in XIV renders Luke 15:14: "And aftir that he had ended alle thinges, a strong *hunger* was made in that cuntre." The same passage is rendered in the King James version (1611): "And when he had spent all, there arose a mighty famine in that land." The Geneva Bible, 1560, reads: "there arose a great dearth throughout that land."]

fan   An enthusiast, as of a sport. [Am., prob. c. 1900, with ref. to a sports enthusiast < *fanatic* < Gk. *phanatikos,* person from the temple (FANE, PROFANE). In orgiastic rites, a god-intoxicated person. Many U.S. revivalist sects still work themselves up to a religious frenzy, "coming through" to "speak in tongues," the tongues being a presumably God-inspired gibberish, the intensity of the experience often accompanied by a sexual climax—or watch the sport fans root for the team, especially at moments of tight action, and see if you can distinguish their mania from religious fanaticism.]

fan club/ fan letter/ fan mail These are originally terms developed in response to silent movies, and to the star system of the silent screen. *Fan club* came last. MMM first attests the compound *fan letter* as of 1925.

fen Science fiction. An arch plural of *fan* as if by analogy to *man, men.* But occasionally at least, used for the singular. *Isaac Asimov is a fen—on its way to become a bog.*

fancy Dan   1. A flashy dude. 2. *Boxing.* A fighter who boxes artfully and has fancy footwork, but who cannot deliver a powerful punch, nor take one. [Am. XIX. One might normally expect such slang labels to be reduplications (as fancy Nancy) or alliterative (as fancy Freddy). This one, however, has precedent in Sc., in which Andrew is commonly rendered as Andy or Dandy, whence *Dandy Andy,* altered in Am. to *fancy Dan.*]

fanny   *Slang. In Am.* The buttocks, esp. female buttocks, but *you can bet your sweet fanny,* said to a person of either sex, = you can bet your ass. [In Brit. slang since mid XIX, the external parts of the female sex organs. Usu. glossed vaguely as " < the female given name Fanny." And perhaps so, but why not then *nancy/betsy/fifi?* Perhaps (?) after the all-purpose whore of John Cleland's *Memoirs of Fanny Hill,* published in late XVIII, but suppressed and more rumored than read; which may account for the long lag before the term is attested. All this is plausible, and perhaps even likely, but the final gloss must be *origin unknown.*]

fantastic: trip the light fantastic   To dance lightly, nimbly. [From Milton's "L'Allegro": "Come and trip it as ye go / On the light fantastic toe." Then, shedding the toe, into widespread Am. use c. 1900 in consequence of the wildly popular song by Charles B. Lawler and James W. Blake, "The Sidewalks of New York," the lyrics of which end: "(we) Tripped the light fantastic / On the sidewalks of New York."]

farm   *n.* An agricultural holding for raising crops and livestock or both. (West of the Mississippi, and with some diffusion back into the East, *ranch* is more common, originally signifying cattle ranch, but now extended to everything from *avocado ranch* to *fish ranch.*) — *v.* To work the land in raising crops and in husbandry. [< L. *firmus,* firm. Medieval L. *firma,* lease payment for the use of land. OF and

ME *ferme,* with a gradual sense shift from "lease, land rent" to "land so rented." And the foregoing may be sufficient to explain the etymology, but see also OE *feorm,* feast, in historical note below.]

prison farm Variantly ***state farm/work farm/county farm.*** A minimum-security prison in which inmates cultivate a more or less substantial acreage.

farm club A minor-league baseball club affiliated with a major-league organization. [*Farm* because such clubs are usu. in small cities (out in the country, out in the bushes); and because the major-league organization "raises" future big-league players on these "farms."]

fat farm A luxurious country estate where the overweight rich pay heavily to be starved thin. ***funny farm*** A country insane asylum. ***farm out*** To subcontract work.

buy the farm RAF, WWII. To die in a crash. [Because aviators often said, "When this is over, I'm going to buy a farm." When one crashed and was killed, it was over.]

you can get the boy out of the farm but you can't get the farm out of the boy A common city formula implying: Once a yokel, always a yokel. When said by country folk, it generally means: A farm boy may move to the city, but the solid country virtues bred into him by farm life will remain with him. (Iowa papers, please copy.)

HISTORIC. OE *feorm,* feast, may have influenced the evolution of *farm.* It was long the custom of large landholders to lease lands for a stated fee in money, plus all provisions for one night's feasting. (Since large landholders might lease literally hundreds of farms, some could expect to feast for most or even all of the year.) Edwin Radford, *Unusual Words,* cites the Saxon Chronicle (775 A.D.) to the effect that the Abbot of Peterborough let a parcel of land for fifty pounds a year and *anes nihtes feorme,* one night's feasting. Similar land leases are recorded in the Domesday Book, a land survey and census undertaken in 1085–1086 on order of William the Conqueror, who thought it well to itemize his conquest.

In time the tenant farmers must have learned to skimp on their *feorm(e)* provisionings, for later contracts dropped this provision and leased land for what was called in legal L. *firma alba* payment in *whit-monnaie* (silver). Some leases additionally specified *firma nera,* black rent (paid in heads of livestock and wagonloads of farm produce, or in labor, with no nonsense about what the tenant might take to be enough for a night's proper feasting).

farthingale *Women's fashions.* 1. A webwork of hoops attached by struts to a waist belt to give a skirt something like the fullness of a bell-shaped bird cage. 2. The petticoat(s) and skirt(s) worn over such a contraption. [A complex evolution that offers a glimpse into medieval ladies' wear, in which such devices were made of flexible light boughs (withes) attached to a waist belt, God knows how. At root: "green branch, withe." < Sp. *verde,* green, *verdugo,* withe, *verdugado,* contraption made of withes. Altered in OF to *verdugale, vertugalle.* Whence in XVI Eng., via such transient forms as *verdingale, vardingale, fordingale* → *farthingale.*]

featherless biped Man. [L. *animal implume bipes,* a featherless biped animal. In a surviving learned joke, Plato is said to have offered this definition of a man; whereupon Diogenes is said to have ridiculed him by bringing a plucked cock to the agora and flinging it down scornfully, asking if that was Plato's man.

Captain William Golden, USN (ret.) of Richmond, Va., writes me that he has a letter in his possession written by an XVIII Virginia gentleman, who may have known of this story and used it as the basis of an unusual racial slur in which he referred to a Negro slave as *"an ebony biped."*]

fecalemia *Vulgar exuberant medical school formation.* A mock medical name for the disease known to the layman as shit in the blood, i.e., cowardice. [*Fecal,* the adjectival form of feces, excrement < L. *faex,* dregs; with *-emia,* of the blood < Gk. *haima,* blood (HEMOSTAT). Advanced cases of *fecalemia* can lead to terminal *coprolithia. Coprolite* is the technical name for a fossilized turd. (It has also been too long neglected as a select bit of invective. Everyone knows at least one poop who is at soul's essence a coprolite.)]

feud 1. A continuing bloody vendetta between two families, clans, or groups; usually self-intensifying, each act of violence touching off a more bloody reprisal. (In early societies, honor demanded that a slain kinsman be avenged by the law of an eye for an eye, a life for a life, the family or clan being disgraced if it failed to retaliate. Blood feuds were common in Europe through the Renaissance, and survived in Am. XIX among southern mountain folk, and exist to this day among various ethnic groups.) 2. (The sense softened with the general passing of the blood vendetta:) Continuing bad feeling between two groups (or, Don't walk Newark at night). [OE *fēhida,* feud. Also with collective prefix *ge-, gefāh,* feud (collective hostilities). < *fāh,* hostile; *fāhman,* foeman, foe. Ult. < IE *peig-,* inimical, of evil inclination. Via Gmnc. with p/f and g/h → to the OE forms given above. And with variant p/f and g/k → Gmnc. skeletal form *fʾk-* → Eng. *fuck* (the form is not attested in OE, perh. because of a verbal taboo).]

fib A white lie. [< L. *fabula,* a spoken tale (FABLE). < L. *fari,* to speak. (The present part. is *fans,* speaking. With neg. prefix *in-* → *infans,* infant, i.e., not speaking, with effective sense: "not yet speaking.") In XVI *fible-fable,* nonsense (the sort of stuff fablers spin); a redupl. based on *fable.* Whence *fib* by back formation from *fible.* It is unusual for a new word to be formed from the echoing rather than the base element of a redupl., but it does happen. *Zoot suit* is a Black English rhyming redupl. based on *suit,* with *zoot* as the echoing element, and also the base of *zooty.* (See *zoot suit,* Vol. I.)]

fiery cross A wooden cross set up in front of the house of a hated person and set afire as a dire, anonymous warning. In U.S. firmly associated with the racist Ku Klux Klan, though any brutalized hate group can plant a fiery cross, as any racist can paint a swastika on the wall of a synagogue.

HISTORIC. In the Middle Ages a small, light, fiery cross was used as a call to military service. At declaration of war, the necromancer-alchemist-astrologer, in ritual with the liege lord, prepared the cross, lighted the four ends, performed some mumbo-jumbo, and then put out the four fires by plunging the ends in turn into the bloody guts of a sacrificed animal. (Symbolism, anyone?)

The charred and bloody cross was then given to a runner, who carried it to the lordling of the nearest village on the lord's estate, handing it over with no word spoken except to name the assembly point. The local lordling sent the cross forward at once by one of his runners, and the pattern was repeated until all men subject to military service had been notified.

Any man who was so notified and did not appear was, by his failure, a traitor and subject to death by sword (blood and gore) and by fire (drawn, quartered, and burned). Thus a doubly dread symbol: first, of war, and second, of the punishment awaiting those who failed to heed.

filibuster 1. *Am. XIX politics.* A prolonged speech with no purpose but to delay action on a pending bill, esp. when the legislature is about to adjourn. 2. *Earlier.* A military action against a small country by mercenaries who seek booty or concessions. [XVI Du. *vrijbuiter,* pirate < *vrij,* free, *buit,* booty. Lit. "one who makes free with the booty." → Fr. *filibustier;* Sp. *filibustero.* The political sense is prob. based on the idea: "one who stages a raid on the legislative process."]

fin   *Slang.* A five-dollar bill. Also *finnuf/finnif.* [These variants are Yiddish forms based on OHG *finf,* five. In Brit. slang c. 1835, a five-pound note. These forms were common in Brit. horse racing slang before being transmitted to American tracks c. 1900 via the internationalism of horse racing.]

finance   *n.* Large-scale economic management or manipulation. —*v.* To supply the money for a large-scale venture. [A word with many changed and changing senses. ME *finaunce,* settlement of a case by paying a fine or by forfeiting property. Lit. "the act of putting an end to a claim, account, court case." But OF *finaunce* had the primary sense "wealth" (what one has left after settling all claims —in current Am. that sense could be rendered by "bottom line"). Ult. based on Fr. *fin,* the end.]

fish: he eats no fish   He is not a Roman Catholic (and may therefore be trusted). [The ref. is to the fact that Roman Catholics ate fish on Friday. The saying, now obs., but common in Elizabethan and XVII English, is based on the Englishman's distrust of Roman Catholics as agents of a foreign power. For though Henry VIII's break with the Vatican and the seizure of RC church properties was variously motivated and caused continuing dissent in Britain, most Britons felt a deep insular distrust of foreign powers in their land, in part from deep feelings stirred by the many earlier invasions of the British Isles.]

fit as a fiddle   1. In precise order. 2. In vibrant good health. [A simple metaphor. A well-made and tuned fiddle is a precise arrangement of many exactly ordered parts. Whiting, *Am. Proverbs and Proverbial Phrases, to look like a fiddle,* 1792 (but with no source given): "This day the Ship was completely rig'd, Hold stowed, and in every respect in readiness for sea. She looked like a fiddle!"]

flagstone   A more or less flat slab of stone used for paving, flooring, patio flooring, and for laying a path or a series of steppingstones.

Flat pieces cut from a mass and polished or rough-polished, as plaques of marble, pass as flagstones if laid on the ground, as in Vermont, where marble is common. But generally flagstone implies stratified sedimentary rock, as sandstone, with natural cleavage planes between strata. [At root: "flat stone." (Implies some substantial area as distinct from a flat pebble.) Ult. < IE *plak-*, flat. With common p/f and k/g in Gmnc. → ON *flaga*, layer of stone; and into ME under Dane Law (IX–X) as *flagge*, piece of sod. The variant form *flok-* does occur in OE but as *flōk*, flatfish (FLUKE).

The same IE stem with a nasal infix, perhaps in Italic → L. variant *plancus*, flat; *planca*, plank, is the source of Eng. *plank*.]

flat   A floor, or part of a floor, of a multi-unit dwelling, commonly a walk-up in a tenement. With the slightest touch of elegance (as an electric elevator), a flat becomes an apartment, and with a further upgrading (as in the Waldorf Towers), a suite. [Ult. < IE *plat-*, flat, a level expanse. With common p/f in Gmnc. → OE *flett*, a dirt floor, as a threshing floor, but also with ref. to the dirt floors of early cottages. In a late OE sense, an enclosed flat space, a hall. And so Sc. *flet*, the inside of a house.]

flea   A bloodsucking, wingless insect parasite of the order *Siphonaptera*, which is < Gk. *siphon*, tube, and *ptera*, feather; hence, flying thing, with neg. prefix *a-;* hence with root sense: "non-flying thing with a (sucking) tube." [IE *plou-*, flea; with p/f in Gmnc. → OE flēa(h). As an element in compounds, *flea* readily suggests (1) annoyance, (2) infested condition; hence, cheap and shabby. Whence:] ***flea bite*** A trivial annoyance. ***flea-bitten*** Undesirable. Cheap and shabby. ***flea market*** An odds-and-ends market for used stuff. Originally a street fair held at stated times, as Rome's Sunday morning Mercato di Porta Portesa; then commonly a permanent establishment, as the Parisian Marché aux Pousses, flea market being a translation of the French term. ***flea*** Any object sold in a flea market. (For generations now, the ladies of Chautauqua have been donating fleas to the annual church flea market and buying them back from one another, only to redonate and rebuy them.) ***flea in one's ear*** An annoying hint one is left to think about. Also, a stinging rebuke.

flog   To beat with a whip or similar object, usu. on the back or buttocks. [A vowel-modified back formation from *flagellate* < L.

flagellare, to whip.] *flog (beat) a dead horse* To persist pointlessly. (See *horse: flog a dead horse* for the nautical derivation.)

fluke An odd lucky chance. *fluky* With the various distinct senses: Oddly lucky. Unpredictable. Queer. [NWD notes, properly, the use of *fluke* in XIX billiards slang with the sense: "lucky shot" and adds " < ?" I lack attestation and can only suggest that the origin is in fishermen's slang with ref. to catching a fish by the odd chance of getting a hook, not into its mouth, but through a fluke or fin. And *fluke* is also, of course, a flatfish.]

footsie/footsy *Am. only.* 1. *In XIX nursery talk, and surviving.* A child's foot. *little footsie-wootsie.* Hence: 2. *In amorous prattle.* The foot of one's cutesy tootsie-wootsie. 3. The act of touching feet or of rubbing knees under the table flirtatiously or as a signal of intimacy. 4. The act of signaling covertly (under the table) by touching someone's foot, or by stomping it, or by kicking a shin. *Every time I tell that story, my wife plays footsie with a spike heel.*
  play footsie with To be covertly intimate with someone, amorously, flirtatiously, or in plotting together. *Organized crime has always played footsie with crooked cops.*

for crying out loud *Am. Dating uncertain. Prob. c. 1900.* Exclam. of anger, vexation. [A minced oath. As if one had started to say, "For Christ's sake!" but stopped after "For Chri—" and switched to the meaningless but inoffensive "—ying out loud!" And cheese and crackers, that's the doggone truth of it.]

forlorn hope A lost cause. [The idiom would appear at first glance to be a natural combination of Eng. words. It was, in fact, borrowed in late XVI < Du. *verloren hoep,* a lost band of soldiers; in Dutch military usage, a vanguard, rear guard, or other expendable unit; what we would now call a suicide squad. Du. *verloren* is the p.p. of *verliezen,* to lose; *hoep* is cognate with *heap,* a quantity, and also with *hoop,* a band, as in barrel hoop.]

Forum The central marketplace of Rome and seat of the government in the Republic. [At root: "place out of doors." < IE *dhwer-,* door. The voiced stop *dh* regularly shifts to *f* in Latin, whence L. *foris,* out of doors, *forum,* place out of doors. But the root sense has receded from the word, to be replaced by the associated sense: "place of discussion," because the Roman forum was the place of public discussion.] *forum* 1. A place for discussion. 2. A more or less open public discussion, now invariably in a large room or hall. 3. *Loose usage.* A radio or TV panel blathering away at a public issue, usu. chaired by a moderator not much better informed than anyone else, but with the master talent of making clichés sound like profound utterances.

fossil poem As used in these notes, a word or idiom formation notable for the poetic quality of its root imagery or association of elements. [I have taken the term from Richard Chevenix Trench, Anglican Archbishop of Dublin, an early, deeply erudite mid XIX etymologist. He seems a bit quaint today for his slightly pompous intrusion of moral preachments into his etymology, and his work suffers for lack of more than a century of scholarly advancement in the field, but few men have been his equal in his grasp of so many languages and of their interrelations. Had our present knowledge of Indo-European and Proto-Indo-European been available to him, he might well have become the most notable etymologist of all time. He may, among other distinctions, be said to be the godfather of the Oxford English Dictionary, for c. 1850 he addressed the British Philological Society and was so brilliant in making a case for a dictionary based on historical principles that the society responded with the ultimate expression of passion known to the British—it formed a committee, and that committee organized the enormous and sustained work that resulted, almost 75 years later, in the publication of the OED.]

foul [IE *pu-* is commonly rendered by scholars as "rotten, to rot." It is obviously, however, an echoic root, still surviving in the Eng. expressives *pew!/pee-u!/phew!* "Ugh, it stinks!" Via Gmnc. with p/f (and note same variant in *pew!/phew!*), and suffixed *-l-* → OE *ful*, ME *foul*, foul.] *adj.* A whole cluster of senses based on the opposite of "good": Base. Dirty. Disgusting. Messy. In violation of decency and good order. *foul-mouthed, foul play, foul weather.* In sports, with the sense: "in violation of the rules." *personal foul, foul line.* Also "out of fixed limits." —*n. Primarily in sports.* A violation of the rules. *He has four fouls.*

   In nautical usage. foul/fouled/afoul Tangled. Snarled. Snagged. **run afoul of** Be caught, snarled, tangled in. *And in generalized ext.* To become tangled in. *run afoul of the law.*

   foul-up Slang. 1. A mismanged situation. 2. A boob who mismanages everything. *foul ball* 1. *Baseball.* A ball hit outside the foul lines. 2. An oaf who cannot stay inside decent limits. One who fouls up constantly. [But the sense "disgusting" also functions here.]

And see *fulsome.*

freebooter   [For etymology, see *filibuster.*] 1. A pirate of the Spanish Main. [He makes free with the booty.] 2. *Politics.* A grafter on a large scale. [One who loots public funds.]

freehole   *Primarily prison slang.* A pushover. A worthless person. A punk. [Dating uncertain. Prob. post WWI. In the savage sexuality of our prisons, an inmate whose anus is available to any pederast. Hence, the bottom of the prison pecking order.]

free lance   An independent agent who is available to anyone who can uses his services. In current use, most commonly *free lance writer/ photographer,* one who offers his work for sale to various publishers with whom he is not formally affiliated; or one who will accept specific assignments without becoming a regular employee. [But originally a mercenary knight. One who, lacking commitment to a feudal lord, offered the services of his lance to any who would pay.]

HISTORIC. The Crusades of XI–XIII drew many knights to fight for the freedom of the Holy Land for reasons of religion and knightly honor. In practice they regularly turned out to be expeditions for carnage and plunder over which competing lords fell to bickering. Old feudal ties were often rent by death and dissent. Many unlucky knights, their liege lord dead, made their way home by offering themselves as itinerant mercenaries.

In 1507 "Cardinal" Cesare Borgia, "nephew" of Pope Alexander VI, having lost papal protection on the death of his "uncle," was killed in Spain while fighting as a free lance. He must have been one of the last in the maverick knight tradition that evolved primarily from the Crusades. The longbow and the crossbow had already dented knighthood, and gunpowder was already in process of blowing the last of it out of the saddle.

fret[1]   To be gnawed by anxiety. [And "to be gnawed" is the root sense. One would not readily recognize *fret* to be root-related to Ger. *essen,* to eat, yet both derive from a Gmnc. form, prob. *itan,* to eat, of which *essen* is a variant; the existence of the Gmnc. form being pointed to by OE *etan,* to eat. The Ger. intensive prefix *ver-* (as in *spielt,* played, *verspielt,* played out) took the form *for-* in OE

→ *foretan,* and later *fretan,* to devour. And so to ME *fretan,* with the modern sense: "to vex."]

fret² [Of obscure Gmnc. origin. Evidenced by OE *fraetwan,* to adorn, to ornament; *fraetwa,* treasure. Akin to OF *frete,* fretted, i.e., of intricately interwoven ornamental work; the form almost certainly of Gmnc.-Frankish origin.] A cross ridge on the finger-board of a stringed instrument.

fretwork Ornamental wood or metal work more or less intricately chased with delicate patterns of cross lines. *fretsaw* A fine jigsaw for cutting such patterns. Also for cutting out intricate curved patterns by inserting the blade in bored holes. [And if such work be conceived as "an eating out," one might make an inviting (but unattested) case for a common origin of fret¹ and fret².]

fulsome Disgusting. Revolting. [See *foul* for full etymology. Commonly misused as if *ful* = *full,* hence with the sense "cloyingly replete." It is, in fact < OE *ful,* foul.]

HISTORIC. On a TV interview, candidate Reagan went on too long in answer to a question, remarking at last that his remark had perhaps been "a bit fulsome." It hadn't been quite that. He intended, of course, long-winded ("in the manner of being too full"). And *fullsome,* if so written, would be understood. To that extent, therefore, it is a working word. It is, however, not listed in standard Am. dictionaries, and properly so, inasmuch as Am. speech has no way of distinguishing between *l* and *ll* in this case. Reagan's confusion, it follows, must remain disgusting.

And note *fulmar* A species of gray Arctic gull, *Fulmarus glacialis.* From ON *ful,* stinking; *mar,* gull, whence *fulmar,* stinking gull, so called because of the foul-smelling secretion with which it coats its feathers to waterproof them.

funeral The ceremony attending an interment, entombment, or cremation. *it's not my funeral* A common disclaimer of interest in and sympathy for someone else's bad luck. *It's no skin off my corpse. that's your funeral* Implies "not mine." Also implies no interest in joining the mourners. [Late L. *funeralis,* funereal, preserves the untraced stem, **funer-,* of L. **funus,* funeral. The stem may (?) be akin to *fumus,* smoke, by association with the crematory pyres commonly burning in an early necropolis. (See *bust,* Vol. I.)]

fur: make the fur fly   To have a violent fight. (As if two animals clawed and bit so violently that bits of hair and hide filled the air.) [But the idiom (XIX) is a hyperbole beyond nature. I have seen cat fights and dog fights, and I have watched every nature film I could find on TV. I have never seen furred animals, even in deadliest combat, make fur fly. I have, however, seen a weasel all but explode the feathers from a hen. *Make the feathers fly* was Brit. XVIII, with ref. to cockfighting. I must take *make the fur fly* as a careless XIX adaptation of the earlier cockfighting image.]

futz around   *Slang.* To putter about aimlessly. Implies not only purposeless fooling around, but the obstruction of others who are trying to go about their business. [Am. street slang based on Yiddish *arumfartzen*, to fart around.]

G

gab *Slang. n.* Loquacity. Prattle. Drawn-out busy talk, usu. about nothing much. —*v.* To prattle on and on. ***gabfest*** Any session marked by loquacity, esp. a buzz-buzz session of gossips. ***gift of gab*** The native talent for speaking fluently, and sometimes persuasively, though not necessarily sincerely. ***gabby*** Inanely loquacious. [Some refer the word to Sc. *gab*, mouthful, lump, but the Sc. ref. is to food. "Mouthful of food" to "mouthful of talk" would be a simple transfer. But Du. *gabbelen* and Eng. *gabble*, both meaning "to chatter on and on inanely," suggest a common though untraced Gmnc. root, prob. echoic in origin.]

gaff *n.* 1. A substantial hook secured to a pole for boating large fish once they have been reeled in. (And this is now the one functioning sense, though originally:) 2. *Cockfighting.* The razor-sharp spur (heel) attached to the back of a gamecock's legs. [Various Brit. slang and natuical specialized usages do not function in Am. < Sp. **gafa* with cockfighting sense.] —*v.* To boat a fish by gaffing.

   stand the gaff To bear up under punishment, pain, stress. [< Cockfighting; to keep fighting though raked by the opponent's spurs.]

   (But not *gaffer, old gaffer*, old man. < *g'father, gaffer*, grandfather.)

gallon as in ***ten-gallon hat*** cowboy's sombrero, has nothing to do with liquid capacity. [It is < Sp. *galón*, ribbon, which in the commonest context on the SW frontier implied ribbon worn between the broad rim and crown of a sombrero.]

   HISTORIC. Men's hats are still variously beribboned. In Mexican custom, ornate ribbons and bands of worked silver or gold were common items of male swagger. The larger the hat, the more *galones* were possible. *Diez galones*, ten ribbons, was probably hyperbolic, but signified an unusually large sombrero.

In evidence of the power of words, the Hollywood legend has since grown that cowboys commonly watered their horses out of their ten-gallon hats. Under extraordinary circumstances, as in scooping water from a seep in rocks the horse could not climb safely, a cowboy might have watered his horse in this way. Normally, a horse led to water is capable of drinking for itself, and is instinctively better at finding it than is the cowboy. It is conceivable, too, that a traveling horseman who carries grain to keep the horse healthy on a long ride might use an outsize sombrero as a feedbag. But the rest is a Hollywood cliché compounded of dream dust.

galoot An awkward, oafish guy. The most ordinary sort of stiff. [In dispute, for much is known about this word, all to no conclusion. First attested in Am. during War of 1812 as a name for a green soldier. C. 1835, a Brit. sailors' disparaging name for a marine. The form suggests a Du. origin, and the variant *geloot* is attested in late XVIII, though the sense is uncertain. Weekley thinks to derive the word < Du. *genoot*, companion, and the n/l dissimilation has precedent, but the sense does not conform with military and naval senses above. P. *Slang* looks to Du. *gelubt*, eunuch (with sense ext. to "one not capable of rendering manly service"?). All guesswork. Galoots remain persons of unknown origin.]

gambit 1. *In common usage.* An opening move, as in chess, war, or any elaborate negotiation. *But strictly speaking:* 2. An early sacrifice designed to gain a later advantage. (The common chess gambit is the act of sacrificing a pawn in order to establish an advantageous position.) [It. *gamba*, leg; *gambetta*, act of tripping up. In the example given, to trip up a pawn is to knock it over; in the basic war metaphor of chess, to kill the pawn (foot soldier). Ult. < IE *kamp-*, to bend → Gk. *kampē*, bent. Then with k/g and p/b → Late L. *gamba*, leg ("thing that bends"), and also, hook ("bent thing").]

gang [The Eng. form is already recognizable in IE *ghengh-*, to go afoot. Via Gmnc. to OE *gangan*, to go, to walk. The root sense remains firmly pedestrian. It is simply not idiom, for example, to say "a gang of horsemen."] 1. A wandering and prowling group. [And since early England was infested by wandering groups of dispossessed persons, mendicants, and rogues who prowled the countryside, up to no good, the word early acquired a pejorative sense. Hence:] 2. A more or less organized group of criminals.

gangster. 3. A group of chums from a given neighborhood who meet regularly at a fixed place, as on a street corner. *that old gang of mine.* Originally a propinquity group banded in friendship. Later an organized group of city youths that often engage in lethal fights with other gangs to "protect the turf." *youth gangs.* 4. A crew of workers who move about from one work assignment to another. *work gang.*

chain gang State or county prisoners, esp. in the southern states, sent out by day to work on public projects, esp. along the roads. [So called because they were earlier chained together or to a heavy iron ball to prevent escape. Now more commonly *road gang.*]

gang bang A gang orgy in which all the boys or men go at the girl(s) in quick succession and in various combinations, as in a multiple rape, though sometimes with the consent and even solicitation of the girl(s).

gang up on To attack as a group.

gangway / gangplank A footbridge between ship and shore. *gangway!* Make way! Clear the way! [These forms are direct survivals of OE *gangan,* to walk.]

garb   1. Clothing. 2. *Archaic.* Regalia. *Masonic garb.* [AHD says: "Clothing, especially the distinctive attire of one's occupation or station." Perhaps. But is it in Am. idiom to say "garbageman's garb"? The base of the word, < obscure Gmnc. sources, is It. *garbo,* style, grace, elegant appearance and bearing. In late XVIII, Denham, writing in praise of Cowley's poetry, fixed precisely the distinction between garb and clothing:

> To him no author was unknown,
> Yet what he wrote was all his own.
> Horace's wit and Virgil's state,
> He did not steal but emulate!
> And when he would like them appear,
> Their garb but not their cloaths, did wear.

Denham means that Cowley did not snatch rags from the masters, but cut his own cloth to their high style.]

garble   To mix things in a disorderly way. To jumble. To scramble. *George McGovern's political speech-making sounded like a garbled version of chopsticks, but less lively.* [The word has undergone a radical sense shift from "to sift (and select)" to "to make a mess of." In XVII with the now obs. sense "to select in biased way." Earlier: "to sift, to select." In legal Latin circa XV *garbelagium,* the act of sorting goods, esp. groceries, in preparation for selling them. But the more immediate source is It. *garbellare* to sift < *garbello,* a sieve; and ult. < Arabic *ghirbāl,* sieve. It. *garbuglio,* however, similar in form to *garbello,* meant "a confusion, a disorder, a hubbub," and from it XVI English derived *garboil* with the same senses. *Garboil* is now obs., but it seems to have lasted long enough to reverse, or nearly to reverse, the meaning of *to garble.*]

HISTORIC. In medieval England there was once a legal officer called a *spice garbler* who functioned as what we might call a pure food and drug inspector. He had the right to enter any shop at any time and to examine and to sift any spices, drugs, or other small goods, and, by garbling them, to make them clean. I do not know surely, but must suppose, that if the goods could not be made clean by sifting, the *spice garbler* had the power to condemn it.

gargoyle 1. In the convention of medieval cathedral-building, one of a series of grotesque stone carvings, usu. of the upper torso and head, of a humanoid or bestial form, in effect representing a fiend, and for practical purposes placed in rows along cathedral heights to serve as rainspouts. Often comical in their distortion, they made the religious point that the fiends, too, were subject to God's plan. 2. Any grotesque person. [Root sense: "gorge." IE *gwere-,* to swallow. Suffixed -*g*- in L. *gurguliō,* windpipe, throat, gorge (GURGLE). The sense shift was from "to swallow" to "thing with which one swallows." In gargoyle (OF *gargouille*) the sense is reversed to "thing that spews from its gorge."]

HISTORIC. In pious legendry, Romans, bishop of Rouen in VII, is said to have slain a dragon that lived in the Seine and preyed upon his people. (The legend illustrates to what extent clerical duties have become limited of late.) The name of the dragon was *Gargouille,* which must have been understood as the Maw, hence the Devourer.

garote/garotte (Accent second syllable.) *v.* To snap the neck with a two-handled wire or thin strong cord. (Not to be confused with strangulation, which takes time. Death by garoting is caused by a broken neck and is almost instantaneous. A victim dropped through the trap door of a gallows dies in the same way, not of strangulation but of a snapped neck. —*n.* The device used in garoting. [OF *guaroc,* with the early sense "club" and later: "stick used in tightening a tourniquet."]

HISTORIC. In medieval Spain, *garotta* labeled an iron collar equipped with set screws for tightening after this friendly harness was placed around the victim's neck for torture or execution. The later sense of the related OF *guaroc* suggests that the earlier method was to strangle a victim by tightening a tourniquet around his neck, a slow process, though it might end with a snap. Man has been characteristically ingenious in his dungeons. *Garote,* as a noun, is now specific to the neck, but medieval torturers and executioners applied the *guaroc* to various parts of the body, often as a headband. A related device was the *Spanish boot,* a metal device akin to the *garotta* but applied to the foot as a form of torture for extracting confessions. By the time the boot had been applied to both feet, the victim would have confessed to anything, and would have been left without a legal leg to stand on. I once dreamed that I was in a Spanish dungeon and had just confessed that Isaac Asimov was my mother.

garret The space just under the roof of a multistory house. Am. favors *attic,* but *garret* survives when this unheated, commonly unfinished space with at least one slanting wall is used as the wretched lodging of a student or impoverished artist (though a number of artists on today's rising market have gone from garrets to penthouses). [The immediate source is OF *garite,* watchtower. Ult. < OE *wer-,* to protect, to defend (WARD, WARDEN). Via Gmnc. → OE *warian,* to guard, to defend (WARY). In It., derivatives commonly begin with a *gw* sound, as in *guerra,* war, *guardia,* guard; in Fr. with a hard *g* sound *guerre, gare;* in Eng., either with hard *g* or *w, guardian, garret, warranty, warden.* The sense shift of *garret* has been from "high watchpost" to "shabby place under the roof."]

gat *Am. Late XIX.* A pistol. At first a revolver. Later also an automatic. [By back formation < *Gatling gun,* the first effective machine gun, invented by Richard J. Gatling (1818–1903) and developed for U.S. Army use shortly after the Civil War. The Gatling gun had a cluster of barrels that fired in turn as they were hand-cranked around an axis. Until the slightly earlier development of the repeating rifle, only the early six-shooter was capable of a limited rapid fire. Hence *gat* as the "little rapid-fire thing" as opposed to Gatling gun, the big one. As a note from our British cousins, Edwin Radford, *Unusual Words,* explains *gat* as "doubtless due to the American predilection for words which exaggerate size." Or Brit. *geyser* (pron. *geezer*) for a gas-operated hot-water heater?]

gate [OE *geat* is assumed to be of obscure Gmnc. origin. ME *g(e)ate, gat.* The earliest sense was "opening in a fence," then gradually with additional ref. to "device that seals and unseals the opening."] 1. An opening in a fence. 2. Movable device for closing or unclosing such an opening. 3. One of the various entrances to a section of seats in a sports stadium. 4. The number of people who pay for admission to (primarily) a sporting event. 5. The amount of money so collected. *a million-dollar gate.* 6. *Horse racing.* A wheeled device with a number of stalls equipped with forward gates that spring open simultaneously to ensure all horses an equal start. When all horses are *in the gate* the race can begin.

gateway 1. A more or less imposing opening to / exit from a palace, piazza, city. Commonly fitted with a portal or movable metal grille, but the primary ref. is to monumental stonework at either side, and usu. across the top. 2. A common label for a city conceived as the essential passage to a region that lies beyond it. In the common ballyhoo of civic boosters *the gateway city.*

gate-toothed / gape-toothed / gap-toothed Having spaces between one's teeth, especially between the front teeth. [These forms are all corruptions of ME *gat-toothed,* now obs. Chaucer describes the Wife of Bath as gat-toothed. A folk belief, of which Chaucer was certainly aware, holds that such teeth are a sign of a lecherous inclination.]

swinging like a (rusty) gate Baseball. In the hubba-hubba of "talking it up," a fixed phrase for taunting a batter who has taken a powerful roundabout swing, and missed.

give/get the gate To dismiss/be dismissed summarily. Includes to fire/be fired from a job. But most commonly to jilt/be jilted by a lover, steady sex companion, fiancé.

gate crasher Also *crasher* One who attends a social affair without an invitation, or who slips into a public performance or other event without paying for admission. [Am. Early XX. P. *Slang* notes its Anglicization (with curious but uncertain precision, "in late 1926"). What, no day, date, and hour?]

The many other idioms based on *gate* are more or less self-evident and lacking in interest.

gay *adj.* 1. *Traditionally.* Revelsome. In a lighthearted mood. Festive. [< Fr. *gai,* via Frankish < Gmnc. stem **ga-hi-,* impulsive, impetuous, unrestrained.] 2. *But now.* Homosexual. Lesbian. (Lesbian activists spurn the title homosexual, but only out of ignorance of the language, taking *homo* to be < L. man, when it is in fact < Gk. *homos,* the same—at root: "erotically attracted to the same sex"—the antonym being not *femmesexual* but *heterosexual* < Gk. *heteros,* other.) [Bruce Rodgers, *The Queen's Vernacular, A Gay Lexicon,* offers: "fr. 16th century Fr. *gaie,* homosexual man." But this is an inadequate gloss, for the traditional senses remained active.] P. *Slang* notes Brit. early XIX *gay,* sexy; c. 1830, *gay bit,* a harlot; c. 1900, *gay house,* a brothel; and in the same period *gay in the arse,* said of a woman eager for sex (which is from earlier Fr. *avoir la cuisse gaie,* gay in the thigh).

The slang implication "sexy," semantically flavored by "merry/ the merry life," came into use post WWII, when homosexual activists for equal social rights came out of the closet and propagandized for Gay Liberation. In ad-agency terms *gay* is certainly a more palatable term than fag, homo, queen, queer, pervert, etc. Homosexual activists seized on it because they needed it as the most acceptable term for "social merchandising." I need it too, and can no longer use it as I would wish to, but their need is prob. greater; let them have it and may we all be merry, if not gay.

Toward a dating: I once owned, but lent and lost, an anthology of lighthearted short prose by such authors as Dorothy Parker, Robert Benchley, Ring Lardner, and Damon Runyon. I have forgotten the title, but I recall that it was published in 1940, and that it was subtitled "A Gay Anthology." That subtitle may be very nearly the last time "gay" was used in its traditional and innocent sense, "merry."

gazinta   In elementary school forms of yesteryear, the essential word for reciting the tables of division: *2 gazinta 4 twice, 2 gazinta 6 three times,* etc. See *ampersand.* From time to time, some newspaper columnist reports that children in rote recitation render the oath of allegiance as "I pledge a region to the United States of America and to the Republic for Richard Stans, one nation* on the windersill with libitty and just this for all." I will add, from *Hamlet:* "So I have heard and do, in part, believe." Children will slur the sound of words they do not understand. So colonial children slurred *son of a sekonk* (son of a skunk) to *son of a sea cook* (see *sea cook,* Vol. I). The newspaper version quoted above, however, is too archly sustained; one gazinta perhaps, maybe two, but I doubt four.]

HISTORIC. *Too many will have forgotten, and most of the young will never have known, that during the Eisenhower administration there were inserted at this point two words in violation of the principle of the separation of church and state, God being argued to be beyond sectarianism (and perhaps not related to any church?). The fact remains that citizens who do not accept the asserted mythology are unreasonably excluded from making a full declaration of loyalty. I, for one, will not recite the asterisk words. I propose that they be replaced by "in the universe"; a self-evident placement. Those who believe the universe to be Godly will be served, and so will those who believe it to be physical (by God!).

genuflect   In passing before an altar or other sacred place or object, to touch one knee to the floor or ground, rising again in a single motion (if one's knees permit). *genuflection* In Brit. *genuflexion* A passing reverence as distinct from kneeling, which is the act of going down on both knees and remaining so for a discrete period of time. *Verbal ext.* To humble oneself. *In genuflecting to the almighty dollar, Mazie was forever on her knees to rich clients.* [At root: "one knee bend." < L. *genu,* knee; *flectere,* to bend (FLEX). The form *genuflectere* does not occur in classical L. but only in church L. and not until the fifth century A.D.]

Georgia cracker   A native of Georgia. [The idiom converges from several sources. 1. *Wisecracker.* Variant of *wiseacre* < early Ger. *wiss segger,* OHG *wizzago,* soothsayer. The sense shift in English has been from "one who speaks sooth" to "one who speaks a lot, and usu. too much." 2. *Corncracker.* One who shells corn and cracks (pounds) it to make corn meal, a basic southern country chore; hence, by association, a rustic. (See *yokel.*) 3. *Crackerbarrel.* Rustic. One who sits around the general-store cracker barrel, munching, bragging, and making wisecracks. The name was originally (dating?) applied to Georgians pejoratively, connoting a shrewd but ignorant would-be wise country bumpkin, but then adopted by Georgians as a proud label as if, ignorance deleted, "wise, shrewd, not to be deceived." Kansans have similarly adopted the once bloodily opprobious *Jayhawk(er)* as a proudly asserted nickname.]

Gesundheit   [Ger. "good health (to you)."] The Ger. term has passed intact into Eng. as the remark one makes when a person sneezes. [In It., *salute,* may you be hale and whole. In Eng. one also says,

"God bless (and preserve) you." In L. *absit omen*, may that not be taken as a bad sign.]

HISTORIC. I have read that in some of the plagues that swept Europe, sneezing was an early symptom of infection. In that context, any of these remarks would have had the intermediate sense: "I hope you haven't caught it."

At ultimate root, however, all such remarks relate to primitive man's belief in daemonism, including the belief that the soul can be expelled from the body. Sneezing, as a powerful ejection of breath, might blow the soul out, whence any such formula would have the root sense: "May no part of your daemon essence have escaped." It remains a sentiment worth saying a thank you for.

gibberish   Incomprehensible prattle. [In XVI only as a verb, *to gibber*. Shakespeare, *Julius Caesar* (1604): "The graves stood tenantless and the sheeted dead / Did squeak and gibber in the Roman streets." And the form is readily argued as a simple expressive rendering the sound of incomprehensible and outlandish chatter as *jibby-jabber*. But one must at least mention Jabir ibn Hayan, eighth-century Arabic alchemist, occultist, metaphysician, and philosopher. Some of his many works were translated into Latin in XII and XIII and were widely known to European alchemists, his name being rendered as Geber and also Gabar. In Old It. *gabare* meant, among other things, "to prattle, to hoax." And though the noun form *gibberish* did not emerge until XVIII, the OED offers as a variant spelling *geberish*. If *gibber* is taken to be an expressive, there is reason to suppose it was at least influenced by *Jabir/Geber*, if not directly derived therefrom.]

Gipper   Nickname of George Gipp, 1895–1930, one of Knute Rockne's football players at Notre Dame until he contracted a disease that left him only a short time to live. *(let's win this) one for the Gipper* Let's go out and win this football game for the (dying) Gipper. [Probably the most disgusting slob sentiment in American history. When it became known that the Gipper could not play, and that he was terminally ill, Rockne psyched up the damp souls of his jocks by urging them in trembling pseudo-sincerity (worse yet, he was probably sincere within the narrow limits of his own psyche) "to win this game for the Gipper." Worse yet, his jocks accepted the plea as a true soul's call to dedicated mayhem. And abysmally worse yet, the dying Gipper probably felt that he was involved in a mortal sentiment and that his death could serve no better purpose than to inspire his fellow morons to another football victory.]

gnomon [Gk. *gignōskein,* to know. Gk. & L. *gnomon,* one who knows. But since Late L. the term has been specific to:] The spindle of a sundial, the vertical member that casts the time-telling shadow. Unmoved, its moving shadow tells (knows).

HISTORIC. The gnomon is a natural poetic symbol, though so fixed in its possibilities that it has expired of overuse. The Chinese character meaning "serenity" is an ideogram of a gnomon. The ideogram may be described as an inverted capital *T.* In mathematics (a usage I am unable to explain) a gnomon is what is left of a parallelogram after a similar, smaller parallelogram has been taken from one corner. (Perhaps because the remaining figure "knows" what it was?)

gofer *Originally theatrical, but long since generalized.* The most junior assistant on any crew. He is available for all incidental chores. [As to "go fer" coffee, tools, props, scripts, newspapers, or at need, the battered replica of the Holy Grail. Cf. *cookie pusher.*]

good grief *Exclam.* Originally of regret, but since generalized for all purposes. [Dating uncertain, but prob. in use by at least late XVIII Am. A minced oath. Though rarely recognized as such, it is, at root: "God's grief!" a ref. to Christ on the cross. As such, a powerful oath, as if "By God's grief." But rendered innocuous in the mincing.]

goo-goo[1] Baby talk. Hence, amorous prattle. *goo-goo eyes* 1. Moon eyes full of loving invitation. 2. Large, innocent, bug eyes. [Prob. in late XIX use, popularized by the c. 1920 song "Barney Google" ("with the goo-goo-googly eyes").]

HISTORIC. The impresario Billy Rose, once secretary to Bernard Baruch, and the winner of various shorthand speed contests, decided to write a popular song. Systematically, he analyzed the most successful popular songs of the preceding years, and came to the conclusion that the common characteristic was a lot of repeated *oo* sounds. He proceeded to write "Barney Google" and it was an instant hit with even a sort of funky survival.

goo-goo[2] *Boston regionalism.* A do-gooder, esp. one working for political reform. [Prob. influ. by *goo-goo*[1] but adapted from *Good Go vernment Association.*]

goose hangs high, the   All's well. Earlier (XVIII) signified "clear weather." [Because geese, esp. when migrating, fly high when the weather is clear. There is no evidence that *hangs* is a corruption of *honks,* and in any case the sense and image would remain the same. C. 1800 there was a country sport in which horsemen rode past a gander tied to a tree, its neck greased. If the horseman could grab the neck on the run and pluck the goose from its bindings, the prize was his. Some have sought to derive the idiom from this game, and perhaps so, but though the evidence is uncertain, the idiom prob. preceded the game (which at best was a passing fashion). Prob. a simple farmer's observation that migrating geese were flying high, thereby signifying good weather.]

gorgeous   *adj.* 1. Dazzlingly attractive and desirable. 2. *Colloq.* Stunningly beautiful. And with noun force in the common colloq. *Hello, gorgeous,* which is, of course, a short form of *gorgeous one.* [The origin, though much speculated at, is unknown. AHD timidly suggests a derivation from *Gorgias,* c. 483–376 B.C., Greek sophist and rhetorician. But ? The earliest forms are late ME *gorgeouse* and XV *gorgyas, gorges, gorgayse,* all traceable to OF *gorgias,* which occurs only with ref. to elegant raiment, panoply, and court appointments. Most conclude that the OF form is of unknown origin, but let me borrow a turn from Partridge and "trepidate" that there are possible cognates in Old Sp. *gorga,* what hawks gorge on (GORGE), Old It. *gorga,* throat (GARGOYLE), and L. *gurges,* whirlpool (GURGLE, REGURGITATE); and that if these are in fact cognates, the root sense might be (?): "filling one with a passion to devour." Cf. the common Am. colloq. *you look good enough to eat* for *you are gorgeous.* And note that the *i* of OF *gorgias* is there only to soften the sound of the preceding *g.* But these, too, are mere speculations to be trepidated without assertion.]

gorilla   1. *Gorilla gorilla,* the largest and most powerful of the apes, a native of equatorial Africa. 2. *Obvious ext. (a)* A powerful, hairy man. *(b)* A thug. A strong-arm man. [The custom of most dicts. is to refer the term to Gk. *gorillai,* an African tribe of hairy men. Origin unknown.

But something is known. In V or VI B.C. a Carthaginian navigator named Hanno sailed beyond the Pillars of Hercules and explored the west coast of Africa. He wrote a record in Punic of his voyage, in which he mentioned a hairy tribe of men called (in whatever the form might have been in Punic) *gorillas.* There is no way of identifying the tribe he mentioned, but his log was translated into Gk., establishing the name as *gorillai,* as above. The word remained in Gk. in legendary obscurity until, in 1847, it was applied to the giant ape, which had recently been observed and described by explorers. More than 2,000 years passed between Hanno's obscure record and the application of his word to the great ape. But gorillas are inland equatorial jungle creatures, and though various explorers and traders had long been familiar with the west African coast, it was not till mid XIX that Europeans began to explore the interior. I have been unable to identify the taxonomer who exhumed the Greek name of that mysterious tribe of hairy men and applied it to the ape.]

gosh   *Exclam.* 1. Of surprise. *Gosh, is that pony for me!* 2. Of sadness or disappointment. *Gosh, I ripped my pants!* 3. Of protest. *Gosh, Ma, I don't want to go to bed yet.* [< *God.* A minced oath, perhaps one of the mildest of mincings. Am. early XIX, and though I cannot attest, prob. in use in XVIII.] **gosh oh gee** Minced form of *God oh Jesus.* And akin to **golly** Identical with *gosh,* and a similarly minced form of *Goddy/Lordy.* Variantly **gosh a-mighty** and **my gosh.** [*American Dialect Dictionary* cites *gosh* for *very* in 1895 usage in Ky., Tenn., and N.C. "We've been having a gosh wet spell." And also *gosh-dinger* for *humdinger,* western Ind., 1912.]

go west, young man   Popular XIX slogan urging ambitious young men to seek their future in the undeveloped West. (So popular was the slogan that it still survives as a general encouragement to strike out along new lines.) [Coined by John Babsone Lane Soule in an article in the Terre Haute, Ind., *Express,* 1851.]
   HISTORIC. Soon after its first appearance, Horace Greeley (1811–1872) adapted the slogan in an editorial in his New York *Tribune:* "Go west, young man, and grow up with the country." Picked up from the *Tribune,* the slogan was endlessly repeated, and attributed to Greeley, who never claimed it as his own, his editorial acknowledging Soule as his source.

grapefruit   The large citrus fruit, yellow-skinned when ripe, and the tree on which it grows, *Citrus paradisi.* [The name is from a persisting error. Some, including NWD, explain it by the "fact" that the fruit grows in grapelike clusters—one of those errors clerk-lexicographers borrow from earlier clerks. I have owned grapefruit trees and must insist that not even the crudest sense of metaphor could conceive the fruit to grow in grapelike clusters.

In 1814 the botanist John Lunan, in his *Hortus Jamaicensis* (The Garden of Jamaica), mentioned a variety of this fruit that tasted like grapes. Perhaps. Or perhaps Luhan's taste buds were addled. In any case, *grapefruit* came off his tongue and into ours.]

HISTORIC. The grapefruit varieties common in the U.S. have been developed from the *C. paradisi* of Jamaica, from stocks of *C. grandi*, which is indigenous to Malaya and Polynesia. Early European explorers called the fruit of *C. grandi* "pummelo," which would seem to be some combination of Fr. *pomme* and L. *malus*, both meaning simultaneously "fruit" and "apple."

An intermediate name, still surviving in Jamaican English, is *shaddock*, after an unidentified Captain Shaddock, who is said to have introduced the tree to Jamaica. If so, what he brought from his Pacific voyaging must have been *C. grandi*, which in the new environment became the distinct species *C. paradisi*, later hybridized into the various species of common and pink grapefruit now grown in the U.S.

grapevine   The often astonishingly accurate rumor circuit of a large, intricate, and more or less self-contained organization. [First in use in Civil War, the original term being *grapevine telegraph*, i.e., not the straight strung wire of the telegraph but the intricate web of the army's nervous system. Later in commonest use in prison slang, but also generally disseminated. *The Wall Street grapevine is buzzing with talk of mergers.*]

Greek calends   Every 30th of February. **until the Greek calends** Never. [L. *ad calendas Graecas*, a British university joke. The Romans reckoned time by calends. (See *calendar.*) The Greeks had no calends except in months beginning with a double moon, and then only in the reign of Pope Joan, which had not yet begun because the Greeks were never able to calculate how many years B.C. they were taking place in.]

greet   [At root: "to address upon meeting." IE *gherd-*, to call out. With metathesis and d/t in Gmnc. → OE *grētan*, to speak to, to call out to upon meeting. ME *greten.*

The same stem functions in ON *grāta*, to bemoan ("to cry out in grief"), whence Eng. *regret*, in which *re-* serves as a frequentative signifying "to mourn over and over again," but not necessarily aloud, the root sense being submerged in Eng. The primary sense of *to greet* in Eng. is the root sense, above, but by association:] 1. To welcome. But also: 2. To receive in a hostile way. *Napoleon greeted the advancing Austrians with salvos of heavy artillery.*

greetings and salutations A fixed form of address, written or oral. [Lit. "a calling out to you with wishes for your good health."]

grippe Same as *influenza* (variantly *flu*), which see. [Fr. *grippe*, a seizure; *gripper*, to seize. Via Frankish < Gmnc. *gripan*, to seize. Ult. < IE *greib-*, to seize (GRIP). Akin to IE *grebh-*, to seize, to reach for (GRAB, GROPE). Because during the virulent XVIII epidemic, French physicians, lacking knowledge of viruses, were groping for an explanation of what was grabbing their patients. As Italian physicians of the time, similarly at a loss, ascribed the disease to the *influenza*, influence (of the stars), at root: an "inflowing" of astrological forces. So the Fr. "seizure."]

grizzly bear *Ursus horribilis*, lit. "horrifying bear." The grizzly is more or less in a tie with its bleached cousin, the polar bear, as the largest and most ferocious predator of the North American continent. [IE *gher-*, to rub, to grate, to chafe; and by ext. "to chafe the mind" to the idea "horror." Zero-grade form *ghr'*, prob. suffixed -*s*- in Gmnc. → OE *grislic* ("grisly-like"), horrible, horrifying. Perh. influ. by *grizzled*, having gray hairs among darker ones, but hair style is not likely to be the thing one notes first on meeting a grizzly at its own social level.]

Gulf Stream A current of warm water arcing northerly and easterly from the Gulf of Mexico. [Name coined by Benjamin Franklin in 1769.]

HISTORIC. Among his many dazzling accomplishments, Franklin prepared and published, in 1769, the first chart of a major ocean current, which he named the Gulf Stream. He began with the knowledge that colonial ships, on average, crossed the Atlantic in two weeks less than British ships. Colonial skippers had learned to sail east with the current, and to avoid it when sailing west. Charting their courses, and gathering data on water color and temperature, Franklin charted a substantially accurate flow of his "Gulf Stream." The name now strikes us as inevitable, as if from nature itself. I take that fact, too, as an evidence of Franklin's genius. A more pretentious man might, in the current academic manner, have called it "the northeasterly arc of the pelagic confluence."

gung-ho   *adj.* Impetuous. Full of élan and esprit de corps. Hence, boy-boyish. Hence, eagerly inane. [Chinese, "work together." In WWII adopted by Lt. Col. Evans F. Carlson, USMC, as the hubba-hubba slogan and battle cry of Carlson's Raiders, on the well-tested principle that boys will die more or less enthusiastically when they are given something to shout. The shout need not make sense, but only assert a conditioned commonality.]

gut   [In extraordinary fact < IE *gheu(s)*, to gush out, to pour. Via Gmnc., all but unaltered in form or sense → ON *gjusa*, to gush (GUSH). Suffixed *-t-* in Gmnc. → OE *geotan*, to pour; *guttas* (the form is plu.), an outpouring. Since the guts are the source of excretion, the root association seems to be with diarrhea! Yet this root suggestion of ancestral soupiness has receded from the word.] *n.* An intestine. —*v.* 1. To eviscerate. 2. To demolish the insides of a structure, leaving the shell, usu. by fire, but also by a demolition team prior to a thorough interior remodeling.
    bust a gut To make an all-out effort. [To strain so hard as to rupture an intestine. In effect, to kill oneself trying.] ***catgut*** Dried sheep intestines used as the strings of a musical instrument. [*Cat* is fanciful; prob. because of the screechy sounds produced on the strings by a beginner.] ***gut feeling*** A deep intuition. What vague persons offer in place of reason. ***gut issue(s)*** The essential core. The heart of the matter.
    gut bucket *Black English.* 1. A bucket placed under the tap in a barrel house to catch any drippings from the tap. [This is the one surviving usage in which something like the idea "diarrhea" may be said to survive.] 2. *In jazz.* A style characterized by a deep syncopated bass. [Way down deep.]
    guts 1. Entrails. 2. *By association.* The belly. 3. Courage. [Deep inner quality.] ***bag /sack of guts*** A worthless person, esp. a fat one, conceived as no more than a skinful of entrails. ***hate his/her guts*** To hate him/her utterly.
    gutless wonder In WWII. A G.I. term of scorn for an officer who was gung-ho on the parade ground but who tended to stay back in combat while he sent his men forward. [*Wonder* < *ninety-day wonder*, because officer candidate school was a ninety-day training course.]

gymnasium   *In Am.* A usu. large building with facilities for physical training and indoor sports. *In Germany and various other European countries.* (Always with a hard *g.*) What Am. calls a high school, but at a more insistent level of literacy. [< Greek *gumna-sion*, place for training naked < *gumnos*, naked. Because Greek boys trained naked in open-air *gumnasia;* at sports, horsemanship, and the arts of war, whence Am. *gymnasium;* and in reading, writing, rhetoric, philosophy, mathematics, etc., whence the European academic *gymnasium*.

At root: "place of nakedness." Ult. < IE *nogu-*, naked, which comes to Eng. variously through three separate evolutions. 1. Via Gmnc. with g/k and suffixed -*d*-, the prob. form being *naku-'d* → OE *nacod*, naked. 2. Via Italic with g/h and suffixed -*d*-, the prob. form being *nahu-'d* → L. *nudus*, naked (NUDE).

Naked and *nude* have acquired distinct and powerfully operative overtones in English, which I may perhaps illustrate by a few lines I once wrote as an elegy for a strip-teaser:

> She stripped herself of all except pretense.
> By nature, she and nature lived to feud
> Over two words. Her life explains their sense:
> Born naked into the world, she left it nude.

3. Via Hellenic with the aphetic variant *(no)gu-* → *gu-* and suffixed -*mn-* → Gk. *gumnos*, naked; *gumnasion*, place of nakedness.]

NOTE. Readers of T. S. Eliot will recall his "gymnosophic banyan tree." *Gymnosophists* were an ancient sect that meditated or taught while sitting naked—here, under a banyan tree. The form is from Gk. *gumnos*, as above; *sophos*, wise. *Sophist* has since acquired the sense: "one who deals in elaborated false wisdom." Eliot's phrase permits that late sense, but is primarily a reference to wise men of the East who squat naked to meditate and to counsel believers, who bring an offering and sit at their (crossed) feet.

Gypsy, Gipsy [C. 1500. < *E(gypci)an*, earlier form of *Egyptian*, because Gypsies first reached Europe in XIV, Britain in late XV, and were believed to be nomadic Egyptians.] 1. A nomadic, subethnic (splinter) group with its own language (Romany), customs, religion, and a self-issued license to swindle and rob all outsiders, though rigid in observing the tribal moral code. (See *thug*, Vol. I, for a note on the *thugees*, a group similarly withdrawn from general society, but given to violent robbery and ritual murder, whereas Gypsies, as a rule, swindle and pilfer nonviolently.) Leaving India, Gypsies wandered the Middle East and North Africa for uncounted centuries, but are now all but unknown except in Europe and U.S. (where the pickings are good, and the society large enough to be somewhat tolerant). Many large U.S. cities have more or less fixed Gypsy communities, though some Gypsies still wander in motor caravans. 2. *Ext.* Any garish, gadabout, untrustworthy person. (Implies rejection of established values, but not necessarily pilferage and flimflam.) —*v.* **gyp** To cheat, to swindle, to short-change. (Implies petty pilferage.)

gypsy moth An Old World moth that has infested most of the U.S., its caterpillars ravaging foliage. [It came by the same route the Gypsies took and is an even worse pest.]

gypsy cab [Originally NYC but now also in other large cities.] A taxi that is supposed to operate only in response to phone calls or on radio dispatch, but that ignores the law and cruises the streets for fares.

HISTORIC. NYC originally issued, at a more or less reasonable fee, a fixed number of medallions as identification of a cab licensed to cruise for fares. In subsequent cab-owner to cab-owner sales, these medallions have been bid up to recent highs of over $30,000. For the pleasure of overworking himself in city traffic, an independent cabby must invest $40,000–$50,000 in his cab, medallion, garaging, insurance, and other start-up charges. The gypsies are illegal cruisers, but they are more than $30,000 cheaper than the law, and continue to compete with medallion cabs, the Hack Bureau regularly issuing statements that it is powerless to stop them.

H

hack   A taxi. (In Am. a *cabby* drives a *hack*. *Hacky* does not occur for a cabdriver, but a *hackney license* is commonly required.) [< Brit. *hackney coach,* a large, public, horse-drawn carriage. *Hackney* originally signified the breed of horse that commonly drew such coaches; after *Hackney* (earlier *Hakenei*), an administrative district near London, because *Hackney horses* were bred there. And also:] **hackneyed** Trite. Dully repetitive. Overused. [Like the all but unvarying daily (and nightly) routine of a *hackney coach* and of its horse.]

haddock   A cod-like North Atlantic food fish. [ME *haddok* < OF **adot, *hadot*. But there is no evidence that the OF labeled the same fish we call haddock. Pious legend has it that St. Peter caught a haddock in the Sea of Galilee (which is really a freshwater lake, the haddock being a saltwater fish). It is purported to have had a coin in its mouth. The two characteristic spots on either side near the fish's gills are said to be the impressions of Peter's thumb and forefinger when he picked up the fish. If that was Peter's normal way of handling fish, he did well to give up the trade of fisherman. He was already halfway to the miraculous in catching a haddock in fresh water. And what sort of coin can one expect to find in the mouth of a fish that wasn't there, and that had probably already slipped through one's fingers and back into the water?]

hail-Mary pass   *Football.* A long pass attempted against all odds but prayer, usu. in the desperation of time running out, leaving no chance to score if the go-for-broke attempt fails. [*Hail-Mary* as a generic for prayer. Akin to the WWII Air Force formula: *coming in on a wing and a prayer.* (Question: If things get worse and the pilot has to let go either the wing or the prayer, which does he choose?)]

124

halt¹ *v. To stop. —n.* A stop. [A root reversal < IE *kel-*, to impel, to drive or to move forward swiftly (CELERITY, ACCELERATE). But with k/h and suffixed *-dt-* in Gmnc. → OE *healden,* to hold (HOLD), esp. with ref. to husbandry (HOUSEHOLD) and the driving of flocks and herds. I can only speculate that since driving livestock leads to its penning, the root sense "to drive" was slowly replaced by its opposite, "to bring to a stopping place in the croft, pen, or fold": from "to drive" to "condition driven to."

In Am. *halt* is commonly replaced by *stop,* except as formalized in the military command, but:] ***call a halt (to)*** and ***bring to a halt*** 1. To stop temporarily. *The noon whistle brought the machines to a halt.* 2. To stop permanently. To put an end to. *The air raids brought Japanese war production to a halt.*

halt² *adj.* Lame. —*n. The halt.* Those who limp or who walk with crutches. [IE *kol-*, to strike, is a variant of IE *kel-* in preceding entry, but with the sense "to drive forward by striking blows." So with same k/h and suffix in Gmnc., but with a vowel shift → OE *hild,* war ("the act of driving the enemy by striking blows"). Variantly, OE *holt,* a stand of trees ("things that can be hacked down"). And so, as a hacked branch hangs askew, OE *lemphealt,* limping, having a bent or broken leg.]

handwriting on the wall The idiom is invariably understood as meaning a warning or omen of evil to come. (Cf. *lion's share,* which is everywhere understood as "the greater part," though the original Aesopean sense was "all of it.") *Joe Kennedy saw the handwriting on the wall and sold out before the crash of 1929.* But though there was some small delay in deciphering the handwriting on the wall, the message was not a warning, but a writ of summary execution, saying in effect, "You're dead."

HISTORIC. Daniel, Chap. 5, tells how Belshazzar, in drunken revel, called for the sacred vessels that had been taken from the temple in Jerusalem by his father, Nebuchadnezzar, "that the king and his princes, his wives, and his concubines, might drink therein."

For this sacrilege, the God of Israel sent a detached hand to write on the wall "MENE, MENE, TEKEL, UPHARSIN," which, after all the other wise men of the kingdom were unable to decode it, Daniel explained as: "God hath numbered thy kingdom and finished it. Thou art . . . found wanting. Thy kingdom is divided, and given to the Medes and Persians." I doubt that any four words in any language known to man could express all the meanings of Daniel's freely elaborated translation, but that night Belshazzar was slain and Darius the Mede (who must have been standing by in the wings) took over the kingdom. The point, among others, is that once the judgment has been delivered, the end is not to come, but at hand.

happy as a clam   Very happy. [Am. In colonial times *happy as a clam at high tide,* because the water then was too high for clamming. It is simple enough to suppose that the happiest one can make a clam is by leaving it alone.]

HISTORIC. As a random inquiry into the nature of idiom, I have asked hundreds of people what they supposed could make a clam happy. Very few, in fact almost none, knew of the earlier and lengthier form, yet all understood the clipped form accurately. I am not inclined to generalize about language. My only conclusion has been repeated several times herein: Language does what it does because it does it.

Sometimes idiom wanders far from its original source and sense, as in *mad as hops* (what can that mean?) < *hopping mad.* And see *cold shoulder,* which has kept the sense while shedding its original image.

At other times the later idiom seems to have lost all touch with its earlier form. So *Land of Nod,* the Biblical wilderness east of Eden into which Cain was driven for killing Abel, has become in nursery English baby's sleepy-bye land. Language does what it does because it does it.

happy hour   *Saloon merchandising.* A cocktail "hour," usu. 4–6 P.M. or 5–7 P.M., in which bars offer drinks at substantial discounts, often at half price, and often with other little inducements, such as hors d'oeuvre. At standard bar markups, 50¢ worth of whiskey comes out to $2.50–$3.50 a mixed drink. Half price still leaves a substantial margin of profit, and may attract customers. And there is always the hope that customers pre-lubricated at happy hour rates will stay on for more of the same when the happy hour ends and drinks are restored to full price.

hassock   1. *In most common Am. use.* A stuffed footstool or low seat. An ottoman. 2. A stuffed pad for kneeling on at a priedieu or in church. (The latter now commonly replaced by a hinged padded board running the length of a pew or row of seats, but still called a hassock. 3. *Root sense but rare.* A clump of matted vegetation. [OE *hassuc* (of unknown Gmnc. origin), ME *hassok,* a clump of matted vegetation including the interlaced roots.]

HISTORIC. Trench, *Dictionary of Obsolete English,* offers the most useful note: "Already in Phillip's New World of Words, 1706, the *hassock* was what it is now [mid XIX], 'a kind of straw cushion used to kneel upon in churches'; and some of us may remember to have seen in country churches *hassocks* of solid tufts of coarse black grass which had so grown and matted together that they served this purpose sufficiently well. But this is only the secondary and transformed use of the word. It was once the name by which this coarse grass growing in these rank tufts was itself called, and this name . . . in Norfolk it still bears."

hasty pudding   In early Massachusetts Bay Colony, corn meal mush, but later, with the beginnings of prosperity, with added goodies and molasses. Culinary terms are forever shifting as housewives improvise, but corn meal mush remains the base. [< Brit., in which the name labeled oatmeal porridge, often with various seasonings. A whimsically fanciful name for a staple of poverty's kitchen. Cf. *Scotch woodcock* for scrambled eggs on toast with anchovies or anchovy paste. (Fancy enough but not quite up to woodcock.) And *Welsh rabbit* (or *rarebit*) for melted cheese over toast.]

> And there we saw the men and boys
> As thick as hasty pudding.
> —*Yankee Doodle*

haul over the coals   To tongue-lash. To deliver a severe reprimand. [But at origin even more so. Hauling over the coals of a slow fire was a standard inquisitorial treatment of accused heretics, and capable of some subtle adjustment. A fast haul over relatively cool embers with the wretch face up could blister his hide (*to blister one's hide* is surviving idiom). A slow haul over hotter coals could remove the hide. A slow haul face down would normally put an end to the discussion. God is served in many ways.]

hay and grass: between hay and grass   Between youth and old age. [Am. XIX, perhaps in use by XVIII but attestation is lacking. Still survives regionally to describe one no longer in the green of youth but still able to function.]

NOTE. A reversed idiom. *Between grass and hay* would express the normal order of things. Once an idiom is established, however, native speakers ignore incongruity and reversed order. What is more absurd than a *time clock?* (What else is a clock for?) Why *head over heels in love?* Isn't the head properly above the heels?

What's sauce for the goose is sauce for the gander is of proverbial age in English. It seems to say that what is good enough for a woman is good enough for a man. But there was no such sentiment current in that male-dominated society, which would have thought "what is good enough for a man is more than good enough for a woman."

It is foreigners learning English who are puzzled by these curious reversals; native speakers, long habituated, tend to ignore them.

head   An addict. [One whose head is set on some addictive substance.] *juice head* Also *whiskey head.* An alcoholic. [Both terms occur in the lyrics of early XX jazz songs, suggesting an origin in late XIX Black English.] *hophead* A narcotics addict. [< XIX street slang *hop,* opium. And so *hopped up* originally, in an opium haze; later, high on any drug.] *pothead* One addicted to marijuana. [In Mexico, until recent anti-marijuana legislation, marijuana cigarettes were available by the pack, and those who chain-smoked them were known briefly in Am. slang as *vipers.*] *shithead* Now also means worthless person who has shit for brains, but at root, early XX, a heroin addict, *shit* being once common and still surviving slang for heroin.

hearse   Earlier a horse carriage, now commonly a motor van, for the ceremonial conveyance of the corpse in funeral rites. (In backwater towns it commonly doubles as an ambulance.) [But earlier signified a three-sided metal rack, sometimes on wheels, to be positioned around the bier to hold votive candles. One side was left open for close viewing and for kneeling in prayer. The form, if only fancifully, resembled the Roman harrow, L. *hirpex;* prob. < Osco-Umbrian **hirpus,* wolf, the common sense element being "teeth." Via L. variant *herce* → OF & ME *herse,* hearse.

Unattested: The sense shift from *candle rack on wheels* to *burial conveyance* suggests that at some stage in the evolution of funerary rites, the coffin rested on the metal candle rack, and could be so wheeled up the church aisle. Hence the sense: "corpse conveyer," shifting by association from the candle rack to the funerary wagon. In earlier times, of course (before churchyards became filled), no funeral wagon was needed from last rites to interment, and the candle rack could be wheeled or carried just outside the door and the body put down. (And see *rehearse.*)]

Hell¹ The Teutonic equivalent of Greek *Hades,* Roman *Dis* or *Infernus,* the dark underworld of the dead. [As Dis is named after the mythic king of the underworld, so in Nordic myth the name derives from Hel, daughter of Loki, god of discord and mischief. He is in many ways like Greek Pan (he who causes panic), and like English Puck or Robin (Hobgoblin) Goodfellow. Hel rules the underworld and to it go the souls of all who did not die in battle. The warrior dead go to Valhalla. Hel corresponds to Greek Proserpine, daughter of Ceres (Mother Nature) and part-time wife of Pluto, king of the underworld. It is easy to see that all these variants derive from some common legend now lost in the Dawn Age mists.

Ult. < IE *Kel-,* to conceal, place of concealment. With k/h in Gmnc. → Hel, as above, "goddess of the place of (ultimate) concealment" (HULL, HALL). The same IE root without consonant shift → L. *cella,* small room, hovel (CELL).]

HISTORIC. Most early mytho-religions assert an underground to which all or most souls are consigned for eternity. The myth is obviously an elaborated equivalent of the grave, and of the horror associated with being sealed into the ground. The physical details of the Christian hell are not specified, though the imagery of it largely derives from Dante, and by association with the Titans, brutish earth creatures, and with volcanoes conceived as the flues of enormous hellish fires, though the Greek and Roman underworld was commonly conceived as a cold dark place of mournful souls. The idea that those who die in battle ascend to a supreme heaven, escaping the dark cave of death, occurs in many forms, especially in Islamic and Teutonic belief. Again, these variants derive from some common ancestral myth series now lost in the mists of time.

hell² A many-purpose once taboo word. Used as an exclam.: *What the hell!* Also as an intensive: *Hell, I don't care.* Literally: *May you fry in hell.* And to indicate rough male approval: *a helluva fellow.*

The Gk. form *Hades* functions as a more or less acceptable minced form. Through XIX, those who felt required to write the word minced it by blanking out the spelling as *h——l,* and orally the same effect is achieved by spelling out rather than pronouncing the word. A word with so many connotations will not be reduced to any one definition, but some examples will illustrate. And see Vol. I for *hell or high water, hell-bent,* and *hell-on-wheels.*

what the hell! 1. Exclam. of surprise, anger, dismay. [In Am. sometimes minced as *What the Sam Hill!* for "What the damn hell!"] 2. Said with a shrug, expresses resignation. *What the hell, let's get it over with.* 3. As an intensive, expresses dismay, disapproval, or suspicion. *What the hell are you doing? Who the hell is that?* 4. Expresses rejection or indifference. *What the hell do I care?*

go to hell 1. To fall into deep sin or ruin. *He went to hell because of bad companions. The business went to hell when the neighborhood changed.* 2. As an imperative, expresses contemptuous dismissal or refusal. *go to hell in a handbasket* A fixed formula. I have heard it time and again but must confess I do not know what it means or how it came about. [Comments and suggestions eagerly solicited.]

get the hell out of here Intensive imperative. 1. *To a confederate.* Clear out! Danger! 2. *In contemptuous dismissal or rebuff.* Get out! Scram! (And stay out!)

raise hell 1. To make a scene. 2. To have a riotous good time. 3. To assail. *Naval fire raised hell on Guadalcanal. raise hell with* 1. To berate. 2. To use to create tumult. *The sniper raised hell with that rifle.* 3. To join with in a riotous good time, in berating, or in attacking. [At root, as in medieval black magic, the act of summoning a fiend from hell. Hence a powerful violation of good order. Faustus, literally, raised hell.] *full of hell* [At lit. root: possessed by a devil. But that evil implication has receded, leaving the more genial senses:] Lively. Mischievous. Ready to take part in any frolic.

Hell's Canyon A 7,900-foot canyon cut by the Snake River on the Idaho-Oregon border. [*Hell* because deep in the earth.] *Hell Gate* In NYC, a narrow channel in the East River, a tricky passage of often fast-flowing water. It was notoriously dangerous for sailing vessels. [*Hell* because it led many a man to his death, it being an easy basic assumption that no sailing man goes to heaven.] *Hell's Kitchen Am. XIX.* The west side of New York, north from 42nd St., indefinitely into the 60's. This area as an Irish immigrant slum. [Hot, steamy, stinking, infernal place. The kitchen would certainly be the hottest part of hell. Hot, by transference, teeming, and in context, evil.]

give 'im/'em hell 1. To chastise severely. 2. As a cry of encouragement, as in battle. Pour it on. Send them to hell after making a hell on earth for them.

hell around To roam about in search of riotous fun or violence. *catch hell* To be on the receiving end of *give 'im/'em hell.*

a helluva time Depending upon the context, an ordeal or a rousing good time. The same ambiguity of good or evil pertains in *helluva guy.* *a helluva lot Intensive.* A great deal. [Enough to fill the chasm of hell.]

hell diver 1. Originally the dab chick, either the European or the American grebe as an expert diver. 2. WWII. *Transfer sense.* A naval dive bomber.

heller One who raises hell. Either an evil person or, approvingly, a rough and ready guy.

hellish 1. Infernal. 2. *Colloq.* Damn(ed) good. *We had a hellish good time.*

hell hound/ hound of hell (Pejorative only.) 1. An evil person. 2. A fiend as the tracker of souls. [The original ref. is to Cerberus, the fierce and merciless three-headed hound that guarded the entrance to the underworld in Greek and Roman myth, permitting souls to enter but none to return to earth.]

hellkin An imp. A minor fiend. Variantly, a mischievous or evil child. [Harlequin, now a clown in a pantomime, or a masquerader in a coat and tights marked with diamonds, was in the Middle Ages a name for a devil and is cognate with hellkin, as in It. *arlecchino,* and esp. in OF *hellequin.*]

like a bat out of hell At balls-out speed. [A rhetorical flourish. Bats at dusk emerge from caves in a great rush. Had a bat thought to lodge in hell one day, it would be driven out the faster by the sulfurous fumes.]

hot as the hinges of hell Very hot. *not till hell freezes over* Never. [Both rhetorical flourishes based on the idea of hell as the base of a volcano.]

hen's teeth: scarce as hen's teeth   Hyperbolically scarce. In fact, nonexistent, in that a hen has no teeth. But in idiomatic usage implies great scarcity rather than nonexistence. [Am. Attested in the *Congressional Record,* Oct. 2, 1893; but so natural a metaphor in an agrarian society that the expression may well have been in use for a century or more before finding its way onto the floor of the Congress.]

hermit   A recluse. *hermitage* 1. The place where a hermit lives. 2. A remote monastery or abbey where monks who have retired from the world live their secluded and ritual lives. 3. *In loose usage.* A retreat, usu. in the country. A second house, or summer house, in which one can manage the illusion of solitude at dawn, though the place commonly warms up to clattering cocktail parties. I once received an invitation to a cocktail party "at our hermitage" and found myself in a traffic jam of stand-up martini drinkers. [Ult. < IE *er-, ere-*, far (ERRANT). → Gk. *erēmitēs,* (person) of the desert < *erēmos,* solitary, deserted. The sense shift from IE to Gk. was from "far away" to "apart from all others." Eremites of the early Christian era often dwelt in the Sahara, but the Gk. sense was not "of the sandy wastes and desolations" but "in unpopulated and uncultivated places (deserted of people)." Some eremites lived in forests, on unpopulated islands, on crags, or in remote back country. The essence of the term is solitude, not sand.]

herring choker *New England, esp. in fishing ports.* A Nova Scotian. [Nova Scotian herring, more esteemed in foreign markets (as Japan) than at home, are caught in gill nets as much as 100 feet long. These nets are (or once were) hauled across an open fish hatch, or simply across the bows of a small boat by heroically thewed Nova Scotian fishermen. Those fish that did not shake out had to be grabbed by the gills and pulled (choked) out.]

hidebound *adj.* 1. Labels a morbid condition of cattle. Healthy animals have a layer of fat between hide and flesh, permitting the hide to ride easily on the body's motion. This layer makes it relatively easy to flay the new-slaughtered animal. But in emaciated cattle the hind binds to the flesh, so closely at times as to hinder motion. 2. *Ext.* Said of trees with a bark so thick and contracted as to hinder growth. 3. *Metaphoric ext.* (And now the primary sense unless the context is specifically veterinarian.) Labels a person so set in his opinions that he is incapable of alteration or intellectual growth.

hiero- *Prefix.* Sacred. [< Gk. *hieros,* sacred.] **hieroglyphics** Early Egyptian picture writing. [*Hiero-;* with *glyph,* carving (< Gk. *glyphē,* carving; *glyphein,* to carve). Because the first hieroglyphics were chiseled in stone. Early Greeks, on first seeing these inscriptions, named them "sacred carvings," perhaps because they took the invention of nonspoken communication as a godlike increase in man's capabilities, but more likely because these prealphabetic inscriptions were made of stylized images of gods, sacred creatures, and totemistic animals.]
  hierarchy [*Hier(o);* with *-archy,* rule by priests. (< Gk. *archein,*

to rule; *archon,* ruler).] 1. *Root sense.* Rule by priests. (The pha-
raohs and some of the Roman emperors went this idea one better
by declaring themselves to be gods. So, too, until desanctifying
Douglas MacArthur, the emperor of Japan.) 2. *Among early Christian writers.* Rule by the Pope. Whence: 3. The ranks and orders
of authority within the Roman Catholic Church. 4. *Ext.* The pecking order within any complex organization. 5. Any established or
asserted order of importance, including the relative ratings of
things. [So in an ultimate degeneration of the word, a *N.Y. Times*
report, July 21, 1980: "Alfred Sloan (of General Motors) developed
the annual model change and a carefully ordered hierarchy of
models." (From which one may suppose that a Cadillac Fleetwood
is more sacred than a Chevrolet.)]

high and dry   In a bad way, with little or no means of rescue or
recovery. [*Am. mid XIX nautical.* Said of a vessel driven ashore
beyond the normal high-water mark; hence with little prospect of
being refloated.]

highway robbery   1. *Lit.* Armed robbery on the open road (earlier
called the king's highway). But: 2. *In common ext.* Used to describe
extortionate prices charged when goods are in short supply, or
exorbitantly inflated by high-chic shops and fancy restaurants. *New
York hotel rates these days are highway robbery.* Or: *We buy steak
once a month from the highway robber who calls himself a
butcher.* [Am. Dating unknown. But the sentiment has early precedent in many languages. In Roman dialect, It. *amazzati,* kill yourself, becomes *amappati.* I have often heard Roman housewives say
to a merchant who charged a high price, *"Amappati, che prezzo!"*
which in extended translation would read: "You should kill yourself
for charging such a price!"]

hind tit   A common rural (and diffused) colloq. for (to mix metaphors)
the bottom of the pecking order, the least desirable position. *suck
hind tit* 1. To get the least (the worst) of it. 2. To be left with
nothing. [Am. XIX, and perhaps earlier. The metaphor is based on
the competition of animal litters for the maternal spigots. Various
veterinarians I have consulted tell me: *(a)* that the rear teats produce less milk than the forward ones; *(b)* that there is no significant
difference fore and aft. Where doctors disagree, let laymen hold
their peace.
It does happen that a given litter outnumbers the available

spigots. Then, in the competition for food, the runt(s) of the litter is/are squeezed out, often to die of starvation. It seems, now, to be impossible to trace the idiom with whole assurance, but *hind tit* may be a figure of speech for *no tit at all,* a ref. to the excluded runt(s) left with nothing, the hindmost tit of all.]

hires Employed persons. [May this usage be stillborn, but so in a multiple-atrocity three-column head on page 1 of the *N.Y. Times,* Aug. 11, 1981: *Half of the City's New Hires Are Minority Workers.*]

history [A complicated evolution < IE *weid-,* to see. That sense readily extended to "to understand." Suffixed form *(w)id-es-ya,* id-e'-'a → Gk. *idea,* idea (IDEA). Variant *(w)id-es-tor* → Gk. *histor,* learned man. (One who sees and understands. And certainly the wise men of primitive tribes were those who knew and understood the past of their people.) L. *historia,* the pursuit of learning by seeking out the facts.] Any account of past events that seeks in some way to explain how one event led to another. History, however, cannot be allowed to mean "that which happened." Event is what happened. History is a style of writing based on discrete assumptions about which events are important, and about the mechanisms by which one event leads to another as if by cause and effect. Marxist histories of a given period rarely resemble the accounts of non-Marxists. U.S. and British schoolbooks on the American Revolution barely seem to describe the same engagement. Events happen; more events than any scholar can hope to identify. History must be written. And yet, of course, in common usage *history* is taken to mean "that which happened."

    case history The recorded data taken to be pertinent to a case in medicine, psychiatry, social work, and the like. *make history* To do something so notable that it will be remembered by future generations.

hobby Any activity, from the bumbling to the highly skilled, with which one whiles away the idle hours. *Sex used to be Jim Whitehead's hobby before he took to meditative bourbon.* [Earlier a gentle old nag ridden at a walk and especially suitable for small children. So ME **hoby* (perh. < *hobbled* but as likely < *Hob, Hobbin,* pet form of the once common given name Robin, and often applied to pet animals). Then, by a simple association, a stick with a more or less crudely carved horse's head at one end, "ridden" astraddle by children at play. (Also *cock horse.*) Whence by a further association, playtime activity.]

> ***hobby kit*** A package containing all the components for assembling a "do-it-yourself" project. ***hobby shop*** If not the cathedral, at least the chapel of the American religion of "do-it-yourself" after it has been pre-done and pre-packaged with step-by-step instructions.

hog 1. Generic name for a pig. 2. *In Am. practice.* A pig weighing 120 lbs. or more. 3. *Simple ext.* A glutton. [OE *hogg.* Of obscure Celtic origin. At ult. root < IE *su-,* swine.]

> ***hog it (all)*** To take all the food (or anything else) for oneself.
>
> ***hogwash*** 1. Pig slops. [First attested OED, mid XV, as *hoggyswasch* < ME *hoggys,* genitive case of *hogge,* pig; with *wasch,* here with the sense: "slops" (liquid food).] 2. *In XVIII.* Utter nonsense. [Stuff as worthless and disgusting as pig slops. Used as a formula of indignant rejection.]
>
> ***hog wild*** In a screaming, physically violent frenzy. [Cf. the common idiom *scream like a stuck pig.* An injured or otherwise frightened pig screams and lunges in blind panic. In somewhat softened but obvious ext. describes a person in a screaming rage.]
>
> ***road hog*** A driver who straddles lanes, preventing other vehicles from passing.
>
> ***live high on the hog*** To eat (live) well. [*High,* here, meaning above the belly—where the best cuts of pork are.]
>
> And see *whole hog.*

holding pattern 1. *Air traffic control.* A flight path and altitude assigned to aircraft that may not, for safety's sake, be allowed to land at a congested airport, esp. in poor weather. The waiting aircraft are usu. required to fly circles around an established radio beacon at intervals of at least 500 feet of altitude. Such planes are said to be ***stacked up.*** Except in declared emergencies, air controllers, unless the field is closed and the planes given another destination, clear planes for landing from the bottom of the stack or landing pattern. 2. *Metaphoric ext.* In abeyance. Holding off. Delaying a commitment. *Their romance is in a holding pattern, but they do have a date for Tuesday night.*

hole in the wall A shabby room or flat. [A still-current survival of massive medieval city walls, which were often studded with warren-like shops and hovels for the poor. Collaterally, may be a ref.

to British debtors' prison, in which inmates were given food and lodging only if they could buy it, the indigent being forced to beg alms through holes in the outer walls of the prison. In either case, the term connotes wretched living.]

Hole in the Wall Gang A legend-encrusted outlaw band of the Frontier West, the leader being a larger-than-life-size post–Civil War desperado named Butch Cassidy, his lieutenant being the Sun Dance Kid. Among other embellishments of the truth, the gang's hideout was said to be in a secret canyon that could be entered only through a passage in a cliff (the hole in the wall) that was concealed by a waterfall. Hollywood has made overmuch of this detail—an all but incredible geological formation. The bare fact is that the gang had some safe hideout beyond a narrow rock pass, or simply that it was clever enough to make itself hard to find.

hollyhock   The marsh mallow, *Althaea officinalis,* native to China. It was cultivated in England as a garden flower by VII, and escaped the garden to grow wild. Its recorded presence in medieval England is evidence that many unrecorded trade routes operated between the Far East and western Europe, prob. with terminals in Byzantium and Arabia, and again in Venice. [But as with many flower names, *mallow* or *hock* prob. labeled different plants at different times. OE *hoc,* hock, mallow. Prefixed *holi,* holy → *holihoc,* holy mallow. Pious legend associates this flower (whatever flower it was) with St. Cuthbert (d. 687) because it was said to grow profusely around his hermitage on the Isle of Farne.

At this point all becomes uncertain. If St. Cuthbert's flowers were what we now call hollyhocks, there was hardly time for the plants to escape from their first cultivation and to make it to the Isle of Farne in time for St. Cuthbert's death (though getting birds to fetch a few seeds would not be much of a miracle for a true saint).

It may be that hollyhocks grow there now, and were assumed to have grown there in the saint's time. More likely the "holy hock" was a different flower, for the Welsh name was *hocys bendigaid,* blessed hock, or blessed mallow, and prob. labeled a different flowering plant because *A. officinalis* was not known in England until VII. Or, to give confusion its full due, the Welsh name may have arisen late, as a translation of ME *holihoc.* It is a tangled garden.

Then in XIII, to tangle further, the name was modified from *holihoc* to *hollyhock* by association with the holly, perhaps because hollyhock buds resemble holly berries, esp. when the flowers are blue and are just peeping through the bud. In that case the XIII hollyhock would be *A. officinalis,* though our present garden strains have been so hybridized that their seeds do not breed true but produce paler and paler flowers in successive years.]

homage   A formal act of respect, admiration, honor. (There is no verb form *to homage,* that function being expressed by using an auxiliary verb, commonly *to pay homage (to),* and earlier *to do homage.*) [Root sense, with ref. to the feudal system: "manhood act" of swearing oneself as one's lord's man, honor bound to his service by one's manhood, religiously bound to it by the established sanctity of the feudal pecking order, a socioreligious flow-down from the "divine right of kings." < L. *homo,* man; *-age,* act of. Medieval L. *hominaticum* → OF and ME *homage,* first with the feudal ref., then generalized to the modern sense, as if paying respect to a "lord" of intellect, goodness, benefaction, great personal achievement.] *an homage to Archibald MacLeish.*

homely   1. Plain, unattractive, ugly. *Isaac Asimov is the homeliest man in town, or in any three or four towns you care to mention.* 2. Crude, homespun, inelegant. *Only his wit is homelier than he.* [But up to XV with the sense "secret." < Ger. *heimlich,* which labels a "home" (family) matter not to be discussed abroad. Also, earlier, *be homely with,* to be on intimate terms with. *To be homely with Isaac is to shine by comparison.*]

honcho   The main man. The big macho. The powerful one. [An etymology in search of an attestation. After ten years of searching this form out in Spanish sources, I have pieced slender clues to a still-tentative conclusion that it developed in overseas army use during the Korean War and that it is a corruption of some Korean or perhaps Japanese word I cannot locate. The help of any knowledgeable reader is hereby urgently requested.]

hoodlum   A roving thug. [The unattested derivation may be far-fetched, but no other seems available. San Francisco c. 1880 was infested by gangs of such thugs centered on the Barbary Coast but roaming free. One dominant gang was headed by a man named Muldoon. The story has it that a newspaper reporter writing about the depredations of this gang, but reluctant to name Muldoon for fear of reprisals, spelled the name backward, labeling the thugs *noodlums,* a compositor changing the initial *n* to *h* to make *hoodlums.* There is the smell of spook etymology about this derivation.

Nor have I been able to find a trace of the Muldoon in question. The reader is free to ponder this derivation before concluding "origin unknown."]

hooey   *n.* Hogwash. Bunk. Baloney. —*Exclam. or interjection.* In effect, That's a lot of bunk! [Am. c. 1900. Commonly glossed as an expressive akin to *ugh, oops, phew.* But there is clearly precedent in *ballyhoo(ey)* and in Brit. *ballyhooley,* popular in British musical halls c. 1880, and at root (though influenced by ballyhoo) it is a minced form of *bloody-holy, bloody,* at that time remaining arbitrarily offensive in Brit. use.]

Hoosier   A native of Indiana, the Hoosier State, the local self-assertion being that a true Hoosier can outdo any man. [The origin, now overlaid by many strata of spook etymology, must prob. remain forever in doubt. The common suggestion that the term is a corruption of an Indian term is merely random since no one has been able to locate such a source.

   In mid XIX Middle Border dialect, a man of great physical strength, one who could outwork, outdance, outrun, and outfight all comers, was called a *husher,* one who could make all others hush up. *Husher* was also once common on the Middle Border for "bully." *Hoosier* may (???) be an alteration of *husher* in the sense "powerhouse of a man"—as Hoosiers would still like the term to be received.]

hoot[1]   The cry of an owl. [Echoic.] ***hoot and holler*** 1. To be boisterous. 2. To complain loudly. (My father-in-law once came up with the mixed metaphor, *He hooted and hollered like a stuck pig.*) ***hoot owl*** 1. A small barn owl. 2. Any owl. 3. *On wstrn. frontier.* An outlaw. [One who travels at night and signals his confederates by hooting like an owl.] ***hoot-owl trail*** The course of an outlaw's life. ***take to the hoot-owl trail*** To become an outlaw.

hoot[2]   Nothing. ***not care a hoot*** Not care at all. [Am. XIX. This *hoot* is a corruption of *iota* by aspiration and with a terminal intrusive *r,* as if "h'ioter," though that form is unattested. *Hooter,* however, is amply attested. James Russell Lowell, 1819–1891, uses it in a less than memorable rhyme:

> And again to impress on the popylar mind
> The comfort and wisdom o' going it blind—

To say that I didn't abate not a *hooter*
O' my faith in a happy and glorious futur!

In which *not a hooter* might be rendered in formal English, "not one iota."]

horn [IE *ker-*, horn, head. With k/h and suffixed -*n*- in Gmnc. → OE *horn*.] 1. A bonelike projection on the head of many hooved animals. 2. The nonbony projections on the heads of snails; the projecting feathery tufts of owls. [Not really horns but giving the visual impression of them.] 3. *Music*. *(a)* Originally, an animal horn blown as a signal. *(b)* A brass instrument. 4. *Jazz*. Any wind instrument.

blow one's own horn To brag. To seek to make a big impression. [Since earliest known times, important personages have been announced with a sounding of animal horns, and later with a flourish of trumpets. One who blows his own horn is busily announcing his own importance (since no one else will announce it for him, or even recognize it). Matthew 6:2: "Sound not a trumpet before thee, as the hypocrites do in the synagogues and in the streets."]

horn in (on) To intrude. As in *stick one's nose* into somebody else's business. *Horn* suggests a goring, hence a grosser intrusion. [P. *Slang* cites the idiom as Am. (undated); into Brit. c. 1930.] **lock horns** 1. *Of animals*. To attack head to head, as male deer do in fighting off rivals for their harems. It sometimes happens that in butting their antlers together, they become locked and cannot separate. Skeletons of large hooved ruminants have been found with their horns so locked. 2. *Of people*. To fight head to head. **pull in one's horns** To back off. To stop being belligerent. To recant. [To me, a puzzling idiom. It suggests the action of a defeated stag, buck, bull, or ram in withdrawing from a fight. Yet the only creature I can think of with retractable horns is a snail. First attested XIV.]

hornbook *Am. colonial and XIX*. 1. Not really a book, but a wooden paddle faced with a sheet of parchment on which the alphabet and the numbers are printed as models, the parchment being covered with a transparent sheet of horn on which beginning students may copy the models on the parchment, easily wiping away what they have written. 2. *Ext*. A primer.

horn of plenty The cornucopia, an ancient symbol of abundance spilling from a ram's horn about the size of a tuba. **horn spoon** See Vol. I.

horns/the horns Immemorial symbol of the cuckolded husband. (See *hornswoggle*, Vol. I. Also *cuckold*.) I have never discovered why the cuckold is said to sprout horns. Fools and court jesters have sometimes worn caps bearing cloth horns. A man who has been cuckolded has been made a fool of, but he might better be said to sprout ass's ears. Are the horns to be taken as the penises stuck into one's unfaithful wife, and left to stick out of one's head (identity, honor, being)? For to be cuckolded was a blood-and-honor offense before it became a footnote to modern living.

horn spoon See Vol. I. *horns of a dilemma* See *dilemma,* above.

horny Sexually aroused. Originally with ref. to a male erection protruding as stiff and hard as an animal's horn (ah, sweet dreams!), but at least since WWII, liberated women have taken over the idiom for their own feelings of sexual desire.

horny-handed Callused hard by labor. Commonly in *horny-handed son of toil.*

around the Horn 1. *Nautical.* The passage from the Atlantic to the Pacific (or vice versa) around Cape Horn, or through the usually tempestuous Strait of Magellan. *The missionaries came to Hawaii around the Horn, and their land-grabbing descendants have been blowing it ever since.* 2. *Baseball.* The act of relaying the ball from third base to second to first for a double play, or in the rarest of baseball feats, a triple play.

hors d'oeuvre (Sing. & plu., though *hors d'oeuvres* occurs as a common, though ignorant, plural.) [Fr., apart from the work. < L. *foris opera.* In earliest use as an art term meaning "apart/aside from the main body of an artist's work." In Fr. with the sense: "aside from/ not properly a part of the meal" (the meal being conceived as a coordinated work of the high cuisine).] In Am. usage labels little varied appetizers, hot or cold, served with cocktails, usu. but not always before a meal. If served as a platter at table before a meal and consisting of various cold cuts and vegetables, the term is *antipasto.*

NOTE. In any true cuisine one sips wine or wine and bitters along with the hors d'oeuvre, but cocktails are taboo because alcohol tends to numb the taste buds, the martini being especially villainous as an affront to the chef who in concept or fact has planned the meal as a sequence of subtle tastes, each course being matched to the wine selected for it. Liquor, usu. brandy, is for after the meal.

horse-and-buggy   *adj.* Primitive. Passé. Not adjusted to modern living. [The idiom could not have occurred before XX and the general replacement of the horse and buggy by the automobile. *Hayburner* for "horse" is, similarly, an idiom that could have arisen only after a specific historic change. Only after the railroads' *iron horse* had been established as a *woodburner* and, later, *coalburner* could it have meant anything to call a horse a *hayburner.* MMM's first attestation is dated 1921.]

horsefeathers   Rot. Bunk. Common as a term of contemptuous dismissal. [Prob. Am. though not so noted in NWD. Not entered in P. *Slang.* Prob. from c. 1800. *Cowgills, frogswings, snakeshooves, beesmanes,* might have expressed the same nonesuch nonsense, as does *mare's nest,* for example. The question is, "Why *horsefeathers?*" And here all sources are mute except for Charles Earle Funk, who reports in his book titled *Horsefeathers* that old New England carpenters used "horsefeathers" to label "rows of clapboards (feathering strips) laid with the butt edges against the butt edges of shingles and clapboards to provide a flat surface" (over which new siding might be applied). Funk offers no attestation, but he was not a man to invent etymological data to suit his convenience. If one will accept his, so to speak, "field report," as I do, *horsefeathers* is clearly an alteration of "house feathers," for "house feathering strips." The sense "ludicrous" or "inferior" would then follow logically from the fact that such housefeathering / horsefeathering was a gross method, inferior to stripping off the old siding before applying new. Funk wrote in mid XX, having been born in late XIX. "Old New England carpenters" would take the term back to early XIX, and with a reasonable lag between origin and common use, back into colonial Am. As noted, this derivation lacks full attestation and may, accordingly, be called into question. But Funk was an accurate reporter, and the root "house feathers" makes clear the form and also the sense.]

horse: flog a dead horse   To rage insistently and pointlessly. [Flog away: the horse is dead.]
    HISTORIC. But though seemingly a natural folk metaphor, as of an angry plowman urging on his horse after it has dropped dead, the origin is not agricultural but nautical. (And be it noted that the stupidest of plowmen would know when his horse was dead and beyond command or flogging.)
    On late XVIII Brit. merchantmen, the *dead horse* was the work

time, usu. a month, for which sailors were paid in advance when they signed on. Many sailors drank away their dead horse before sailing (watched over by a boatswain enforcer and a shore crew, to keep new men from skipping with their pay?). In any case, they drew no pay until the dead horse was worked off (flogged).

Kemp, *Oxford Companion to Ships and the Sea,* writes that it was once custom on British merchantmen, on flogging off the dead horse, to parade a crude straw effigy of a horse's head, singing, "Old man, your horse must die," then hoisting the effigy to a yardarm and cutting it loose to fall into the sea. If the ship carried passengers, the effigy was first auctioned off to them, the proceeds being divided among the crew.

Kemp adds an obscure note that to *flog a dead horse* was to get extra work out of a ship's crew while the men were still working off their dead horse. But has not the captain the right to call for extra duty hours at any time?

Among the vagaries of language, this nautical origin has all but entirely receded from the idiom, overpowered by the image of the angry farmer beating his dead horse. In an informal survey, I have asked several large college classes to interpret this idiom, and I found no American student who was aware of its nautical origin.

horses: hold your horses   Wait just a minute. Don't go racing off in anger. [Always with the plu., hence with original ref. to a team of horses drawing a wagon, carriage, stagecoach, or the like. As if: "Now, don't just gallop off in anger (and without knowing where you are going)," hence "Stay put, and let's talk it over." Cf. later, *hold the phone.*]

hot dog   The frankfurter in a roll as the basic American calorie. Originally with some combination of ketchup, mustard, pickle relish; now with these and all sorts of additions, from sauerkraut to chili sauce. Especially associated as a festive snack with ball games and a day at the shore. [First attested 1901 in a comic strip by the popular Tad Dorgan, and who knows what goes on in the mind of a man who draws funnies? There was at one time a joke that these sausages were made of ground dog meat. A wiener in a bun (projecting at either end) has been conceived as a dachshund wearing a blanket. Whatever the conceiving image or association, *hot dog* came into being c. 1900 and is firmly established in Am. with festive associations extravagantly beyond the merit of the wiener in a bun as food.]

hot dog! And in elaborated form *hot diggity-dog!* Am. exclam. of delight. [By association with the hot dog as festive food at the baseball park and at the shore. I have seen this term asserted as a minced oath, *dog* being *God* in reverse; a case, I believe, of over-subtle invention. The quality of the exclam. is sufficiently explained by the festive associations.]

hot dogging A recently popular form of suicide on skis. It con-sists of acrobatic leaps, somersaults, and aerial twists performed at breakneck speed on a slope studded with moguls, terraces, and other irregularities. [An elaborated form of skiing; perhaps so called by association with festive exuberance; perhaps because the skier is likely enough to end up as dog meat.]

hotfoot   A moronic practical joke. The prankster wedges a match between shoe sole and upper of a victim who is talking, drinking, or sleeping. He then lights the match and waits for the victim to leap up in pain when the flame scorches the shoe leather. The leather remains painfully hot after the match has burned out. The result is an often painful blister and, of course, the prankster's unbearable ha-ha at his own trite ingenuity. [Origin uncertain, but the "joke" depends on shoes (boots) with soles and uppers into which to wedge the match, and on friction matches, which were not available until early XIX (see *locofoco*, Vol. I). The NWD marks this term as an Americanism. Technology dates it to the early XIX.]

hotfoot it To run fast. [So fast that one's feet heat up. A simple metaphor. Cf. early jazz slang *feetswarmers,* as in Dixieland record-ings labeled "Sidney Bechet and his New Orleans Feetswarmers," based on the fact that a hard Dixieland beat makes one stomp until one's "feets" get warm. *Go hot foot* is attested in ME, but *hotfoot it* is Am. and prob. late XVIII, early XIX.]

hoyden   A sassy, high-spirited girl.—*adj. hoydenish* Possessing a bouncy, graceless, but infectious charm. [Now specific to girls and perhaps women, but earlier applied to either sex, implying crude, country manners. < Du. *heiden,* heathen.]

HISTORIC. *Heathen* now means non-Christian. It once meant one who lives in the wild back country without knowledge of city ways, i.e., a dweller in the heath. Missionaries from Rome first brought Christianity to the cities, the heath dwellers retaining the old religions along with their uncivilized manners and crude dia-lects. (And note that *civilization* is, at root: "of the city.") The heathen was once what we might call a hillbilly, redneck, clodhopper, stumpjumper, and the like. The religious connotation came about VI–VII A.D., the heath dwellers being the last to be converted to Christianity. *Pagan* is similarly from L. *paganus,* an outlying district, and also one who lives there.

hubbub 1. The sound of a shouting mob. 2. Any stir and clatter involving many people, as in the intolerable clamor of any stand-up cocktail party (to which please do not invite me unless I can expect a chair and a table or coffee table on which to set my drink and ashtray). [At origin, a Celtic war cry. "They (the attacking Celtic foot soldiers) came running with a terrible yell and hubbabowe, as if heaven and earth would have gone together." —Edmund Spenser, "The Present State of Ireland," 1596.]

hugger-mugger *Brit. Rare in Am., but occurs. adj.* 1. Secret. *a hugger-mugger operation.* 2. Confused. *Things are all hugger-mugger.* —*v. Does not occur in Am.* To keep secret. —*n.* A secretive, seemingly muddled, but acute person. [Redupl. based on *mugger,* which was originally ME *moker* < **mokeren,* to hoard, to hide. Hence ME *hoker-moker,* secret. In XV *hoder-moder;* XVI *hucker-mucker;* all meaning "secret, concealed." The sense progression has been from "secret, concealed" → "not clear" (in XVII) → "all in a muddle."]

hum: make things hum To get everything working busily and efficiently. [Am. XIX. I take the ref. to be to the hum of machinery running smoothly and busily.]

hurdy-gurdy 1. At obscure origin, a medieval instrument on the lines of a lute, but played by street nonmusicians who cranked a rosin-covered knobbed wheel against the strings to pluck a single tune, a change of tune requiring a change of wheel. The antique French instrument called *la vielle,* which resembles a mandolin topped by a small ark, was played by a musician rather than by a hand cranker, but must have resembled those early hand-crank lutes. 2. *Am. Rare since 1930's.* A barrel organ. [Echoic of the droning mechanical sound of the instrument; as if it played only *ur-di-gur-di,* which is a reasonable rendition of what it did indeed play.]
   HISTORIC. Up to the 1940's, the hurdy-gurdy man or organ grinder, almost invariably attended by an elaborately costumed

monkey trained to hold out a tin cup for pennies, nickels, and the rare dime, was a common figure of the street scene.

In 1938, when I was a senior at (then) Tufts College, the dramatic society, Pen, Paint, and Pretzels, undertook an ill-advised production of Maxwell Anderson's unbearably windy *Winterset.* One of the street scenes called for a hurdy-gurdy man and there was none to be found until an aged Sicilian was exhumed from Boston's North End. He had retired when his monkey died in, as I recall, 1934, but he still had his hurdy-gurdy, and after preposterous insistences, he agreed to crank his organ on stage for three nights. In my childhood the hurdy-gurdy man was as common as the scissors grinder who backpacked or wheeled his grindstone through the streets, calling hoarsely for scissors or knives to grind for nickels or dimes. The scissors grinder has vanished, and the old Sicilian *mustacchio* Tufts exhumed in 1938 was my last experience of his species. He was also a naturally memorable actor—especially downwind.

husk   *n.* The outer covering of various seeds and fruits; in Am. esp. of corn. (In the South the more common term is *shuck.*) —*v.* To remove the outer covering, esp. of corn. (Pea pods and nutshells are technically husks, but in idiom one shells peas and cracks nuts. But note the common *shelled pecans,* pecans whose shells have been removed.) [ME *husk, huske* < MD *huskijn,* house. Akin to ON *hus,* house (HUSBAND, HUSBANDRY, HUSSY). The sense shift < "place lived in" → "outer covering" is paralleled by the use in mechanics of "housing," a protective covering around an engine, a flywheel, a drive shaft, etc. The husk of an ear of corn is, in this sense, its housing.]

   husking bee Earlier also **husking frolic** From early colonial days to the time all the farmer's children had fled to the city, the husking bee was a harvest festival lasting for many days, all the members of the community taking turns in husking each family's corn. Husking is hard work. It was made light by many hands and by forfeits and by prizes of kisses and by a general gaiety.

In "Hiawatha," Longfellow says husking was a frolic of Indian women, and that a girl who found a red ear would win a handsome husband.

> And whene'er a lucky maiden
> Found a red ear in the husking,
> Found a maize ear red as blood is,

Nushka! cried they all together,
Nushka! you shall have a sweetheart,
You shall have a handsome husband.

The American farm frolic was for both sexes and was described by Joel Barlow in "Hasty Pudding," a mock epic written in 1796. (A *smut ear* is an ear blackened by fungus spores. In Barlow's account girls, but not boys, are allowed to blacken all the boys with a smut ear. A boy who gets a red ear kisses all the girls; a girl who gets one gets to choose which beau she will kiss, but not all of them.)

The laws of husking every wight can tell;
And sure no laws he ever keeps so well:
For each red ear a general kiss he gains,
With each smut ear she smuts the luckless swains;
But when to some sweet maid a prize is cast,
Red as her lips, and taper as her waist,
She walks around and culls one favored beau,
Who leaps, the luscious tribute to bestow.
Various the sport, as are the wits and brains
Of well pleas'd lasses and contending swains;
Till the vast mound of corn is swept away
And he that gains the last ear wins the day.

Cornhusker A Nebraskan. [A self-chosen nickname.]

hypocrite   One who pretends to be what he is not, and even perhaps what no one is. [Gk. *hypokrisis,* an actor ("one who is different from the role he plays"). < *hypo,* under; *krisis,* act of separation from. Hence with root sense: "less (other) than one appears to be."] "Hypocrisy and alcoholism are the two minimum adaptations to the social order." —Fabrique du Jour, *Inenmerdable,* trans. by Rigid Wildboare.

I

icebox   Up to the age of electric or gas refrigeration, a wooden cabinet with metal grilles for shelves (to facilitate air circulation) and one large upper compartment, usu. zinc-lined, to hold a block of ice. The zinc-lined compartment had a drain for meltwater, which was usu. collected in a basin under the box. (In the age of linoleum flooring for kitchens, the basin, if allowed to overflow, could cause a bone-breaking slick on the linoleum.)

HISTORIC. Iceboxes were in XIX use and common until c. 1930 (later in the boondocks), when they were generally replaced by electric refrigerators. Pond ice was used until c. 1920 (it wasn't always dirty), when *icehouses* began to manufacture it, usu. in hundred-pound blocks. *Icemen* delivered the ice by horse wagon along regular routes and issued cards to be placed in a window. The cards were about 14 inches square and each side had a number: 25, 50, 75, or 100 (pounds). By placing the desired number uppermost, a housewife signaled the weight of ice desired. Breaking the hundred-pound block with his ice pick, the iceman cut it to the desired weight and brought it to the house, the small blocks carried by tongs at his side, the large blocks slung by tongs over a rubber sheet he wore attached to his neck to hang down in back. A delivery of ice meant a trail of droplets across the kitchen floor, to be mopped up by the housewife.

Elegant houses had large iceboxes backed against an exterior wall, and behind the icebox, a hutch door through which the ice could be delivered from outside without dribbling through the house. Such houses also used copper tubing connected to the icebox drain to allow the meltwater to drip outside the house (until the tube froze in winter and the water backed up—but that was simply a problem for a now legendary creature called a maid or a cook).

It was once common idiom to say of a cold room *it feels like an icebox in here.* I cannot remember when I last heard the idiom so put, probably before WWII. Nowadays one says *it feels like a deep-*

freeze in here. Language is usually quick to register technological change.

I could care less   I couldn't care less. [A baffling form that has recently come into common illiterate usage, and that has all too commonly passed into the colloq. usage of the presumably literate. I have heard it from the mouth of a professor of literature, but a professorship, of course, no longer implies literacy. It is easy, of course, to swallow the *-n't* suffix of *couldn't,* and the clipped form is commonly pronounced cŭnt. I still cannot understand how the essential negative can be ignored. So, too, *anymore* for "nowadays." (See *any more / anymore,* Vol. I.)]

idiot   A person of the lowest measurable intelligence, commonly incapable of speech and even of recognizing danger. One of a mental age below 3 years on the Binet scale, and an I.Q. below 20. [The generalized stem *idio* refers to self or to a specific thing. So L. *id,* that ("that specific thing apart from all others") (IDIOM, IDIOSYNCRASY, IT). The curious sense shift occurred in Gk. *idiōtēs,* a free citizen of the lowest class; one not competent to hold public office, hence one who lives apart from the state and for himself alone. The same aristocratic assumption functions in Engl. *lewd,* the original sense being "laic, not of the clergy," but implicitly "one too ignorant (and low and common) to be a clergyman" (benefices being generally the perquisites of younger sons of the gentry). The sense "lascivious" (the way low, common people live) did not develop until XIV.]

    idiot card A card held up behind the camera as a way of giving TV or movie actors their lines. [Am. A bit before 1950, the term originating in TV. The work of idiot cards is now done by an electronically printed reel mounted by the camera lens.]

ignominy   Disgrace. Dishonor. [Root sense: "loss of one's (good) name." L. *ignominia,* condition of being without a name; hence, dishonor. < *Nomen,* name, with neg. prefix *ig-.*]

    HISTORICAL. The Romans used clan and family names (*cognomena*) as titles of honor and went so far as to commit suicide if a vile or cowardly act caused them to "lose their good name." Surnames (originally sir names or *twa names,* second names) did not come into British use until after the Norman Conquest, and then slowly, and at first restricted to the nobility. Once established, however, surnames became a matter of family honor.

Browning's "My Last Duchess" is about an Italian duke's demented pride in his "nine-hundred-year-old name." To lose (blemish) one's honored name was easily equated with being nameless, hence base-born, for commoners were slow in acquiring family names (beginning c. XVI). Hence, to be "disnamed" was to lose one's place in the pecking order of Britain's rigid caste system.

imbecile   An adult or adolescent with a mental age on the Binet scale of a 3–7-year-old, and an I.Q. of 20–50; a classification between *idiot* and *moron,* which see. [Root sense: "feeble (minded)," but with the root image: "feeble and with no walking stick to lean on," the idea of halting feebleness transferred to mental incompetence. < IE *bak-,* walking stick → L. *baculum,* same sense, dim. form *bacillum,* and with *im-* (syncopated form of the neg. prefix *in-*) → *imbacillum,* weak (lit. "lacking the support of one's little walking stick"). The IE root *bak-* with b/p and k/g in Gmnc. is the base of Eng. *peg,* as in *peg leg.*]

inch of candle auction   In XVII–XVIII Brit., a form of auction in which a one-inch candle was lit as each lot was placed on the block, the bidding continuing until the candle guttered out, whereupon the property was knocked down to the last bidder. [In earlier Fr., this form of auction was called *à l'extinction de la chandelle,* though the Fr. phrase also meant to the last breath, as in a deathbed scene. *Sale by inch of candle* was in use in early XIX and is listed by D. E. MacDonald, *Dictionary of Quotations,* 1810, but this form of auction had fallen out of use by then, only the phrase surviving, though prob. solely as a matter of antiquarian interest, for what could it have meant to a generation that had forgotten this form of auction?]

indent   [IE *dent-,* tooth. O-variant *dont-* (PERIODONTAL) → Gk. *odōn,* tooth; L. *dens,* Late L. adjectival form *dentalis,* of a tooth, of the teeth. Same stem via Gmnc. with the prob. form *tanthuz* → Saxon *tōth,* teeth. In Brit. in various legal forms, and in some current Am. usage *to indent* implies to make a tooth-shaped mark or marks, to serrate.] 1. To set back the spacing of a line of writing to indicate the beginning of a paragraph. 2. *Old-style legalism.* To make fair duplicate copies of a document on a single large sheet, which is then cut into two parts by serration. The matching of these irregular indentations, when fitted together again, validates the documents.

indenture 1. *Surviving legalism.* A binding document. 2. *Earlier.* To impose or to accept status as a bondsman for a stated number of years, with recompense as stipulated in the document. *indentured servant Esp. in the early American colonies.* A person so indentured. (See *kidnap.*) [Both terms derive from the fact that the legal documents establishing the indenture were serrated (indented) as above. *indentation As in sense 1 of* indent. A setback in a more or less regular line. *an indentation in the otherwise regular coastline.*

Indian file   One behind the other. [There were natural reasons for Indians to move through wooded country in single file. What is less generally known is that when they had reason to hide their passage, each man in the party took pains to step in the footprints of the first man, the last in line dragging a leafy branch to erase, or at least obscure, the line of footprints.]

indolent   Lazy. Habitually lazy. [At root: "feeling no pain." < L. *dolens,* feeling pain (present part. of *dolēre,* to feel pain); with neg. prefix *in-* → Late L. *indolens,* painless. The sense evolution is by association with "painstaking" to describe hard work, hence "taking no pains," hence "putting forth no effort." In medicine, what is now commonly called a *benign tumor* (if there can be such a thing), or better, a *nonmalignant tumor,* was once commonly an *indolent tumor,* now all but obsolete. Of the three labels, the one now used least seems in every way to be the most accurate.]

Inferno   *n.* 1. Hell. 2. A hellish place. Esp. a place of raging fire and stink. —*adj.* *infernal* Hellish. [The form is It. < L. *infernus,* the underworld. Akin to *infra,* under, as in the bastard form *infrared.* Also akin to *inferior,* lower (in position, quality, worth). So in archaic Eng., *the inferior regions,* hell. The now primary association with fire is late. The myth of Vulcan, who had his smithy and forge at the base of Mount Etna, suggests fire in the infernal regions, but in Roman myth the underworld was generally a place of misty darkness, a dark, damp inclosure more nearly suggesting the grave than a magma. Dante was probably the prime mover in associating the Inferno with fire, though his ultimate hell is of ice.

infernal machine Archaic. A bomb. [Anarchists of late XIX and early XX set off *infernal machines,* so called because they were hellish and would blow people to hell.] The devices used by terrorists since WWII are generally called *bombs, plastique, grenades,* or *booby traps.*

influenza   And commonly *flu.* An infectious respiratory disease, usu. with muscular pain and irritation of the digestive tract and sinuses. [It. *influenza* (L. *influentia*), influence ("flowing in") of the stars. As if the disease were caused by astrological conjunctions. This label applied to the disease by Italian physicians during the virulent European outbreak of 1743; in effect, a confession that they, lacking knowledge of viruses, did not know what was killing their patients. In Fr., *grippe,* which see.]

HISTORIC. Now not normally fatal except to patients in otherwise weakened condition, but several deadly epidemics are on record. The viruses that cause influenza mutate rapidly, altering the severity and some of the symptoms of the disease. In 1918–1919 an esp. virulent strain caused widespread death in the U.S. Annually, with the coming on of winter, outbreaks, commonly called Asiatic flu, blue flu, Hong Kong flu, decimate (which see) work forces, usu. for about a week. Some epidemiologists, citing the rapid mutations of the virus, and past deadly outbreaks, have speculated that some esp. virulent form of the virus could cause something very much like plague death.

injury   [IE *yew's-,* to incant a religious formula, to perform a rite. Slightly modified and with s/r assimilation → L. *jurare,* to swear solemnly at law. With *in-,* neg. prefix → *injuria,* a harm done in violation of the law.] 1. *In common usage.* Bodily harm. *He was injured in an automobile crash.* (But not said of inanimate objects: the driver was injured, the car was damaged.) 2. *At law.* By the unlawful action of another or of others, any harm done to a person's body (as battery, mayhem), or reputation (as slander, libel, defamation), or property (as malicious destruction), or by violation of one's rights (as illegal seizure, peonage).

interfere   To intervene and impede. [But not adequately rendered as if L. *inter,* between, with *ferre,* to carry, with effective sense: "to carry (bear forward) a thing or oneself between (two other things)." The root is L. *ferire,* to wound (It. *ferita,* a wound). The root sense, therefore, is "to strike one another." Into Eng. in XVI with the specific sense (still used in the schooling of horses): what a horse does, in performing certain gaits, when it strikes a hoof against the opposing hoof or leg.]

interval   [The root ref. is to the space between the inner and outer walls of a Roman stockade. L. *intervalla* < *inter*, between; *valla*, palisades (WALL).] 1. A distance, in either time or space, between two similar things. 2. *Geography*. A low flatland between acclivities. 3. *Music*. The difference in pitch between two similar tones.

   at intervals Separated in time, space, or both. *The last of the marathon runners came in at increasing intervals.*

   NOTE. L. *vallum*, a palisade, and *murus*, a wall, were often used interchangeably. From *murus* English derives *intramural*, lit. "within the walls" (of, commonly, a single college); and *intermural*, lit. "between two different sets of walls" (colleges). The language convention, in answer to need, has assigned distinct senses to almost identical and root-related forms. Cf. *liquid*, a form of matter; *liquor*, alcoholic drink; *liqueur*, after-dinner cordial; and *delinquent*, apart from expected standards—all from the same IE roots, *liek-wo-*, to go away (from), to depart. (See *liquid*.)

intricate   *adj*. Composed of many interwoven elements. [L. *intricatus*, pp. of *intricāre*, to entangle (in many trifles) < *in-*, into; with *tricae*, minutiae, trifles. In It. *intrecciare*, to weave, to plait, to intertwine; *intrecciatura*, weaving. In It. ballet *capriola intrecciata*, a leap in which the dancer kicks the heels or crosses the legs as many times as possible (as if weaving). Altered in Fr. to *entrechat* (which see) but in Eng. rendered by *intricate*.]

intrude   To thrust into. **intrusive rock** *Geology*. Upwelling lava that forces its way into earlier rock formations. [L. *intrudere*, to thrust into. Ult. < IE *treud-*, to press in upon, to compact, to squeeze. Via Gmnc. with slight modifications → OE *thrēat*, subjugation, oppression (THREAT). *A threatening intruder thrust in with two six-guns protruding.*]

iron maiden   An instrument of torture or execution. A mummy-shaped box in which the victim was strapped. The door of the box was studded with spikes that had screw threads permitting them to be lengthened or shortened. When the door was forced shut, the wretch in the box had the spikes driven into his body. The best known of these devices was the Iron Maiden of Nuremberg (Germany), whose spikes must have been set for a slow death since this form of execution was reserved for the worst of crimes, among them matricide, patricide, and high treason.

irony   Writing or speech in which the true meaning is the opposite of what is said. (Not to be confused with sarcasm, a cutting remark. *Of course I believe in Spiro Agnew's innocence* is irony. *He was only collecting Maryland retirement benefits* is sarcasm. [IE *wer-*, to speak, speech (WORD). Variant *(w)er-*, *er-* → Gk. *eirein*, to speak. Substantive *eirōn*, one who speaks falsely. Whence with an altered sense *eirōneia*, irony. The Gk. sense progression was from "to speak" → "to lie" → "figure of speech that twists the truth to its opposite (but understood as a figure of speech and not as a lie)."]

isolite   *In TV sportscasting, esp. in football.* A special form of replay in which a single key player appears in a ring of light, other players appearing in a visible but dimmer background. [The roots would suggest "equal stone," but the form is a portmanteau of "isolated" and "lite" (for "light"). Isolite replays were briefly popular in the mid 1970's, and were then abandoned. Why? They were effective.]

J

jack   [Most sources, as the AHD, derive the term < Du. *Jankin*, dim.
form of *Jan*, John. And *Jack* is the common nickname form of John.
But following the Norman Conquest, Fr. *Jacques* (1. A common
name; 2. A generic term for a peasant) was in common use as a
man's name; and while it is not necessary to refute the Du. origin,
French was certainly closer to hand.]

Jack has become a more or less all-purpose whatchamacallit
word in English.

As working gear, primarily, a tool for raising a heavy load by
leverage, cranking, or hydraulic or electric power. But it is also
used to label a wedge driven by a sledgehammer. And in this sense,
it is the probable origin of *jackhammer* A pneumatic trip-hammer
device for driving a wedge-tipped steel bar through rock or other
hard material. Nautically, *jack* is a prop or support, or a crosstree
on a mast. Also *telephone jack* A female socket that accepts a
prong, thereby making the service connection for a phone. In all
these usages *jack* has the sense: "a special thingamajig sort of device."

In a second special sense, corresponding to Fr. *jacques*, peasant,
a fellow, a laborer, a working stiff. Whence *jack-of-all-trades, man
jack* Redundant but for effect, as in *I want every man jack of you
on deck*. And so *cheap jack* A low, worthless fellow. And *jack tar*
At root: an ordinary seaman. As a generic first name, *Jack Frost* The
personified figure of winter and cold. And see *jackanapes*, Vol. I.

In a third sense, something common, and serviceable, but less
than ideally desirable. A rough and ready thing. So *jackboot*. A
heavy boot that can be drawn up over the knee, though often worn
folded below it. When applied to animals and plants, implies a
coarse, inferior species, as *jackass* 1. A male ass/donkey. [*Jack*,
here, for "male."] 2. A stupid, often loud, person. And so *jackdaw,
jack mackerel, jack rabbit*. Also *Jack Mormon Among Mormons
(and generalized)*. A Mormon who professes the faith but does not

observe its rules and restrictions. [One who runs from the "straight and narrow" like a jack rabbit in brush.]

In gambling. One of four playing cards in the standard deck. Earlier called a *knave.* **one-eyed jack** Two of the knaves are portrayed almost full-face, with both eyes visible. The jacks of hearts and spades are portrayed in profile, with only one eye showing. In frivolous games of poker, one-eyed jacks are sometimes designated as wild cards. *jackpot In draw poker.* A hand that can be opened only if the declarer holds a pair of jacks (or better). Since several rounds may be dealt and passed for lack of such an opening, and since the players ante each time the deal is passed, a jackpot is likely to come to more money than an average hand. Thus *hit the jackpot* To win a large pot. (Whence the use of the term with ref. to slot machines, to signify the "big win.") [*Pass the buck* is a related idiom. In common early poker playing (and still surviving) the winner of a jackpot was given a marker (the buck), indicating that when he next dealt, he was required to deal a jackpot. The buck was passed to him, and if he chose to, he could pass it to the player on his left.]

jack light A light for luring deer into range of a hunter, for deer are attracted to such a light source. Hence *to jack deer* To hunt deer in this way. The practice is illegal in most states, perhaps in all, and subject to heavy penalties.

hijack v. To stop a moving vehicle and commandeer it, steal it, or take goods from it. —*n.* The act of so doing. [Origin in dispute. Some refer it to *jacking deer,* but hijacked vehicles are forced rather than lured. *To jack* has long had the sense "to raise" (see *jack up,* below). By association perhaps, "to cause to raise one's hands," as in a stickup. And to do so on a highway. Whence (perhaps?) to *highway-jack.* But no such form has been attested, and this suggested derivation can only be speculated, not asserted.] Whence the recent *skyjack* To commandeer an aircraft in flight and divert it to a destination specified by the *skyjacker(s).*

And variously: *jack up* 1. To raise physically, as by a tire jack. 2. To raise the price. 3. To boost someone's spirits. 4. *Rare.* To steal. *"I jacked them up for their wallets and their watches," said the endearing boy who had suffered a bad family background.* (Sometimes *jack off.*) *jacks* A child's game consisting of picking up small objects (*jacks,* in the sense "whatchamacallits") between various ritual acts of bouncing and catching a ball. *jack* An ensign (subordinate to the national flag) flown at the bow of a ship to indicate national origin. *the Union Jack.* *yellowjack* 1. Such a jack flown to indicate contagion aboard ship. It requests medical aid, or signifies that the ship is in quarantine. 2. Yellow fever. A once commonly fatal disease spread by mosquitoes. [Sailing crews in tropical and semitropical ports often broke out with yellow fever, thereupon flying the yellowjack, as above. The ensign and the reason for flying it then came to share the same name.]

jailbird 1. One behind bars. [Like a bird in a cage.] 2. One who is habitually in prison. [And perhaps sufficiently explained by "caged behind bars." But in earlier England minor offenders were commonly placed in cages and put on public display. Those "birds" were commonly women adjudged to be immoral, shrewish, or malicious gossips. Men might become "birds" for drunkenness, brawling, profanity, disturbing the peace, or uttering unpopular sentiments.]

jamoke *Street slang.* A punk. A worthless guy on the streets. A chump. [At root: "a jackass." < Brit. slang, *moke*, lit. ass, donkey, but in effect: "person of no consequence." Ult. < Romany *moxio*, ass, donkey. Into Am. as if *jack-moke*, jackass, and contracted to *jamoke.*]

HISTORIC. If this term appears in any listing of Am. slang, I have missed it. Yet it was in common use in the 1970's in a TV series titled *Baretta*, starring Robert Blake.

Romany, the language of the Gypsies, is not commonly recognized as a source of English slang. Yet British Gypsies often worked together with native British rogues, and a number of Gypsy terms have been passed on via thieves' cant. Some of the most common are: *pal, masher, cosh, posh,* the Brit. slang term *narc, shiv,* and also *rum go,* for which see Vol. I.

java Coffee. [After the bags of coffee beans once prominently stenciled JAVA, the place of origin. (Cf. *Mocha.*) P. *Slang* glosses the term as of early XX Canadian origin, and meaning not only coffee, but also tea. In Am. *gimme a cup a' java,* gimme a cup a' coffee. In Am. navy usage, *cup of joe,* prob. by way of an intermediate (but unattested) form "cup of J."]

jejune 1. Lacking substance. (Originally, lacking substance for the body. Hungry.) Whence, metaphorically: 2. Vapid. Inane. (Lacking nourishment for the mind.) Whence: 3. Sophomoric. Inane. Childish. [L. **jejunus,* hungry, unfed. Prefixed *dis-* → L. *disjejunus,* not hungry, fed, well fed. Much altered → OF *disner*, to eat, to dine. → ME *dinen*, to dine. In Eng. the sense "lacking physical nourishment" has receded, to be replaced by "lacking matter for the mind."]

Jesus H. Christ An exuberantly elaborated form of *Jesus Christ* used as an oath or exclam. [I can find no merit in the pointlessly scholarly assertion that the "H" is from the common crucifix rubric *in hoc signo (vincit)*, in this sign he conquers. Slang, and esp. profanity, is commonly prompted to elaborate flourishes for sweet style's sake. *John Public*, a useful personification, soon became John Q. Public, and John Q. Fucking Public. The art of cussing is to sustain and elaborate the rhetorical roll of the profanity. Who would settle for the exclam. *Jesus Christ!* when he could unroll *Jesus H. Christ in the blue-burning, snake-bitten, bone-sucking foothills of perdition?* In the age of Jackson a gale of this sort of exuberance broke upon the American language. It has never blown out entirely, and along its course it blew through the spaces of Mark Twain's mind to become the howling, lusty force of his style.]

jim-dandy *n.* An outstanding person or thing. *The Kid was a jim-dandy.* —*adj.* First-rate. *And they gave him a jim-dandy hanging.* [Am. XIX. Generalized rural. *Dandy* as in *fine and dandy. Jim*, here, as an intensive, as in *jim-cracker*. Akin to *tom* in *tomfoolery*, *jack* as in *crackerjack*. Am. has tried many such compoundings, of which *jim-dandy* and *crackerjack* have become established. Among many that have fallen from use are (c. 1900) *joe-dandy*, *joe-darter*, and *jim-hickey*, the last surviving as *doohickey* for a whatchamacallit.]

john (Lowercase only.) A toilet. (What people named John call a richard.) [In XVIII Am. *Cousin John*, or *cuzjohn*, for Cousin John's Privy. Various histories of Harvard cite the 1735 Harvard College regulation: "No freshman shall mingo against the wall or go into the fellows' cuzjohn," and this seems to be the first attestation. (*Mingo* is from L. *mingo*, I piss, *mingere*, to piss.) The Harvard form is certainly influ. by Brit. university slang *coz, cuz*, which Partridge, *Historical Slang*, defines as "a defecation." Partridge derives the Brit. term from Hebrew *cuz*, a large metal refuse container outside the temple of Jerusalem.

Hebrew was an essential part of the university curriculum, and the sense "refuse container" is readily adaptable to privy, but "large metal container" baffles me, for it was always starving time in Jerusalem, and any large metal object would attract thieves, who could fence the metal for melting down and resale. The Vandals (see *vandal*) seriously damaged the Colosseum to remove from it the large vertical iron bands that once reinforced the stone courses of the outer walls. Perhaps the temple *cuz* was protected by a religious taboo.

Hebrew aside, *coz, cuz,* was a long-established term for cousin, and it rather than the Hebrew seems to be the operative element in the Harvardian *cuzjohn.*]

John Bull   1. The British equivalent of Uncle Sam. Hence: 2. An Englishman.

HISTORIC. The War of the Spanish Succession, 1701–1714, was both bloody and financially ruinous. Dr. John Arbuthnot, 1667–1735, physician, mathematician, and man of letters, attacked it in a series of pamphlets published in 1712, first separately, and then together under the title *History of John Bull.* In this allegorical satire, Arbuthnot attacks the follies of Lord Strutt (Carlos II of Spain), Lewis Baboon (Louis XIV of France), Nicholas Frog (the personified Dutchman), and John Bull (the personified Englishman). The four are presented as foolish neighbors who squander their substance in a series of endless lawsuits. (The first of the five pamphlets was titled "Law Is a Bottomless Pit.")

Arbuthnot's John Bull is depicted as a crusty, blunt, honest fellow who is quick to anger. The British people seemed to like this description of themselves and identified gladly with John Bull.

So enshrined in the Briton's self-estimate, he later emerged as a cartoon figure depicted as a British squire wearing a low top hat, a cutaway coat, britches, boots, and a vest marked like the British flag. (And see *Colonel Blimp,* under *blimp.*)

Johnny Appleseed   An endearing figure of American history. The nickname of John Chapman, born Leominster, Mass., 1774, died near Fort Wayne, Ind., 1845, after almost fifty years of planting apple orchards in the wildernesses of western Pennsylvania, Ohio, and Indiana, as a visionary gift to the settlers who would be advancing into this first western frontier.

HISTORIC. Chapman appeared in western Pennsylvania sometime before 1800, well before there were settlements there, and began to plant apple orchards in suitable glades. He continued his work into Ohio and Indiana up to the time of his death at age 71.

What first stock he brought with him is not known, perhaps no more than a bag of seeds that he germinated in wilderness nurseries. He could not have made trips east for new stock, for he was notably eccentric in dress and manner, and legends of his comings and goings would certainly have multiplied along his trail through the settlements, as they did not.

It follows that he must have germinated his first seeds in isolated places, setting out sprouts, and returning in subsequent years for new stocks from his established plantings. He did not plant trees at random but in well-planned orchards. It was an indefatigable and touching labor, a gentle solitary's gift to those who would come after him.

joint   [In standard Eng., a substantive ("point of jointure/meeting") from the p. p. of *join,* to come together with.] 1. A low, often illegal den. [First attested 1883 by MMM from *Harper's* magazine: "I have smoked opium in every joint in America." And diffused almost immediately into Brit. slang. *What I didn't learn at my mother's knee, I picked up at other low joints.*] 2. A house, apartment, nightclub, suite, etc. Implies expensive decor and furnishings. *He's got a fancy joint on Sutton Place.* 3. In the opposite sense, a dive. *He owns a fly-specked beer joint on the Bowery.*

   case the joint *Criminal slang.* To study a place one plans to rob. [Make a case study of the place.]

   the Joint *Criminal slang.* State prison or the penitentiary. Implies a long-term home away from home, as distinct from a jail. [Because a penitentiary is a meeting place (and trade school) for criminals.]

Jordan almond   (The *l* is silent.) 1. Technically speaking, the Jordan and the Valencia almond are the two common cultivated varieties, once grown primarily in Spain and to a lesser extent in Italy, and now, with new strains, in Israel and California. 2. In common usage, a sugar-glazed toasted almond once used as confetti before confetti turned into inedible bits of colored paper. [Gk. **amugdalē,* almond. L. *amygdala,* OF *amande, almande.* ME *almande.* The almond now cultivated is indigenous to SE Asia. It was introduced into what is now Israel at an unknown date, but in time for XII crusaders to find groves of the trees along the banks of the Jordan. The designation *Jordan* is, it follows, geographical, and follows a common pattern of naming new fruits and other plants after their last known place of origin. The designation is slightly confused by the fact that OF *amande dou jardin* and ME *jardyne almaunde* are at root: "garden almond," i.e., cultivated almond, to distinguish the cultivated species from various wild, bitter European species that are inedible and even poisonous. (Almonds are related to the peach, whose pits contain prussic acid. In WWI schoolchildren collected peach pits and turned them in to be used in the manufacture of poison gas.)

The confusion of *Jordan* and *jardin* is further complicated by the glosses of various Webster's dictionaries which explain *Jordan* as "a proper name." So it is, if the proper name is of the river Jordan. The ref., however, seems to be to a person named Jordan, in whom I can place no faith, on the grounds that his appearance on the scene would outdo coincidence. I have nevertheless searched for him, and have found no trace. Unless the various Webster's dictionaries can identify him, they would do well to re-edit the gloss.]

jot *n.* 1. The least bit. 2. *Obs.* The letter *iota.* (It was earlier also written *jota.*) [< Gk. *iota,* called "the least letter," consisting of a vertical stroke with a dot above it. Hence the associated sense: "least thing."] —*v.* To write hastily and in short form. [A fanciful ext., as if encoding in dots and (vertical) dashes—which is a loose, but passable, description of shorthand.]

not care a jot *Archaic.* Not care the least bit. **nor jot nor tittle** (Archaic but well within the recognition vocabulary of the literate.) Not in the least. [*Tittle* < L. *titulus* (in ME *titel*), a diacritical mark; here, the dot over the *i.* At root, therefore, and with the sense fully expressed = not so much as the stem of the letter *i* nor the dot over it.]

jug Prison. **in the jug** In prison. [But not, as will be commonly supposed, put away in a jug and the mouth corked with a stopper. This "jug" is < Sc. **joug* (prob. akin to *yoke*), an iron (or reinforced wood) yoke or pillory with enclosures for the head and hands. Minor offenders were so clamped and placed on public display.]

HISTORIC. What we call minor offenses, including even petty theft, were commonly capital offenses in earlier England and punishable by hanging or beheading. The *jug* or *joug* was for such offenses as public drunkenness, profanity, brawling, disturbing the peace, malicious gossip, being a public scold, or even for the expression of unpopular sentiments.

jughandle On divided highways, a right-turn loop that re-abuts the highway, usu. at a traffic light, to make possible what is in effect a left turn. [A direct simile. On a road map such a loop looks like the handle of a jug.]

jukebox A coin-operated phonograph with push buttons for making one's selection of records to be played. Early jukeboxes were gaudily decorated and aglow with shifting and flashing lights. They are now much more complicated systems, with remote-control selection boxes placed along the bars and booths of beer joints and diners. [< Gullah *juke* (of untraced African origin), misbehavior, disorderliness, riot. whence late XIX *juke house,* a brothel ("disorderly place"). The jukebox, however, did not appear until c. 1920. In early XX New Orleans, *jass house,* whorehouse, whence *jazz,* because jass houses were the first places that black Dixieland musicians found a chance to play for pay. *Jukebox* is about twenty years later than *jazz* but named after the same association of loud music with bawdyhouses.]

junco The common small North American bird. It is a dark gray with a light gray underside. [L. *juncus,* rush, reed. Via Sp. *junco,* at first with the Latin sense, then applied to the bird by early Spanish settlers because it is light enough to perch on rushes and reeds. Hence, at root: "reed bird."]

jungle [Ult. < Sanskrit **jāngala,* wasteland. Into Eng. from the outposts of Empire in late XVII via the Hindi form *jangal.* As in many languages, "wasteland" implied an uninhabited place, whether desert or forest land.] 1. A dense tropical forest in which predators roam free. 2. Entangled place difficult to pass through. *the jungle of legal procedure.* 3. Place apart from civilized order. *the inner-city jungle.* 4. A trackside encampment of railroad tramps. *hobo jungle.*

  jungle gym An arrangement of uprights and crossbars, as if the skeleton of a large crate, for children at play to climb and swing through, as if they were monkeys in the jungle. As *Junglegym,* a registered trade name coined by the manufacturer.

junk 1. Refuse. Rubbish. 2. Salvageable scrap. 3. Any more or less worthless stuff. 4. *Am. colloq.* The clutter of one's personal possessions. *Pack your junk and go back to California, Ron.* 5. *Narco slang.* Any narcotic, esp. heroin. [In XV nautical usage, *junk* labeled frayed ends of rope (and prob. other worn-out ship's gear), good only for picking apart to use as oakum, or for sale to port scavengers. (See *slush fund.*) All later senses are consonant with this XV usage, the term being regularly dismissed as "of unknown origin."

Which it may be. But there is L. *juncus,* reed, rush. Through the Middle Ages and well into XVI the great halls and passageways of European palaces and castles were not carpeted, but strewn with rushes. Crushed underfoot, these had to be swept out and replaced regularly, prob. in each morning's clean-up. I cannot assert that yesterday's rushes thrown out as this morning's refuse caused a sense transfer from L. *juncus* to Eng. *junk,* but neither can I resist the speculation.]

junkie An addict, esp. one hooked on heroin. [Am. street slang. Dating uncertain. But the common drugs of XIX were opium, morphine, and cocaine. Heroin, a morphine derivate, first used as a painkiller 4 to 8 times more powerful than morphine, did not enter the hospital pharmacy till c. the 1890's. It is unlikely, therefore, that *junk* as a street name for heroin could have come into use before WWI, and it probably did so later.

junk mail Nuisance mail consisting of commercial or charitable solicitations, once sent out in bulk and addressed to "Occupant," the mailman being required to leave one piece at each address. Now commonly personalized by use of computers and word processors, but still junk.

junkman A collector of salvageable odds and ends. As a figure of American mythology, he once rode through American city and suburban streets with a horse and wagon, crying hoarsely, "Junk? Any junk?" He paid pennies for odds and ends he hoped to resell for nickels. His counterpart is now the scavenger truck that drives along collection routes on trash collection day to "garbage pick" (primarily in affluent suburbs) before the garbage truck has collected its loads. **junkyard** A place for storing resalable scrap. Now esp. an automobile graveyard from which people with old cars can cannibalize parts. When equipped with an enormous press for crushing old cars into small blocks, a junkyard can be a lucrative business.

junket   1. A dessert of custardy sweetened milk and curds with rennet. 2. A picnic. 3. Any short festive outing. 4. *Am. only.* A pleasure trip by a congressman or a government official, purportedly on official business, but in fact a vacation trip at government expense.

[These variant senses find a common ground in L. *juncus,* a rush used in weaving baskets (JONQUIL), and by transfer, the basket so woven. The dessert was once packed for sale in small baskets. Picnic food was stored in larger baskets; hence, gala outing, and so by association, any festive trip.]

K

keep your shirt on   Don't get angry. Calm down (and let's talk this over). Be patient a while longer. [All senses derive from the Am. colonial and XIX custom of removing one's shirt before starting a fistfight. Removing one's shirt was not an invariable custom but a common prudence at a time when a homespun shirt was an especially valuable object, not easily replaced. (Because scratches, scrapes, bites, and other skin wounds would heal, whereas a good shirt might be reduced to unwearable tatters.]

ker-   Indo-European stem meaning "to grow, to cause to grow." It is the base of a discrete cluster of words whose kinship is not commonly recognized.

   Kerēs The Greek goddess who causes things to grow, a sort of classical Mother Nature. In L. *Ceres,* originally with a hard *c.* In Eng. with the *c* commonly pronounced as if *s.*

   cereal The main crop grown under the patronage of Kerēs/ Ceres.

   kr- The zero-grade (vowel swallowed) variant form of *ker-*: *increase* Via L. *crescere,* to grow. *crescent* Now said of any sickle moon, whether waxing or waning, but originally specific to a new (growing) moon. And so, in music: *crescendo* At root: "growing (louder)."

   sincere (See Vol. I.) Not, as commonly supposed, < L. *sine cera,* without wax. But < Gk. *sun,* syncopated form of *sum, sym,* with; and stem *ker-,* to grow. Hence "to grow together with (as one unadulterated thing)."

   accrue Which see.

   Cereal is the sincerest accrual of the crescent bounty of Ceres.

kettle: a pretty kettle of fish   *Ironic.* A nasty mess. [As now used implies a gooey mess, as a kettle full of boiled fish. And such a kettle, esp. one filled only with leavings to be scrubbed out, has been asserted to be the root image, it being not at all pretty. And perhaps. But in XIV–XV, a *kittle net* or *kittle* (origin unknown) was a fish trap. A *pretty kittle of fish* would at that time have meant "a fine haul of fish." In feudal England all game and all fishing rights on waters within the manor were reserved to the feudal lord. But feudal England was also hungry, and such *kittles* must have been fair game for poachers. With these as the known facts, the rest must be conjectured, and even conjecturally no one has come up with a satisfactory explanation of the idiom, or of its acquired ironic twist.]

Khayyám, Omar   Widely known as a Persian poet, c. 1100, author of the *Rubáiyát,* the title meaning "the quatrains," the form in which the poems were written. (Persian *ruba,* four; *ruba iyat,* quatrain.) Popularized by the extraordinary translation of XIX English poet Edward FitzGerald. Later translators have accused FitzGerald of taking gross liberties with the original text, but in so doing he created a masterwork of English poetry, which none of the merely accurate have managed to do.

Called the Tentmaker, because the poems are written as if by a wise but uneducated and dissolute artisan, Omar was in fact a scholar-mathematician who pioneered the use of graphic devices to represent and project algebraic functions. Robert W. Marks, *The New Mathematics Dictionary and Handbook,* cites the following quatrain (italics mine) as deriving from Omar Khayyám's work as a mathematician:

> *For "is" and "is not," though with rule and line*
> *And "up and down" by logic I define,*
> *Of all that one should care to fathom,* I
> Was never deep in anything but—wine.

kibitzer   [< Yiddish *kibitsen,* to meddle in the affairs of others. < Ger. *kiebitzen,* to observe; obscurely, by way of some real or imagined folk observation of nature < *Kiebitz,* plover, lapwing. (I do not know the lapwing, but I have kibitzed the plover, never with any sense that it was kibitzing me.] A pest who looks over the shoulder of cardplayers, and who cannot be restrained from commenting until he is bound and gagged, or evicted, or shot as an act of justifiable homicide.

kick tires   [The basic image is of a prospective automobile buyer "inspecting" a car and discussing price. Buyers who are as mechanically ignorant as I am seem to think that to kick the tires and find that they are solid is somehow an appraisal of the car's value. Hence:] 1. To examine an automobile with some thought of making a deal for it. 2. *Generalized*. To think about making a deal. In a recent telephone call, the caller said to me, "We kicked tires on a lot of other possibilities but we followed up in these three areas."

kidnap   To abduct a person. Now implies to abduct and hold for ransom, but the abduction is per se kidnapping, whether or not ransom demands are made. [The second element, -*nap*, is < the Gmnc. stem *napp-*, to seize, the more common variant being *to nab. Kid* for "young child" was well established in XVI, a natural and endearing simile for expressing the friskiness, shagginess, and general smelliness of the run-about young. Hence originally to abduct a child, the form arising in XVII when, before the large-scale development of Negro slavery in the American colonies, there developed a foul trade in abducting children to be sold in the American plantations as indentured servants and laborers, in effect as slaves.]

King Cotton   Cotton as the crop that ruled the economy of the pre–Civil War southern states. [It was first so dubbed in a speech made on the floor of the U.S. Senate in 1858 by James H. Hammond of (I believe, but with some doubt) North Carolina.]

kitty   1. In card games, and esp. in poker, the sum of the antes and all bets on a given hand. 2. A small percentage of each pot set aside as the house cut, or to pay for refreshments. 3. A jar or bowl in which to put money for the musicians. It was once commonly placed on the piano with a sign reading "Feed the Kitty." 4. A restaurant or bar pool into which all tips are thrown to be divided among the servers when the place has closed. [XVIII Brit. *kitty*, with sense 4 above. Dim. form of earlier *kit*, tub.]
    feed/sweeten/fatten the kitty Gambling. To add to the pot by betting. (Not to be confused with *raising/upping the ante*. One feeds the kitty by repeated betting at the stated stakes. To *up the ante* is to increase the size of the stated stakes.)

knight in shining armor   [A survival from the array and panoply of the pure knight of chivalric romance.] 1. *In girls' dreams.* The symbolic figure of male splendor. Mr. Right on horseback with plumes and dazzling armor. 2. *In politics.* An idealistic reformer with a heroic stance. When used by the opposition, implies that the reform candidate is an impractical dreamer, and that no one can be that pure in the first place. Variantly *knight on a white charger.* [*Shining* and *white* are fixed symbols of purity in European myth and religion.]

knock on wood   *From surviving primitive magico-religion.* A formula invoking good luck or (the same thing) averting bad luck. Commonly accompanied by tapping on a wooden object or, in self-deprecation, one's own head, a sufficiently common wooden object. [There is some pious distortion in the common assertion that this phrase means "touch a crucifix." To begin with, one does not *knock* on a crucifix (as if to see if Jesus is home), and *touch* is a poor substitute for *knock.*

Yet there was in earliest times a religious significance in the gesture. Early Greeks are known to have knocked on an oak tree (Gk. *drus*) in order to summon the gods or a specific god. *Drus* is, at root, tree, and akin to *druid,* at root, one who worships trees. The precise forms of such dawn-age rituals are in doubt, but to tap on a tree, especially upon an imposing great tree ("A tree that looks at God all day/ And lifts its leafy arms to pray"?) was once a means of invoking the gods. If they responded favorably, that was good luck.]

knuckle   [A complex evolution from IE *gen-* with senses: 1. To compact. 2. To squeeze into a ball. These developing to: 3. To bend. 4. To project. 5. To strike. The form is based on the zero-grade form *gn-,* with g/k in Gmnc., and suffixed → MLG *knokel,* bodily joint (ankle, knee, elbow, wrist, knuckle), and with these senses borrowed into ME *knokel.* Prob. akin to *knee.*] 1. A finger joint, esp. the joints connecting fingers and palms. 2. *By association.* The fist. 3. The part of a hinge through which the pin passes. [A survival of the root sense: "to project."]

knuckle ball Baseball. An often erratic slow pitch for which the ball is gripped between the thumb and knuckles. Also *knuckler.*

knuckle duster Also *brass knuckles* A thug's weapon consisting of a metal bar with ringlike holes for three or four fingers. The most lethal have projecting knobs, or even spikes, but even plain ones are enough to deliver a punch that can maim or kill.

knuckle down To work hard. [Lit. "to bend to the work." Survival of root sense 3, above.] *knuckle under* To give in (to). To yield under pressure. [Root sense: "to bend (joints of the body)" as in submission.]

give the knuckles to 1. *Slang.* To strike with the fist. 2. *Boys' slang.* To rub hard with the knuckles, esp. along someone's scalp in the boyish torment called *giving (someone) the barber's itch.*

Ku Klux Klan   1. A secret society of night-riding terrorists organized after the Civil War to reassert white supremacy by lynching Negroes. 2. The Knights of the Ku Klux Klan, formally organized in Georgia in 1915 in the image of the earlier society. [Prob. at root: "knights of the (inner) circle," prob. < Gk. *kuklos,* circle, with Klan added for "clan" (blood-related social unit).]

HISTORIC. The circle has been a prominent symbol of the clan. The burning cross (see *fiery cross*) has been its symbolic dire warning. Klansmen have commonly dressed in white sheets with white conical head covers into which eye holes have been cut; this uniform both to ensure anonymity and to inspire terror. Its cabalistic name was also meant to inspire terror.

The Klan once had a powerful following in and around Freehold, N.J. About fifty years ago (I have lost the exact date) N.J. Klansmen held a demonstration in Perth Amboy, inspiring such hatred in the largely immigrant townspeople that a riot broke out in which many Klansmen were brutally lynched, some of their mutilated bodies being stuffed into sewers.

la-di-da *adj.* Airily affected in manner. —*n.* Airily affected speech and manner. *After five minutes of Katharine Hepburn's la-di-da the audience begins to sweat sugar.* [As if one's speech consisted of the la, di, dah refrain of some song—with gestures to match.]

lam¹ To wallop. To thrash. *I'll lam you one.* [< ON *lemja*, to beat, to thrash.]

lam² *Am. slang.* Also **take it on the lam** 1. To get out in a hurry. 2. To escape. [< *lam¹*, prob. influ. by Brit. cricket slang, to hit hard (c. 1855), and Brit. schoolboy slang, same as *lam¹* (c. 1875). The sense shift in Am. slang was from "to beat (someone) hard" to "to beat the ground hard with one's feet in running off."]

lambaste To thrash severely. [*lam¹* (which see) with *baste*, to strike rapidly and repeatedly. Some take *lam* to be < OE *lama*, lame, and explain *lambaste* as "to lame (someone) by rapid and repeated hard blows." But this rendering would be more persuasive if supported by the dating, as it is not, the ON root having passed into ME under IX–X Dane Law.]

lariat *Wstrn. frontier.* A cowboy's throwing rope. In pride of craft, cowboys judged a man by his way of handling a lariat. The true cowboy (see *quirt*) would have nothing to do with "boughten" rope, but wove his own, meticulously, of horsehair, carrying it as a proud and prized possession. [< Sp. *la reata*, the rope. < *reatar*, to bind. < L. *reaptare*, to make apt (for a given purpose) < *aptare*, to arrange for use; with *re-* as intensive prefix.]

lasso (lăs´-oo) *n.* A lariat.—*v.* To use a lariat. *Bill Decker once lassoed a grizzly for breakfast.* [Into wstrn. frontier idiom from Sp. *lazo*, a lariat, but also, and earlier, a snare, a noose. < L. *loqueus*, snare.

At root: "woven loop." Ult. cognate with Eng. *lace,* which is made up of many loops.]

laundry Variously, the act of washing clothes, the place for washing them, the clothes about to be washed, being washed, or freshly washed. [IE *lou-,* wash. With simple u/v and vowel modification → L. *lavare,* to wash. Late L. and Old It. *lavandaria,* OF *lavendier,* ME *launderie,* launder. And see *lavender.*]

lavender 1. Any of a genus of plants related to mint, with pale purple flowers, and yielding an aromatic *oil of lavender.* 2. *Color.* Pale purple.

HISTORIC. *Launder* and *lavender* are anciently associated. Launder is etymologically earlier, but for centuries of drudging, and let us hope loving, domesticity, women have strewn sprigs of dried lavender in the folds of ironed laundry to scent it pleasantly; and this immemorial touch of domesticity gave its name to the plant, lit. "the laundry herb."

lead by the nose To dominate. [In the past, various animals, as half-wild performing bears, were kept in restraint in this way, but the best-known example is certainly the bull with a metal ring in its septum. When a hook attached to a stout stick is passed through the ring, a twist of the stick causes such pain that the beast is rendered docile. In time, the memory of past pain can so condition the animal that a simple rope passed through the ring will dominate it. And so it is that the root image is generally taken to involve a rope rather than a stick and a hook. Isaiah 37:29 specifies a hook, as if through the ring in a bull's nose, but confuses bull and horse, for declamatory effect, by adding a bridle: ". . . therefore will I put my hook in thy nose, and my bridle in thy lips, and I will turn thee back by the way by which thou camest."]

learn 1. To acquire knowledge. [Root sense: "to track down," implying deliberate and systematic pursuit. Ult. < IE *leis,* trail, spoor, to track down. Via Gmnc. with untraced alteration → OE *leornian,* lit. to follow a trail, but with effective sense: "to pursue (track down) knowledge." ME *lernen,* till XIII, also meant "to impart knowledge," now expressed by "to teach," but surviving in dial. and now substandard *to learn (larn) someone a lesson.*] 2. To come upon information by chance. [Usu. with *about* or *of. I learned about/of it by accident.* This sense, though a natural extension, is away from the root sense of deliberate tracking (though, of course, a tracker can pick up any number of side trails along the way.] *learning* n. A body of knowledge.

    book learning Theoretical, academic knowledge, as distinct from hard, practical experience in the competitive rat race. [Always used pejoratively by those who lack it and who pride themselves on having succeeded without "academic frills." These arrogant ignorances usu. vaunt themselves as "self-made men." Most of them might have done better to seek professional advice in their own amateur making. No formula more certainly identifies a smug fool than the one beginning, "I never was much on book learning, but . . ."]

lee   Commonly but not exclusively nautical. n. 1. The side more or less away from the wind. 2. *Nautical only.* Sailing direction away from the wind. Commonly *alee/hard alee.—adj.* Of that sheltered side. *leeward* To (toward) the lee. [IE *kel-*, warm. (→ L. *calor*, heat.) Variantly *klē-, kleu-*, with k/h in Gmnc. → OE *hlēowe*, warm. The simple shift has been from "warm/warm place" to "side sheltered from the wind" (that side being generally warmer than the exposed side). So OE *hlēo*, ME *le*, shelter. The OE form is clearly cognate with ON *hle*, which has the same sense; and also, though without the aspirate, with Du. *lij.*]

left-handed compliment   An insincere or ingenuously awkward compliment that is in fact a derogation. *My ma said to thank you for my dinner. It sure was good, what there was of it, and there was plenty, such as it was.* [A survival of the ancient assumption that right is the side of honor, and left the side of inferiority.]

left-handed monkey wrench   An inane nonesuch by which underdeveloped "old hands" send an ignorant new boob on a wild-goose chase to locate one. Variantly, the new boob is sent for a bed stretcher or a bucket of steam. The person to whom he is sent recognizes the dull joke and refers him to someone else, and that idiot to another, all hands having a belly laugh over the boob's gullibility.

leg: shake a leg   A command to hurry up. To bestir oneself. [Of Brit. nautical origin.]

    HISTORIC. In the early British navy *show a leg* was the boatswain's command to hit the deck for duty muster. The command

in full was *show a leg or a pusser's stocking, pusser,* here, for
woman, just as *puss* is still used as a term of endearment, and slang
pussy for the vaginal sheath. (At root: "furry thing.")

For in XVI and early XVII women sailed with men on both
naval vessels and merchantmen, some as wives, and many as a
subpart of the crew, slinging their hammocks in quarters they
shared with the men. The call, in effect, summoned the men to
deck muster, but allowed the women to remain for a while to
undertake their morning preparations in "privacy." And see *son of
a gun,* under *gun,* Vol. I.

lemon sole   Sole sole. [A root redundancy now firmly established in
the tradition of French restaurants in the U.S. Even good restaurants seem to think this entry on menus written in English implies
a touch of elegance. But *lemon* is a corruption of Fr. *limande,* sole
< L. *limus,* mud, the flatfish being bottom dwellers. (*Mudfish sole*
would be an etymologically sound redundancy, but might be said
to lack something in elegance.)]

Lent   The forty days of mourning that precede Easter in Christian
observance. It begins on Ash Wednesday and ends on Easter Sunday. Devout Roman Catholics abstain from meat during Lent.
They and others commonly vow to "give up" some customary
pleasure in this period (as sex, tobacco, alcohol, cardplaying). [The
English name is at root: "spring" < OE *lengtan, lectan,* to
lengthen, whence, as a substantive, "period when the days
lengthen." In most other European languages, the root sense is:
"the forty days," as in It. *la quarantesma,* the forty (days).]

lesbian   A woman erotically attracted to other women. [< *Lesbos,*
the Greek island on which Sappho, the great Greek poetess of VII
B.C., and a lesbian, lived and wrote, away from men, in the company of her retinue of ladies.]

HISTORIC. Lesbian activists reject the label *homosexual,* insist-
ing that it labels male-male eroticism. Whatever their public
relations point, it is made in ignorance of the language, for it
takes *homo* as if from L. *homo,* man. *Homo* is in fact from Gk.
homos, the same, and the antonym is not *femmesexual* but
heterosexual < Gk. *heteros,* other. A homosexual is one erotically
attracted to his or her own sex. (*Sexual* < L. *sexus,* of unknown
origin.)

lily: gild the lily   To elaborate pointlessly. [Am. Well established in XIX but with no firm first dating available. This absurd idiom of gilding, gold-leafing, or spray-painting a lily is a corruption of Shakespeare, *King John,* IV. ii: "To gild refinèd gold, to paint the lily." Shakespeare intended two images of absurdity: to go to pains to make pure gold purer, and to paint the lily in an effort to make its perfect whiteness yet whiter. The now established Am. idiom redoubles absurdity by collapsing the two metaphors into one.]

limousine   Before the advent of the *airport limo* (which turns out to be either a shuttle bus or a cab that takes multiple passengers, each paying a fare for, usu., being crowded too close by greed), a long chauffeur-driven automobile with elegant appointments, especially in the rear seat(s). As such, a symbol of opulence. In early XX an open touring car, later equipped with a folding top, and still later with a fully enclosed, spacious rear compartment, the roof of which did not extend over the chauffeur's seat, an obvious class distinction. [The name implies "covered," by ref. to a long flowing black cape once commonly worn by the people of *Limousin,* a former French province just west of central France. Limoges is in the region still called Plateaux du Limousin.]

lion's share   The largest and choicest part. [From the Aesopian fable in which the lion goes hunting with weaker companions. In the original, the lion took half of the kill because he was the lion, and a quarter for his mate and her cubs. That left one quarter available to anyone who would fight him for it, and since no one dared, the lion's share was, effectively, all of it. The error by which "all" became "most" remains unexplained, and a purist might fairly insist on using the idiom in its original sense, but the error has long been so firmly established that purity would only lead to confusion. As a reasonably Aesopian moral: "Don't be so right that you will be misunderstood."]

liquid   *n.* One of the three basic forms of matter, a substance whose molecules flow more or less freely in relation to one another, hence unlike a solid, but without tending to expand indefinitely, like a gas.—*adj.* 1. *Lit.* Having the qualities of a liquid. 2. *Metaphoric exts.* (*a*) Moistly smooth. Limpid. *liquid eyes.* (*b*) Free-flowing. *liquid sounds, music, versification.* (*c*) Readily available. *liquid assets.* [One of the choicest fossil poems of the language. IE *leik-wo-,* to go away. → L. *liquere,* to be liquid, to make liquid.

Hence the root sense: "that form of matter that goes away." A liquid may "go away" by flowing (and that is prob. the primary sense). It may also go away by evaporation, by percolation, or in the way bourbon disappears from my bottle; and if "to flow" is the primary, these other "goings away" are consonant ambiguities, as in a good poem.

With a nasal infix and *de-* prefix → L. *delinquere,* to be delinquent. And delinquency, too, is a form of going away (from desirable norms).

Then, because the language needed other labels → *liquor* An alcoholic beverage (what daddy goes away on at times). And the Fr. form of the same word: *liqueur* After-dinner drink, usu. of low alcoholic content but highly flavored. *Bon voyage.*]

loafer 1. An idler. 2. A low, slip-on shoe resembling a moccasin but with finished uppers and stitched-on soles like those of a shoe. [Originally *Loafer,* a registered trade name, post WWI.] *loaf* To loiter idly. [The verb form is first attested in England in Joseph Neal, *Charcoal Sketches,* 1838. Dickens uses it in *Martin Chuzzlewit,* and by mid XIX it had become common in Am. The original Eng. form is *loafer,* based on Ger. *laufen,* to run, a seemingly strange sense reversal, except for the intermediate Ger. *Landlaüfer* (Du. *landlooper*), lit. "one who runs about the countryside," but with effective sense "tramp, hobo." The *Landlaüfer* did not run through the countryside, but idled about through it without working, looking for what he could find to feed his idleness; and with this intermediate sense understood, the sense of Eng. *loafer* is sweetly consonant.]

loll To lounge about. To be idle. [Much altered from the root sense: "to be forever muttering prayers," whence "to be pious," whence "to be a pious hypocrite." ME *lollen* was taken intact from the Du. with the sense "to mutter," of echoic origin, as if forever saying "lo-lo" or "la-la."

Lollard In XIV–XV Britain, a follower of John Wycliffe (died 1384, aged about 60), English clergyman and Bible translator. But the name is from Du. *lollaerd,* mutterer; effective sense: pious person forever muttering prayers; and in ext. "pious hypocrite." The derivation of *dunce* from the name of John *Duns* Scotus is a similar case. (See Vol. I.) The name was originally applied, c. 1300 A.D., to Dutch sectarians, the *lollebroeder,* the (piously) muttering brothers, who were satirized in England as *the Flemish Beghards.*

Lollard is first attested in a sermon delivered in 1382 to denounce the doctrines of Wycliffe, then still alive.]

HISTORIC. Wycliffe is remembered for his translation of the Vulgate into Middle English, a work in support of his belief that the faithful should have access to Scripture without clerical mediation of the Hebrew, Greek, and Latin texts. He also believed that laymen should be permitted to preach, that the English church should be independent of the Vatican, and that many elements of the Mass were idolatrous, necromantic, and an offense to the spirit of Christ. His followers even opposed the insistence on virginal nuns, believing that celibacy led only to hypocrisy and abortion.

In Roman Catholic medieval England, Wycliffe was a proto-Anglican, and even a proto-Protestant, who extolled the individual conscience as superior to dogmatic decree. He won substantial support from laymen but the enmity of orthodox clerics, who denounced and persecuted his followers as heretics. (It cannot be said that he simply lolled about.)

lollipop/lollypop   1. A piece of hard candy on a stick. A sucker. An all-day sucker. [Generalized Brit. dial. *lolly*, tongue; with *pop*, thing put (popped) into the mouth.] 2. *In sticky ext.* A term of endearment for "sweet thing." *John Williams is a lollipop with a boozy breath.*

long gone   Sthrn. dial., now widely diffused colloq. Out of reach. [The original sense was "left so long ago as to be beyond pursuit." So in sports: *Had Franco Harris had one more step on the tacklers, he would have been long gone* = he would have been beyond all pursuit and would have scored a touchdown. So in baseball: *That ball is long gone* = it is a home run, i.e., out of reach. And so, from the dialogue of Late Late Show big-house movies: *Once I get over that wall, I'll be long gone* = beyond pursuit and recapture. (Ha!)]

loon   1. A fish-eating, freshwater diving bird of subarctic and north-moderate latitudes. [In XV *loom* < ON *lomr*, at root: "creature (bird) that cries out." Ult. < IE *la-*, an echoic base widely dispersed in words referring to animal calls. So L. *latrare*, to bark. And perh., though uncertainly, in the third syllable of *ululate*. But early associated with Sc. *lown* and dial. *loun*, fool, oaf, clown, deranged person. Whence:] 2. A deranged or foolish person. [In part, by association with *loony* for *lunatic*. But:] *crazy as a loon* Wildly and noisily demented. [Because the call of the loon, heard most commonly across lake water, beginning at twilight and repeated at intervals during the night, is a long, eerie wail, followed by a sort of yodel, followed by what sounds, to human ears, like maniacal laughter.]

lord 1. The master of a household. [The form is the etymological equivalent of *lady* (Vol. I). *Lady* is at root: "she who kneads the bread," hence "she who has the keys to the larder (in which the flour is stored)," hence "mistress of the house." *Lord* is, similarly, "guardian of the bread (food)," with the effective sense: "master of the house, manor, fief." In OE *hlāfweard* < *hlāf*, bread (LOAF); with *weard*, custodian, guardian (WARDEN, WARDER). ME *loford, lord.*] 2. A title of nobility. [At root: "master/ruler of a fief." In the linked structure of feudalism, one to whom feudal underlings pledge service and loyalty, he in turn pledging his to his liege lord, and all finally pledging themselves to the king as sovereign lord.]

lord and master [A redundancy that has become a fixed formula.] 1. The dominant male. 2. *Now more or less mockingly, but XIX–early XX.* A husband. *the Lord* God. *House of Lords* A British gentlemen's club. The titular upper chamber of Parliament, consisting of peers of the realm, though now all but powerless in contrast to the House of Commons. *lord of the manor* 1. *Earlier.* The ruler of a fief. 2. *Now.* The owner of an estate. 3. *More or less mockingly.* The lord and master of a household.

lord it over To display one's position and power by forcing underlings to be deferential.

lout A clumsy oaf. A dull-witted inferior person; inferior, that is, by the reckoning of the old caste system. [Of lost Gmnc. origin. The stem *lut-* occurs in ON *lutr*, bent, stooped over, and in *luta*, to bow, to stoop. Hence, as a substantive, an inferior person ("one who bows"). The root image is of a heavy-handed field worker bowing and scraping before a lord (the lord graciously condescending to feel superior). OE *lutan*, ME *lutien, louten*, to bow. So obs. verb *lout*, to bow and scrape (and tug the forelock). So Chaucer, *The Monk's Tale:* "To which image both yonge and olde/Commanded he to lout and have in dread." So Shakespeare, *1 Henry VI:* "And I am louted by a traitor villain."]

love *In tennis.* Zero. No score. [A simple and undramatic extension from *love* with the sense "nothing." So *all for love, not for love nor money, love's labor lost.*]

HISTORIC. A common spook etymology asserts this term to be from Fr. *l'oeuf,* the egg, prob. by association with Am. slang *goose egg* for "zero." But French has never used *egg* in this sense. (Chrétien de Troyes does have "not worth an egg," but the sense here is akin to Hamlet's "Exposing all that fame and fortune dare/ Even for an eggshell," i.e., merest trifle.) Nor would *l'oeuf* be the natural French form. *Un oeuf* would be more likely (if at all), which (still supposing) might have passed into English as something like *nine, new,* or *nuff.* The fact is that French has always used *zéro* in tennis scores, counting *zéro-quinze, zéro-trente,* etc. The spook etymology is perhaps a bit more dramatic than the true one, and pretends to a more learned awareness of language, but spook etymologists always prefer drama and false learning to the truth.

lucre   Ill-gotten wealth. Hence the fixed phrase *filthy lucre* Money. [Note that an insolvent person is said to be "cleaned out," and that the rich are commonly said to be "filthy with money."

Ult. < IE *lau-,* usually rendered as "gain, profit." But the root was formed before money was used as a medium of exchange. (See *peculiar.*) The early measure of wealth was by heads of livestock. The IE root, therefore, must have meant in first usage: 1. Increase of flocks and herds. 2. Booty, plunder. (Whence prob. the sense of "evil gains.") *Lau-,* suffixed *-kr-,* emerges as L. *lucrum,* monetary gain (LUCRATIVE), whence ME *lucre,* money, long stigmatized as the "root of all evil." So. L. *radix malorum est pecunia,* money is the (filthy) root of all evil.]

lugger   A fishing or coastal sailing vessel having two or three masts with trapezoidal *lugsails* attached at the top to a spar fixed obliquely to the mast. Lugsails have no yard at the bottom, but are secured by long sheets attached to cleats. A lugger also carries two or three jibs. [*Lugger* does not appear in Eng. until XVIII, about a century after *lugsail,* and some have speculated that the name derives from *lug,* to haul. But this form of sail was called in XV and XVI a *bonaventure,* good luck sail; and in Fr. *voile de fortune,* luck sail. I have been unable to find why these sails were so associated with luck, but the precedents indicate that *lug* is a corruption of *luck.*]

lunger   1. In XIX Am. and up to the virtual conquest of tuberculosis and the closing down of sanitaria for the tubercular (was that c. 1950 or slightly earlier?): One who suffered from a respiratory ailment, esp. from tuberculosis. But in street slang: 2. A wad of phlegm, conceived as being hawked up from the very lungs. ***hawk a lunger*** To bring up such phlegm with a deep, guttural rasp. [*Hawk*, here, as in *to hawk*, to peddle in the streets in the deep, hoarse voice of a pitchman.]

macho [Sp. < L. *masculus,* male.] *adj.* 1. Virile. 2. Overassertively virile. —*n.* A man who makes a display of his virility. *He is into playing the big macho.* Also **machismo.**

malady Ailment. Disease. [Many have been prompted, on surface evidence, to see this term as a reversal of dismal < L. *diēs malī,* bad days (see *dismal,* Vol. I), as if < *malī diēs,* but the evolution is quite separate. Ult. < IE *ghabh-,* to give, to receive. With g/h, prob. in Italic → L. *hab-, habere,* to have, to own, to be in possession of ("to receive what is given"). P. p. *habitus,* held, owned. Whence L. *male habitus,* in possession of evil, ailing. Then, by an unattested contraction in Medieval L., and with b/d → It. *maladia,* illness. And so OF *maladi,* ME *maladie.* The final syllable resembles Old It. *di,* day; which survives as the final syllable of the names of the days of the week, as in It. *lunedì,* Fr. *mardi.* It is possible, therefore, that the Medieval L. contraction and consonant shift was influenced by some form of L. *malī diēs,* but in the absence of firm evidence, one can only speculate.]

manure Animal (or chicken) dung used to enrich soil (after a year or so of storage, in which the acids are leached out; variantly—but why?—the stuff may be spread fresh from the source and the field left fallow for a year). *A gentleman farmer is one to the manure born.* [Root sense: "work of hand." Closely cognate with *maneuver,* work of hand < Medieval L. *manu operari,* to work by hand. OF *manoeuvrer.* ME *manouren, manour.* Not necessarily with the implication "spread by hand" (though the true farmer does not disdain to get his hands dirty) but because tillage and husbandry are works of hand; and in one sense, to spread manure with a spade or fork is a work of hand.]
    horse manure! 1. Nonsense. [Worthless stuff. (Though no countryman would dismiss manure as worthless. And as a suburbanite,

I buy it expensively in dehydrated, pelletized, fortified, vitamin-ized, USDA-enriched form.)] 2. Exclam. of derision, disbelief, indignant rejection. [Am. Dating uncertain. Prob. in colonial use. And cf. the ruder forms *horse shit!* and *bull shit!* with identical senses.]

Marathon   A plain of about 10 square miles on the northeast coast of Attica, approx. 24 miles from Athens. [So called because it is covered with wild fennel, called in Gk. *marathon.*] There in 490 B.C. the outnumbered Greeks under Miltiades managed to exploit a compound series of errors by the invading Persians. An unknown Greek ran to Athens with news of the victory. Some attribute the run to Pheidippides, a famous athlete, but he was in Sparta, to which he had run (a considerably greater distance) the day before to seek aid against the Persians. The aid could not possibly have reached Marathon in time. I do not understand why the Greeks did not think to send a man on horseback, though the road was rocky and Greek horses were not shod—or even a relay of horses —but the whole action at Marathon was a blundering improvisation.

marathon   1. A long-distance road race. The most famous of such races is the Boston Marathon, run annually since 1897 on April 19 over a distance that is now set at 26 miles 385 yards. This distance was established by the British Olympic Committee in 1908, when the Olympic marathoners started at Windsor Castle and ran to the Olympic Stadium, a distance of 26 miles, to which the committee added 385 yards in order to place the finish line in front of King Edward's royal box. The "Edwardian" distance is now the commonest, though marathons in other parts of the world are so varied in length that no world records are kept for this event. 2. Anything that goes on at great length.

marble   1. A form of limestone made dense and crystalline by deep earth pressures and heat. It is either white, or tinted and streaked by mineral admixtures. Marble takes a high polish, and has been prized for the facings of stone buildings, and for sculpture. 2. A plaque, monument, gravestone, or sculpture of marble. *the Elgin marbles.* 3. A small ball of stone or clay conceived to resemble marble, esp. in the child's game of lagging such balls to a line or at a glassy. 4. *By analogy to "small ball."* A testicle. [A complex evolution from IE *mer-*, to rub, to seize. Via Gmnc. → ON *mar,* incubus ("creature that seizes and grates the soul of a sleeper").

And so the *mare* of Eng. *nightmare.* And also OE *mearu,* soft ("that which is easy to grasp and rub").

Via Hellenic the same stem yields Gk. *marmaros,* stone ("thing that can be seized by hand," and perhaps also "thing to be rubbed smooth, as in sculpture"). But influ. by Gk. *marmairein,* to shine; whence the sense shift from "stone in general" to "marble" ("the stone that shines"). And so L. *marmor,* OF *marbre,* ME *marbre.*]

lose one's marbles To become mentally deficient. **not have all one's marbles** To be mentally deficient [See sense 4, above. With *marbles* for testicles, a man who has lost a testicle is "not all there," and "not all there" means "mentally deficient."]

go for all the marbles To be a high-roller. To risk all in the hope of winning all. In slang, to go for broke. [See sense 3, above.]

to marble To mark with curving striations. **marbled** So marked. *With ref. to meat.* So marked by streaks of fat, normally a sign of tenderness.

to marbleize Same as to marble.

martinet A harsh and inflexible disciplinarian. One who goes strictly "by the book," making no allowances for individual human urgencies or possibly exonerating circumstances. [Originally with exclusive ref. to military discipline, but early extended to any situation in which a robot is given controlling power. Eponymous. Fr. XVII. After General Jean Martinet, who introduced and rigorously enforced inflexible regulations for officers and men under his command.]

martyr 1. One who clings to a religious belief against all persuasion of torture and death. 2. *Ext.* One who sacrifices all (or at least much) to support any cause, esp. one who dies for the cause. 3. *Loose ext.* One who professes to endure great suffering for the good of others. *Everyone has at least one aunt who is a professional martyr.* [< Gk. stem **martur-, martos,* witness. Then in the Latin of Christian writers to describe those who died for the faith, *martyr,* at root: "Witness to Christ." In It. *martiri,* suffering.]

masher A man who habitually solicits women for sexual favors. [We have the term, via Brit. thieves' slang, from Romany, the language of the Gypsies, in which *masha* signifies "fascinating person," a trickster who is good with a spiel and at winning confidence.]

mater   (Pronounced mā́-ter or mä́-ter.) Mother. [Rare in Am. L. *mater*, mother. < Gk. *metra*, womb.]
  mater dolorosa (Second pronunciation only.) The Virgin Mary as the bereaved mother. [L., sorrowful mother.]
  alma mater (*Mater* takes either pronunciation.) [L., step-mother.] A nostalgic name for one's college as a kindly intellectual stepmother, if Am. colleges may yet be said to deal in intellect.
  And cognate *matrix* Plu. *matrices* 1. That which contains and gives shape to, as a casting mold. [As above, < Gk. *metra*.] 2. *Mathematics.* An array of numbers or symbols in horizontal rows and vertical columns.

mawkish   [Root sense: "infected, maggoty." Ult. < IE *math-*, vermin, growing and teeming thing (MOTH). Via Gmnc. → ON *mathkr*, small vermin. Transmitted to ME during IX–X Dane Law as *mawke*, maggot. In XVII, nauseating, nauseated. In XVIII, inanely sentimental.] *adj.* Nauseating. Cloying. Offensively tasteless. Insipid. Jejune. [But with ref. only to conversation, opinions, manners, the earlier specific ref. to spoiled food having receded from the word.]

meat-and-potatoes   *adj.* Basic. Cf. post-WWII *gut*, as in *gut issues*. **meat and potatoes** *n.* The basic issue(s) at stake. "Herein lies the real meat and potatoes of the political process."—Duluth *Budgeteer*, Oct. 15, 1980. [Am. Dating uncertain. An established metaphor. As meat and potatoes are conceived to be the basis of all diets, so as a figure for the core of any issue.] **let's get down to meat and potatoes** Let's get down to the basic facts. Let's talk turkey.

medicine   [Ult. < IE *mē-*, measure, to measure (METER, METRONOME, MEASURE). Variant *med-*, to take appropriate measures. Hence the root sense: "the science of taking appropriate measures concerning one's health."] 1. The variously practiced art/science of the diagnosis and treatment of diseases, and of their prevention. 2. *By analogy.* Any dosage used in treating disease. 3. *Among Amerinds and other tribal peoples.* A benign or evil spirit power affecting the well-being of an individual or a tribe.
  big medicine / strong medicine As in sense 3. A powerful daemonology.
  medicine man 1. In many tribal cultures, the priest/magician/healer whose spells and incantations are supposed to control the daemon forces that threaten individual well-being and the affairs

of the tribe. *Medicine man* is most commonly used with ref. to Amerind tribes; *witch doctor,* with ref. to other tribes, esp. African. In either form, this priest is a survivor from the earliest rites of black and white magic, and usu. believed to be able to lay on evil spells and to counter or remove them. 2. *Am. XIX.* A traveling quacksalver.

   medicine ball *Body building.* A large, soft, heavy ball thrown from one exerciser to another, primarily to be caught in the belly to tone stomach muscles (or at least to bruise them).

   take one's medicine 1. *Lit.* To swallow a medical dosage. [Until recently (within my lifetime) many medicines were prepared in powdered form, a single dosage being measured out into a small paper envelope. This powder, often bitter, was dissolved in water (or simply put into a glass of water and stirred without dissolving) and gulped down as best one could endure the bitterness. Hence:] 2. To face up to the bitter consequences of one's actions, presumably for one's own good.

medicine show   A wandering quacksalver's pitch for public attention. Medicine men in XIX Am. favored garishly painted wagons and an outlandish companion or two, often an Indian (said to know mysterious medicines), or a tumbling dwarf, or an unemployed circus clown. These tumbled, juggled, and variously attracted a crowd, to whom the medicine man would make his pitch for his elaborately labeled bottles of cure-alls.

   The price of such bottles was commonly $1, at a time when land could be bought for 25¢ an acre. And they usually sold fast, great-grandmother saving her butter and egg money to buy them by the clutch, knowing that the medicine would make her feel better. And it would, for she was commonly though unknowingly addicted to the narcotics common in such mixtures, and every junkie feels good when he has a fix.

   For before the Pure Food and Drug laws of the 1890's and later, there was no systematic control of the substances one could put into a usually alcoholic liquid thereupon called a "medicine." Nor was there any control of the claims one might make for the stuff. A commonest admixture was laudanum (opium dissolved in alcohol). Morphine was another common additive. The predecessor of Coca-Cola, called French Wine Coca (see *dope,* Vol. I), used cocaine as a stimulant, though in 1896 the present Coca-Cola Company, having acquired manufacturing rights, changed the stimulant to caffeine. The Sears, Roebuck catalogue for 1897 offered "tincture of laudanum" in a 4-ounce bottle for 28¢, $3 a dozen. (A dozen would equal a quart and a half of the stuff, but laudanum became a prescription medicine in 1898.)

The regulation of false claims came later. The Sears catalogue continued to make shameless claims for its patent medicines. The 1902 catalogue offered "A perfectly safe and reliable cure of the Opium and Morphia habit," a true quacksalver's pitch (and also evidence of the widespread use of narcotics in XIX America). The size of this "kick-the-habit" bottle is not specified, but the catalogue copy adds: "cannot be sent by mail on account of the weight."

mess   [L. *mittere,* to set in place. P.p. *missus,* set in place (commonly, though not exclusively, as a meal or a course of a meal is set in place on the table). Prob. ult. < IE *(s)meit-,* to throw (TRANSMIT). ME *mes,* a meal, a dish of food, a group of people, as soldiers and sailors, who habitually eat together (MESSMATES).] *n.* 1. A meal. 2. Enough food for a meal. *a mess of fish.* 3. A disorderly condition. *This room is a mess.* [By association with the litter left on a table after a meal.] 4. A military or naval group that eats together. *Officers' mess.* (Also the place of eating.) —*v.* 1. *In military and naval usage.* To eat a meal. 2. *Nursery.* To have a bowel movement. [See noun sense 3.]

mess about/around To putter. To stir aimlessly. [As the scraps of a meal while one lingers at table.] **mess around with** 1. To have to do with aimlessly. 2. To associate with ill-chosen companions. **mess up** 1. To make a muddle of. 2. To batter. *A thug messed up his face.* **don't mess with me** Leave me alone. **mess jacket** A semiformal, close-fitting, waist-length jacket. Once commonly worn by naval officers at formal mess.

HISTORIC. To my knowledge, R. C. Trench, *Dictionary of Obsolete English,* is alone in pointing out that *mess* once meant "a group of four persons or things." Trench speculates that "in the distribution of food to large numbers it was found most convenient to arrange them in fours."

Whether or not Trench's speculation is valid, his citations establish this sense conclusively. A *mess* at the Inns of Court consisted of four. A phrasebook published in London in 1617 bears the title *Janua Linguarum Quadralingus, or A messe of Tongues, Latine, English, French, and Spanish.* Trench further cites a XVII sermon: "There lacks a fourth thing to make up the mess." Also, Shakespeare, *3 Henry VI,* I. iv: "Where are your mess of sons to back you now?" (the ref. being to the four sons Edward, George, Richard, and Edmund). He also cites from Fuller, *A Pisgah Sight of Palestine* (which I have been unable to locate and date, but guess to be XVII): "Among whom [converted Jews] we meet with a mess of most eminent men." [Whereupon four are mentioned.]

Mexican stand-off A potentially violent confrontation from which both sides, being equally matched, back off. [*Stand-off* is the earlier term. *Mexican*, a racial slur implying that Mexicans will not fight unless they have a clear advantage in numbers and arms, was added in mid XIX by southwestern American cowboys, as part of their generalized contempt for Mexicans. Cf. *Irish bull*, under *bull*,[2] Vol. I.]

milestone 1. A stone highway marker incised with the number of miles to or from a given place. 2. *Ext.* Any significant event in the affairs of a nation, an organization, or a life.

HISTORIC. Since all roads were said to lead to Rome, Augustus caused to be set up in the Forum a base-stone marker called a *milliarium*, of the thousand, and distances along the highways were measured from it, stone markers being placed along the highways every thousand paces *(mille passuum)* and numbered outward consecutively. These stones were placed every 5,000 feet, very nearly the distance of the modern mile. Five feet will hardly do for a man's pace. The Romans must have intended a horse's pace, though even that seems a brisk clip for an unshod horse (the Romans had no horseshoes) over rutted stone roads.

mini [< *minimum*. A dress designer's fad term of the 1960's, applied to brief skirts. Whence *maxi* < *maximum*, for full-length skirts.] *mini-skirt* First, an above-the-knee skirt, soon followed by the crotch-height skirt to be worn with panty hose. "If they get any shorter, girls will have to wear their hair in an up-do and powder their cheeks." —Attributed to Bob Hope one night when he was cut off the air.

mini-series TV. A series of special, and usu. highly touted, programs, planned to run for less than a full season. "NBC . . . broadcast its multimillion-dollar 'Shogun' miniseries the week of Sept. 15." —Chicago *Tribune*, Oct. 12, 1980. [And so the *Trib.* I believe the form is better hyphenated as mini-series. *Miniseries*, almost crying to be pronounced *min-is´-e-rēs*, is too likely to *mizle* (which see) the reader.]

minus   [L., less.] *prep.* 1. Less. 4−3 = 1. 2. *Colloq.* Lacking. Without. *He found himself minus his wallet.* —*adj.* 1. *Mathematics.* A negative quantity; a quantity less than zero. 2. Low in a given scale. *a grade of B minus.* —*n.* 1. The minus sign. 2. A negative quantity. 3. *Colloq.* A disadvantage. *His manners are a social minus.* [In Renaissance mathematics written $\overline{\text{min}}$., the overlining indicating that the form was an abbreviation. In written mathematics, then, the *min.* was deleted and the overline became a dash. The symbol − was first used in print in a book on mathematics by Johann Widman, *Behende und hübsche Rechnung,* Leipzig, 1489.]

miracle   1. A benign supernatural intervention in human affairs. [L. *miraculum* has the sense: "thing to wonder at," but the ult. stem is IE *(s)mei-,* to smile (upon). Orthodox religious thinking in the Judeo-Christian tradition has always treated miracles as benign supernatural interventions. When a supernatural damnation thunders down, as in the destruction of Sodom and Gomorrah, that is not discussed as a miracle but as an example of God's wrath. Miracles are the work of a smiling God. In early (and perhaps surviving, but I don't know) procedures for canonization, a minimum of three miracles must be proven to be the work of the candidate saint. Even by canon law, how does one prove the impossible three times without the help of a smiling God?] 2. A chance or coincidence within the possible permutations of chance, but so unlikely as to seem miraculous. 3. *Loose ext. but implicit in L.* miraculum. A thing to marvel at.
    miracle play Variantly **morality play** A pious medieval drama based on the lives of the saints, who always arise in glory from martyrdom while various fiends and evil pagan tyrants rant and bluster and are overthrown.

mizle   (Pronounced mĭ´-z'l.) To lead astray. To lead up the garden path. To deceive. [A common arch form based on the deliberate mispronunciation of *misled. He mizled and bed-raggled her.* Compare such joke forms as: *No, doctor, I've never been X-rayed, but I've been bed-ridden and ultra-violated.*]

modicum   1. A small amount. *a modicum of saffron.* 2. A minimum observance. *a modicum of respect.* 3. The least trace. *There is not a modicum of truth in him.* [< L. *modus,* measure, *modicum,* a short measure of quantity or of time. The sense "brief period of time" has receded from Eng. *modicum,* but was securely part of the L. sense. In Am. we do not say, "I'll be with you in a modicum (short while)." Yet in the Vulgate, Christ says to his disciples, foreseeing the crucifixion and the resurrection: *"Modicum et non videbitis me, et iterem modicum et videbitis me."* A little while and you shall not see me, and again a little while and you shall see me.]

mogul 1. A powerful person. 2. *Ski parlance.* A small mound of snow on a ski course. [Root sense: "heap." Ult. < IE *muk-*, a heap. (Whence Sc. and dial. *muckle*, much. *Many a mickle makes a muckle.*) With k/g in Gmnc. → OE *muga, muha*, heap of grain. Via same evolution, and with *l* as a dim. suffix → ON *mūgl*, little heap, whence the skiing sense.

   The word has often been presumed to be of Oriental origin because in 1526 Baber conquered most of India, founding a vast Moslem empire. He was known in the West as the *Great Mogul* ("the super heap"?).] In Am. almost exclusively in the alliterative form *movie mogul.*

mold [IE *med-*, to measure, a measure. → L. *modus*, measure, means of measuring; dim. form *modulus* → OF *modle*, and with a metathesis → ME *molde*, a matrix.] *n.* A matrix. It gives form to a plastic substance poured into it and left to harden. —*v.* 1. To shape in such a matrix. 2. To form into a particular shape according to the matrix one selects. 3. *Generalized ext.* To give form to in any sense. To train someone's character. *Horatio Alger's father, in molding him to fundamentalist religious principles, drove him from neurosis to psychosis.* Not to be confused with stamping an image upon metal with an intaglio die, as in coining, and by ext., in giving form to.]

   God (nature) made him and then broke the mold Asserts that the person referred to is unique and that his like will not be seen again. So the common Italian eulogy for Caruso (the image shifting from mold to stamping die): *"Natura lo fece, e poi ruppa la stampa."* Nature made him and then broke the stamp.

molecule The smallest particle that can display the physical and chemical characteristics of a compound. [Root sense: "a small great-big." In the New Latin of Renaissance alchemy, *molecula*, particle of matter, whence Fr. *molécule*. The second element, *-cula, -cule*, is a dim. suffix. The first element, *mole*, is etymologically complex. The immediate base is L. *mōlēs*, a great mass, a massive structure or earthwork; whence Eng. *mole*, a breakwater. But ult. < IE *mo-*, labor, exertion, burden, to work hard, as, for example, in building a mole. The sense shift has been from "hard labor" to "massive thing built by hard labor." The IE root, suffixed *-l-* → L. *molestus,* laborious, burdensome; whence OF *molester,* ME *molesten,* to put a burden upon, to weigh down, and hence, to vex (MOLEST).]

Molotov cocktail   In WWII, an improvised incendiary antitank grenade first used by the Russians against invading Nazis. It is simply a glass bottle of gasoline with a gasoline-dipped rag attached to the stopper. The rag wick, ignited before throwing, touches off the splashed gasoline when the bottle breaks. If done properly, the heat of the fire drives the crew out of the tank, to be shot down. Later in the war, widely used by guerrillas and partisans. [I believe, but cannot attest, that Loyalists first used such incendiary bottles in the Spanish war of the 1930's; but the device has taken its whimsical name from V. M. Molotov, the old Stalinist Bolshevik who served as Russia's foreign minister 1939–1949, and again 1953–1956, before being expelled from the Communist Party in 1961 by the Khrushchev forces he had opposed.]

momentum   The inertial force of a moving body, the product of its mass, density, and velocity. [L. *momentum,* movement < *movēre,* to move. Ult. < IE *meu-,* to drive forward, to impel.] *moment* 1. An instant in the (forward and away) course of time. 2. *Archaic.* Importance (at a critical moment). *matters of great moment.* Yvor Winters, "Before Disaster," uses *moment* for momentum, instant of time, and critical instant, all at once: "But should error be increased/Mass and moment are released."

   momentous Of great importance. *momentary* At/of an instant of time. *momently* 1. *In current Am.* In an instant. 2. *Archaic.* From instant to instant. *He stood on the scaffold, his doubts increasing momently, until he caught the hang of it. momentarily* 1. In a moment. 2. For a moment only. *I loved Mimi only momentarily, but it was momentous.*

monger   1. *Am.* A pejorative term, used in compounds only, for one who deals in evil things. *rumormonger, gossipmonger, warmonger.* 2. *Brit. only.* In common use, with no pejorative sense, for what Am. would call "a small retailer." So *ironmonger,* one who sells hardware; *costermonger,* one who sells fruit and produce (originally an apple seller, after *costard,* a variety of apple); and *fishmonger.* [IE *meng-,* a small thing, to supply with small articles

→ Gk. *manganon,* a sorcerer's charm, amulet, fetish, (and also, taking a pejorative turn) worthless thing with which a mountebank cheats the gullible. Whence L. *mangō,* an unscrupulous dealer, a swindler.]

HISTORIC. The pejorative sense attached to this word stem by the Greeks, together with the admiration of sharp dealing so often expressed in Greek mythology, seems to indicate that Greek street merchants had immemorially heavy thumbs on the scales, and fast fingers for short-changing. In a number of European languages the word for Greek has been used to mean sharpie, swindler, cheat. In XVII Brit. slang *Greek (it)* meant to cheat at cards. At about the same time Sp. *gringo,* a variant of *griego,* Greek, became a term for a despised and unreliable foreigner.

Am. *monger* has preserved the pejorative sense the Greeks attached to the stem. Brit., by long habituation, has generally made *monger* a neutral label for a small retailer, though a pejorative sense still surfaces in *warmonger* and the like; and who, for that matter, conceives a fishmonger as a model of honesty?

monkey: cold enough to freeze the balls off a brass monkey   A round rhetorical flourish meaning very cold. [P. *Slang* glosses the term as c. 1900, "mainly Australian," but without any citation. If this language formula is indeed Australian, I feel that all language reasoning must stop, to be superseded by admiration, for the Aussies have their own wild, whirling way with language, and I take their rhetoric to be beyond the reach of any non-native.

There is, however, a rumor, loud in the land, and repeated by many of my correspondents, that *balls* here refers to cannonballs, and *brass monkey,* to a rack for holding them. The cannonballs of wooden ships must certainly have been held in some sort of rack to keep them from rolling about the deck. The projectiles of the big guns on steel warships, on the other hand, are passed up from an ammunition hold.

Partridge's dating is more apt to steel ships than to wooden ones. I have searched through a dozen books on wooden ships and nautical language, and have turned up no reference to a cannonball holder called a *brass monkey.*

In cold weather, brass and iron would contract at different rates, but never with enough difference to spill the balls from the rack. The figure, even if the Australian navy had such racks, is a wild, whirling hyperbole. If the reference is, literally, to a brass statue of a monkey, it is still sufficiently hyperbolic.

In the past, readers have supplied me with clues that had eluded me. I have now been eluded for years. If any reader can give me a firm reference to nautical *brass monkey* for "cannonball rack," it would be my grateful pleasure to pass on the information in a future edition.]

moon: she thinks he hung the moon (and stars)   She adores him as if he were God. The formula clearly implies that he is not, and therefore that her love is blind. Variantly ***you'd think he hung the moon*** (to hear her carry on about him). [Frederic G. Cassidy, writing in the *N.Y. Times,* Sept. 7, 1980, asserts this idiom (on, I believe, insufficient evidence) to be a Southernism. But if it was so once, it became widely diffused. Growing up in Boston in the 1920's, I heard it frequently as a formula of old wives' gossip.]

moron   A person whose mental development remains at the 7–12-year-old level on the Binet scale, the I.Q. being 50–75. Cf. *idiot* and *imbecile*. [Gk. *moros,* neuter *moron,* foolish, silly, inane, dull. Ult. < IE *mouro-* with same senses. And see *oxymoron*. *The achieved aim of the American school system is lesson less for moron more.*]

morris dance   A traditional folk dance of Britain in which costumed dancers perform various tales and legends, primarily about Robin Hood. Dance is one widespread form of reenacting tribal history, esp. among peoples without a form of writing. The pre-tourist hula, danced primarily by old ladies, was one such. The Moors performed such dances around their campfires, and variations of the Moorish style, diffused into Spain, France, and Britain, give us the English form. [ME *Moreys, Mores,* of the Moors. Fr. *danse mauresque,* Moorish dance. An especially long-bladed pike in use in Britain in XV was called a *morrice pike.* Shakespeare, *Comedy of Errors,* IV. iii, has: "He that sets up . . . to do more exploits with his mace than a morris pike."]

mortgage   1. A long-term loan with real property as collateral and a fixed schedule of payments, the property subject to foreclosure for failure to pay. 2. The document establishing the lending agreement and lien on the property. 3. The lender's claim on the property. [< OF *mort,* death; *gage,* a pledge → *mortgage,* death pledge (to pay upon the death of the borrower). I cannot pretend to understand the intricacies of how such a pledge applied to an entailed estate, which could not be sold and which reverted to the crown if the landholder died without a legal heir.]

motel   An inn offering, along with a high level of mediocrity, free parking spaces for guests, most of whom arrive by car. [*Mot*(or) with (hot)*el*. Doris E. King, *Palaces of the Public, A History of American Hotels*, Harvard University Press, traces the name to San Luis Obispo, Cal., where in 1925 a roadside establishment offering separate cottages with attached garages was advertised as a *Mot-el Inn*. Similar establishments developed on the East Coast (and in mid-America) in response to the motor age, but they were called *tourist courts* or *tourist camps* until c. 1946, when *motel* took over nationally. As more and more elaborate high-rise establishments (in effect, hotels with one free parking space per room) have moved into the expensive real estate of downtown areas, *motor hotel* has become common.]

   No-tel Motel Whimsical name for a motel used primarily for sexual assignation. Streetwalkers and barroom hookers have regular arrangements with such establishments to rent rooms by the hour. They are also known as *hot pillow joints,* the turnover conceived as being so rapid that the pillow on which one's head is laid is said to be still hot from the head of the last laid occupants.

   swingers' motel Conceived in California and dedicated to sexuality, these motels offer exotic decor (Moorish whorish), elaborate mirroring, including mirrored ceilings that allow couples to observe themselves in the sexual act, water beds, and closed-circuit pornographic films for sexual stimulation. Though sometimes conceived as dens of exotic and perverse sexual practices, swinger motels, according to various sociological reports, are most commonly patronized by couples who are married (to each other) and who have reached the age at which a little added stimulus makes the difference.

Motown   1. Detroit. [< *Mo(tor)town*. Originally Black English. Coined c. 1941 by the many black workers who migrated from the South to work in defense plants in Detroit, remaining primarily as auto workers after the war.] 2. A distinctive sound and jazz style that evolved after WWII from the abundance of black musical talent in Detroit. 3. The label of the vastly successful Jobete Music Co., Inc., founded by Berry Gordy (Robert L. Gordy). It was the first large recording company completely owned and operated by blacks. *The Motown Era,* a songbook published in 1971 by Jobete, notes: "No publisher can match Jobete's . . . record of . . . more than 345 new hit songs since 1958." Jobete became one of the top ten U.S. recording and music publishing houses, moving its main offices to Los Angeles–Hollywood. It has since been acquired by ABC.

Ms.   (Pronounced *miz.*) A perhaps once necessary but ill-chosen invention of Women's Rights activists. Activists, though right and valiant, tend not to be language sensitive. The intent was to find a social and business label as neutral as Mr., which designates sex without specifying marital status, at the same time asserting the writer's or speaker's awareness of Women's Liberation and demanding that it be respected. The premise being that the label *Miss* implies junior, inferior, or old maid status. And so it once did, though the success of the equal rights movement has removed the earlier connotations from *Miss.* May the cause continue to advance, but may *Ms.* be rejected, as I believe the language process will eventually reject it (*ms.* is the abbreviation for *manuscript,* and most manuscripts should properly be rejected). As a spoken title, moreover, *miz* is dialect of the South as a form of address for a woman, and too folksy for formal use. It will be a pleasure to vote for a qualified female presidential candidate, but I will predict without any reservations that she will not let herself be called Ms. President, but rather *Madam President,* by analogy to the established *Mr. President.*

mule: suck-egg mule   A nonesuch idiom in the sthrn. rhetorical flourish *well, I'll be a suck-egg mule!* Exclam. of surprise, vexation. [See *egg suction.* A mule is not physically equipped to suck eggs except in sweet rhetoric, but could it do so, it would be as remarkable a critter as a fiddling cow.]

multiplication, division, and silence   The qualities most desirable in a corrupt machine politician; in essence, the mathematics of graft, to multiply its sources and to divide it wisely among members of the machine, along with the ability to keep one's mouth shut. [Common in late XIX Am., and for reasons I cannot explain, in vogue at that time in Philadelphia. William Marcy ("Boss") Tweed, 1823–1876, was from 1859 to 1871 the leader of Tammany Hall, and hence the supreme power of NYC machine politics. When asked what he looked for in selecting political aides, he responded with this (once) much-publicized formula. It is no longer current but still exhales a fine aura of the American political past.]

muscle   [At root: "mouse," because of fancied resemblance in shape. This metaphoric linkage is first evident in Gk. *mus*. 1. Mouse. 2. Fleshy bulge. Muscle. Ult. < IE *mu(s)-*, mouse. OE and L., though by separate evolutions, have the identical form *mūs*, with the same double sense. L. *mūsculus*, little mouse → Eng. *muscle*.

ODEE cites a similar metaphor in L. *lacertus*. 1. Lizard. 2. Upper arm muscle. Fr. *souris* also has the double sense, mouse and muscle.] 1. Any of the bodily bundles of fibers that contract and expand to produce motion. 2. Brawn. Strength. 3. *Slang.* Influence. Clout. ["power to get things done."] 4. *Criminal slang.* Coercive force. *(a)* A thug. *(b)* A group of thugs. *(c)* The threat of using thugs, perhaps together with influence (sense 3).

muscle in 1. To force an entry. Esp. to infringe upon or take over a racket or a legitimate business.

muscle-bound 1. Lacking litheness and bodily coordination because of overdeveloped, bunched muscles. 2. *Ext.* Stupid. Sometimes rendered *muscle-bound between the ears.*

muscle man 1. A body builder. 2. A thug.

Variantly *mussel* A bivalve mollusk found in both salt water and fresh. [Also < L. *mūsculus* and based on same metaphor. The Eng. form influ. by MHG *mussel* and MD *mosscele. The mousy muscle man ate mussels redundantly.*]

NOTE. *Thews* and *sinews* are synonymous with *muscle*, sense 1, but have acquired no extended senses. One might say archly, "I wouldn't flex a thew (or sinew) to help him," but in normal usage *thews* and *sinews* occur in plu. only.

Thews is ult. < IE *teu-*, to observe closely, with ref. to religious ritual, i.e., to do the proper thing. So OE *theaw*, custom, observance of custom. ME *theawes*, good qualities (of observance); whence a further extension to "good (strong) bodily qualities." Same IE root → L. *tueri*, to watch closely in observing ritual → TUTOR, TUITION.

Sinew, in sing. (rare), means tendon; in plu., bodily strength. Ult. < IE *sei-*, a binding, a band. Variantly *sneu-*, sinew. And so with only minor alterations in Gmnc. → OE *sinu, seonu*; ME *sinewe*, sinew. The IE variant *(s)neu-*, suffixed *-ro-* → Gk. *neuron*, sinew (NEURON). Similarly with u/v and metathesized → L. *nervus*, sinew (NERVE). The common element in all variations is "bodily chord, thread, ligament."

nadir   1. The celestial point opposite the zenith. (See *zenith.*) 2. *Accurately.* The lowest point in the affairs of a nation, organization, or life. 3. *Inaccurately.* A low point. A slump. [< Arabic *nazīr (as-semt)*, opposite (to the zenith).]

nailed to the counter   Exposed as a fraud. ***another (damned) lie nailed to the counter*** Another deceit exposed. [These forms, now rare, were common in the political and journalistic rhetoric of XIX Am. Originally with ref. to counterfeit coins, but soon generalized.

   HISTORIC. Counterfeit coins were pestilently common in the XVIII colonies and later in the states. Tradesmen, having identified them (too late), often nailed them to the counter—or they were said to do so. A counter well-covered with such coins could do little more than advertise the gullibility of the storekeeper; it could not be much help in identifying the counterfeits. Small steel nails were not commonly available till the very end of XIX. The storekeeper would have had to use a heavy iron nail, mashing the lead counterfeit he was nailing. And to what purpose except to make a mess of his countertop? Yet language is as much of legend as of fact, and the idiom was received in XIX as if most of America's countertops were covered with nailed lead nickels.

naked possession   A legal term in common use when the West began to be tamed to the point of legal administration and the recording of deeds. The term labels long use of land without a formal deed to it, and was applied primarily to the legal status of large ranches and their long-established use of public range land. In one sense, it is legally equivalent to *squatter's rights* though many a naked possessor fought off squatters on "his" land. In post–Civil War actions *naked possession* and *squatter's rights* were sometimes upheld by the courts and sometimes not. Inevitably some of these

land disputes turned bloody before property rights were settled
and legal deeds registered.

narc   In Am. slang, a contraction of *narcotics agent.* [But in Brit.
XVIII and XIX *nark* was a police informer or a stool pigeon, and
that form is traceable to Romany *nak, nahk* (spelling?), nose; a nark
being one who "noses" into things.]

nasty   *adj.* 1. Stinking. Filthy. Disgusting. 2. Of these same qualities
extended from the physical to the moral. Hence, indecent. 3. *Further ext.* Mean. Spiteful. 4. *Further ext.* Unpleasant, trying, causing
discomfort, annoying. *nasty working conditions.* 5. *Still further
ext.* Grievous. Having dire consequences. *a nasty accident.* [If one
will allow an ignoble but vivid imagery, this etymology is a fossil
poem. It is also a specimen case of how humankind creates language from existing language, for as soon as two words are available, there is the possibility of combining them to form a third; and
from the three, more; and from that more, still more. So from the
early IE roots *ni-*, down (NETHER), and *sed-*, seat, to sit (SEDAN), our
Aryan language fathers formed *nizd'-*, nest, "sit down place (for a
bird)." Whence L. *nidus,* It. *nido,* Fr. *nide,* nest. And among British gamekeepers, *a nide of pheasants* ("as many as hatch from one
nest").

So for the southern evolution. Our Gmnc. language fathers
made the further observation that where the bird sits it drips,
and that after the rites of spring, a nest becomes a befouled and
reeking thing in the heat of summer. To express this observation they evolved the adj. *nestig,* lit. "like a nest," but with the
root sense: "beshat and stinking." This hypothetical form may
be adduced from OD *nestich* and OE *nestig,* whence, with
a slight vowel modification, and with the common shift of OE
g to ME *y* (as in *hunig* → *honey*) → *nasty,* at root: "shitty-
stinking."]

neap tide   An especially low tide that occurs when the sun and moon
are on the same side of the earth, combining their gravitational
pull. [Root sense: "shut tide." Ult. < IE *ken-*, to close, to shut. The
zero grade form *kn'-*, with k/h in Gmnc. and probably suffixed *-p-*
→ OE *hnappian,* to nap ("to shut one's eyes") and by association,
"to reach a low point of activity." ME *nepflood,* neap flood, neap
tide ("shut tide").]

near 1. Not far from. 2. Close in time. *near noon.* 3. Almost. *near famished.* 4. *Colloq. and dial.* About ready to. *I'm near to taking his block off right now.* [Of obscure Gmnc. origin → OE *nēah,* near; *nēar,* nearer. Mod. Eng. *nearer* is, radically, a double comparative, "more nearer." Mod. Eng. *next* is < OE superlative *nēahst,* nighest (which, with h/g → *nēag'st,* next). And see *neighbor.*]

 near miss In artillery fire, and esp. in aerial bombing, a hit just to one side of the target. [The form might as readily have been *near hit,* but the elves in charge of language decide these matters at their own whim. As an added complexity, supplied by technology, a near miss scored in bombing a ship is commonly more effective than a direct hit. Such a hit on an armor-plated deck could cause damage without sinking the ship, whereas a near miss, transmitting its detonative force through incompressible water, could spring the hull plates, sending the ship to the bottom. Just off to one side turned out, in practice, to be "more nearer."]

neck verse Brit. The first verse of Psalm 51, beginning "Have mercy upon me, O God." [So called because the ability to read it in Latin could save a condemned felon's neck.]

 HISTORIC. From the Middle Ages into XVII, British law offered *privilegium clericale,* benefit of clergy, whereby a person condemned at law, even if found guilty of murder, went free if he showed he could read the Bible in Latin. When the condemned person claimed the benefit, the ordinary (court chaplain) came forth with a Bible and pointed, by long-established tradition, to the beginning of Psalm 51. If satisfied with the reading, the ordinary announced, *"legit ut clericum":* he reads like a clergyman, and the man was released after being branded on one hand, prob. as an information to his church superiors that he might well be reviewed by a church court.

 In time, even illiterate rogues were pre-coached to read the neck verse, and these, along with other abuses, led to the rescinding of the benefit in XVII. In XVI, it had been rescinded in cases of treason.

nectar 1. *Greek myth.* What the gods drink in the feasts of Olympus, ambrosia being their food. 2. *In various exts.* Any beverage said to be fit for the gods. 3. The liquid secreted by flowers and gathered by bees, who make it into honey. [Root sense: "drink that dissolves death (hence conferring immortality)." Ult. < IE *nek-,* death, to die (NECROPOLIS). Suffixed *-ta-,* to dissolve, to melt (THAW) → Gk.

nektar, drink of the gods ("that which causes death to melt away").
The sense evolution from "death" to "beyond death (immortality)"
is identical to that of *ambrosia,* which see. But this root sense has
receded from the word, the present active connotation being "delicious (with no implied extension of life expectancy)."]

 nectarine A variety of esp. juicy peach with a smooth waxy skin.
[By back formation from *nectarine peach,* delicious peach. < Earlier adj. *nectarine* (last syllable pronounced *īn*), of/like nectar.]

negotiate [The root sense may be variably rendered: "to be busy (not
idle), to be ill at ease." < L. **otium,* leisure, idleness, ease (OTIOSE);
with negative prefix *neg-.* L. *negotiare,* to carry on business. And
cf. It. *negozio,* place of business.] 1. To work long and diligently at
complex matters. *negotiate a treaty.* 2. *Finance.* To work out the
complex details of a business transaction. 3. To overcome a considerable obstacle. *negotiate the Burma Road.*

neighbor One who lives nearby. [Ger. *bauer,* farmer, dweller, is akin
to *be, being.* Also has the senses "to make things grow, to bring into
being, to exist." *Neigh-,* near. Of obscure Gmnc. origin. (See
near.)] **neighboring** In the vicinity of. [And note that *vicinity* is, at
root, "dwelling place." < ON *vic,* place of residence, dwelling.
Modified to *-wick* in English → *bailiwick.* And a common element
in place names (CHADWICK, STANWICK, FENWICK).] **neighborly**
Solicitous. Friendly. [Disposed to kindly community exchanges.]
neighborhood 1. The area around one's residence. 2. Such an area
conceived as having particular characteristics, commonly ethnic,
but also physical (having parks, clean streets, well-kept homes—or
not), and traditional (served by community centers, clubs, YMCAs
—or not).

 the neighborhood is changing It is losing its desirable characteristics, as above. Always implies change for the worse. Commonly
implies that ethnic "undesirables" are moving in, real estate values
are falling, housing is deteriorating.

nemesis (Accent First syllable.) 1. The cause of one's downfall. 2. *In
common sports usage.* An unbeatable rival. *In the end, Ali was his
own nemesis.* **Nemesis** The Greek goddess of retribution. [Her
name derives < *nemein,* to allot, to distribute, to mete out. At root,
therefore, her function was to apportion just punishment or just
reward. But the Greeks must have sensed that there is nothing to

hope for in true justice. As everyone knows his own faults, ultimate justice can only punish. I can find nothing in the various legends of Nemesis, "the Allotter," to show she ever rewarded. She is—or she became early in her legendary career—the goddess of just retribution. As a projection of the Greeks' own psyche, she is a figure of the guilt any reasonable man can confess to himself, whatever he may say to others.]

neon   An inert gaseous element. Traces of it occur in our atmosphere. [< Gk. *neon,* neuter of *neos,* new. Hence "the new (element)." The name was given it upon its discovery in 1898 by British chemists M. W. Tavers and Sir William Ramsay.]

   neon sign A usu. advertising sign consisting of glass tubing filled with the gas and intricately bent to resemble printing, handwriting, or simple sketching. When the gas is ionized it gives off a brilliant red light. [First called *neon lamp* in Brit. But in Am., since the first appearance of such advertising gimmicks in the early 1920's, *neon sign,* and as they became more familiar, *neon* or *neons.* Now in wide use with signs whose tubes contain other ionizing gases which give off a whole range of colors, but *neon* labels all such in all shades.]

   neon adj. Bright. Glaring. Garish. *Jimmy Gleason turned up wearing a neon plaid sports coat.*

nice   [Root sense: "ignorant." So L. *nescius,* p.p. of *nesciere,* to know not < *scire,* to know; with neg. prefix. (*Scire,* p.p. *scius,* substantive *scientia,* is the root of SCIENCE.). OE *nice,* simple-minded, witless, silly; ME *nice,* silly, foolish, bashful; and these are clearly root-related senses, but thereafter modern Eng. *nice* developed a range of senses that defy explanation. In XVI, fastidious, overly fastidious. Hence, hard to put up with. And also, minutely accurate. In XVIII, appetizing, pleasurable, attractively delicate. It is these XVI and XVIII senses that survive, the root sense having receded from the word.] 1. Indicates general approval (in the XVIII senses attractive, as *nice-looking girl;* pleasurable, as *We had a nice time,* and also, warm, sympathetic, congenial, as *What a nice thing to do!*). 2. Precise. *a nice distinction* (which, in context, may mean "exactly discerning" or "pointlessly fastidious," a distinction without a difference; these senses being from XVI).]

   nice and . . . *Colloq. formula.* Agreeably. *nice and cozy, nice and easy.*

   nice guy Sympathetic, congenial, generous, moral, outgoing person. Can be applied to either sex. *Lynn Freedman has been a nice guy to Stan, but wait until she finds out.*

nice nelly A prim, fussily fastidious person of no consequence. Said of a man, implies that he is a milktoast. [Am. adaptation of Brit. *nice nanny* (governess), *nice as a nanny.* The governess conceived as a cooingly genteel nonlady trying to act like one.]

Mr. Nice The Am. colloq. equivalent of Chaucer's "verray, parfit gentil knight." The nice guy personified. But usu. in negative constructions. *That does it—no more Mr. Nice* = That's a last offense—from now on I will do no more favors for you.

ninety-nine Medical formula. Patients under stethoscopic examination of the upper chest are instructed to repeat this number. If the lungs and bronchial tubes are in good condition the sound rings clear, but it is muffiled if there are congesting fluids present. May your *ninety-nine* ring clear forever, or at least until you die of something else.

nix No. Nothing. *As a command.* Don't do it. **nix (it)** To forbid or reject (it). **nix,** fem. **nixie** *Scottish superstition.* An evil sea spirit. **nixie** *Post Office Department jargon.* An undeliverable piece of mail. [This last prob. from slang *nix* in the sense "it's no go." All senses < Ger. *nichts,* nothing. And see *Old Nick.*]

no-account Worthless. [Not worth entering in any account book.] *That no-account hound dog should have its tail docked clear up to its neckbones.* [Now standard in sthrn. wstrn., and Miss. Valley dialects, but with precedent in late XVIII Brit. dialect and colloq.] **the count of no-account** A worthless person who puts on airs of being important. [An Am. elaboration, from c. 1850, or perhaps a bit earlier.]

nob A person of elegance and high social standing. **nobby** Fashionable, classy. (In Am., variantly *knobby,* but the form is a more or less accepted misspelling.) [Brit. slang, but also in XIX (and surviving) Am. use. J. R. Bartlett, *Dictionary of Americanisms,* cites (1877) a "hat Seller's Advertisement" (no source given): "If you would dress yourself cheaply, neatly, *nobby,* and stylish, give us a call." Edwin Radford, *Unusual Words,* says British university rosters of alumni entered *nob* (for *nobilitatis*) after the names of graduates of noble blood. The most notable Am. use is in the name of San Francisco's **Nob Hill,** the exclusive section of San Francisco where those who had struck it rich in or after the gold strike of 1849 built their mansions. Prob. a convergent evolution, for though *nob, nobby,* were established Am. forms, the name may be a corruption of *Nabob* (< Hindi , *nawab,* governor of an Indian province during the Mogul Empire, and in XVIII–XIX as *nabob,* an Englishman who had returned home with a great fortune made in India).]

Nod: Land of Nod   1. The wilderness to which Cain was banished by the Lord for the murder of Abel. [Genesis 4:16: "Then Cain went out from the presence of the Lord and dwelt in the Land of Nod, to the East of Eden."] 2. *Nursery English.* Sleepy-bye land. [Obviously based on *nodding* as in *nodding off to sleep.* Yet the nursery form is an extraordinary evolution, and probably a recent one. I am unable to date the nursery usage, but had it evolved before late XIX, it is all but certain that preachers would have thundered against its use as a debasement implying that the sleeping child has been sent off to the wilderness of the first murderer, in an exile beyond the presence of God.]

Norman French   The language spoken by the XI Norman conquerors of Britain, but more specifically the language of the conquerors' courts and of royal decrees for the next two centuries or so. Since court proceedings and government records were generally well preserved, they have been a major etymological record of the shifting language in these two centuries.

nose   [The form evident in IE *nas-,* nose. Via Italic → L. *nasus;* via Gmnc. → OE *nasu,* nose.] 1. The bump in front of one's face for smelling, to catch colds in, to poke into other people's business, and for getting bloodied when they react properly. 2. *Aeronautics and aerospace.* The forward part of a plane or rocket, whence: ***nose cone*** The heat-resistant forward shield of a rocket ship or space vehicle, designed esp. to shield the vehicle from the heat of reentry into earth's atmosphere. Of airplanes: ***nose dive, nose down, nose heavy, nose wheel*** and, when a plane crashes on landing and flips forward onto its back, ***to nose over.***

Of the nose as the organ of scent, and by ext., of sniffing and poking about: ***nose around*** To sniff out information. ***nose for news*** *Journalism.* The ability to sniff out a newsworthy story. ***poke (stick) one's nose into someone else's business*** To be meddlesome. ***nosy/ nosey*** *adj. Slang.* Prying. Meddlesomely inquisitive. ***nosegay*** A clutch of flowers. [To make the nose feel gay.]

Of the nose as an identifying feature: **nose job** *Slang.* Surgery to change the shape of one's nose. **big nose** In the Orient, a pejorative term for an Occidental. **count noses** To take attendance. (A simpler method than counting feet and dividing by two.) **hawk nose, Roman nose** A capacious, downcurving nose. [For reasons I am unable to trace, *Romannose* is a common surname among today's Oklahoma Indians.] **pug nose** A small nose with an upward tilt. [Like the nose of a pug dog.]

Idioms from animal behavior: **nose open, nose aside** What a dog does in opening a door. **lead by the nose** To dominate utterly. [From the practice of forcing a stout metal ring into the tender cartilage of a bull's, sow's, or boar's septum. The animal can then be led with a hook on a stout stick, the pain caused by twisting the ring dominating even a dangerous animal, e.g., a husband.] **hard nose** A tough customer. **by a nose** 1. *Horse racing.* To win by no more than the length of a nose. 2. *Generalized ext.* Just barely. **get the wind up one's nose** To become wary, excited, restive. [As does a horse spooked by a threatening scent.]

In Brit. nautical: **nose-ender** A wind from dead ahead. [Straight up one's nose.]

And miscellaneously: **brown nose** A sycophant. [An ass-kisser who nuzzles the dominant person's rectum for favor, thereby acquiring a touch of local color.] **nose habit** An addiction to cocaine. **stick one's money up one's nose** Squander one's money on cocaine. **stick it up your nose** *Slang.* A formula of contemptuous rejection. [As if said scornfully to an addict.] **rub noses** To cuddle. To be gently intimate. **nose to nose** In closest confrontation, as in a slugging match. **bloody one's nose** To hurt, not fatally, either physically or metaphorically. *The Hunts got their noses bloodied to the tune of about two billion dollars when they tried to corner the market in silver.* **pay through the nose** To pay painfully, extortionately. [The liquid equivalent of the pound of flesh.] **get one's nose out of joint** To become jealous. Morose. [As if one's nose had been broken in a fight.]

More or less self-evidently: **cut off one's nose to spite one's face** To be perversely vengeful. **(right) under one's nose** Said of one who cannot find a thing sought though it is just in front of him. **turn up one's nose** To snub, reject, show contempt.

And as a dramatic antiquity: **nose stitch** *Nautical.* The sailmaker's last stitch in sewing a dead man into a canvas shroud for burial at sea; it went through the canvas and the dead man's nose to keep him from tumbling down into the shroud. Rigor mortis might stiffen a bloke to proper parade standards for sea burial, but the seagoing imperative was to get rid of the dead before they became infectious, and rigor mortis takes time to set in. Nor would any true salt who is dead enough for burial at sea object to a simple nose stitch in the name of good order.

nucleus The central, more or less compact core around which a larger mass coheres. *nucleus of a cell.* And by ext. *nucleus of the new army.* [Akin to *nut.* < L. *nux,* nut (stem *nuc-,* nucleus, deriving from the dim. form *nucella,* little nut. Ult. (by a complex evolution) < IE *ken-,* compact mass. Zero-grade form *kn-,* with k/h and suffixed *k → (h)n'k) →* L. stem *nuc-.* By a similar Gmnc. evolution → OE *hnecca,* neck ("place where the body becomes compacted into a small space").]

nut [For etymology, see *nucleus.* Root sense: "compact mass."] 1. A seed, usu. of a tree, encased in a more or less hard shell. 2. The human head. ["hard-shell dense mass."] 3. An enthusiast. *Maggie, a nut about bolts, was screwy.* 4. A threaded metal cap that receives a bolt. 5. A lunatic, a zany or an erratic person. **nut house** *Derisive slang.* An insane asylum. [As in sense 5, but also with sense 2 and the added idea "cracked."] **nutty** *adj.* 1. Having a taste like that of a nut. (Said esp. of sherry. *a fine, nutty dry sherry.*) 2. Insane. Zany. Ridiculous.

a hard nut to crack A difficult problem. **nuts and bolts** The hard practical aspects. *get down to nuts and bolts* To turn from generalizations and get down to the hard practical aspects of a problem, situation, or given case. *in a nutshell* In brief.

nuts in May A frivolous nonesuch. [Except in the tropics, nuts are gathered in the fall.] *here we go gathering nuts in May* A traditional song refrain. [The effective sense, as now understood, is "here we go to do our frivolous merry nothing." But *nuts* is a corruption of earlier *knots* (of flowers to be knotted into wreaths and garlands)—in either case a frivolous merry nothing, but with a substantially altered root image.]

nuts Slang. adj. 1. Insane, erratic, zany. *He's nuts.* 2. Excessively fond. *He's nuts about anything female.—n.* The testicles. ["hard compact masses."] *Also in sing.* A testicle. Esp. in the common expression *left testicle. He'd give his left testicle to have a real pair of balls.* [I cannot explain why the language convention is so set toward the left testicle. Left, of course, is the established side of inferiority or dishonor, but there is no evidence to indicate that the left testicle is inferior to the right. This idiom implies that one would give a good deal, but note the common: *He'd give his right arm* (to be ambidextrous).]—*exclam.* Variously expresses annoyance, frustration, indignant rejection, ridicule. [At prob. root: "my balls to you!" but influ. by "you're nuts," while also expressing the speaker's sense of burly manhood.]

HISTORIC. In the winter of 1944–1945, the Germans staged the last massive counterattack of WWII against the U.S. forward line whose key point was at Bastogne in southeastern Belgium. The engagement is called the Battle of the Bulge. The defending U.S. forces nicknamed themselves the Battered Bastards of the Bastion of Bastogne.

The German surprise attack achieved a substantial early success, whereupon the German commander sent an officer with a flag of truce to offer terms of surrender. The U.S. commander is said to have replied with one word: "Nuts!" The Germans are said to have been puzzled by the reply, but anyone native to American slang will recognize it as expressing the whole complex range of contempt—in a nutshell.

There is also the fact that *testicle* is at root: "witness (to one's manhood)." "To smite one's thigh," in Biblical translation, was in fact to cup one's testicles in swearing an oath; to say in effect, "I swear it by my manhood." At deep roots, "Nuts!" is "to reject utterly, by every power of one's manhood."

nuthatch   A small bird, family *Sittidae*, with a long, powerful beak. It is remarkable for having learned to wedge nuts into a fissure in bark, and to peck them open while so held in place. [Whence its name, not because it hatches nuts, but that it, so to speak, "hatchets" them. < OF *hache*, ME *hak*, hatchet (HACK, HASH, HASH MARK).]

obloquy [L. *ob-*, against (OBNOXIOUS); *loqui*, to speak (LOQUACIOUS) → *obloqui*, to speak against, to denounce, esp. in public, as in the senate.] Accusation, denunciation, defamation, vituperation.

ogre 1. A grotesque, gigantic, humanoid man-eater. Fem. **ogress** [In some ways akin to the one-eyed Cyclops of Greek legend (Gk. *Kyklops,* round eye), but an ogre is not specifically one-eyed, and in fact not specifically anything but monstrous and man-eating.] 2. *Loose ext.* A brutish, cruel person. *His boss is an ogre—and you should see his wife.* [Fr. *ogre* was first used by Perrault, *Contes,* 1697, but no one knows where he got the word. Perhaps by metathesis and with k/g from It. *orco,* demon < L. *Orcus,* the name of one of the fiends of the underworld, but this is guess only. What is certain is that Perrault's term became established at once in French, and very soon after in English.]

Old Nick The devil. [Prob. directly from, or akin to, Ger. *Nickel,* goblin; but as with most terms of folklore and superstition, influ. by various kindred terms. Prob. by *nix,* fem. *nixie,* in Teutonic myth, an evil water spirit. So, too, the MHG formula for an evil or revenant spirit, *nihtes niht,* the nothing which is nothing. The root idea in all these forms is "absence of being"; in Eng. spook formula "the death in life" or "the undead"—all surviving as formulas of spook/horror movies. All ultimately based on IE *ne-,* a generalized negative.]

orchestra [IE *er-gh-,* to move swiftly, to jump about → Gk. *orcheisthai,* to dance. The same root in Sanskrit, *'rghā,* has the sense "to rant and rave." The now primary sense of *orchestra* arose only in XVII with the development of the large musical group. Gk. and L. *orchēstra* was specific to the curved apron or pit in front of a stage. There the chorus chanted (and danced). And so today's **orchestra**

pit in which large musical groups commonly perform for operas and musicals.] 1. A large performing musical group made up of various sections of strings, woodwinds, brass, and timpani, and sometimes with additional instruments, as accordions, a piano or pianos, and most recently electronic instruments. 2. *Theater.* [By association with Gk. *orchēstra,* space in front of the stage.] *(a)* The seats on the first level of a theater. *(b)* Such seats from the front of the stage or orchestra pit to the overhang of the balcony.

    orchestrate 1. To arrange a musical score for performance by a full orchestra. 2. *Federalese and corporate robotic.* To combine many elements into a single plan. *Eisenhower orchestrated the Normandy invasion and the final assault upon the Third Reich.*

orchid   1. Any of the dazzling variety of flowers of the genus *Orchis,* widespread in the temperate zone but found mostly in the tropics. [At root: "testicle flower" < Gk. *orkhis,* testicle; the name used by early naturalists including Pliny the Elder, because its double root was said to resemble a pair of hairy testicles.] 2. A compliment, an homage. [Orchids were once the almost exclusive corsage flower sent to a lady one was to squire for the evening. Walter Winchell, the prevailing noise on Broadway from the 1920's to the 1950's, took to the formula of approval, "Orchids to so-and-so for such and such," the counter-formula of disapproval being "Scallions to . . ." This sense has had some survival, but seems likely to pass with the highly perishable memory of W.W.]

orphan   A child whose parents are dead. If one parent survives, *motherless child* or *fatherless child.* [IE *orbh'-,* to separate, to thrust apart, with common b/f → Gk. *orphanos,* child separated from its parents, and since the Greek clan was patrilinear, with the primary connotation "child separated from its father," since separation from the mother was not taken to be the critical condition. In various early-manhood rituals, surviving as what we call confirmation, the essence was to be separated from the mother, who could only bear babies, and to be ritually reborn of the men of the tribe, who alone could pass on manhood.

    In ancient societies one principal way to be separated from the father was to be enslaved, commonly by being taken captive in war. So, in a side evolution, the slightly altered stem *(o)r'b'-* became Old Slavonian *rabu,* slave (and, thereby, one taken from the father). In a further evolution this stem → Czech *robota,* slavery, drudgery, whence English *robot,* and what, by nature, is more orphaned than a robot?]

overwhelm   To inundate and overpower. [The root image is of stormy seas breaking over the sides of an early (Viking) ship, an image that pits the force of the sea against the best that puny man can do. Except in this compound, *whelm* is obs. It is akin to *helm.* In early Teutonic ships (really large canoes), the helm was a long sweep-oar extending over the starboard side (at root: "steering side"). IE *kel-,* to conceal, protect, with k/h in Gmnc., is the base of *whelm,* and also of *hull,* the outer protection of a ship. So by association with *helm* (at origin: "thing over the side") and with *hull, to overwhelm* is what the sea does when it comes in over the side of a ship and swamps it. And whimsically, of course, *to underwhelm,* as in *I am underwhelmed by the power of positive thinking.*]

NOTE. T. S. Eliot wrote near the beginning of "Prufrock," "to lead us to some overwhelming question." He concluded, "Till human voices wake us and we drown." I believe that he used *overwhelming* as the first sounding of a sea image that is developed through the poem and resolved in the last line. In my experience, few readers can recognize what the poet is doing when he uses the language at this depth and as if the poem were a musical structure. Some are ready to accuse the critic of inventing into the poem what the poet could not possibly have intended. One of the purposes of this book is to show that a word is not only a denotation, but a sound, an image, and a unique history; and that good poets use words at a depth far beyond that of normal usage.

oxymoron   A figure of speech based on conjoining incongruous elements. *As a Ronald Reagan watcher, I waver between enthusiastic indifference and acute apathy.* [Gk. *oxumoron,* a seemingly absurd but effectively witty remark. At root: "a sharp-dull." < *oxu-,* combining form of *oxus,* sharp (AX, ACUTE); with *moron,* dull (see *moron*).]

$\mathcal{P}$

pad: on the pad   *Police and criminal slang.* On the precinct, or other unit, list to receive bribes paid on a regular, usu. weekly, basis not to individuals but to the whole unit, to be divided among all according to a formula established by their own corrupt but scrupulous principles. (Not to be confused with *on the take*, said of an individual cop open to bribery.) [Am. Latter XIX. *Pad*, here, as if *pad of paper*, the secret ledger in which the police bag man kept accounts in blatantly open or in disguised form. Since all officers of a unit were on the pad, some form of accounting was necessary.]

paddle your own canoe   Do for yourself what no one else can do for you (with ref. to a one-man Indian canoe). [Early Am. semi-proverbial. Bartlett Jere Whiting, *Early American Proverbs and Proverbial Phrases*, attests its use in 1802 and again, from a different source, in 1803, the double citation serving as evidence that the phrase was widespread, and probably in oral use from the time the settlers began to push west by water.]

pajamas   *In Am.* A loose two-piece sleeping suit. [*Pajama* (sing.) occurs as an adjective *(pajama tops)* and in the title of the play *The Pajama Game*, which deals with genial bed-raggling. The only instance I have found of its use as a singular noun is in Ogden Nash's playful poem about the one-l lama (a priest) and the 2-l llama (a beast). Nash concludes:

> And I will bet a silk pajama
> There isn't any 3-l lama.

Nash was refuted, however, by various firemen, who insisted they were all too familiar with 3-lllarmers, and also with 4-lllllarmers. (I have long wondered whether or not Nash paid his forfeit and delivered silk pajamas to the firehouse.)

The form is < Hindi *pājāma,* loose Oriental trousers of cotton or silk < Persian *pāi*, leg, with *jāma*, garment. The word is a gift of the British Empire. In adapting the garment for sleeping use as a replacement for the nightgown, early XIX Britons in India added the matching tops. In the U.S., conversely, it is now common to wear long tops without the pants, which is halfway back to the nightgown.]

pal An intimate friend and habitual companion. A chum. [< Romany, *pahl*, *pal*, brother → XVII Brit. thieves' cant with the sense: "close companion, partner in crime." (Gypsies are conspiratorially close. Unless they feud, the bond between Gypsy brothers must be as close a relationship as men can share.] ***palsy-walsy** adj.* Intimate. Thick as thieves. [Early XIX Brit. slang, prob. < earlier thieves' cant. Redupl. based on *palsy*, adjectival form of *pal.*] **be pals** To be close friends.

palace [ME & OF *palais* < L. *palatium*, the Palatine, one of the seven hills of Rome, because it was there Augustus lived, the Caesars who followed him extending the imperial palace and its grounds.] 1. The residence of a ruler. 2. *Ext.* Any imposing residence suggesting imperial splendor. 3. (In French usage more than British or American.) An imposing building housing an important government agency. *Palais de Justice.* 4. A large, ornately decorated place of public entertainment. *Palace Theater.* 5. (In the language puffery of merchandising.) A pretentious name for a store or restaurant with no fair claim to being palatial. *Palace of Furs, Palace of Pizza,* and for a beauty shop, *Palace of Beauty.* And the adj. form **palatial.** *In NYC any apartment one can walk through without sidling is called palatial.*

palaver *n.* A more or less formal and protracted verbal negotiation. 2. *Ext.* Talk. *(a)* Long-winded discussion. *(b)* Self-seeking talk, as flattery, cajolery. *Don't listen to his palaver; his one topic of discussion is your pocketbook.* Also verb, *to palaver,* but commonly in Am. *let's have a palaver.* [< Portuguese *palavra,* a word, a speech, a discussion. From about XVI, Portuguese was a strong element in the Afro-pidgin developed by Europeans and native chiefs for trade negotiations. In that pidgin *palavra, palabra, palavar,* signified a formal discussion toward a trade agreement.

The Portuguese form is based on Church L. *parabola,* parable < Gk. *para,* across; *bolein,* to throw; hence with root sense: "to throw across (a moral, a precept, in the form of a little story)." The root sense is sweetly apt to the situation of native chiefs and traders squatting in formal council to "throw across the language barrier" a trade agreement.]

NOTE. Fr. *parler* and Sp. *hablar* both mean to talk. But Fr. *hableur,* taken over from the Spanish, has the pejorative sense: "one who spiels on and on self-seekingly." Conversely, Sp. took over Fr. *parler* and made it over to *pablar,* to spiel with intent to deceive. At ult. root, Fr. *hableur* is "one who speaks like a (deceitful) Spaniard"; *hablar* is a neighborly assertion of French deceit.

palindrome   [< Gk. *dromos,* a race (HIPPODROME); with *palin,* again, over, and with effective sense: back.] A word or phrase that reads the same backward and forward.

NOTE. *Pop, dud, madam, radar,* are palindromic words. The late John Berryman once asserted that *deified* is the longest palindromic word, but if *releveler* and *redivider* can be defended, they are longer by two letters, and the likely longest palindromic word in English is *kinnikinnik* (this spelling is permitted by Webster's Unabridged Dictionary), a non-tobacco smoking mixture once in common use by the Indians and early settlers of the Ohio Valley.

Word game buffs have worked out palindromes that run to hundreds of words, but they read like delirious rantings, both forward and back.

Among the manageable and deft palindromes is the supposed rueful assertion of Napoleon: "Able was I ere I saw Elba." There is also the pig's elegy: "I'm, alas, salami"; the early XX masterpiece: "A man, a plan, a canal—Panama"; and the charming: "Top step's pup's pet spot."

The beginning of the book of Genesis, as rendered by St. Palindrome, reads: Chap. 1. "Madam, I'm Adam." Chap. 2. "Eve." Chap. 3. "Sex at noon taxes." The rest of the scroll was tragically destroyed in the burning of the library at Alexandria.

palsy   Paralysis, esp. partial paralysis. [Standard into early XX. Now rare. The form, attested in various spellings in XIII, is a typical British swallowing of OF *paralysie,* via *p(ar)al'sie → palsie, palsy.* Nothing is beyond the resources of a people who can make *Chumley* of *Cholomondeley* and *Rotten Row* of *rue du roi.*]

p and q: mind one's p's and q's   To pay close attention to details. [Brit. XVIII. First attested by OED 1779. Allowing for a reasonable lag between first use and attestation, c. 1740 would be a likely date of

origin, and the dating is critical, for the idiom is commonly rendered as a short form of "pints and quarts," with ref. to drinking
accounts kept on a slate by pub owners and their assistants. But in
mid XVIII how many such were sufficiently literate to form the
letters p and q? The old style of account keeping, adapted from the
immemorial counting stick, was a series of vertical marks, each four
slashed across diagonally to make five, and this simple counting
method is still in use.

In mid XVIII, however, with the emergence of a moneyed
middle class, it began to be general custom, for the first time in
British history, for the children of substantial families to be tutored
in reading and writing. Abecedarians often reverse their letters, a
common problem being the proper formation of the vertical loops
of g's, p's, and q's, whence the tutorial admonition *mind your p's
and q's*. Though not conclusively attested, this derivation is certainly more likely than one based on a pints-and-quarts assumption
of a general literacy, or even semi literacy, at the XVIII pub.]

panjandrum   A generalized Lord High Everything. [A made-up
word.]

HISTORIC. An XVIII actor named Macklin boasted that he could
recite anything he had read once. The playwright Samuel Foote
(1720–1777) wrote and offered him a test passage. Macklin scanned
it, and in a fury refused to repeat a word of it. Yet, in the telling
and retelling of this pointless story, the language picked out one
nonsense word and chose to preserve it. Foote's passage read (italics mine):

> So she went into the garden to cut a cabbage leaf to make an apple pie
> and at the same time a great she-bear came running up the street and
> popped its head into the shop. "What! on soup?" So he died, and she
> —very imprudently—married the barber. And there were present the
> Picninnies, the *Joblillies,* the *Guryulies,* and the Great Panjandrum
> himself with the little Red Button a'top and they all fell to playing the
> game of catch-catch-can till the gunpowder ran out the heels of their
> boots.

For reasons beyond me, Foote's passage must have been copied
many times and passed about among the literati as some sort of
howling joke. It must have been a dull season in London. But to
repeat the one possible principle: language does what it does because it does it.

A second all-but-submerged word may have emerged by the

blending of the two words I have italicized. I have not been able to find *gubilooly* in any dictionary, but my wife brought it out of her Missouri farm childhood as the label for any hash, stew, or soup improvised from refrigerator (earlier icebox) leftovers.

paraffin   A hydrocarbon derived from petroleum and having a wide range of industrial uses, primarily in candlemaking, for coating wax paper, and as a protective coating. Once widely used in sealing jars of home preserves, and ideal for the purpose because it resists chemical combination (even with wax beans). [Discovered in 1830 by Karl von Reichenbach, German chemist-physicist. He noted that the substance had little affinity for chemical combination, and expressed that quality by L. *parum affinis,* (having) little affinity. By clipping the L. form *par(um) affin(is),* he coined *paraffin.* Paraffin did not become an industrial product until the American chemist James Young developed a process for its large-scale extraction (patented 1850) from petroleum. Variously refined, it has since been the principal ingredient in candlemaking.

HISTORIC. From c. 3000 B.C., as evidenced by the excavation of Egyptian tombs, candles were in use by the wealthy, the commonest being made of tallow. Superior and brighter candles were made of beeswax. Tallow and beeswax with various additives remained the basic ingredients of candlemaking until XIX and the general availability of paraffin by James Young's process. And soon, then, came Edison, after whom candles became festive and decorative rather than primary sources of light.

parboil   To boil partially, lightly. [But the sense has been reversed from the root meaning: "to boil thoroughly." < OF *parboillir* < Late L. *perbullire,* in which *per-* serves as an intensive with the effective sense "through and through." The sense alteration arises from the mistaken assumption that the altered form "par-" meant "part, partially." And cf. *purblind.*]

parlay   *v.* 1. To re-wager an original bet plus winnings (to let it all ride). To do so once is technically a parlay, but the action commonly implies several such compoundings, one of the dreams of bankrupt horse players being a seven-horse parlay. 2. *Business.* To build a business or a stock portfolio by reinvesting profits. 3. *Generalized ext.* In any context, to start with little and to build it into much. *Starting with a case of psychic body odor, Don Rickles parlayed no talent into perfected revulsion.* —*n.* The act of parlaying. [It. *paroli,* a high roll of the dice. Obscurely < *paro,* equal. Perh. (?) from the roll of twelve, the two highest even numbers. In the standard dice game twelve is craps, but in variants, as in horse dice, sixes are the high roll.]

parlor   1. In XIX American custom, and still surviving in some rural areas, a room set aside for receiving guests, and not normally used by the family, which tended to gather in the large old-fashioned kitchen. 2. This sense of formal sitting room was carried over c. 1880 to *ice cream parlor,* a more or less decorated room with tables and chairs to one side of a soda fountain ("special room for receiving commercial visitors"). Whence: 3. Applied to various commercial establishments whose clients sit about, as *tonsorial parlor, beauty parlor.* 4. In old-fashioned hotels, a small sitting room off the lobby. *east parlor, blue parlor, sunset parlor.* [Church L. *parlatorium* (< L. *parlare,* to speak). 1. A room in a monastery or nunnery where those who had taken vows of silence could meet with visitors from "the world" and be temporarily permitted to speak. 2. In more relaxed orders, a room in which members might meet for occasional suspension of their vows of silence.

OF *parlear* succeeded this cloistered sense, designating a formal room reserved for the reception of guests.]

In the current American life-style, what was the parlor has become the living room, which is not shut off from the rest of the house. In suburban U.S. the living room is commonly replaced by the lower-level *rec room* (recreation room). Rec rooms commonly have wet bars; living rooms, rarely. The living room is now commonly at an angle to an open dining room.

parsley   The curly, richly green herb used both as a choice seasoning and as a garnish. [The stem is Gk. *sēlinon,* but for reasons unknown to me, the Greeks associated the plant with rocks and called it *petrosēlinon* as if "rock parsley"; and that prefix has passed into many European languages in the name for the herb. So L. *petrosēlinon,* It. *petrosino.* In OE *petersilie,* which is identical with Ger. *Petersilie.* And so such variants as Finnish *persilja,* Czech *petržel,* Russian *petrushka.* Whatever the reason for the *petros* prefix in Gk., it is likely that without it, the Eng. name would have been *sillie* or *silly* (which would inevitably have set up a spice shelf dialogue between the *silly* and the *sage*).]

partridge   A game bird resembling the quail but larger (up to 14 inches long), with an orange-brown head, gray-brown neck, and rust-brown tail. Native to Europe, the partridge was imported into the U.S. and has established itself here. [At root: "farter," with ref. to the burring sound made by its wings when it flushes. Ult. < IE *perd-*, fart, to fart. Via Gmnc. with p/f and d/t → OE *feortan*, ME *ferten*, to fart (FART). Same IE stem unaltered → Gk. *perdestai*, to fart; Gk. and L. *perdix*, fart → OF *perdiz, perdriz*; ME *partriche*, fart bird, partridge. And the taxonomical name *Perdix perdix*, fart-fart (bird).]

pea   The plant or the seed of the common vegetable. [Gk. *pison*, L. *pisum* → OE *pisë*, which in late ME became *pease*, the terminal *e* being first pronounced and later not, whence the *pease porridge* of the nursery rhyme. This form was then mistakenly taken as a plural, whence *pea*, as if it were the correct sing. form of *peas(e)*, whereupon, with the concurrence of the language convention, it did in fact become the correct sing. form. Language does what it does because it does it.]

pea jacket   A sailor's short, double-breasted, heavy wool coat with a broad collar that can be turned up to the top of the head as a protection from the wind. [*Pea* by modification to the most proximate familiar form. < Du. *pijjekker*, such a jacket < *pij*, a coarse, heavy cloth; with *jekker*, jacket < OF *jacque*, short overgarment worn by peasants < *jacques*, peasant(s) (JACKET). Occurs in Brit., but first attested in XVIII Am., suggesting a sailor-to-sailor transmission from Dutch.]

peanut   1. The ground-hugging vine (originally native to South America). When its seeds begin to form, the flower stalks grow longer, driving the papery pods into the ground. [*Pea* because the usu. double nut in its pod remotely resembles a blanched pea pod. Also *goober, goober pea*. (See Vol. I.)] 2. *Ext.* An insignificant person. A runt. A small fry.

  peanuts An insignificant amount of money.

  peanut gallery A term of contempt for the loud, ignorant, and jingoistic mob that filled the cheap upper tiers of American theaters, commonly with a bag of peanuts to snack on. If displeased, the mob was readily raucous enough to drive a performer offstage. Performing hams, knowing that the mood of the peanut gallery could make or break them, played to its jingoism and shallowness (and so enter George M. Cohan, Al Jolson, and the other stars of American jingoism and schmaltz). So the common but nontheatrical *any more stupid remarks from the peanut gallery* in which *peanut gallery = the seats of ignorance.*

XIX and early XX theaters had ornately decorated ceilings. In Britain the ceilings were commonly painted with scenes of Olympus, and so in Brit. those who sat in the cheap seats nearest the ceiling were called *the gods of the gallery.*

pearl   [L. *perna,* of obscure origin, first meant back of the leg, ham, ham-shaped; later, mussel (because of the resemblance of the mussel's "flesh," or of the sometimes protruding footlike member (the peduncle), to a calf muscle. (See *muscle.*) By an untraced evolution → OF and ME *perle,* pearl (by association with the nacreous inner lining of mussel shells—pearls were unknown to Europeans except as rarities brought overland from the Far East by camel caravans).] 1. A variously colored and shaped deposit, principally of calcium carbonate, formed around an irritant, usu. a grain of sand, by oysters and some freshwater mussels. Valued as a gem. 2. A person of great value. *She is a pearl of great price.*

pearl diver 1. One who dives into the sea to collect oysters to be searched for pearls. In Japan girls do this work in about 30–50 feet of water, originally by holding their breath, now with scuba gear. 2. *Am. slang.* A whimsical title for a drifter who used to wash dishes in restaurants, now commonly replaced by a dishwashing machine. [He plunged both hands into the water as if diving, and worked over the dishes, conceived to be oyster shells, in which he might find his pearl of great price—or something worth the price of a bed in a flop house.]

mother of pearl Nacre.

pearls in wine Many legends of Arabian opulence refer to dropping a pearl in wine to dissolve and flavor the drink of an honored guest. Cleopatra is supposed to have done so in honor of Antony. Pearls, to be sure, can lose their luster by absorbing body oils and must be cleaned at intervals, but they do not dissolve in wine, and any beverage capable of dissolving them would take out the insides of the drinker. Pearls (and sometimes gemstones) were so dropped in wine as ceremonial gifts by pre-Islamic potentates (before Mohammed, 570?–632 A.D., forbade alcohol). But they were not expected to dissolve, nor did they. (As a party favor, it does beat fishing an olive out of a martini.)

pearls before swine, to cast To squander things of great worth on those who cannot appreciate them. Archly, **to cast false pearls before genuine swine** Commonly, to teach in an American college or university, offering spurious knowledge to swinish students.

peculate To embezzle. [Root sense: "to rustle cattle." See *pecuniary*, which is, at root: "wealth expressed in heads of cattle" (before metal came into use as coinage, the first metal bars being traditionally stamped with a cattle head). L. *peculium*, the sense generalized to any valuable possession, was any property given to a wife or a slave to be held apart from the master's estate. The variant L. *peculiaris*, reserved to oneself alone. And so, via ME *peculier*, modern Eng. *peculiar*, at root: 1. Of oneself alone. *the peculiar properties of mercury.* 2. *Ext.* Queer. Unusual. ("Not in common possession.") 3. *Further ext.* Idiosyncratic. *Or in slang.* Touched in the head. *Cattle rustling is, at root, a form of peculation not entirely peculiar to the old West.*]

peculiar 1. *Colloq.* Odd. Queer. (So the conversational formula, once common and still surviving, "Do you mean funny ha-ha or funny peculiar?") 2. Specific to oneself. *Gerard Manley Hopkins developed a poetic style peculiar to himself.* [Intermediate root sense: "specific to oneself/apart from the state," hence, odd, i.e., not responding to the conceived social norm. At ultimate root < IE *peku-*, wealth expressed in heads of livestock. (See *pecuniary.* Also, *fee*, Vol. 1.)

Heads of livestock, and esp. of cattle, were the earliest means of exchange. Gradually, then, bars of metal, rare and precious in antiquity, began to be used—and were commonly stamped with the head of a bull, as if to explain that they were a form of wealth. Many early coins were also stamped with the head of a bull.

By ext., personal property. ("Held apart from the state.") So L. *peculium*, originally (privately owned) livestock; later, personal property. *Peculiaris*, private, not held in common with others or with the state.

Cf. (Vol. I) *idiot* < Gk. *idiotes*, free citizen of the lowest class (implies not fit by birth or education to hold public office, hence existing for himself alone, i.e., apart from the state.)]

pecuniary *adj.* Of money. [< IE *peku-*, wealth expressed in heads of livestock. (As the Masai of Africa still calculate wealth. As in the still surviving custom in primitive tribal societies of buying a bride for a stated number of goats or other livestock.) In time, bars of metal and, later, coins became a measure of wealth and a medium of exchange; and at first these were memorially stamped with the head of a bull. With p/f in Gmnc., *peku* became fe(ku)-, whence *fee* (Vol. I), and note that in ME *fee house* had the double sense: "cattle shed" and "treasury." See also *peculiar.*]

pelf   Ill-gotten gain. *The Astors are still doing reasonably well on what's left of John Jacob's pelf.* [ME *pelf,* loot, booty. < OF **pelfre. Pilfer* is also derived from the OF form, but for reasons I cannot explain, has acquired the sense "to filch, to steal a little," whereas *pelf* implies a real haul of ill-gotten gains. It takes a lot of pilfering to add up to real pelf.]

person   Among activists for equal rights for women (see *Ms.),* an insistent but offensive sex-neutral designation for an individual. The cause is good, but the language will not long tolerate such absurdity. *chairperson* A disgusting affectation when *chair* is available and sufficient.

> There was a male chauvinist pig
> Who bought a stuffed bra and a wig
>   And started rehearsin'
>   To be a chairperson
> In case Bella Abzug won big.

So, too, *freshperson* A similarly disgusting term for a first-year high school or college student. (In the name of reason, could we settle for *frosh?*) May the cause prosper for all our sakes, but the language insensitivity of its activists is evident and offensive. I have known several to assert *personagement* for *management* in a ludicrous failure to recognize that *man-,* here, is from L. *manus,* hand, *management* being the act of taking matters in hand. I *mandate* that I will answer no letter from any entity, male or female, that subscribes itself a "chairperson," for we obviously do not speak the same language, and how, then, could we communicate?

Pete's sake   Am. Mild exclam. of annoyance. *For Pete's sake, cut it out!* In the name of St. Peter, stop it! But also commonly without the preposition. *Pete's sake, Ma, I don't need another bath!*

phone: hold the phone   1. *Lit.* Please wait a minute without hanging up (there's someone at the door). 2. *Generalized ext.* Now just hold on and think for a minute (before this talk turns into an argument).

Variantly: Hey, stop for a minute and let me think. 3. Exclam. of surprise. *Well, hold the phone, here comes Mehitabel!* [The form was obviously not possible before the invention of the telephone, plus enough time for it to become familiar enough to have the name shortened to *phone;* hence an early XX idiom formation. A variation of earlier *hold your horses* (see under *horse*).]

phosphorus   The chemical element P, in pure form a waxy, nonmetallic solid that glows in the dark (PHOSPHORESCENCE). When exposed to air it ignites spontaneously at room temperatures. [Ult. < IE *bha-*, to shine. With simple bh/ph → Gk. *phaos, phōs* (genitive *phōtos,* light); *phosphoros,* torchbearer ("bringer of light"). In Roman myth *Phosphoros,* the torchbearer, was the morning star (in another manifestation the morning star was Venus), because it rises just before the sun, and was poetically conceived to be the sun's torchbearer. This name was then applied poetically to the element, first discovered in 1669.]

HISTORIC. The element was discovered by the German alchemist Hennig Brand, who came upon it in the residue of evaporated urine. It was a double discovery: first of the element itself, and second of the fact that it occurs naturally in the body (it was later found to be an essential of our diet). Heaven knows what Brand was looking for in the redolence of his simmering pots, but his double discovery stands as some sort of record for chamber-pot serendipity. The element and its extraordinary properties were much discussed but remained scarce because Brand kept his method of extraction secret. Then in 1775, Karl Schiele, another German alchemist, announced a simple method of extracting P much more plentifully from animal bones.

piazza   1. A public square in an Italian town or city. 2. A roofed porch. [In this second sense, common in Am. up to about WWII. *Veranda/verandah* (< Hindi by way of Portuguese, and with root sense: "stockaded enclosure") was concurrently in use from c. 1920. Also *porch* < *perch* and L. *porticus,* entrance hall. And also, esp. in Penna., *stoop* < Du. *stoep,* stairs leading into a house. These stairs culminated in a broad landing, usu. with a small projecting roof over the front door, and commonly with room for a chair on either side of the door. On summer nights one sat on the stoop after dinner to "get the air" and to exchange small talk with one's passing neighbors. *Piazza* (pron. *pyă'-ză, pĭ'-ă-ză, pyä'-ză*) < L. *platea,* courtyard, open space. Ult. < IE *plat-,* flat (PLATYPUS).]

HISTORIC. Covent Garden, built in London, 1631–1634, was modeled on an Italian town piazza with an arcade along two sides, and was first called Covent Garden Piazza. *Piazza,* originally intended in sense 1, soon became associated with the roofed arcade, and was so imported to the American colonies in sense 2, which is now not even in the recognition vocabulary of the young. *Porch, veranda,* and *stoop* are still more or less recognized, but new styles of housing have all but eliminated the referent. The suburban family now sits out on the terrace, patio, or deck.

Pickwickian sense   A whimsical formula for rendering a statement innocuous as soon as any objection is raised. [After Charles Dickens, *The Pickwick Papers.* If any Pickwickian took objection to a thing said, Mr. Pickwick's formula was, "I meant that only in the Pickwickian sense," and all cause for objection was at once removed.]

pie in the sky   Future heavenly reward in lieu of decent living conditions on earth. *Pie,* symbolic of good living; *sky,* heaven, the hereafter. From the late XIX rallying song of the International Workers of the World, called Wobblies:

> Work and pray,
> Live on hay,
> You'll get pie in the sky when you die.
> —It's a lie!

HISTORIC. The Wobblies were generally Marxists. Their pie-in-the-sky song (sometimes attributed to Joe Hill, early Wobbly organizer and martyr shot dead by company police) follows from the Marxist dictum "Religion is the opium of the people." Preachers promised heavenly rewards for those who endured intolerable working conditions on plutocratic earth, but to the Wobblies, "It's a lie!" Their alternative was to fight—as violently as need be—for safe working conditions, a fair wage, and a more rewarding life here and now.

pier six brawl   *Boxing.* A toe-to-toe slugfest. (The way longshoremen were said to slug it out. [I can find no evidence that any Pier 6 was notably more violent than any other pier. I take *pier six,* therefore, to be a generic for any pier on which longshoremen worked, quarreled, and fought.]

pillar [L. **pila,* pillar.] *Architecture.* A freestanding, usu. ornamental vertical member, originally and still commonly of stone, usu. weight-bearing.

pillar of society One who upholds the principles of his social group, "ornamented" by his merits. [This metaphor can be traced at least to 1325: "a pila ariht (aright) to holden up holi church." *Column of society* might have done for this purpose, but misses fatally. *Underpinning* and *prop* lack something. Chaucer called his Monk "a noble post unto his order," but modern *post* lacks the splendid association with Greek or cathedral or palace pillars, or even of courthouse architecture.

(driven) from pillar to post Forced from one bad situation to another. [*Pillar,* here, a corruption of pillory; *post* for whipping post.]

HISTORIC. In earlier England (and in early American colonies) disorderly persons (blasphemers, scolds, drunkards, etc.) were commonly sentenced to stand with their head and hands locked in the pillory, on public view. The sentence imposed discomfort and public ridicule, but was necessarily short, for if left in the pillory until he passed out, the wretch might die of strangulation. Commonly, therefore, the sentence specified a number of hours in the pillory, after which the wretch was taken to the whipping post and given an additional municipal blessing with the cat-o'-nine-tails, all in view of his/her generally approving townspeople.

pinch [Of obscure origin. Perhaps (?) < Gallo-Latin *pinz, pintz* (of unknown origin), to point, to narrow to a point. First attested in OF *pincier,* to pinch (PINCERS, PINCE-NEZ).] *v.* 1. To squeeze between thumb and forefinger. 2. To apply pressure from two or more points. 3. To steal. [To seize by hand. And variantly, with same sense:] 4. To arrest, as a criminal suspect.—*n.* 1. The act of seizing and squeezing hard. 2. The condition felt as a result of such an act. 3. *Slang.* An arrest by the police.

pinch-hit 1. *Baseball.* To substitute for a weaker batter when a hit is urgently needed. 2. To substitute. *Gerald Ford, pinch-hitter President of the United States, struck out. pinch hit* A hit scored by a pinch-hitter. *pinch off* 1. To break off, as a bud, by squeezing between thumb and forefinger. 2. To squeeze a flexible tube, shutting off the flow of liquid or gas. *pinch pennies* To be miserly. *in a pinch* Under cross pressures. *feel the pinch* To feel the strain of being hard pressed.

where the shoe pinches Proverbial. The point at which one feels the strain or the chafing. (Earlier, *where the sandal pinches.*)

HISTORIC. Plutarch, *Lives,* tells of Emilius Paulus, who put aside his wife, and who was questioned by his friends for having done so. He passed them one of his sandals, asking that they examine it and tell him if the leather was not good and the work not well done. When they had all agreed that it was, he added, "And yet not one of you can say where it pinches me."

pineapple   1. The widespread tropical and subtropical fruit. Pineapple-growing requires a ferrous soil. Hawaii offers such a soil and an ideal climate, whence pineapple-growing has become an important industry there, though Hawaiian pineapples were developed from a species indigenous to South America. [ME *pinappel,* pine cone. (Not *pineapple,* for speakers of ME could not have known this New World fruit.) The pineapple, when first found by Europeans (prob. in late XVI, early XVII), was named metaphorically after its resemblance to a pine cone. The pineapple is in botanical fact a cluster of fruit growing together in a shape and outer texture resembling a pine cone. And so, in a further ext. of the same metaphor:] 2. *Am. WWI* (perh. with antecedents in slightly earlier army usage). A hand grenade. [Because U.S. hand grenades (unlike the German "potato mashers" of WWI) have a grooved, diamonded outer texture (which is not a bit of army esthetics, but designed for a secure grip when the grenade is thrown, and for more effective fragmentation when the charge detonates).]

pioneer   1. One who opens the way into new areas of learning and esp. of technology. *pioneers of medicine.* [And in this sense since XVII.] 2. *Primary sense in Am.* One who moves out to explore and settle wild country, as the westward migrants of the shifting American frontier. [And these two associations have given the word an honorific connotation it long lacked, the original sense being "peon, riffraff." Ult. based on IE *ped-,* foot → Late L. *pedo,* foot soldier (as distinct from the lordly cavalry).] 3. Big-footed oaf. [Medieval L. *pion, peon,* a member of the labor force of an army, trained not for fighting but for felling trees, building roads, and generally preparing the way for the fighting army. In XVI called *pioner.* Othello clearly held *pioners* in contempt. Bemoaning the infidelity of which he believes Desdemona to be guilty (*Othello,* III. iii.), he declaims:

> I had been happy if the general camp,
> Pioners and all, had tasted her sweet body,
> So I had nothing known.

And contrast that sense with Whitman's salute, "O Pioneers."]

pirate   1. A sea raider out for personal plunder. (If licensed by a sovereign, he did the same work in the same way, presumably sparing friendly flags, but was obliged to give most of the loot to his licensing sovereign.) 2. *Ext.* A grasping, merciless person. 3. *Ext.* One who issues the work of another without permission of the copyright holder, and without payment of royalties. *Taiwan is a literary pirate's nest.* (And all corresponding verb forms.) [Via L. *pirāta* < Gk. *peiratēs,* a sea raider, and also, one who attacks from the sea, but with the lit. sense: "one who undertakes a venture" < *peira,* a venture, an attempt. In this sense Jason and the crew of the *Argo* were pirates. To the Greeks piracy was a respected and even a heroic trade, especially when one killed only foreigners, all of whom were lumped as barbarians (and who, of course, did not count).]

plea bargaining   (*v. to plea bargain)* An arrangement by the district attorney's office in collusion with the courts, cynically designed to clear the docket of the criminal courts and to reduce crowding in the jails. Prisoners under indictment who cannot post bail often spend a year, or most of two years, in jail awaiting trial. The D.A.'s bargain is to offer a sentence equal to time already spent in jail if the prisoner will plead guilty. A guilty plea will mark the prisoner as a convicted criminal, but many already have a police record, and are eager to plea bargain in return for an immediate release. If, on the other hand, a prisoner is innocent, believes that a trial will establish innocence, and does not wish to be branded a convicted criminal, he or she must remain in jail months, perhaps even years, longer to await trial. So much for ideal justice. As Dante put it in the *Paradiso: "Diligite iustitiam qui judicatis terram."* Love righteousness, you who are judges on earth.

plus   [L., more.] *prep.* In addition to. *Four plus four equals eight.—adj.* 1. *Mathematics.* Positive. More than zero. 2. High in a stated scale. *Calvin Coolidge's grade for life was perhaps a C plus.—n.* 1. The plus sign. 2. *Colloq.* An asset. *His attitude is a definite plus.* (And note, in hard-sell advertising, *plus you get all these extras,* an all but established illiteracy for "plus which, in addition to which.")

plus fours [Short for "plus a four-inch overhang." Originally a tailors' term.] Baggy pants fastened just below the knee but cut full enough to allow a four-inch dependent bag. They were once standard golf wear, passing out of common use in the late 1930's in U.S.

plus sign The sign +. [A stylized form of L. *et,* and. The first published work to use the symbols + and − was a German book on mathematics, *Behende und hübsche Rechnung,* Leipzig, 1489, by Johann Widman.]

Podunk   A generic term for the smallest and most backward of small towns, a spoofing designation. [There is a Podunk, Mass., but the name was once specific, as early as 1666, to the area between Hartford and Windsor, Conn. The asserted Mohegan-Algonquinian original, by whatever distortion it may have passed into English (if it did), is supposed by some to have meant "pocket/neck of land." But most attributions to Indian sources are hazy. MMM gives *po-dunker,* bullfrog (1857), which is likely from a much earlier echoic rendering of frog croaking as *po-dunk, po-dunk, po-dunk;* and this echoic source is not only more natural than a ref. to an unknown Algonquinian original, but explains the comical connotation of the word: "out where the bullfrogs go *po-dunk.*" And see *yokel.*]

poilu   A French army enlisted man in WWI. The equivalent of the Am. *G.I.* of WWII. [And so used in Fr., but first as an adj. meaning "hairy, bearded," and by easy ext. to the earlier French dogface, "he-man," as in Am. "a man with hair on his chest," and so a fond, familiar term for the French fighting man as a virile tough customer.]

poltergeist   A spook that roars, wails, hoots, screams, and generally goes bump in the night. [Ger. *Geist,* ghost; *poltern,* to roar, bellow, howl. *Poltern* is ult. < IE *bhel-,* to roar (BULL, BELLOW). With bh/p and suffixed *-t-* → *poltern,* the infinitive; *polter,* combining form. In one root rendering: "a bull spook (of which the banshee is the cow).")]

pop the question   To propose marriage. [*Pop* (with the sense: "a sudden release of internal forces") is fixed idiom in this context. A logician puts the question, a student asks it, a suitor pops it. Popping the question, once the exclusive function of the male, always implied premeditation (the buildup of the internal forces), but in the stereotypes of the folk mind, the suitor fidgets, hesitates, flusters, and finally blurts out (pops) the actual question.]

porridge *Now.* A boiled mush, typically of oatmeal, commonly thinned with milk to the consistency, and taste, of library paste and devoured at breakfast by overambitious people who then go forth to assault the day. [But earlier, a thick soup ("pease porridge hot, pease porridge cold"); still earlier a soup; and at root: leek soup. ME, *porray* < OF *poree*, leek. Leek soup or onion soup must have been boiled thick in the ancestral pot, but the language has thickened it further in making mush of it.]

posse *In Am. usage, esp. on the western frontier.* A body of men who volunteer to ride with the sheriff in pursuit of a criminal or criminals, and who are sworn in as deputies, usu. without pay, for the duration of the pursuit. [< Medieval L. *posse comitātūs,* power(s) of the county. (A U.S. *county* corresponds more or less to the area ruled by a *count* in earlier Europe. The *posse comitātūs* was a body of knights, squires, and lesser landholders summoned to emergency duty to enforce the law at the count's feudal command. U.S. sheriffs still summon volunteer posses to hunt for lost children, and accident and murder victims, but the armed posse, except in rarest instances, has been replaced by regular deputies, sometimes assisted by state and federal forces.)]

posslq (Pronounced probably, *póss'l-q'.*) An acronym of *p*erson of *o*pposite *s*ex *s*haring *l*iving *q*uarters. [From the 1980 census form.]

HISTORIC. The U.S. Census Bureau functions to count population, not to label the forms of cohabitation. In the past *husband, wife, relative,* and *resident non-relative* sufficed for the count. During the 1970's unmarried marriages became so common that parents took to the forms son-out-law and daughter-out-law.

The bureau, recognizing this new life-style, must have weighed endless possible phrasings before hitting on this form. And so out of the ashes of bureaucracy into the fire of living language, this phoenix of a word—*posslq,* standing by for the love poetry of the future.

> Come live with me, and when you do,
> We'll be each other's posslq.

possum [The common rendering of *opossum,* which is the Eng. version of the Algonquinian word meaning at root: "little white creature."] A North American arboreal nocturnal marsupial with a long, almost bare, rat-like tail. It sometimes sleeps by wrapping that tail securely around a branch and hanging nose-down. Possums have adjusted well to the suburbs, sleeping by day and raiding garbage cans by night, but those that have lived in my yard sleep in whatever tree hollows they can find, not hanging from branches.

play possum 1. To lie still, pretending to be dead. [Because possums behave in this way when they have no other hope of escaping a predator. It must work, at least to some extent, for the possum has survived a long evolutionary trail.] 2. To hide and lie low in order to escape unfriendly notice. (Note to foreign students of American: The idiom is always *play possum;* never *play opossum.*)

precarious Risky. Dangerous. Likely to fail. [At root: "standing in the need of prayer." First into Eng. in XVII as a legalism meaning: "dependent upon another, subject to the will of another." Ult. < IE *perk-,* entreaty, to beseech, to pray (to). Metathesized variant *prek-* → L. *prex,* prayer; *precari,* to beseech, to pray; *precarius,* dependent upon prayer, in need of prayer.]

predicament 1. A bad situation. One that seems to offer no favorable outcome. 2. *In logic.* A set condition. A fixed category. [L. *praedicāmentum* translated Gk. *katēgoria,* category (in logic, argument). < Gk. *kata-,* against; *agorein,* to speak formally in public assembly < *agora,* legislative assembly. Thus *kategorein,* to categorize ("to denounce on the floor of the legislature"). The L. renders the Gk. not by *dicere,* to speak, but by *dicāre,* to proclaim solemnly. Ult. < IE *dik-,* to utter solemnly, as in religious ritual or at law. Prefixed *prae-,* before. Hence the root sense: "solemnly declared beforehand, solemnly prophesied."]

HISTORIC. Any reference to a sign or pronouncement from on high moves the folk mind to a sense of foreboding. *Foreboding* itself is an example. It means at root: "advance news" < OE *bodan,* to announce, *boda,* a herald. ("One who brings an announcement from high authority"). Etymologically the announcement could as readily be good news as bad, but the folk mind has systematically foreseen evil in news from on high. So *omen,* a sign from on high (good or bad) → *ominous.* So *portent* → *portentous.* So *on the carpet* (under official review, for better or worse) → in trouble. And so *predicament* (solemnly prophesied) → bad situation.

Humankind hopes for the best and employs priests to pray for it, but such sense shifts invariably show that the folk mind expects nothing but trouble from higher authority, whether god or emperor, and that man's best hope is to pass unnoticed by the mighty.

prejudice   Unless qualified, implies categorical aversion. So *racial prejudice,* though note that in being averse to one race one must, though bigoted, be in favor of another. [And so L. *praejudicare,* to judge beforehand. But no judgment is possible without evidence. It follows that prejudice must mean: "a preformed assumption that all members of a given class are good or bad." To some extent the sense shift has been from "either for or against" to "against." The assumptions of a democratic society impute social evil to prejudice, yet when qualified, *prejudice* can express simple preference. *I am prejudiced in favor of girls—they are female.*]

press gang   *Archaic, but well into XIX.* A junior officer or petty officer with a detail of men sent out to serve as what we would now call a recruiting team. The term is ambivalent because press gangs once commonly shanghaied men to fill out a crew. One of the issues of the War of 1812 was the British naval practice of stopping U.S. merchantmen to impress some of their crew into British service. [And so it is that in such forced enlistments *press* is taken with the sense "under pressure." As one might say in current Am. slang, the recruits were "pressured" into service. But this *press* is < OF *prest,* ready (money). (Fr. *prêt.*). So XIV *prest money,* an advance payment.]

HISTORIC. An enlistment is, technically, a service contract, and a contract is not valid unless a valuable consideration has been paid. New hands recruited by legal press gangs were, therefore, given *the king's (queen's) shilling* to legalize their enlistment, and the shilling, an advance against their future pay, was *prest money.*

Cf. *soldier* < OF *soulde,* pay < L. *solidus,* a Roman copper coin. In the days of Mussolini the lira (now about $\frac{1}{1000}$¢) was worth about 20¢ and could be changed into 100 small coppers called *soldi,* which is also a generalized It. term for money, mostly in southern Italy. *Soldier,* therefore, has the root sense: "one who serves for pay." So *solid,* a thing of substance. And so *solid citizen,* a person of substance. Like *soldier,* a *solid citizen* is, at root: "one who accepts money," for if he did not accept it he would have none, and

the common community term for a grown man who has no money
is "bum."

procrastinate   To put off doing a given thing (or everything in general). To delay to some nebulous tomorrow. [At root: "to put off
(forward) to tomorrow." L. stem *cras,* tomorrow. (Adj. form *cras-
tinus,* of tomorrow; prefixed *pro-,* forward, for, to → *procrāstinare,*
to put off till tomorrow.]

prolix   Tediously wordy. [< L. pro-, *forward* (here implying motion);
liquere, to flow. (See *liquid.*) → L. *prolixus.* ME *prolixe.* The root
image of ever-flowing water is here transferred to nonstop gab.]
    NOTE. The ultimate root sense of *liquid* is: "to go away" "form
of matter that goes away." To say *prolix as a spring brook* is to use
the language in some depth. To say *prolix as a valedictorian* is to
use the language at ultimate root depth, in that a valedictorian is
one who is "going away."
    If the question is, *Will anyone understand?* the answer is proba-
bly, *Few and rarely.* But if the question is, *Is there a self-delighting
pleasure in using the language to root depth?* then the answer is,
Yes, always. One must choose the level at which one hopes to use
the native tongue, but certainly those who use it at root depth will
use it best and most effectively.

pudding   1. In earliest usage, a sort of sausage. So *blood pudding* A
sausage made of blood, usu. pig's blood cooked with suet and often
cereal additives, and served loose or encased in an intestine. [At
root: "sausage." < L. *botulis,* sausage (BOTULISM). Altered in OF
to *boudin,* and in ME to *pudding.*] 2. *Later.* A mixture of chopped
organs and intestines, vegetables, cereals (usu. oats), and seasonings, boiled in the sewed-up stomach of an animal. Called in Sc.
haggis. 3. *Later.* A mush made of stale bread boiled in milk sweetened with honey, and with whatever additives of nuts and dried
fruits occurred to the cook. *bread pudding* [All these forms suggest
the housewife's attempt to make something approximately edible
of the lowest meats and stale bread, but now:] 4. Any sweetened
dessert variously based on boiled flour, cornstarch, tapioca, rennet,
and all the plenty of the abundant grocery, with additives and
flavorings to the limits of ingenuity, often refrigerated and topped
with ersatz whipped cream, sundae toppings, and whatever the
housewife cares to improvise. [The cooking of common household
dishes is at the whim of the housewife and the availability of

choices. Few things are harder to date than the variations of Mom's kitchen. I have suggested a sequential development from sausage to modern sweetened concoctions, but I have not been able to date the changes, nor have I dared try. Bailey's 1764 *Dictionary* defines pudding as "a sort of Food well known, chiefly in England, as Hog's pudding." Bailey, however, is consistently antiquarian in his definitions, and though he ignores *bread pudding,* it must certainly have been in common use at least a century before his *Dictionary.* Bailey also mentions intestines, suggesting sense 2, above.]

puddin' head A dolt. [A person who has pudding, senses 1 or 2, for brains. Maybe originally one whose head was a sack of boiled haggis. Cf. common *mush head* and *meat head.*]

purblind   1. Totally blind. 2. Partially blind. 3. Stupidly or stubbornly undiscerning. [ME *pur(e)blind,* purely (totally) blind, but also with modern sense 3. Then *pur-* came to be misunderstood as *poor,* whence, "of poor vision." So XIV, blind in one eye; XVII, having poor vision (whatever the cause). And transiently, even obs. *pore-blind* (blind as a pore?). A similar confusion of the first element has changed the sense of *parboil* from "to boil thoroughly" to "boil *par*tially."]

purloin   To steal. [To steal is, in one sense, to cause the object stolen to disappear far and away, and that is the root sense of OF and Norman Fr. *purloigner* < *pur* (L. *pro*), away; *loign,* far (L. *longus,* long).]

puss   *Slang.* A pejorative term for the face, originally for the mouth. *How would you like a poke in the puss?* **make a puss** To pout. [< Gaelic-Irish-Erse **pus,* mouth, and into mid XIX Am. via Irish immigration.]

puzzle   1. A more or less baffling problem or riddle. 2. A game of some complexity designed to test one's wits. 3. A person about whom one cannot form an opinion. A thing one cannot "figure out." *Life is a puzzle any corpse can resolve.* [OF *opposaile,* thing set before one. (Cf. *poser,* a baffling thing.) ME *posolet,* (thing) set forth / in place. But the word was not in general use until XVI, the then forms being *pusle, puzzell,* and the sense: "bewildering thing." OF *opposaile* is almost certainly, though unattested, < L. *pōnere,* to put in place (DEPONE), via p.p. *positus,* put in place.]

pyramid   [From a Greek joke. In Arabic a funerary pyramid was called *pi-mar,* which was exuberantly punned on by Greek soldiers, becoming *puramis, puramous,* wheat cake, with the effective sense: "stack of (Egyptian) wheat cakes."(?) Stacks of wheat cakes do not, of course, come to a point, and in context, the pun seems to be as pointless, but the soldier slang led to L. *pyramis* and Fr. *pyramide,* and a word was born.] 1. *Geometry.* A solid with a polygon (commonly a square) as a base, and whose sides, forming a squared cone, are triangles with a common apex. 2. *In Egyptian funerary custom.* A massive stone structure of this sort erected by the ancient Egyptians to contain and conceal the tomb of a royal personage. (These tomb structures are four-sided forms with a square as a base and are, geometrically, *regular pyramids.* In geometry there are also *irregular* and *truncated pyramids.* If the truncating plane is not parallel to the base, the figure is a *truncated prism.*)

   to pyramid 1. *Strictly speaking.* To buy or sell stocks that show a paper profit and to continue doing so without further investment of new capital. 2. To build a financial complex by means of a holding company that acquires minimum controlling interests in larger companies. [In both cases the root sense is "to pile high," though the image would be more accurate were the pyramid inverted ("piling high and wide from a small base").]

   P.S. As this book was going to press, I received a letter from David Schroeder of Boulder, Colo. I believe that the letter explains the Greek soldier's joke (and thank you, sir):

> The allusion to wheat cakes in the Greek root of the word *pyramid* might relate to a feature of the rock used to construct the Egyptian pyramids. The rock contains a disk-shaped fossil called *nummulites.* These were single-celled animals (foraminifers) that secreted shells more than an inch in diameter. Admittedly, I know nothing of the shape and size of ancient wheat cakes . . . but they, too, must have been disk-shaped and possibly about the size of the *nummulites.*

Q

quadrangle 1. *Mathematics.* A four-cornered plane figure. [L. *quadrus,* four; *angulus,* corner.] Mathematicians classify a figure resembling a bow tie (⋈) as a simple quadrangle. 2. *Architecture and esp. collegiate architecture.* A rectangle or square of connected buildings enclosing an open lawn or terrace, the common access to the central courtyard being through arches which are topped by rooms or passages or both, the arches commonly equipped with gates. Also, in common collegiate usage: *quad.*

    in quad Primarily Brit. but borrowed into XIX Am. with some Ivy League survival. 1. In one's collegiate quarters. 2. *Generalized.* In collegiate attendance. 3. Campused. Restricted to one's college grounds as a disciplinary measure. 4. *Brit. only.* In prison. [Confined to the prison quadrangle.]

quartered *In public executions.* Hacked into four parts; the quarters then placed on public display as dire admonitions. *drawn and quartered* Execution by having the arms and legs secured to four horses that were then driven in opposing directions to tear the wretch apart, a punishment reserved in the Middle Ages for high felons and for heretics.

    HISTORIC. In England, where public executions were so popular a spectacle that hangmen erected boxes around the gallows and sold seats to ladies and gentlemen eager for the sport, this butchery was part of the spectacle until XVIII, when George III (reigned 1760–1820) abolished quartering, the victim instead being disemboweled while still dangling from the rope.

quell 1. To put down a disorder, as a riot or an insurrection. *I tried to overthrow Jane's sense of propriety, but she quelled me.* 2. To allay. To soothe. *Luckily, Joan was there to quell my pain.* [The sense has been much gentled since the IE stem *gwel-,* to die, death. With g/k in Gmnc. → OE *cwealu,* death; *cwellan,* to kill; *gecweald,* slain. In ME *quellan,* with sense 1, above, but "by bloody military means" was implicit. By XVI *to quell,* the sense "to kill" was receding, and the primary sense was emerging as "to suppress disorder." To say that Idi Amin *quelled* his opponents would be etymologically sound, but would not likely convey today the sense of bloody slaughter so central to Amin's tyranny.]

quibble   *n. & v.* An equivocation. To equivocate. [In early XVII, a pun, to pun. And a quibble is, at root, a play on words, but this sense has receded, to be replaced by "evasive phrasing." Bailey's 1764 *Dictionary* offers: "to move as the Guts do," a sense I have not encountered elsewhere, and can only guess to be of echoic dialect origin.

The current sense derives from L. *quibus,* which is the dative and ablative plural of *qui,* who; *quae,* what; and *quod,* which. The sense derives from the fact that *quibus* once appeared over and over in the Latin of legal documents, and came to be identified by those "outside the law" as the specimen word of evasive legal phrasing. *A lawyer is an avarice quibbling its way to the pretense of honesty.*]

quick   [IE *gwei-,* alive, to live. With g/k and suffixed *-k-* in Gmnc. → OE *cwicu, cwic,* alive. ME *quike, quicke,* retains the OE sense and adds "rapid." (Which, of course, one cannot be, once slowed by death.)] 1. Alive. *the quick and the dead.* 2. Rapid. *Jack be nimble, Jack be quick.*

    cut to the quick 1. *Now.* To offend grievously. 2. *But in earlier sword-and-shield warfare.* To deliver a fatal sword wound. [To cut to the very life source.]

    quick step/quick time A marching cadence of 120 steps a minute.

    quicklime Calcium oxide. [So called because it is the first ("most rapidly produced") product derived by kilning crushed limestone.]

quicksand   A pocket of sand that yields to pressure, sucking down heavy objects that fall into it. [*Quick,* as if alive, in contrast to inert, weight-bearing sand.]

    HISTORIC. Quicksand was long a mystery, for wet sand does not normally swallow heavy objects, tending rather to pack hard, as does most beach sand. Only recently has quicksand been reproduced under laboratory conditions, the particles being kept in loose suspension not because they were wet but because water was being forced upward through them, as in nature quicksand occurs above a deep spring whose upward flow keeps the particles from packing together.

quid A chew (chaw) of tobacco. [An unexplained variant of cud. Am. Prob. colonial. Known to be common in XIX. Snuff was in common use in XVIII Britain. I have not been able to locate any ref. to chewing tobacco there. I am left to guess that snuff was used by Britons and upper-class colonials, chewing tobacco being in XVIII Am. use only among farm workers and country lawyers. Antique dealers tell me that XIX Am. spittoons are common, but that only a very few can be dated to XVIII.]

quintessence (Accent on second syllable.) *n.* 1. The most perfect condition of being. *The pure soul is the quintessence of mortal clay.* 2. The transcendent specimen of a given class. *The diamond is the quintessence of carbon.* —*adj.* **quintessential** That without which nothing could exist. The ultimate gist of anything. [Root sense: "the fifth essence." The ancients believed that all things were composed of the four elements earth, air, fire, and water. These four elements, however, were not enough to account for man's God-seeking soul. They posed, therefore, a fifth and purest element, of which the heavens were composed, *ether,* understanding by that term something like "God stuff." The Greeks labeled that fifth element *pemptē ousia,* which was translated into L. as *quinta essentia,* whence OF *quinte essence,* and ME *quintessence.* (In modern Fr. *essence* is the word for gasoline, but no French oil company has ventured *quintessence* for "high-test.")]

HISTORIC. Manichean teaching, embraced by St. Augustine in his youth, asserted that God had placed only a limited amount of God stuff (or quintessence) on earth. The first men were almost entirely composed of this essence. As the population grew, the fixed amount had to be divided among more and more gross bodies, until man became mostly bestial, with only a spark of the God essence in him. Any walk through NYC tends to bear out Manichean theory; but so does any honest introspection.

quirt [< Sp. *cuerda,* cord.] A horseman's whip. On the western frontier, no self-respecting cowboy would buy a quirt or a lariat, both being prized possessions a true man wove meticulously and artfully from horsehair.

q.t. Quiet. [As if *q . . . t*, a once common coy form of circumventing a word one does not wish to commit to paper, or to utter in full, as in the presence of children (who generally know what it means as well, or better, than their parents—or so, at least, by the time they have recovered from milk lip).] ***on the q.t.*** 1. On the quiet. 2. *Ext.* In strictest confidence, secrecy. *No s . . . t, I'm telling you on the f . . . ing q.t.*

QWERTY The now standard keyboard of English and American typewriters. [After the first six letters of the upper keyboard.]

HISTORIC. There were efforts as early as late XVIII to develop a practical typewriter. In these early efforts the keyboard was commonly in alphabetical order beginning with the upper left key. In 1867 Carlos Glidden, Samuel W. Soule, and Christopher Sholes finally developed a workable model, also with the keyboard in alphabetical order. Their first model was slow, however, and the keys tended to stick together. To prevent sticking, Sholes undertook a study of the letters that occurred in most frequent combination in English words, and rearranged the order of the keyboard to keep those letters apart. The result was the now standard QWERTY keyboard. Technical refinements soon solved the problem of sticking keys (to the extent that it will ever be solved in a manner acceptable to my two fingers), and the keyboard in alphabetical order was once again possible, but typists who had trained themselves to QWERTY refused to retrain their fingers, and the QWERTY arrangement has remained standard.

rambunctious   Loud and disorderly. Contentious. [In XIX Brit. *rum-bustius.* In XVIII *robusteous.* [Which Bailey's 1764 *Dictionary,* ever root-directed, defines as "strong like an oak," with no ref. to the unrestrained use of that strength when on a tear. The root, as Bailey cites, is *robust* < L. *robus,* oak; but the sense progression here has been from "strong" to what recent slang would call "coming on too strong."]

ready   1. Prepared to act. *Here I come, ready or not.* 2. Immediately available. *ready cash.* [These are transfer senses from OE *(ge)rǣe-de,* counseled, advised; *unrǣede,* not advised, ill advised. To be well counseled is, in a basic sense, to be prepared to act.

Ult. < OE *(a)re-,* to fit together → L. *reri,* to consider, to take under advisement ("to fit together all the elements of"). Same IE stem *re-,* suffixed *-d-* in Gmnc. → OE stem *rǣed-.* The common OE *gerǣede* survives in early ME *zeredi* (also *iredi*), but later *raedi, redi.*]

HISTORIC. Schoolboys cannot resist a chuckle at the name of Ethelred the Unready, but his name and subjoinder will illustrate. Ethelred II, king of England c. 968–1016, succeeded his murdered half-brother, Edward the Martyr. The circumstances of Edward's death led many to suspect Ethelred of foul play, and more to distrust him. His troubled reign was further complicated by Viking raids and the surviving Danish occupation. But Ethelred, a sort of Macbeth (whether in fact or only in repute), had trouble securing loyal lieutenants and counselors, the lords of England walking wary of him. Hence *Unready,* unadvised, uncounseled. The name is a partial redundancy. *Aethel,* noble, is akin to Ger. *Edel,* with same sense. The suffix *-red* is from the OE stem *rǣed-.* Hence, noble counselor. So the whole name = noble adviser unadvised (or ill-advised).

rebate   *v.* To return to the buyer a portion of a price paid. —*n.* The amount so returned. [But at root, a term from falconry, in which a bird that has taken to flight without being commanded is called a *bating hawk. Bate*, here, cognate with "beat" (as wings). < L. *batuere*, to beat (the wings). OF *batre*. XIII Eng. *bate*, in falconry, an uncommanded flight. Whence *rebate*, to call back a falcon that has broken training in this way.

It is hard to see how the modern sense follows from the original falconer's term, unless one speculates that *rebate* was influ. by *abate*, to lessen. This influ. cannot be attested, but the speculation is the more likely in that most terms of falconry were grossly unknown to most English-speaking people.]

reclaim   [At root, from falconry (and this the only Eng. sense up to XIII), the act of calling a falcon back from flight. < L. *clamare*, to call; *reclamare*, to call back. And so Old It. *reclamo*, the act of calling back a falcon.] 1. To reassert title to. *He reclaimed the stolen property.* 2. *Ext.* To bring (back) to good order and governance. *Proper care has reclaimed many a problem child.* 3. To restore blighted land to cultivation or other good use. *The Israelis have reclaimed great acreages of barren land.*

refrigerator   [IE *(s)rig-*, cold. Via Hellenic → Gk. *rhigos*, cold. (Whence RIGID, RIGOROUS, RIGOR MORTIS, in all of which the sense "cold" has receded and been replaced by "stiff, unyielding." "Cold," however, has remained the primary sense of Eng. words based on L. *frigus*, cold, *frigerare*, to make cold, and this verb, with intensive prefix *re-*, is the base of *refrigerate, refrigerator.*] *At root.* Thing that makes cold.

HISTORIC. I had always assumed that *refrigerator* labeled the mechanical cold box with coolant coils powered usu. by electricity but sometimes by gas; and that *icebox* (which see) labeled the simple chest whose cold derived from the melting of a block of ice. Old-timers still refer to a *refrigerator* as an *icebox*, but the difference between the two is generally observed, except for the young, most of whom have never seen an icebox, and don't know what it is.

Yet all Sears, Roebuck catalogues of the 1890's (up to about 1920, when mechanical refrigerators became popular, though too expensive for most families) advertised iceboxes but called them *refrigerators*, a use fully permitted by the root sense: "device that makes (keeps things) cold." It was only when mechanical refrigerators became general that they took over the name, leaving *icebox* specific to the earlier, nonmechanical, cold cabinet.

POSTSCRIPT. On January 31, 1982, a friend showed me through the Monster Restaurant in Key West. In the amply stocked room for liquor storage I saw an electric refrigerator. Taped to it was a hand-lettered sign that read: "Champagne splits [are] in [this] icebox."

rehearse   To go over and over a part one intends to play, a speech one intends to make, esp. for a dramatic performance, but also in preparation for a foreseeable encounter. *Most affairs are sexual rehearsals for saying goodbye.* [At root: "to go over and over the same ground with a harrow." ME *rehercen,* OF *rehercer* (with *re-* as an intensive and frequentative prefix), to harrow. < L. *herce,* a harrow. And see *hearse.*]

resentment   Offense taken. Continuing bad feeling returned in kind. [A changeling word. < OF *resentir,* which is *sentir,* to feel; with *re-* as an intensive prefix with a frequentative force. Hence with the root sense: "persistent strong return of feeling," and originally of good feeling.

Archbishop Trench, *On the Study of Words,* cites such common XVII and XVIII usages as "a Faithful resenter and requiter of benefits," and the good man's "affectionate resentment of our obligations to God."]

retaliate   To repay a slight or an injury. [But this is a late sense < L. *retaliāre,* to repay in kind, which could imply return of good as well as evil. The modern sense probably stems from L. *lex talionus,* the law of (exactly) measured return, with the effective sense: "an eye for an eye and a tooth for a tooth," though in practice despotic justice added something for good measure, as when a thief who stole a trinket had his hand lopped off.

In XVII "to retaliate one's master's goodness" meant "to return enduring gratitude for goodness received"; whereas today the word is explicit to the return of ill for ill. (And see *resentment* for a similar sense shift.)]

ribald   *adj.* Labels coarse, rump-thwacking humor full of references to sex. [Root sense: "in heat." So Medieval L. **ribaldus,* whorechaser. OF *riber,* to pursue easy sex (RUB), suggests the obscure root *rib-* was Italic. But it could have been Gmnc. *hrib-,* to rub, picked up in Medieval L. In any case, it is widespread in Gmnc. So OHG *hriba*, whore ("easily rubbable women"), MHG *ribe*. The root also occurs in Du. and Icelandic. Prob. ult. < IE *wer-*, to rub; zero-grade form *wr-*, *hwr-*, suffixed *-b'-* in Gmnc.

First attested in XIII Eng. as a noun, *ribalde*, a servant of the lowest order. ("Low, lewd lout.") In aristocratic assumption, "low fellow good for nothing but fucking." In XIV, a scurrilous person. And not used as an adj. until XVI.]

riding the ghost   [A bitter idiom of Depression era cabbies. Now obs., but I once, though briefly, drove a cab in Boston in late 1930's, and had to ride a few ghosts.] Driving an empty hack around town, with the meter thrown, making up the fare from one's own pocket. [Because on each shift, cabbies were required to show a minimum meter reading on pain of being denied a cab on the next work shift. With jobs desperately scarce, cabbies ran up the meter at need, paying up, and hoping to find the corner around which prosperity was said to be.]

rise: get a rise out of   To provoke a more or less strong emotional reaction, commonly by teasing. [From fly casting, in which the angler drops his fly in a likely spot and lets it float on the surface, hoping his dream fish will rise to the bait.]

rite of passage   [IE *rei-*, to fit together, to conjoin. With suffix *-t-* → L. *ritus*, a religious observance ("ceremony properly put together," i.e., "joined, conjoined").] 1. A ceremonial religious observance marking a formal change in one's life and status. 2. *Ext.* A more or less formally prescribed act or series of acts leading to such a ceremony. *the rites of courtship.*

NOTE. *Passage* as a euphemism for "death" and *passing bell* for "death knell" have led many to understand this idiom as meaning "funeral ritual." But *passage* originally had the sense "marking one's passage, stage by stage, through the life of a religious believer." And so Fr. *rite(s) de passage.* Baptism, first communion, confirmation, marriage, and finally funerary observances are all rites of passage through the life of a Roman Catholic person.

robust   [At root: "oak-like," or most specifically, "like a red oak." < IE *reudh-*, red. With regular shift of the voiced stop *dh* to *f* in Latin (as demonstrated by Grimm's Law) → L. *rufus*, reddish, ruddy; and with regular f/b → *rōbus*, *rōbor*. 1. The red oak. 2. *Ext.* Firm, hard, strong. The adjectival form is *rōbustus.*] 1. In abundant health. 2. Sturdy (as an oak). Muscular. 3. Said of hearty and flavorful wine. [It. *vino robusto.*] Also of meat-and-potatoes country cooking. *a robust meal.*

rodomontade/rhodomontade   Loud, empty bragging and bluster. Bombastrionics. [After *Rodomonto,* the loudly self-vaunting Moorish king of the epics *Rolando Inamorato* (XV) and *Orlando Furioso* (XVI), Italian (and esp. Sicilian) retellings of the medieval *Chanson de Roland.* It. *rodomontada,* a bluster of braggadocio; *un rodomonte,* a loud braggart. (I have found no explanation for the r/rh alteration in Fr.)]

romance   *n.* 1. A more or less elaborate tale, originally of knightly deeds and chivalric love. [The form of the word from Medieval L. *romanice loqui,* to speak street Latin, the vernacular rather than the Latin of the classical masters. Also *romanice scribere* and OF *romanz escrire,* to write in the vernacular. (To this extent, *The Divine Comedy* is a romance.) In any case, *romance* came into English as a noun, later acquiring verb functions, as below.] 2. A love affair. [A courtship like those narrated in chivalric romances —except, of course, for a felt shortage of knights in shining armor.] 3. A common and tawdry element in the titles of promotional books and booklets, the function being to give an aura of high consequence to what is merely commercial. *The Romance of Peanut Butter.* 4. (Akin to preceding, and prob. its source.) A quality seemingly inherent in certain objects and places, suggesting that they would have high tales to tell if they could speak. *Ah, the romance that clings to nostalgic old money.* —*v.* 1. To woo. 2. To spin elaborate and deceitful tales. *He tried to romance me into cosigning his note.*

    Romance language A language derived primarily from Latin. Italian, Spanish, and French are Romance languages. English is heavily influ. by them, but is primarily Germanic.

    romantic adj. 1. Concerning love. *romantic whispers from the back seat.* 2. Conducing to love or nostalgia. *romantic islands far away.*

    Romantic literature Beginning in late XVIII, a literary shift from the Age of Reason to an ardent assertion of individual feeling, even of irrational impulse. To risk a gross simplification, the central image of the Age of Reason and of its modes, cadences, and basic beliefs is the minuet, a dance in which many dancers take stately place in fixed relation to an overriding, fixed pattern. The figure for the Romantic Age would then be the waltz, a figure in which two dancers rotate around their own axis, with impulsive variations as the music moves them. The ideal figure for the Romantic would be, perhaps, a solitary waltzer.

rope(s) of sand   A semi-proverbial image for the tie that will not bind, the strand that will neither hold nor hoist. [A. Lee, *Papers* (1783), said of James Madison: "He had rather see Congress a rope of sand than a rod of iron." It is unlikely, however, that Lee coined the phrase and image. I have not been able to locate an earlier source in Brit., but I believe it must be attested somewhere. It may even be of proverbial antiquity, for few images could better express futility.]

row   (Pronounced *rou* as in *rouse*.) A commotion, dispute, noisy revel. [Origin unknown, but in some detail; ult. < widely dispersed Brit. dialect usage. OED dates from 1800 as "slang or colloq." But it is standard in Am. *They were having a row* = they were having a spat. Henry J. Todd in his 1818 edition and enlargement of Samuel Johnson's *Dictionary* labels it "a very low expression," but he must mean that it is of dialect origin, not that it is offensive. Many, including various Webster's dictionaries, seek to derive it from *rouse*, citing *pea* < *pease* as precedent. (*Hamlet*, I. i: "The king doth wake tonight and take his rouse." Note *wake*, here, for "festive seating, wassail.") But the Webster's suggestion ignores the wealth of evidence in *The English Dialect Dictionary*. The 1811 *Vulgar* gives: "*Tow Row*, A grenadier," and "*Tow Row Club*, A club or society of grenadier officers of the line," the implication being, "place of noisy revelry"; but in this sense a late adaptation of dial. *towrow*, which had such conforming senses as: "a noisy disturbance, a hubbub, a revel, to carry on in a disorderly way," and also "to beat severely." There is also dial. *row*, to work hard, especially amid confusion, to rake ashes, to bring up old quarrels. And note that *towrow*, with a common r/d dissimilation between two vowels, could readily (but unattested) yield *to-do*.]
   rowdy 1825. A disorderly person. *rowdy-dowdy 1854.* Redupl. for emphasis. Based on *rowdy. a rowdy-dowdy crew* = a disorderly and down-at-the-heels crew. Also *row-de-dow* [Attested in Brit. 1832.] A reveler's exclam. of enthusiasm. (Survives as an upper New England and esp. upper Maine localism. *Rowdy-di-dow, more fun than a barrel of monkeys!*)

rub To stroke more or less rapidly with a back-and-forth motion. [ME **rubben,* to rub.] *the rub* The difficulty, the problem, the obstruction to be overcome. [In lawn bowling, a bare or uneven patch of grass that deflects the bowl. *Hamlet,* III. i: "Aye, there's the rub." (Shakespeare drew his images from many sources, but the largest single category is country sports.)] *rub out* 1. To erase. 2. *Criminal slang.* To kill. [To "erase" from life.] *rub the wrong way* To annoy. To rile. [As cats and dogs commonly become edgy when stroked against the natural lie of their fur.]

rubber 1. One who rubs. [See *rub.*] 2. The substance, originally dried tree sap (latex), now commonly synthesized and variously treated for use in a wide range of products. [So called because the first use of the latex product (also called India rubber or caoutchouc) was for erasing pencil marks from paper. (The *art gum eraser* is still essentially this form of rubber.)] 3. *Bridge and other games. (a)* A play series that ends when one side has won two out of three games. *(b)* In such a series, the tie-breaking game when the score is one to one. [Origin unknown. Could it be < *the rub,* difficulty to be overcome? The question asked, there is no answer.] 4. A condom. [See Vol. I. Originally (XVIII) made of sheep intestines, but in latter XIX of treated latex.] 5. *Plu.* Low-cut overshoes of rubber or rubberized canvas.

    rubber check A check returned by the bank as unnegotiable. [It "bounces"—like a rubber ball.] *rubberneck n.* A sightseer who gawks in all directions. [As if stretching the neck.] —*v.* To act like such a sightseer. *rubber stamp n.* 1. A strip of more or less hard rubber affixed to a wooden, or other, strip attached to a handle, and having raised letters or symbols. When pressed against an ink pad and then paper, this device imprints a limited prepared message. 2. An underling; one capable of relaying only fixed and limited messages. *Warren G. Harding was a rubber stamp impersonating a President. rubber-stamp adj.* A generalized and limited copy that lacks substance. *Harding was a rubber-stamp President.* —*v.* 1. To imprint with a rubber stamp. 2. To approve routinely, without deliberation. [This ext. seems to assume that rubber stamps imprint only *YES* or *O.K.* One of my favorite rubber stamps imprints a large *NO!* But idiom chooses what it pleases as it pleases, and we go along with it as natives of the idiomatic code, idiom being a systematic illogic we are conditioned to.]

ruffian   1. A thug. 2. *In softened usage.* A mannerless, offensive person. 3. *In intimate banter.* A dear rogue. [Root sense: "Cruddy person." < IE *kreup-*, rough, abrasive. With k/h and p/f in Gmnc. → OE *hrēof*, scab, scurf, crud. And so by sense transfer from physical to moral repugnance → XVI *ruffin, ruffian,* pimp, whore; then generalized to mean any violent criminal, and made specifically male. (It. also has *ruffiano,* with the same senses, as an untraced borrowing from Gmnc.)]

rum   Strong drink distilled from fermented molasses or mashed sugar cane. Strong rum is twice distilled, emerging at a proof as high as 140, which makes it about the strongest liquor one can drink without burning the stomach lining. [Richard Ligon, *A True and Exact History of the Island of Barbadoes,* published 1650, asserted that *rum* derived from *rumbullion,* which he described as a West Indian word, implying that it was native there. It was in fact borrowed from Devonshire dialect (whence it acquired some currency in general Brit., though now obs.), its sense being: "uproar, tumult, wild party." In Barbados the word was obviously associated with the roaring drunkenness produced by strong drink, and hence by association of effect with cause, *rum* as the hell-raiser's drink.]
    demon rum The curse of strong drink. The addiction conceived as a destroying fiend, *rum* as a generic for all strong drink. [*Rum,* here, a survival from colonial America, where rum was the most common strong drink, remaining so among the iron men of wooden ships well into XIX, though the common tavern drink became bourbon or rye, with Scotch as the drink of the elite, never of the American workingman. In the same survival:] *rummy* A sot. [Though many an American rummy has gone to his grave through the valley of delirium tremens without ever having tasted rum. And so, too:] *rumrunner* The invariable Prohibition era term for smugglers who went out in fast boats to rendezvous with ships waiting outside the then three-mile limit, to load up with cases of Scotch and Canadian whisky. Great Lakes rumrunners had no three-mile limit. They ran the stuff to secret coves on the American side. [But whether seaboard or Great Lakes, rum was the rarest of the rumrunner's cargoes.]
    But *rum go* (see Vol. I) is at root *Rom* (Romany) *go,* i.e., a Gypsy (hence a queer) thing.

S

salacious   Lewd. Lecherous. Pornographic. Conducing to sexuality.
[Not "salty" as in *salty joke, salty remarks.* < L. *salire,* to jump;
salax, given to leaping about (with understood ref. to the antics of
many animals and birds in their mating ritual). *Mad as a March
hare* is a similar ref. to the wildly comical mating antics of hares—
comic, that is, to a human observer, though the continuity of furry
things is evidence that the doe takes the performance seriously.]

salver   A tray or serving platter, usu. of silver. (Now generally associated with the small silver tray on which the stage butler delivers a letter to the stage master, but a salver is simply a special name
for a tray.) [In the long history of political poisoning, a tray on which
food and wine are sampled by the butler/wine steward/food taster
before dinner is served. Root sense: "thing that makes safe." Food
about to be served was placed on a sideboard called a *credenza*
(which see). The butler then put samples from every dish and wine
bottle on a *salver* and tasted everything. If he did not die or develop alarming symptoms, dinner could be served. < L. *salvare,*
to save, to make safe (SALVATION, SALVAGE). The imperative *salve,*
lit. "be safe," came to be used as a salutation, with the effective
sense: "your health."]

salvo   The simultaneous firing of massed artillery (as a naval broad-
side) or of small arms, either against an enemy or as a salute. The
firing of a number of pieces in quick succession is also called a salvo,
but in a salute each round is fired in unison. [L. *salve,* imperative
form of *salvare,* to make safe. The sense is "hail, stay well and safe."
Salve Caesar = hail, Caesar (and may the gods keep you safe). And
see *credenza.* Also *salver.*]

Sandman   The figure of nursery tales who comes gently to put sleepy-
bye dust (sand) into the eyes of children who are being put to bed.

HISTORIC. The Sandman is a figure evolved by odd etymological slippages. L. *semi*, half, was rendered in OE as *sam*, and in Saxon and Gmnc. as *sami*. So OE *samblind*, half blind, partly blind. As OE receded, *sam* became an unknown element and was gestalt-modified to the nearest familiar word pattern, *sand*. In *The Merchant of Venice*, II. ii. 36–38, Shakespeare has Launcelot give it an intensive twist to *gravel blind*, totally blind: "O heavens! This is my true begotten father, who being more than sandblind, high-gravel blind, knows me not."

So, by association, the mildly "gritty" sleepies that children rub from their eyes in the morning were said to be the work of the Sandman. (See *Nod: Land of Nod* for another nursery distortion.)

One would suppose on this etymological evidence that the Sandman is specific to English, but German children, too, have their identical *Sandmann* by the identical assimilation of *sam(i)* to *Sand*, the form of which is the same in both languages.

sarcasm   A cutting remark. [At root: "flesh-tearing (as by a wild animal feeding)." < Gk. *sarx*, flesh (see *sarcophagus*, Vol. I); *sarkazein*, to tear the flesh; *sarcasmos*, the act of so doing; and by ext., a verbal laceration.]

sashay   1. *Square dance call*. The call to perform a step in which one foot, moving forward, back, or to either side, is followed (chased) by the other. [Am. corruption of Fr. *chassé*, such a dance step, but at root: "pursued, hunted, chased," it being the p.p. of *chasser*, to hunt, to pursue.] 2. *Ext*. To saunter along more or less aimlessly. To mosey along. [May once have implied *to strut along*, but if so, that sense has receded from the word.]

Saturnalia   An unrestrained revelry. [After the Roman Saturnalia, a festival in honor of Saturn as Chronos, first god of time and father of the gods. It was celebrated for 3–5 days beginning Dec. 17 and was a time of wild excess in which the violation of normal proprieties was religiously licensed. (See *satire*, under *sa-*, Vol. I, and note on the Fescennine Festival.)]

scallywag/scalawag   1. A rascal. 2. *In Reconstruction South*. A white, native, southern Republican, i.e., one who, though born in Dixie, endorsed Lincoln's policies, and was therefore despised as a native-born carpetbagger. (The word has softened in recent Am. use, being used more or less indulgently.) [The origin is in some doubt, but prob. < Scalloway in the Shetland Islands, with an implied ref. to Shetland ponies as mean-tempered runts of the horse family— and perhaps to the dour natives, islanders tending to be gruffly suspicious of outsiders.]

scam   A plot to swindle, rob, deceive for gain. [Am. XIX carnival cant. The carnie crews speak what is perhaps the densest cant in current Am. The object, as with all thieves' cant, is to speak freely in the presence of a victim without having him understand. Perhaps, as most suggest, a simple variant of *scheme*, but XIX Am. traveling carnivals, like most circuses, were made up of international troupes, and one might speculate possible sources from many different languages.]

HISTORIC. It has become a recent fad to use *scam* in compounds, beginning with *Abscam*, an FBI code word for an investigation of corrupt congressmen and other politicians. At root: "Arab scheme," in which agents posed as oil-rich Arabs and offered large bribes for favorable legislation, the entire transaction being recorded on hidden TV cameras. On June 19, 1980, a *N.Y. Times* front-page headline read, in part: *Indictments in Abscam Case.* On the following day, an inside head read: *Jaycee Spirits High Despite "Jam Scam."* The story was about the misuse of money made in a national fund-raising drive for which the Jaycees sold jam. It involved a prominent North Carolina Jaycee leader who purportedly set a record for increased membership and who was in line for the national presidency of the Jaycees, when it turned out that he had siphoned about $190,000 from the intended beneficiaries of the fund drive, and had used it to pay the dues of nonexistent new members in nonexistent new chapters throughout North Carolina.

He was caught with jam on his face. The *Times* may be caught with egg on its stylebook if it does not institute a *scamscrub*.

ADDENDUM. Or, how etymology may be judiciously readjudicated after the fact when a minority group raises an objection. The following item is presented intact from *N.Y. Times*, Aug. 21, 1980:

> What exactly does Abscam stand for?
> When law enforcement authorities first revealed the Federal Bureau of Investigation's undercover operation they said that Abscam, its code name, stood for "Arab scam" or swindle.
> Yesterday Judge George C. Pratt, who is presiding over the first Abscam trial in Federal District Court in Brooklyn, said it was clear to

him that "Abscam" was a contraction of "Abdul scam," a reference to Abdul Enterprises Ltd., the fictitious business that the undercover investigators invented as their front.

Thomas P. Puccio, the prosecutor in the trial and one of the supervisors of the operation, later said that the judge was right. However, Mr. Puccio had made no effort before yesterday to correct news reports that "Abscam" was based on "Arab scam."

The issue came up in court after Judge Pratt announced that he had received a complaint from the American-Arab Relations Committee that the trials "reflect poorly on the Arab peoples and perpetuate the old prejudices against Arabs, even though they had no part in the charade concocted by the F.B.I."

On review of the evidence, I find Judge Pratt and prosecutor Puccio guilty of pusillanimous tampering with the language, and fine each of them a ten-year supply of evasive adjectives in the hope that the truth may yet be found in them.

scenery   [Gk. *skēnē, a tent. But in L. scaena: 1. Stage scenery painted on canvas. 2. A theater. ("place where scenery is used.") 3. A subdivision of a dramatic act. ("action in front of the stage scenery.") Thus the word, originally theatrical, a stage depiction of nature, came to be applied to nature itself.] n. 1. A prospect of nature, especially a pleasant one. 2. A stage setting, esp. the flies and flats. —adj. *scenic* Of or marked by attractive vistas of nature. *scenic highway.*

score   Twenty. "Four score and seven years ago . . ." —Lincoln, Gettysburg Address. [Ult. < IE *sker-*, to cut. But the specific ref. is to the ancient *counting stick*, a branch on which farmers and stewards kept count of livestock, bales, sheaves, etc. by making vertical cuts to indicate "one," and then for convenience cutting across those *notches* at every fifth, tenth, or twentieth count. A *score* was the largest such lateral cut in common use. *Tally*, which see, also derives from this ancient use of the counting stick.]

scruple   [IE *sker-*, to cut (SCAR). Metathesized form *skreu-*, suffixed -p- → L. *scrupus*, a stone with a cutting edge; *scrupulus*, a little sharp stone. But also, a small weight. And by metaphoric ext., a small matter to which one is sensitive, as a bit of gravel in one's sandal.] 1. *Pharmacy.* A weight of 20 grains, 1/24 ounce, 1/3 gram. 2.

Ext. as in the L., but now the primary sense. Moral, ethical, or religious sensitivity to the smallest details of right and wrong.

secular   *Now.* Not of the church. [At root: "temporal," as opposed to the eternity of the church. By many associations < L. *saecularis,* adjectival form of *saeculum,* with the double senses: 1. An age. (A century). 2. A generation!

We think of a generation as occurring approximately every twenty years. Early Romans thought of it as a century, the approximate period of the longest life. Evolving from some obscure Etruscan rite, the Roman secular games *(ludi saecularis)* were a sort of three-day Olympiad combined with elaborate sacrificial rites. They were held (more or less) every hundred years! The Romans always had trouble with their calendar, but 100 years was the intended interval (once in a lifetime), and the earliest recorded observance was in 249 B.C.

World and time equating readily, the term *clerici saecularis,* secular clergy, developed c. 1200 to label priests who lived in the world and served under a bishop, as distinct from monastics, bound by the rules of an order, who served under an abbot or a father superior. These latter were called *religious (religiones),* the root sense being not, as now, "of the faith," but "a person bound by the special ties of a holy order." (See *religion,* Vol. I, for the precise sense of *religione* in the Middle Ages.)]

sedition   1. The act of breaking away from. Esp. the action of a part of a national unit in breaking away from a nation to become a separate nation; usu. taken by the larger nation to be a rebellious action. 2. *By association.* (*a*) An unlawful dissent. (*b*) Treasonous discord. *Alien and Sedition Acts.* **sedulous** Painstaking. [Both seem, on the surface, though mistakenly, to be based on IE *sed-,* to sit, a seat (SEDAN, SEDENTARY). *Sedition* is < *se-,* reflexive pronoun, here with effective sense: "unto oneself"; with L. *ito,* gone; p.p. of L. *ire,* to go, *itio,* substantive, "act of going." At root: *se- itio,* act of going apart unto oneself, but with *d* inserted for ease of pronunciation. *Sedulous* < same prefix; with *dolo,* pain, painstaking; at root: "the act of taking pains unto oneself."]

sentry   A soldier placed on guard at a fixed post or on a fixed patrol, primarily to prevent the passage of unauthorized persons. [Earlier *centry* and so Dryden's *Aeneid,* early XVII, which form may have been by confusion with It. *sentinella* < *centinaia,* a group of 100 (soldiers), as a cohort was 1,000. But to confuse things further, Thomas Nashe, also in XVII, has "to take sentries in the Hospital of Warwick," in which *sentrie* can only mean "sanctuary." However understood, the common sense in all these cases is "security, safety, guard."]

sepulcher In Brit. *sepulchre* [IE *sep-*, to venerate. Suffixed form *sep-l-*, reverent, ritual → L. *sepelire*, to bury with religious observance. The Eng. form is from the p.p. *sepultus*, buried. The earlier sense, "a receptacle, usu. in an altar, for containing a sacred relic or relics," is standard but rare, the Am. primary sense being:] *n.* A tomb or other burial vault. —*v.* *to sepulcher* To entomb. *Ext.* To inter. *whited sepulcher* A hypocrite. [Matthew 23:27: "Woe unto you, scribes and Pharisees, hypocrites! For ye are like unto whited sepulchers, which indeed appear beautiful outward, but are within full of dead men's bones, and of all uncleanness."]

HISTORIC. It was once Jewish custom to whitewash isolated tombs, in part to warn passers-by against desecration of the dead by intrusion; but probably also as a public-health measure, new and imperfectly sealed tombs providing a focus of infection by attracting rats and all crawling necrophages. Several rabbis I consulted tell me that the tombs were whitewashed only once, when the corpse was sealed in. The whitewash would wear away long before the corpse stopped being dead. If the primary purpose was to warn away intruders who might desecrate the dead, the whitewashing should have been a perpetual-care item.

settee A long, high-backed bench, usu. with arms at either end. Variantly, an upholstered piece like a settee. And as a further variant (regional), a sofa for two. [< *settle*, but in Am. regional prob. influ. by *"set (y)e down."* Ult. < IE *sed-*, seat, to sit.]

seven sleepers (of Ephesus) They represent the condition of being dead to the world.

> I wonder, by my troth, what thou and I
> Did ere we loved. Were we not born till then? . . .
> Or snorted we in the Seven Sleepers' den?
> —John Donne

[Gregory of Tours, *The Book of Miracles*, retells the strangely pointless, pious medieval tale of Constantine, Dionysus, Johin, Maximillian, Malchus, Martinian, and Serapion, seven noble young men of Ephesus in Asia Minor. In the year 249 A.D. they hid in a cave to escape persecution. There they fell into a sleep that lasted just under 200 years, from which they woke only to die almost at once. Thereupon, to raise pointlessness to near-mysticism, their bodies were taken to Marseilles, where they are, purportedly, still preserved in an outsize stone coffin in a cathedral there. So at least the legend Gregory recorded, if only to prove that piety is under no need to make sense.]

seventh heaven   The height of bliss. [Though not securely attested and dated, the root ref. must be to the top of the Islamic seven-tiered heaven, as set forth in the Koran. Once the perfected soul has risen to that height, it grows larger than all this earth and develops 70,000 heads, each with 70,000 mouths, each with 70,000 tongues, each able to speak 70,000 languages; and all souls forever, in all these tongues at once, sing the praises of Allah. One might be tempted to settle for less, but if bliss is loud in the seventh heaven, there is nothing skimpy about it.]

shamefaced   Ashamed. Abashed. [Implies "red in the face," "showing shame by facial signs," and so the word has been received following its corruption < OE *sceamfaest* < *sceam*, shame, and *faest*, fast, at root: "held fast (restrained) by a sense of shame."]

she   *Nautical.* The traditional pronoun in referring to a ship (and extended to locomotives, airplanes, and all sorts of admired mechanisms, e.g., steam shovels, bulldozers, and automobiles). [But note from XVII, and surviving, *man of war, merchantman,* and earlier *Indiaman.*]

shindig/shindy   An exuberantly loud and lively party. [< Erse and Irish *shindy* or *shinty*, a violent early form of field hockey played with curved sticks and a ball. Any form of hockey will equate to violence, the spectators providing the noise (and also brickbats). *We went to a fight and a hockey game broke out.*]

shit   [IE *skei-*, to divide. (A metathesized variant of *sek-*, to cut, to cut off. BISECT.) Via Gmnc. suffixed, prob., *-d-* → OE *scītan*, to shit (at root: "to divide from the body"). The form is attested only in *be-scītan*, to befoul (BESHAT). (Toward the universality of natural metaphor: In late XIX, tramp steamers working the western Pacific took on Malayan sailors, Laskars, primarily as stokers. Their pidgin

English had no word for *ashes* but they rendered the word as "shit belongum fire," a metaphor essentially the same as that which underlies OE *scītan.*)

In OE *c* functioned as *k*, regularly altering to the sound *sh* before the front vowels *e* and *i* in passage to ME, in which the form is *shitten*, to shit.

The *c* retained the *k* sound, however, in passing into Sc., and to many dialects including Erse, the most common forms being *skate, skite,* and *scut,* with such varied senses as dirty, cheap, low, of the anus, and "of bodily expulsion," as in spitting and urination. The common and obvious root sense of all these is *excrement / low, worthless stuff.*

Sc. *He played me daughter Kate a fearful skite* = at root: he played her a shitty trick. So *cheapskate* is, at root: a cheap shit (lowest of low persons). So *blatherskite*, at root: a noisy shit. And so *scut,* the tail of rabbits and deer, is the part nearest the anus.

In hospitals, senior staff members list daily assignments for interns, usu. such chores as urinalysis, stool analysis, and other "dirty" jobs that do little or nothing to advance a medical education. The log in which such assignments are listed is called the *scut book,* at root: the shit book. And in common slang *scut work* is unpleasant, drudging, dirty work.]

In all idioms *shit* = low, filthy, detestable, worthless stuff.

n. 1. A defecation. 2. The results of one. 3. Worthless, disgusting, filthy stuff. 4. *Narco slang.* Heroin. —*v.* To defecate.

go shit in your hat (and pull it down over your ears) Common vulgar formula of contemptuous rejection. [As if to imply that the person so rejected is stupid enough to do as commanded, and even to enjoy this form of shampoo.] Variantly **go take a shit for yourself** [Implies: "You're no good for anything else" / "You're most at home in the crapper" / "That will at least get you away from me."] **well, I'll be dipped in shit!** Exclam. of surprise, vexation (the last thing one would want to happen), but also of pleasurable surprise (the last thing one was expecting).

shithead 1. An utterly stupid person. [One who has shit in place of brains.] 2. A heroin addict. [*Head,* common narco slang for "addict."]

shitheel The lowest, most odious of persons. [*Heel,* the lowest part of a human being, here intensified by being shit-smeared.]

But variantly **shit-lucky, he must have stepped in shit,** and *(fall into shit and) come up smelling of roses* All express the idea of incredible, blind, stupid luck. [Origin unknown. I can only guess that in country folklore, to step in shit (as a cow flop) was said to be lucky. It must certainly have been a common enough pasture experience. But lacking attestation of this bit of folklore, I can only conclude ???]

shit! Exclam. of dismay, anger, vexation, disgust. [Clearly vulgar, but the only slightly minced form *shoot/oh, shoot* passes as acceptable even among the genteel, prob. because the origin is not recognized. Cf. *poppycock* (Vol. I), a sufficiently genteel form, though at root: "baby shit." And in the rhetorical flourish of Black English, the variants *shite* and *she-ite.*]

shit list An imaginary roster of persons to be utterly rejected or to be paid in dirty ways for an offense. *be on someone's shit list* To be in someone's black book.

chicken shit G.I. slang. 1. Endless spit-and-polish regulations, esp. in training units. 2. Pointless make-work chores designed for no purpose but to "keep the men busy." [At root, because shoveling chicken droppings is the dirtiest of farm work, but prob. influ. by *chicken* as the common form for a colonel's eagle insignia, hence by association, the sort of shit training command colonels dream up.] *shit on a shingle* (In common WWII G.I. use, but perhaps earlier in the jargon of prewar diners and truck stops.) Creamed, hashed, hot (if one gets to the mess hall in time) corned beef on toast.

And many more, but enough of this shit.

shopping bag lady   A usu. elderly, female, urban derelict. Many shopping bag ladies are eligible for social security, or other state or federal benefits, but have no address to which checks can be sent, and avoid government offices in dread. They make a meagerest living by picking trash (who on earth buys what they gather?), carrying their gleanings in one or more shopping bags. Like male derelicts, they sleep wherever they can. Penn Station in NYC is a common cold-night clubhouse for them, the cops tending to be permissive between periodic rousts for form's sake. [So called because they carry all their possessions in two or more large shopping bags. I cannot date the first use of the term, but it had become common by 1970. The existence of a Skid Row for elderly women is in itself a soul blight. I know of no idiom that better illustrates the decay of the word "lady" in Am.]

silent majority   The vast majority of honest, God-fearing, churchgoing, foursquare, grass-roots Americans who do not raise their voices in public discussion of politics, but whose opinions were known intimately by Richard M. Nixon. It was this silent majority that gave Nixon his overwhelming mandate to say for them what they do not say for themselves.

As a piece of political effrontery, *silent majority* may be the most slickly successful political phrasing of this century, simultaneously asserting the mystique of the humble-but-true American and claiming that all precincts unheard from vote overwhelmingly for Nixon—a neat piece of political embezzlement.

> There once was a slicker named Dick
> Who, no matter how dirty the trick,
>   Invoked the authority
>   Of the silent majority—
> Till he found he could not make it stick.

simoleon *Am. slang, since c. 1830* A dollar. [< Brit. slang (since XVII but obs. by late XIX) *simon,* a sixpence. There is no explanation of the Brit. usage. Simon Magus sought to buy sacramental powers for money, and *simony,* named after him, is the sin of selling the services of the church for money. The money nexus is apparent, but no proper priest will sell out his office for a mere sixpence. Nor is there an explanation of the Am. variation. What is certain is that Brit. *simon* passed into Am. *simoleon,* the monetary exchange rate shifting from Brit. 6 d. to Am. $1.]

sinecure 1. *In Am.* A job that pays well but demands little work, as for example, the position of country club public relations man in charge of losing at golf to important customers and suppliers of the firm owned by your father-in-law, who would have had to support his daughter in any case, and who can, by this arrangement, deduct her allowance as a business expense, while protecting his business by keeping you out of the office. 2. *Brit.* (With the Am. sense, but also:) A church benefice providing a living and perquisites but involving few duties. [L. *sine,* without; *cura,* care. But note that *cura* meant "responsibility for." So Fr. *curé,* parish priest ("one responsible for the good of his parishioners"). So It., *a cura di,* in charge of (said of an editor who assumes responsibility for a publication, or of editing a text). Eng. *care* has taken on many other senses, but the root sense survives in *caretaker* and in the slightly variant form *curator,* both implying "one who takes responsibility for."]

siren [Ult. < IE *twer-*, to seize, to grasp. In a complex evolution substantially beyond my grasp, tw/sw, perhaps in Hellenic, and doubly suffixed *-y-* and *-n-* to some such skeletal form as *su-y-n-* → Gk. *Seirēn,* siren ("she who seizes").] 1. *Greek myth.* An evil sea nymph who lures seamen to their destruction by sitting on rocks and singing with such irresistible sweetness that the helmsman steers straight for the singing, and the crew, entranced, cannot intervene. [The Teutonic **Lorelei* or Rhine Maidens are identical except for being a freshwater species, but they are not necessarily borrowed from the Greeks. The far greater likelihood is that the Greek and Teutonic siren myths are separate evolutions from a common ancestral legend lost in deepest antiquity.] 2. *Ext.* An irresistibly attractive woman. A *femme fatale.*

3. An air-raid warning signal. [Did not occur in this sense until 1939, the beginning of WWII in England. Perhaps with antecedents in factory tooters, the British developed a device consisting of a whirling perforated metal drum into which air or steam could be forced under pressure to produce a wailing, whistling, penetrating sound. The wag who bent *siren* to this service had the idea "danger" on his side, but he must have been thinking of the banshees.]

skate A steel blade variously attached to the shoe for gliding on ice. (Roller skates, a much later technological development, were so called by a simple association of no substantial etymological interest.) [Du. *schaats,* skate → late XVI Eng. *scates.* The terminal *s* was mistakenly taken as a plu. ending and dropped almost at once to yield *scate, skate.* (Thus sparing us such a pure plu. form as *skateses;* and such verb forms as *to skates, skatesing, skatesed.*)

Some point out that Du. *schaats* is akin to OF *eschasses,* stilts, and a skate is, in a sense, a low-level stilt. But *schaats* is more nearly related to Ger. *Schacke,* shank; *Schackebein,* shinbone. And the historical fact is that early skates (some museum specimens have been dated as early as 600 A.D.) were made of split and polished shankbones of horses, the heavy bones bored to receive straps for attaching them to a boot. It does sound awkward, but young energy makes do. Metal blades were a much later development. Jonathan Swift refers to them in early XVII as recent innovations.]

(Not to be confused with *cheapskate* and *blatherskate/blatherskite,* for which see *shit.*)

sleazy *n. Brit. XVII, XVIII. Now obs.* A fine cotton or linen cloth used for linings. Also *sleazy holland,* in which holland is a generic term for this sort of cloth; *sleazy* functioning as an adjective. (Cf. *shoddy,* Vol. I, for a similar noun–adjective evolution based on inferior cloth.) —*adj.* 1. Cheap. Worthless. Fine-seeming but inferior. 2. Tawdry. Garish. Put forth as if of true value but obviously false. *a sleazy argument.* 3. Sleek. Slinky. Imitating elegance. *dance hall girls in sleazy imitation satin.* [All forms are a corruption of *Silesia,* earlier part of Germany, now a coal-mining district of western Poland. The XVII, XVIII cloth was manufactured there, probably as fine cloth for linings, but deteriorating in quality as it was imitated (keeping the corrupted name *sleazy*) in other places. Earlier also *sleasie, sleasy, sleesy, slesey, slazey.*]

HISTORIC. Bailey's *Dictionary,* 1764, gives: "*Sleasy,* after Silesia," adding: "but the term is commonly used for a thin slight holland." (*Holland,* cloth of Holland, first so named because made in Holland, then a generic name for light cotton or linen cloth made in other places and deteriorating as it was imitated.) Bailey also gives, as a separate listing: "*Sleazy,* slight or ill-wrought, as some Sorts of linen cloths are."

The OED follows Bailey in listing *sleasy* and *sleazy* separately, but goes so far as to suggest that the two forms are of different origin. This separation must ultimately have been the decision of the don who worked up the OED's notes for one section of the words beginning with *s.* He gave no reason for seeing two separate words here. He may have been thinking of *sleeze,* which the *English Dialect Dictionary* gives as a widespread dialect noun (no adj. form) meaning "loosely or badly woven cloth."

One might also look to dialect *slay, sleigh, slaze,* a weaver's rod. But all cloth, good or bad, required the use of a reed worked at right angles to the threads of the loom (the warp and the woof). I cannot find a dialect adjectival form *slazey, slayzey,* and I do not see how an adjective meaning "of the weaver's reed" could mean "ill-woven." There is also the fact that all relevant variant forms given by EDD are of XIX dating.

As I read the evidence over the ghostly don's shoulder, I must conclude that all dialect variants are from XVII, XIX, and are based on the original corruption of *Silesia* to *sleasie, sleasy, sleazy,* which like *holland* was originally fine linen or cotton, but deteriorated as it was imitated in various "sleazy" mills.

slush fund   *Am. XIX politics.* A cash fund not officially carried on the books, to be used for political payoffs, bribery, and other forms of corruption. [Originally Brit. maritime from XVII to the passing of sailing ships. *Slush,* in nautical usage, was rancid grease from the ship's galley. This, along with frayed rope ends (see *junk*) and outworn ship's gear, was saved till the ship reached a port where bum boats (bargelike scavenger tubs) bought it for salvage and resale. The receipts were called the *slush fund,* and were generally used for providing small comforts for the crew.]

snafu   *n.* A mismanaged mess. *The operation was one snafu after another. —adj.* Mismanaged. Snarled. *another snafu operation.* [A WWII service acronym expressing the civilian soldiers' resigned disgust at the standard operating procedure (SOP) of the services. An acronym for *s*ituation *n*ormal—*a*ll *f*ucked *u*p. Often rendered reticently as "all fouled up," but let your own sense of services idiom decide whether *fouled* or *fucked* was the original G.I. phrasing.]

soldier   *n.* 1. One of an army's rank and file as distinct from a commissioned officer. 2. One who makes a profession of arms, officers included. 3. An ardent supporter of a cause. *soldier of the Lord.* 4. *Organized crime.* A "made" (i.e., initiated and sworn) man of a crime family. His function is not to make policy but to carry out orders, asking no questions. [At root: "one who works for pay." Hence a mercenary, though Roman legionnaires, not necessarily mercenaries, were the most prominent class of men to work for pay and booty at a time when most European males worked the soil and traded by barter, living with practically no pay in money. < L. *solidus,* up to fifth century A.D., the most common Roman small coin. Whence It. *soldi,* money; OF *soulde,* pay; *sould(i)er,* soldier, mercenary.] *—v.* 1. To serve in the army. Esp. to show that one is tough enough to meet the demands, challenges, dangers, and injustices of military life. 2. Conversely, to avoid work. To goldbrick. To stand or lounge about, doing nothing while others work. [This sense is from the British seaman's scorn of marines, who have no ship-handling duties, and who stand about as sailors scramble up the rigging, or perform any of the thousand tasks of handling the ship and keeping it trim.]

Solomon's ant   Solomon twice mentions ants. Proverbs 6:6: "Go to the ant, thou sluggard; consider her ways and be wise." Proverbs 30:25:

"The ants are a people not strong." In both references he praises the ant as a model of industry and orderly living. In the first reference "ant" is clearly used generically, rather than as an individual creature. Yet Mohammed takes the story as if Solomon had had a single ant in mind, and includes that one ant among the ten dumb creatures allowed to enter paradise. See *bees: telling the bees.*

so long Common colloq. form of "goodbye." Usu. with the sense: "till we meet again" (Fr. *au revoir*), but in sentimental usage, a farewell to the dead. *So long, old buddy* (which is Fr. *adieu,* at root: "to God"). [Originally Brit. but absorbed into Am. At ult. root, Brit. nautical, prob. late XVIII, as British ships became more and more common in Islamic ports. A British sailor's corruption of Arabic *salaam,* peace be with you, which is the common form of salutation on meeting and departing. It is a bit hard to explain the transformation of *salaam* into *so long,* but the British have traditionally manhandled and even mauled foreign expressions they have taken over, and even swallowed and distorted native forms as *maudlin* for *Magdalene, bedlam* for *Bethlehem,* and *Rotten Row* for *rue du roi,* king's (bridal) path.]

solstice [L. *solstitium,* point at which the sun's course (north or south) is halted. < *sol,* sun; *sistare,* to bring to a halt. It. uses cognate *sostare,* to park (a car).] One of the two terminal points of the sun's apparent course north and south of the equator. South and north latitudes 23°30'.

winter solstice Dec. 21–22. First day of winter in the northern hemisphere. The sun is then at its southernmost point, bringing the fewest hours of daylight to the northern hemisphere; the most, to the southern. Also called *the dead of winter.*

summer solstice June 21–22. First day of summer in the northern hemisphere. The sun is at its northernmost point, bringing the most hours of daylight to the northern hemisphere; the fewest, to the southern.

SOP Armed services. *S*tandard *O*perating *P*rocedure. (Commonly translated by civilian soldiers as *hurry up and wait,* or as *snafu* (which see).

soup [Of obscure Gmnc. origin, via Frankish → OF *soupe.*] 1. A liquid food made of boiled anything, ideally with some fat in the mixture. 2. *Am. slang.* Nitroglycerin. [A gross generalization. Were slang meticulous rather than impulsive, the right image would be consommé, or at least broth. (But who can imagine an oil field roughneck using consommé to bring in a well?)]

soup and fish Am. XIX slang. White tie and tails. [Because that was the proper attire for a formal dinner, beginning with a soup course, followed by a fish course, and going on. *from soup to nuts* A full formal dinner beginning with soup and continuing through many courses to nuts, fruit, etc. [In Roman formula, *ab ōvo usque ad māla,* from the egg (first course, probably deviled) to the fruit (last course).]

soup kitchen A charitable dispensary to the destitute of inexpensive but nutritious food. *in the soup* In trouble. [As if chopped up and boiled.]

soup up To add power, most commonly to an automobile engine, by installing superchargers and other devices and by tuning it fine. [< Sense 2 above. As if giving the engine an explosive new power.]

spaghetti [< It. *spago,* string; plu. dim. form *spaghetti,* little strings. So named in early XIV when Marco Polo, returning from China, introduced Italy to this "dish of the little strings." (But what on earth did Italians eat earlier, always bearing in mind that they did not begin to eat tomatoes until XVII?)] 1. A non-bored, stringlike form of Italian pasta. 2. *Radio, electronics.* Insulating tubing for fine wire, esp. with color-coded sheaths for fine inner circuitry. *spaghetti bender* A pejorative name for an Italian. [But in reason's name, how is one to eat the stuff except by curling (bending) it around a fork? Answer to question: In Sicilian festivities, men sometimes have spaghetti-eating competitions with their hands tied behind their backs. A quantity of spaghetti is dumped on a stone tabletop (or on oil cloth) in front of each sport, covered with *ragù,* and the signal given. The first man to finish his mound of the stuff is King Pasta. The game is a bit like bobbing for apples after they have been made into applesauce.]

spoil *v.* 1. To turn rotten, as overripe or mildewed or frozen or insect-infested fruit. 2. To deface or damage a thing. 3. To interfere in a process, flawing or upsetting it. 4. To harm by overindulgence and mollycoddling. *spoiled brat.* And as an intensive, *that brat is spoiled rotten.* 5. *Archaic.* Variantly **despoil** To slaughter and pillage. [Sense 5 is closest to the root in L. *spoliare:* 1. To skin an animal. 2. The act of stripping armor, weapons, jewelry, sandals, etc., from a dead or defeated foe (skinning him of his armor and other valuables). It. *spogliare*, to undress; *le spoglie*, the remains of a dead person, the corpse at a wake.]

spoiling for a fight Eager to exchange blows. [XIX. Is the root sense: "eagerness to defeat and loot"?]

spoils system *Am. politics.* The practice, after an election, whereby the new "ins" fired all appointed officeholders of the defeated party in order to give the jobs to their own loyal supporters. Now somewhat modified by civil service and the "merit system," but baldly practiced in XIX, and politicians still find ways to reward their own at the expense of opponents. [So called because "to the victor belong the spoils."]

spook etymology In these notes, I use this term to label etymologies invented by language spooks who thrive on free association with no regard for attestation. (An alternative term might have been "guess etymology.") Spook etymologists have long haunted the language, and have been shamelessly ingenious in making up nonfacts in support of their inventions.

A common and simple spook etymology derives *asparagus* from *sparrow grass* (which is easy to do if one ignores Gk. *asparagos*, a vegetable shoot). Commonly, then, the spook will go on to explain that sparrows are compulsively drawn to asparagus, and even that it works upon them as catnip works on cats. These are ludicrous assertions apart from the observable facts of nature, but they are the natural food of spooks. See *love* (in tennis) and *ass in a sling* for specimen spook etymologies, but I have noted many more in these notes.

Spook etymology is not to be confused with *folk etymology*, the common and often poetic process by which we have *daisy* < "eye of day" / "day's eye," as well as *cowlick* and *cowslip* (see *cow*).

sport 1. Diversion, amusement, pastime. 2. *Plu.* Athletic games and competitions. *organized sports.* 3. One who plays by the rules of the game. *good sport, bad sport.* 4. A form of address. [An honorific form of *guy*, implying that the person addressed has *sporting blood* (the inclination to play and to take a chance).] 5. *Genetics.* A mutant. [All these usages share the sense "outside the common, laborious routine of making a living." < earlier *disport*, which is Fr. *porter*, to carry a load, to labor (PORTER); with neg. prefix; hence "not engaged in labor."]

to sport To display gaily. *sporting a flaming red necktie.* *make sport of Primarily Brit.* To tease. To mock. [< Sense 1.] *sports car* A small, low-slung, two-passenger automobile designed to resemble a racing car, but more common as the prowl car of cruising adolescents, and of insecure shrinks who are trying to pretend they have not had their fortieth-plus birthday. *spoilsport* 1. One who will not play by the rules of the game. 2. *Ext.* A wet blanket. One who holds back and casts a pall on the gaiety of others. *be a sport As an entreaty.* 1. Join in the play. 2. Take a chance.

> One night in a dimly lit bar
> I was smoking a ten-cent seegar,
>   When a girl of a sort
>   Said, "You look like a sport,"
> And my wife, in the shadows, said, "Harh!"

spouse   One's husband or wife. Either of a married pair. [But earlier, a betrothed person, one's betrothed. So It. *i promessi sposi,* the betrothed couple. < L. *spondere* (RESPOND), to make a ritual pledge. P. p. *sponsus* (as a substantive), fiancé; and so *sponsa,* fiancée. L. *sponsalia* was the ritual not of marriage but of drawing up the marriage contract, the betrothal, whereupon the couple, in Eng., became *espoused.* (Cf. *espouse a cause.*) The *n* of the L. was dropped in Old It. *sposa* (masc. *sposo*); the form slightly altered in OF *espous, spous;* whence ME *spuse, spouse,* all with the root sense: "betrothed." The modern sense began to emerge in XVIII. Bailey's 1764 *Dictionary,* the tendency of which is always toward the root sense, defines the term as "a Bridegroom or Husband, a Bride or Wife." His definition catches the term just in the act of turning from the root sense to the modern, *Bridegroom* and *Bride* being the betrothed at their wedding; *Husband* and *Wife,* what they thereupon become.]

stack up against   To compete. To measure up to an opponent. [Poker term. A ref. to chips stacked up before the players. It is an axiom of poker that in a no-limit game, a good player with a large stack (or many stacks) can "freeze out" a good player with limited resources. Hence commonly in the negative: *You can't stack up against the big money. Norman Rosten is generally willing, but he just doesn't stack up against Muhammad Ali.* = Ali is not what he used to be, but Norman is smart enough to be chicken.

starters 1. *In standard Am.* The officials who start a race. 2. *In slang.* An opening action, proposition, assertion. Esp. in *for starters For starters, Gentle Jerry broke both of Fat Freddy's legs and kicked in his teeth. Then he went to work seriously.*

stationer A seller of writing supplies, paper, business and legal forms, office supplies, etc. [Because this tradesman earlier did business out of a station, or stall. But so, for that matter, did most other retailers, any of whom might have been called a stationer, except that the language convention, for no traceable reason, chose one, and locked the others out of idiom.]

steeplechase A cross-country horse race over a course that has been fitted out with obstacles. [Originally (XVIII) a game played by hard-riding British gentry, who picked a steeple in the distance and raced toward it in a straight line over all fences, ditches, water, livestock, and tenant farmers.]

step- Prefix indicating family relationship resulting from the remarriage of a widowed parent (now also by remarriage after divorce). [< OE *stēop*, bereft. Ult., via Gmnc. < IE *steu-*, pushed out of. The earliest forms were OE *stēopćild* (*ć*, here, to render *c* as *s*). Also *stēopbearn*, step-baby, orphan. And *stēopfaeder*, *stēopmōder*, *stēopsunu*. Orphan, < Gk. *orphanos*, also has the root sense: bereft. < IE *orbh-*, to thrust asunder.]

stink [OE *stincan*, to stink. Of obscure Gmnc. origin.] *v.* 1. To give off an unpleasant odor. 2. *Ext.* To be offensive. *You stink!* —*n.* 1. A foul odor. 2. *Slang.* An unpleasant scene. *Don't make a stink.* (Cf. the Yiddish proverb translated as: "If something stinks, don't stir it.") *stinker* A rotter. An offensive person or thing. *The obstacle course is a real stinker, and so is the coach.*
　　stink pot 1. A chamber pot. 2. *Ext.* A person conceived as a psychic, social, and personal chamber pot. 3. *Nautical.* A sailing man's pejorative term for a steamship. [Mid XIX. Because the new steamships emitted stinking coal smoke from their stacks.]
　　stinking *Slang.* A generalized pejorative. 1. Worthless. Lousy. Unbearable. Rotten. *a stinking job.* 2. Reeking. 3. Inebriated. [Reeking of liquor fumes.] Also variantly *stinko.*
　　NOTE. *Stink* and *smell* are commonly confused in illiterate usage. *To stink* is to emit a bad odor; *to smell*, to detect one. Early radio operators, be it said in their praise, got it exactly right

in their now archaic slang: *to stink*, to transmit; *to smell*, to receive.

stoic 1. *At root*. One who follows the philosophy of Zeno, whose central tenet was that man's fate is determined by the gods, whereby the good man can only seek such limited virtues as reason reveals, accepting the decrees of fate impassively. 2. *Ext.* A person who accepts the turns of things impassively. Hence *stoic / stoical adj.* Emotionally impassive. [The sense is from the teachings of Zeno, the label from the place in which he taught, a colonnade (Gk. *stoa*) in the *agora* of Athens. So Gk. *stoikos:* 1. Of the *stoa*. 2. Of Zeno's school.]

strategy An overall plan of action that coordinates many tactics. [< Gk. *strategos*, general. Generals plan and command campaigns and battles, detailing specific assignments to tactical field officers.]

sudden *adj*. Hasty. Unexpected. *There comes the sudden discovery that "year" (which see) is a cognate.* [IE *ei-*, to go → L. *ire*, to go → *subire*, to move by stealth ("under cover"). The idea "stealth" has receded, replaced by the associated sense "unforeseen," the present sense being a further association with the fact that the unforeseen happens fast ("before we know it"). So It. *subito*, quick, soon, < L. *ito*, p.p. of *ire*, prefixed *sub-*, under. The form altered to OF & ME *sodain*, sudden.]
 all of a sudden At once and unexpectedly.
 sudden death *Sports*. A tie-breaking extension of play in which the first team to score wins. In golf, more than two players may be in the playoff, the winner being the first player to gain a stroke over the other(s).

sullen Sulky. Ill-humored. Antisocial. Withdrawn in a dark mood. The opposite of outgoing. [At root: "alone, self-enclosed." (See *boudoir*, at root: "pouting room.") < L. *solus*, alone. OF *seul*. The existence of an OF variant, *solein*, alone, though unattested, may be inferred from ME *solein, solain*, solitary, hence "withdrawn into oneself," hence "sulky."]

Sunday: knock (someone) six ways to Sunday To beat up thoroughly. [Am. rhetorical flourish. Dating unknown, but prob. XIX, and perh. from the exuberant language outburst of Jacksonian democracy.

Mark Twain's style is a full flowering of that language exuberance, and this idiom would fit natively into his style, though I have not turned it up in his works (and yet continue to believe it must be there somewhere).

The six ways to Sunday are, of course, the six days of the week, and must be taken in order, leaving nothing out; whence the idea "to be systematic and thorough (in delivering a beating)."]

superheterodyne   A fading word. In the late 1920's and through the 1930's, when radios were made to resemble the lower facade of a cathedral, and their innards glowed with a congregation of variously sized glass tubes with mysteriously different inner grids, *superheterodyne* was the advertiser's and salesman's magic label, the word rolling off the tongue as if a paean to advanced technology. And then came the transistor and the chip. [A polyglot formation. < L. *super*, above, more than; with Gk. *heteros*, other, and *dyne*, force; in effect a superior device for coordinating different (other) electric forces into one superior sound.]

supermarket   A large, lavishly stocked retail outlet, primarily for food but with a great variety of other goods displayed to prompt impulse buying. The essential features are variety, self-service, and checkout counters where the customer must endure long lines in return for "bargains." The essential preconditions are the automobile-refrigerator-freezer technoculture, permitting customers to shop and stock once for a week or more. [So called because the first such markets dwarfed the traditional grocery stores and meat markets in size and in the variety of goods offered. Soon, however, identified by their self-service and by the checkout counter. Whence:] *superette* The last stand of the local grocery store–meat market, which, though it could not compete with the variety of goods offered by the supermarkets, reduced the number of clerks by installing self-service and the checkout counter. [So paradoxically, "a little great-big."]

HISTORIC. The young may need to be told that the old-fashioned grocery store featured long counters that divided the customer from most of the goods. (Some of it was commonly displayed in bins and baskets in the customer area.) Clerks stood behind the counters and fetched whatever the customer asked for. Most local stores offered home delivery, taking orders over the phone, and commonly extended credit to established customers. It was a relatively high-overhead, personalized service, and doomed almost at once by the lower prices and the greater variety offered by the low-overhead, high-volume supermarket.

Clarence Saunders of Memphis, Tenn., converted his Piggly Wiggly chain to self-service in 1916, but the first supermarkets on today's model were opened in Los Angeles and Texas, and soon after in Oklahoma, in the early 1930's. The shopping cart, now indispensable, was introduced in Oklahoma City in 1937, and patented by Sylvan Goodman, owner of a supermarket chain, in 1940. (Customers, out of old habit, resisted the use of carts until owners hired people to push them around the market, pretending to be customers.) Shopping malls with huge parking areas proliferated after WWII, and the new era of merchandising had arrived, inevitably, and at reduced prices, but with a considerable imposition upon the customer, who must wait out tiresome lines at the checkout counter.

surprise *v.* (With corresponding noun sense.) 1. To overtake unexpectedly. Hence: 2. To startle. Hence: 3. To cause wonderment. *Ticonderoga was surprised in the dead of night.* [< Fr. *sur,* over; with *prise,* taken; p.p. of *prendre,* to take, to seize. ME *surprysen.* Samuel Johnson (I cannot now locate the source of the story) is said to have been dandling a chambermaid when his landlady entered and exclaimed, "Dr. Johnson, I am surprised!" To which he is said to have answered, "No, madam, you are astonished. I am surprised."]

surprise attack An unforeseen assault. *taken by surprise* 1. *Earlier (with some survival).* Said of a military position taken in an unexpected assault. 2. *But in generalized Am. usage.* Caught off guard.

surprise party A party to which the guest of honor is not invited, but in which he is ambushed by festivity in the course of his normal rounds, everyone shouting inanely, "Surprise! Surprise!" as the poor fool (who has already guessed from the number of cars parked in his drive and at the curb) enters his house, and pretends to be overwhelmed by the outpourings of friendship and laughter.

SWAK *Acronym. Sealed With A Kiss.* [Common Am. puppy-love inscription on the envelope containing a more or less intimate letter.]

synod A deliberative assembly of church officials from various districts and divisions of a church. [At root: "(assembly come to) by road." Gk. *syn-*, by (syncopated form of *sym*), with *hodos*, road, travel. (The supreme council of the U.S. Lutheran Church is called the General Synod, but there are also Particular (or District) Synods. And see *diet*.]

tabby 1. In loose usage, generic for a domestic cat; but accurately, a brindled and striped cat with markings resembling those of watered silk. [< Obs. *tabis,* watered silk. < ME and OF *atabis,* watered silk. Ult. < *Attab,* a prince of Baghdad, whose palace, outside the city, was called in the Arabic of XIII caravan traders *al 'attāb-īya,* the name also serving for the community near it, and finally for the fine watered silk manufactured there. *Tabis* was in high vogue among men and women of fashion in XIV England and remains an elegant fabric to this day, but as other fabrics became the British vogue, the name *tabis* passed from use except, as modified, with specific ref. to a cat. Earlier, too, with the sense: "a gossip," as in *those old tabbies,* but the sense was clearly: "those old cats gathered together to gossip," with no ref. to their markings.]

talesman The old-fashioned but surviving word for a juror. [In earlier Brit. law, one summoned by a *writ of tales* to fill vacancies in a sitting jury. So called because the writ was addressed in legal Latin to *tales de circumstantibus,* such persons as may be standing about. < L. *tales,* such (persons); nominative plu. of *talis,* such, such a person. At one time British judges could reconstitute a jury diminished by illness, death, or other causes, and could do so simply by issuing the writ to be served on any freeman who might be passing the courtroom or sitting in it as an observer. I do not know what procedures (if any) were used to bring that early talesman up to date on the evidence.]

talisman Plu. **talismans** Any object said to have magic powers in fending off evil, as hexes and spells, esp. one small enough to carry on one's person, as a charm or amulet. [Errantly < Gk. *telein,* to complete (a rite) (TELEOLOGY). Also, to initiate into a religious mystery. (Such an initiation would confer a magical protection flowing from the god one serves.) Medieval Gk. *telesma,* charm, sacred image. The word passed into Arabic alchemical and metaphysical use as *tilsam,* plu. *tilsaman,* returning to Europe metathesized as Sp. *talisman,* It. *talismano,* prob. in XIV. The It. form inevitably suggested *tale mano,* that hand, such a hand, suggesting a magic charm or amulet (as in surviving *witch's hand,* a sewn amulet containing whatever passed as anti-hex ingredients). First attested in Eng. in XVII.]

tally   *n. & v.* A count, as in taking an inventory. To count, to take an inventory. [Earlier, and immemorially, *counting stick,* a smooth branch on which farmers and stewards kept count of livestock, sheaves, sacks, bales, as they were brought in, making a notch for each one, and then for convenience in counting, scoring the notches horizontally by fives, tens, and scores. (See *score.*) Ult. < L. **tālea,* such a counting stick. Whence Fr. *tailler,* to cut (TAILOR, TALLY), and It. *taglio,* cut (INTAGLIO).]

tantalize   To fill with great desire, only to deny its satisfaction. [< Greek myth. After the punishment of Tantalus.]
        MYTHO-HISTORIC. Tantalus, king of Lydia, was the demigod son of Zeus and the mortal maiden Himantes. As a demigod he was admitted to Olympus and to the table of the gods, dining on nectar and ambrosia. He sinned by stealing the food and drink of the gods and bringing it to mankind, the sin being the more grievous in that nectar and ambrosia conferred immortality, thus creating a dangerous possibility of immortal men who could rival the gods. (Variantly, immortality was a consequence of the ichor that flowed in the veins of the gods as blood flows in the veins of man.) Tantalus was banished to Hades and condemned to stand forever in a pool of clearest water under boughs bursting with perfect fruit. Damned to eternal thirst, he could not drink, for the waters receded when he bent to drink. Damned to eternal hunger, he could not eat, for the branches swayed just out of reach when he raised an arm for the fruit. So the myth.
        But myths are usually elaborated parables of early human events. The Titan Prometheus was said to have stolen fire from heaven and brought it to humankind. He was punished by being chained to a mountain peak, where he was visited eternally by an eagle that breakfasted daily on his liver, the liver growing back painfully every twenty-four hours, becoming fully reconstituted just in time for the next serving. Clearly, his myth memorialized

humankind's discovery of fire (a thing that can both serve need and create disaster).

The punishment of Tantalus is in many ways similar to that of Prometheus, and for a like offense. The fascinating question is, What does the myth of Tantalus memorialize? The answer, I will suggest, is the discovery of wine. We still say, "This wine is nectar," and "This food is ambrosia." And wine, so long as its influence works upon the drinker, can make him feel as if immortal.

Such a guess cannot, of course, be attested, but what are such mythic symbolisms for, if not to prompt likely speculation, if only as a stirring of shadows?

taps 1. The military bugle call signaling "Lights (fires) out. Go to sleep." [From *tap*, a drumbeat. Because the earliest form of this military call was sounded on a drum.] 2. Since c. 1870, the last call sounded at burials with military honors, whence its use as a common requiem.

HISTORIC. Oliver Wilcox Norton, later a lieutenant in command of Negro troops, first served in the Union Army as the bugler of Gen. Daniel Butterfield's Brigade. In a privately printed war memoir published in 1903 by O. L. Deming, Chicago, Norton discusses Butterfield's intense interest in military calls as an essential of battle in those days before radio communication. When the men of his brigade were mingled with others, for example, Butterfield composed a brigade identification call that the soldiers rendered as DAN, DAN, BUTT-er-FIELD. The men of his brigade then knew that the next bugle command was to them.

Norton reports that in July of 1862 the general called him to his tent to play a new taps he had composed because "the regulation [bugle] call was not very musical and not appropriate to the order which it conveyed." Taps, as composed by Gen. Butterfield, was (and is):

Put out the lights, Go to sleep, Go to sleep, Go to sleep, Go to

sleep. Put out the lights, Go to sleep, Go to sleep.

Adopted by Butterfield's Brigade, this call struck a chord of nostalgia. Other units, hearing Butterfield's new call, adopted it, and by 1863 it had replaced the earlier regulation taps throughout the Union Army. After the war, as old soldiers began to die, Butterfield's taps came into use as the last call over those who were buried with military honors, and so to its now generalized use as a ceremonial farewell to the honored dead.

tarnal Eternal. [By aphesis and vowel modification. Widely dispersed in Brit. dialect, and common in Am. dialect from earliest colonial days.] *tarnation* A mild minced oath, as if substituted for "damnation" but with the root sense: "the eternal creation." *What in tarnation are you up to?* What in the everlasting creation are you doing? [And clearly influ. by such dial. forms as *botheration, thunderation.*]

tarred with the same brush Of the same bad sort. [In Britain, sheep that graze on open moors are still marked for identification by a brush mark on the fleece. A commonly offered suggestion is that tar was once used for this purpose. Tar, however, tends to come in a limited range of identical shades of black, a fact that led to earmarking, or to the use of more distinctive dyes, which did not make the handful of dyed wool worthless. And since sheep do not tend to be evil, the sense cannot be said to concur.

Sailors are commonly at work with tar brushes; in cramped quarters they often tar one another (and themselves) with identical brushes; and the idiom has many nautical precedents. All the evidence tends to exonerate sheep and to fix this idiom to a nautical origin.]

Tartar Variantly *Tatar* 1. A native of Tartary, most of whose tribes had allied with the Mongol Empire by c. XIII, making up part of the Golden Horde. Under Genghis, or Jenghiz, or Chingis Khan (1162–1227), this fierce cavalry carved out an empire stretching from the Pacific to the Dnieper. 2. The fiercest, bravest, and cruelest of warriors. [As part of the Mongol strategy, this cavalry was encouraged to rape, torture, and kill when looting cities that had resisted the attack. After days of riotous bloodshed, the Tartars allowed a few survivors to escape to spread word to other cities of what would happen to them if they dared resist.] *catch a Tartar* To be in a situation in which one can neither advance nor retreat. Implies that in catching a Tartar one is oneself caught and soon to depart this earth. [Various stories are told of the Russian warrior who charged into a thicket and called to his captain that he had caught a Tartar. When ordered to bring the Tartar in, he is said to have replied (in perhaps his last words): "He won't let me!"

The story has an authentic folk flavor, but *catch a Tartar* is a simple variant of proverbs in many tongues. English has *have a tiger by the tail.* Terence, prob. making use of a Latin proverb, has *Auribus teneo lupum:* I have a wolf by the ears.]

tea caddy   A more or less airtight box of tin, porcelain, or other material for keeping tea dry and easily accessible. [Via pidgin, with some unexplained alteration, < Malayan *kati,* a weight of approximately 21 ounces. Possibly because tea was once packed in containers of that weight.]

terrier   Any of the widely various breeds of usu. small and pugnacious hounds originally developed to pursue small game into burrows. [At root: "earth (burrow) hound." < L. *terra,* earth, soil, dirt. In OF *terrier* meant "burrow," whence *chien terrier,* lit. "burrow hound." (As an example of the plasticity of word roots, obs. Eng. *terrier,* a survival from Norman Eng., was once the legal name for a land registry book, lit. an "of the land book.")]

Terry Parker   A once common street name, unnoticed by any who have dealt with Am. street slang. Regardless of ethnic origin, every big-city ethnic slum of the Northeast (and, I am told, Chicago) had a number of dudes known as Terry Parker, usu. runners for bookies, prize fighters, would-be flashy gents, and small businessmen. In common use in the 1920's and 1930's, suggesting an origin c. 1900 and a possible eponymous Terry Parker who swaggered about in late XIX, though I have not been able to find a trace of him. Yet the name existed (and traces survive) with the force of idiom, for everyone understood that a man who called himself Terry Parker was reaching for a sort of flash, and that he did not want his real name to be used.

Tetons/Grand Tetons/Great Tetons   A range of rugged, sharply peaked mountains, dramatically visible from Jackson Hole, Wyo. [Their name is a gift from the rough humor of the voyageurs, lit. the "big tit" mountains. < Fr. *téton,* which is *téte,* tit, with the majorative suffix *-on.*]

thirty *Journalism.* When written in Arabic numerals, "30," the traditional journalists' way of indicating "end of story." [< The telegraph and Morse code, which came into use in 1840. Various signals began to develop at once as a code within a code, among them the transmission of "30" to indicate end of transmission. Any such assignment of meanings is partly arbitrary, but "30" in Morse code is . . . — — — — — — —, the series of seven dashes following three dots being distinctive and unmistakable.]

thrill *n.* An intense, piercing emotion. —*v.* To cause or to feel such an emotion. [At root: "to drill, to bore," hence with associated sense: "to feel to the core of one's being." Ult. < IE *ter-*, through, to pierce, to bore. With t/th and suffixed in Gmnc. → OE *thyrl, thyrel,* a bored hole. Then by metathesis (as *bryd* → *bird*), *thyrl* → *thrill. Nos(tril),* at root: "hole (as if bored) in the nose," is cognate. *Dentists are thrilling men.*]

HISTORIC. OE *thrall,* captive, slave, is etymologically distinct from *thyrl,* yet the two forms must commonly have been associated, for in early England thralls were marked by having their ear lobes *thrilled* (drilled) somewhat as livestock is still earmarked. In Jewish tradition, too, an indentured servant who had served his time but chose to remain with his master as a slave had his ears drilled as the mark of his voluntary slavery. (It beats starvation.)

through/thorough [Originally variants of the same word with the root sense: "to pass between, among, across, by means of." The double form is already established in OE *thurh, thuruh.* Then as if not to waste the variant, the language evolved two distinct (though related and at times somewhat confused) words.

through 1. By way of. *We took the route to California through West Roxbury.* 2. By means of. *Q. Is the way to a man's heart through his stomach? A. It all depends on what he is hungry for.* 3. Finished with. *You may say I am through with Jane Fonda.*

thorough [In a sense a frequentative form that may be rendered "through and through."] 1. Utter. Absolute. *He is a thorough scoundrel.* 2. Meticulous, accurate, complete to the last detail. *a thorough analysis of the facts.*

NOTE. But in splitting one word into two, Eng. has sometimes confused the forms. The adverb *throughly* is now obs. but did once function for *thoroughly. Thoroughbred* is based on sense 2 of *thorough,* but *thoroughfare* is clearly in place of *throughfare.* And so common Am. *throughway,* a main highway. (N.Y. State road signs point the way to the *Dewey Thrwy.* Is that toll road on its way to becoming the *Dewey Threwey?*)

tick: on tick   On credit. [XVII Brit. slang *ticket* was used in the sense: "account due," i.e., "amount for which one has been ticketed." And since one must have been given credit in order to have such a ticket, the shortened form *tick,* credit.]

tidbit   1. A choice morsel of food. 2. *Ext.* Or of gossip. [Brit. *titbit.* At redundant root: "a small small." BIT; with dial. *tid,* small, a small amount. Akin to the first element of *tiddlywinks.*]

tide   [< IE *da-,* to divide, a division. With d/t, vowel modification, and suffixed -*d*- in Gmnc. → OE *tid,* time, season ("unit into which time is divided"), and also *tide* (one of the most apparent of temporal phenomena).] *Archaic but surviving in compounds.* A season. *Yuletide, springtide.*
    tidings 1. News of the season. *tidings of comfort and joy.* 2. News of this given time.
    tide one over To take care of one's basic needs for the time being. ["for the next division of time."]
    betide Befall. [The form is archaic but recognized, esp. in *woe betide you,* may woe be your portion in the next period of time.]
    tide The rising and falling of water levels of the oceans in response to the gravitational pull of sun and moon. ["phenomenon that happens in divisions of time."] *sail with the tide* To leave port just as the tide turns from high to ebb, there being then ample water and a favorable outbound current.

tinsel   *n.* Cheap, glittering strips of thread or decorative material. — *adj.* Shining, sparkling, but worthless. *the tinsel dreams of Hollywood.* [Trench, *On the Origin of Words,* properly referring to OF *étincelle,* sparkling, which he defines as "cloth shot with silver and gold threads," supposes the word once implied "thing of great value." But *étincelle,* when applied to cloth, meant what *lamé* now means (at root: "thin metal plate, lamination"). *Étincelle* is, at root: "sparkling (thing)" < L. *scintilla,* spark, ult. < IE *ski-,* to shine (SKY).
    Earlier called *cloth of silver* or *cloth of gold,* this fabric was once shot through with fine threads of silver or gold, and was, to be sure, beyond the reach of the homespun masses, suggesting regal splendor, as at the battle of Agincourt, called *the field of the*

cloth of gold because of the *lamé* splendor of the royal tents. Yet, though of precious metal, such threads were almost as fine as gold leaf, being more expensive for the labor of the weaving than for the metal content. To the best of my knowledge, history records no one who made his fortune by picking the metal threads out of even regal lamé.]

TLC   In the baby-talk jargon that generally mars the profession of nursing, *T*ender *L*oving *C*are, the gentle application of which commonly redeems the profession (but why won't those girls shut up, or at least try to be less inanely cheerful?).

togs   Clothing. *all togged out* Dressed in one's best. [The equivalent Brit. form is *in one's best togs.* In XVIII Brit. thieves' cant, *long tog* was a full-length topcoat or overcoat.

Though commonly considered to be colloq. or at least substandard, the term, in all forms, has a firmly classical ancestry < L. *toga* < L. *tegere,* to cover (INTEGUMENT); and beyond, to IE *(s)teg-,* a covering, to cover. (And see *detective.*)]

tomfoolery   Absurd antics. *tomfool* An utter dolt. A damn fool. [ME *Thome Fole* (Tom Fool) was a common name for a half-wit. Cf. *Tom o' Bedlam* for any of the harmless insane released from the asylum of Bedlam to wander the streets and beg for food (sometimes, the more appallingly, in chains). But even in ME *Thome Fole* must have been, at least in part, a minced form of *damne fole,* damn fool.]

tommyrot   Bosh. Nonsense. Mental garbage. [Our standard Am. dicts., in borrowing errors from one another, commonly gloss, as does the estimable AHD: "*Tommy,* pet form of TOM + ROT." In doing so, they ignore *tommy* as a common British workers' term for "bread, food."

Edwin Radford, *Unusual Words,* points out that a British miner's lunch pail is still called his *tommy can* and that it contains his noon *tommy.* Radford also points out that before the Truck Act of 1831, many workers were paid part of their wages in food, and that they had to go to the company's *tommy shop* to draw their food payment and whatever cash might be due them after withholding for rental of a company shack. The inferior rations they drew at tommy shops at inflated prices were called *tommy rot.*

I cannot attest, but cannot resist a qualified assertion, that *tommy* is a variant of *tummy,* the sense shift having been from "stomach garbage" to "brain garbage."]

ton   In Am., a weight of 2,000 pounds. [< *Tun,* a large cask. < Medieval L. **tunna.* ME *tonne,* a tun. The large cask and its contents would have a formidable weight, but not till XVII did *tun* become specific to the cask, and *ton* to weight.]

    come down on like a ton of bricks Come down on hard. Reprimand severely [*Ton,* here, generic for "great weight." A single brick falling from a scaffolding can make an impression. Descending in any aggregate quantity, bricks become emphatic.]

    tons Colloq. 1. A lot. *tons of money.* 2. Very much. *I love you tons.*

    two-ton Powerful. Capitalized, a once common nickname for an especially powerful person, as Two-Ton Tony Galento, in 1930's a graceless but powerful hulk and heavyweight title contender who trained on great quantities of beer.

    ten-ton truck Up to c. 1940, a generic for enormous power. *mash someone like a ten-ton truck.* Ten tons will still do for mashing, but seems relatively unimpressive today. The idiom is from early XX, when trucks were still replacing horse-drawn wagons and when a ten-ton load seemed mystically heavy. At that time *going sixty* and *a mile a minute* expressed a speed that fairly passed for a miracle.

    ton of lead An enormous weight. [Fanciful. A ton of lead is no heavier than a ton of down, but "lead" suggests heaviness, and even if the ton is made up of five-pound castings, the suggestion of heaviness persists.]

tontine   A form of mutual insurance in which all the members of a tontine group subscribe an equal amount. The total sum, along with accrued interest and profits, goes to the last surviving member of the group. Variantly it is divided between or among any who survive to a set date. [It. *tontina,* after Lorenzo Tonti, Neapolitan banker, who introduced this group insurance plan in France in XVII. (The Borgias would have liked Tonti's plan and might have poisoned their way out of many a merry *tontina,* but they were effectively out of business about 150 years before Tonti sold his idea to the French.]

tony   Swank. Stylish. Posh. Elegant. [Am. XIX. < *High-toned,* an expression much in use in XIX Am. society to label a cultivated elegance that combined morality, good breeding, and an opulence made possible only by daddy's dirty money.]

torch 1. A flambeau. In the commonest early forms, a stout stick with flammable material tied to one end, oiled or tarred if possible, and ignited to provide illumination; or variantly, a stiffened rope, frayed at one end and tarred, to be used in the same way. 2. *Brit. only.* A flashlight. [The common sense is "portable light."] 3. *Am. criminal slang.* An arsonist (usu. professional). 4. An intense flame, as in *acetylene torch, cutting torch.* [L. *torquēre,* to twist (TORQUE). The ref. is to tarred twists of frayed rope, as above; but could apply equally to flammable materials twisted about the end of a stick.]

torchbearer 1. One who lights the way for another, as a servant once bore a torch for his master. 2. One who leads the way, as in a cause. **carry the torch for** *Am. slang.* To mourn a lost love. (Implies some public display of grief.) [But at origin (see historic note, below): 1. To mourn in a funeral procession. 2. To carry a funerary torch for pay as a professional mourner. *torch singer* A female singer who exhales husky blues ballads of lost love(s).

HISTORIC. Roman funerals were held at night, perhaps because of the superstition that a priest or magistrate was made ceremonially unclean if a corpse was carried across his path. The funeral procession was lit by torches of tarred and twisted ropes, as above. Latin **fūnus,* death, funeral (FUNERARY), and *fūnis,* rope (FUNIC-ULAR), are so similar that they fused as the basis of Eng. *funeral,* that blending assisted by the use of *fūnis* for a funeral torch.

The number of torches carried in procession was taken as a mark of the respect in which the deceased was held. Professional mourners and the poor were commonly given torches and paid to bear them in procession, to the greater honor of the deceased.

As a mark of dishonor Roman traitors were buried without lit torches. In the Christian tradition, suicides (who were held to be self-damned and already in hell) were similarly buried *a lumi spenti,* with stifled torches (in effect, with unlit torches), and were further denied burial in consecrated ground, their graves being commonly in the weeds near crossroads. (Some say at a crossroads and under the pavement, and that did happen, but rarely, it being too much trouble to dig up the road, and then to tamp and repave it for secure passage. The nearby weeds commonly turned out to be good enough for symbolic purposes, and the real point was, in any case, not to tear up the roadways but to deny suicides Christian burial in holy ground.

Tory   A shifting political label. From 1689 labeled the political party opposed to the Whigs (see *Whig*). Since 1830 in Britain the party label has changed to Conservative. In the American Revolution, a monarchist. *tory* A conservative. A reactionary. [< Irish *tōruidhe*, robber. At root: "one who pursues in order to plunder." < Gaelic *tōir*, pursuit; the Gaelic noun form becoming the Irish verb *tōir*, to pursue. This term was first applied, c. 1645, to the dispossessed Irish who formed into guerrilla bands to harry English soldiers and to kill and plunder English settlers. Like *Whig*, the term was originally pejorative (in effect, "murderous raider") but later proudly accepted by those so labeled. In 1679–1680 the label, as if unemployed elsewhere, was applied to those who opposed the exclusion of James, duke of York, from succession to the throne of England.]

trade-last   Also *t.l. In childish formula.* An offer by B to report a compliment someone paid to A if A will first report a compliment someone paid to B. If A has not heard a compliment paid to B by a third party, a personal compliment by A (who is not required to be sincere but only to pretend to be) will usually do in place of a third-person report. The child is father and mother of the devious adult.

transpire   1. *Now primary Am. sense.* To happen. *The White House has not revealed what transpired at the cabinet meeting.* 2. *In technical accuracy.* To breathe through, as in the emission of water vapor by leaves. [L. *trans*, through; *spirare*, breathe. And to breathe through (emit) was the only sense until XVII, when, by metaphoric ext., the sense changed to: "to emit, to emerge (and take place)," whence in XIX the specifically Am. sense: "to happen," which is reasonably frowned upon by many, though by now a firmly established distortion.]

trespass   [First element modified in Fr. < L. *trans*, through; *passare*, to pass. In OF *trespasser*, Fr. *trépasser*, to die ("to pass through this life"). But into XIII Eng. and surviving, as:] 1. Transgression. "Forgive us our trespasses as we forgive those who trespass against us." [At root: "to pass through (go beyond) God's commandments."] 2. *In legal English since XIV.* An actionable offense. A tort. 3. *Except in prayer, the now primary sense.* To pass into or through the land (not the house and buildings) of another without permission, esp. when that property is posted. So the common sign: *No trespassing. Violators will be prosecuted.* (In a case involving a light plane that came down in posted pasture land, the court held that the pilot was blameless of trespassing, that having done no damage, he was not liable, and that he had the right to make necessary repairs and fly away. It also implied that trespass must be willful.) 4. To infringe upon another's privacy. *People who drop in without an appointment trespass upon my day's work.*

tribe No definition can cover all cases. In general, a more or less primitive social unit with a distinct language (or dialect), religion, way of life, and a limited genetic pool believed to derive from common supernatural parents who are sometimes conceived as miraculous animals or spirits of nature. The tribe, as the term is now commonly understood, is generally ruled by a chief or king. In many primitive cultures he was chief, king, father, priest, god, medicine man, and rainmaker. [But though the term is now restricted to primitive cultures (except as applied to large families and their clan of relatives, as in "the uncles of my tribe"), it had its origin in early Roman history. Ult. < IE *bhu-*, to grow, to multiply, to be. Prefixed *tri-*, three → L. *tribus*, the three peoples, the three conditions of being. The ref. is to the Latians, the Sabines, and the Etruscans, the three peoples who merged to form the Roman city-state.]

HISTORIC. The various early migrations into the Italian peninsula from the sea and from the north were prehistoric, and can only be guessed from legend. By about VIII B.C. the three tribes mentioned above had emerged as separate but related units. As these developed into something like city-states, they evolved a common practice of dividing the community into ten *curiae,* subdivisions roughly corresponding to our city wards, though the divisions were ritual as well as political, and must, at root, have been enlarged clans. The *curiae,* officials in charge, were a sort of ritual aldermen. The form is < L. *co-*, with, together; (assembly of) leading men. By sometime in VII B.C. Rome had developed thirty *curiae,* the number providing a rare confirmation of historical fact, for it makes it clear that each of the three merged "beings, conditions of being," had kept its ten.

As a minor etymological turn, Italian *tribù,* in shedding the *s* of the Latin, returned to the pure form of the IE roots; and so, too, French *tribu.*

tried (in the balance) and found wanting Tested and rejected.

HISTORIC. In early Egyptian belief, souls were variously

weighed in scale pans at death, to determine their merit and eternal fate. In one variant, the good one had done was weighed against the evil. Somewhere I have read that some cultures believe that the soul, at death, is weighed against a feather, but I never understood what was intended. The symbolism survives in the common representation of blindfolded Justice holding the scales aloft. (But if she can't see, how can she tell which way the scales tip unless she puts her thumb in one of them—which, in a possibly deeper symbolism, may signify how the courts do, in fact, work.

true 1. Not false. Genuine. 2. In strict alignment. 3. Faithful. Loyal. ("In strict alignment with one's given word.") [At root: "like a tree." < IE *dreu-*, tree. With d/t in Gmnc. → OE treowe, ME *treue*, tree; and also, true. (The IE stem, suffixed *wid-*, to see, hence, to understand, to know → *dreu-wid-* → *druid*, one who "knows" about trees, i.e., who knows how to invoke their daemons. The early Teutons were druidical tree worshippers, the ideas "true" and "tree" being, among them, religiously conjoint.]

true blue Staunchly loyal. Absolutely reliable. [An aristocratic assumption. *Blue* < *blue blood*, which was supposed to run in the veins of aristocrats and fill them with the *noblesse oblige* of which the fickle plebeians were not capable.]

true to form As expected on the basis of past performance. *out of true* Said of mechanisms, structures. Not properly aligned. Awry.

truism A truth so obvious as to make its assertion pointless. *All else being equal, success in marriage depends, at least in large part, on how well the marital partners get along with one another.*

turkey shoot 1. *Military.* A firefight resulting in a heavy enemy kill with negligible losses to one's own side, as if a marksmanship contest rather than a battle. [Am. Civil War. And perh. earlier.] 2. A competitive target shoot at inanimate targets, in which the competitors pay entrance fees and the winners get turkeys as prizes. A common gun club fund-raising event, commonly with the contestants sorted into groups according to their established ratings, as with golfers grouped in classes according to their handicaps. 3. But in colonial times, a shoot for a fee at live turkeys.

HISTORIC. James Fenimore Cooper, *The Pioneers*, Chap. 17, offers a detailed description of a New York State turkey shoot in 1793. Competitors shot from 100 yards, paying one shilling, about 12½ cents (there was no U.S. coinage until 1797), for each shot. The turkey was packed in snow, with only its head projecting. Any least nicking of the head or head feathers won the bird. Any shot below the head and into the snow, though it killed the turkey, did not win possession of it.

U

ugly as sin Physically disgusting and spiritually revolting; as ugly as one can become. [The first attested use of this now fixed formula was in Sir Walter Scott's *Kenilworth,* 1821.]

ult. A once standard, now rare, business-letter abbreviation meaning "last month." So *ninth ult.* = the ninth of last month. [< L. *ultimo mense,* last month. So *inst.,* this month < L. *instanto mense;* and also *prox.,* next month < L. *proximo mense,* next month.]

ultima Thule (Pronounced thōō´-lĕ.) 1. In the mythology of early geographers, including Ptolemy, the northernmost region of the habitable world, a fantasy place said to exist north of beyond. 2. *Ext.* Any goal, especially if it is unattainable.
  Thule 1. The mythical capital of this northernmost region. 2. (Pronounced tōō´-lĕ.) A village of about 600 frostbitten people on the northwest coast of Greenland. 3. A USAAF air base established there in WWII. [An air force legend once had it that a G.I. sentenced by court-martial to any punishment, including hanging, would be pardoned and promoted to lieutenant colonel if he would volunteer for a four-year hitch at Tooley, but that when notice to that effect was posted in all air force prisons, there were no takers.]

umpteen An indefinite large number. [The form is generally taken to be colloq., and is common in the usage of children, yet the evolution is classical. From XIX Morse code. (Samuel Morse patented his telegraph in 1840.) Based on *M* for many, prob. based on, or at least influenced by, Latin *M* for thousand. In early Morse code, *M,* umpty, signified dash; *N,* enty, signified dot. (Cf. printers' spacings by *ems* and *ens*—wide space, short space.) In all senses: "large, many." And so *umpteen,* umpty-ten, many tens, many times ten. It was probably the genteel superfinicky grammarians of XIX who discouraged the acceptance of the word as standard Am.—those starched fussbudgets who invented the distinction between *shall* and *will*, and decided that *ain't* was not a fit contraction for *am I not.* They are not to praise, and I ain't going to, not umpteen times.]

under the table   1. Covertly, as in money changing hands secretly, or in cheating at cards. Also in giving a concealed signal. (See *footsie.*) 2. Labels the condition of a passed-out sot, so drunk he has slid out of his chair and is lying under the table.

    drink (someone) under the table To outlast a fellow sot in competitive drinking, he (figuratively or literally) passing out and sliding under the table while the winner goes on drinking.

under the weather   Ailing. [Said by many to derive from nautical Eng., but if so, not attested until late XIX in Robert Louis Stevenson's *The Wrecker:* "You must not fancy I am sick, only over-driven, and under the weather." RLS must have believed he was speaking established maritime Eng., but was he? Since he disclaims sickness, he must have meant "hard-pressed and in unfavorable circumstances." The idiom caught on, however, acquiring almost instantly the sense RLS denied. Idiom turns as it pleases the language gremlins.]

university   An institution of learning made up of various more or less distinct colleges. In traditional Am. usage a college gave only bachelor's degrees, but in the general puffery of language many colleges have tacked on some feeble, if not maimed, so-called graduate course toward a master's degree in applied sandbox, in order to call themselves "universities." ***multiversity*** Began to be used in the 1950's for such huge and expanding institutions as Berkeley. [< L. *universitas,* the whole. Commonly rendered as "all the colleges together." At root: *uni-,* one; *vers-,* to turn, hence "to turn (gather, assemble) into one." But earlier *universitas literarum,* the whole of literature. In British universities, this whole consisted of all Greek literature and of the Latin classics (up to about 400 A.D.). To qualify as a classicist one was expected to know everything in this range, and need not have read a word written later.]

unkind   1. Not genial. 2. Unmerciful. Harsh. Cruel. [At root: "not of our (gracious and honorable) sort." < OE *cyn,* kin; at root: "of our (superior and admirable) clan." Ger. *Kind,* child ("one of ours"), is cognate. So, too, English *king.* (See *gen-,* Vol. I.) Thus, to be unkind was to violate the (high) principles of one's (self-esteeming) clan/ kinship. So Chaucer, "unkind abominations" = incestuous abominations (violations of clan standards). So Hamlet's "kindless villain" = person in violation of all standards of our (elite) clan.]

unstrung *Archery.* The condition of a bow when the string has been loosened at one end, or removed entirely. *be/come/become unstrung* To lose emotional control. [The root ref. is to the English longbow, a once powerful weapon almost invariably fashioned from yew wood. If the bow was left strung for long periods, the wood set in its curve and lost resilience. Archers on the march carried their bows unstrung. In the case of a surprise attack, therefore, they were caught unprepared and had to endure some seconds of panicky defenselessness while they restrung their bows, a situation that might well cause the less hardy to come unstrung in the extended emotional sense of the idiom.]

unwashed/the unwashed/the great unwashed A contemptuous aristocratic term for the lower classes, the rabble. [In widespread Brit. use to label the rabble in arms of the French Revolution (1789– 1799) and after, but with antecedents back to OE *unwaescen,* unwashed (in the modern sense). Variantly, Shakespeare, *1 Henry IV,* III. iii. 205: to come "with unwashed hands," i.e., without pausing to wash one's hands (or to make other preparations), *i.e., at once. There is no truth in the charge that Rep. Richard Ichord is all wet; he is as unwashed as the Sahara.*]

upholsterer One who covers padded furniture with fabric, leather, or with the synthetic everything now available in place of everything else. [And so since XVII, but in XIV–XVII an auctioneer's or a merchant's assistant who held up goods, and especially fabrics, for display and inspection by the buyer. In XVI, one who arranged goods for attractive display in the manner of a modern window dresser. The common earlier form was *upholster,* an upholder.]

Up Mike's, down Jake's (Where you got the hot cakes) A taunting or sassy child's jingle for turning away the question, "Where have you been?" [I have never found this fading idiom in a dictionary or listing of slang. I have never come upon it in print. I have no clue, therefore, to its date of origin. I can only enter it as a formula familiar to me when I was growing up in metropolitan Boston in the 1920's. I take *Mike's* and *Jake's* to be "here and there (and none of your business)"; and I take *Where you got the hot cakes* to be a probably later rhyming addition, as in many redupl. forms. I enter it here that it may be at least once recorded, and in the hope it may jog the memory of some older reader who may have a clue to its proper dating and point of origin.

The idiom is in many ways similar to "Pudding and Tame/Ask me again and I'll tell you the same." This formula as a way of parrying the question, "What's your name?" (See *Pudding and Tame*, Vol. I.) In Am. sometimes rendered "Pumpkin Tame." This formula and variant, however, can be traced to medieval demonology, Pudding of Tame being a grotesque name for a demon.

upshot A result. An outcome. [From medieval competitive archery, the last shot in an archery competition; as if "last time-up shot." (And see *debut*.) The effective root sense is "immediate result," for in competitions between expert archers the *upshot* could determine the winner on the spot. This root sense, however, has been somewhat perturbed by XVI *in the upshot*, final result, at last, which could be taken to mean "in long-delayed consequence of," which is better expressed by *in the aftermath* (see *aftermath*).]

up the spout Gone forever. [In XVIII Brit. slang *spout* labeled a sort of dumbwaiter used by a pawnbroker in sending pledged goods to secure storage in an upstairs room. By synecdoche, it also did for the pawnshop ("place where the spout is"). Theoretically what went up the spout could be redeemed and repossessed, but a natural pessimism denied redemption, and *down the spout* never became idiom.]

HISTORIC. From c. 1150 north Italians (Lombards) began to spread through Europe as moneylenders, brokers, and pawnbrokers. By XIV *Lombard* was established in Brit. for "pawnbroker." In Brit. a *lumber room* is roughly the equivalent of Am. *attic, storage attic,* a room for storing things not in use, or simply accumulated household junk one felt was too good to throw out. *Lumber room* is a Brit. corruption of *Lombard room,* room in which a pawnbroker stored pledged goods, commonly above the pawnshop. The *spout* was some sort of dumbwaiter, or perhaps a flight of stairs, leading to the lumber room. The destitute musician who pledged his instrument would have watched it go *up the spout* with a dismal sense that he might never see it again, and this is the sense the idiom has retained.

Utopia   Any ideal place, esp. a prosperous, pleasant, peaceful, and perfectly governed country. [After *Utopia,* title of a book (1516) by Sir Thomas More, who coined the name for an imaginary island with a perfect society and political structure. In essence, a "nowhere." More coined his name < Gk. *ou,* not, no (akin to Gk. neg. prefix *a-*); with *topos,* place (TOPOGRAPHY). *Utopia* means simultaneously "ideal" and "nonexistent."]

U

valet   A gentleman's gentleman in intimate attendance and in
particular charge of wardrobe. Perhaps the rarest of two-legged
creatures in the U.S. today, but the word survives in the trade
name *Val-A-Pak,* a case for carrying suits when traveling, and
valet parking, common at airports and hotels, which has no connection with either clothing or intimate attendance, but signifies
merely: "We, your commercial servants, will park your car for
you and drive it back on demand, ideally without dents, and in
any case *not responsible for theaft or damage."* [The word is a
late spin-off from OF *vaslet, varlet, valet,* a warrior in service to
his feudal lord (honorable term). In ME *varlet* was a squire in
attendance upon a knight, a bachelor aspirant to knighthood (also
an honorable term). By XVII *varlet* had lost these honorific associations, the sense degrading to "inferior" and almost at once to
"scoundrel," and soon after to "servant," and by late XVII to the
present "gentleman's gentleman." All these senses fogged off in
Am. as the servant problem became resolved by the lack of servants.]

Valhalla   [At root: "(heavenly) Hall of Valor." ON < *valr,* the brave
(those slain in battle); *hōll,* hall, place, place of assembly. In Old
Norse myth, the place in heaven reserved for those who die in
battle. It is what modern servicemen would call "good duty," an
eternity of feasting and beautiful women.]

   HISTORIC. In many early religions (and see Iran today) those
who die in battle ascend at once to heaven. A Moslem warrior so
slain is translated to seven hundred years of bliss among the heavenly peris, at the end of which a new shift of girls comes on and
another seven hundred years of bliss begin, and so ad infinitum.
Such beliefs are clearly useful to a warlike people, for with such
retirement benefits, the boys would be not only brave, but eager
to get killed for God and the tribe.

vamp¹ The part of a shoe that covers the front part of the foot. [And so since XVII. But in XIII with ref. to hose, and specific to the part of the hose that covers the foot; foot here conceived as "forward part of the leg." And "forward" is the root sense < OF *avant,* forward; with *pié,* foot → *avantpié,* and by aphesis *vantpié,* modified again → van(t)p(ié), and *n* syncopated to *m* before *p* → ME *vampey.* And cf. obs. *vambrace,* a piece of armor covering the forearm. (A pity *vamplay,* in connection with *vamp³,* did not come to mean sexual foreplay.)]

vamp² *Music.* An improvised and generalized accompaniment or bridge. [An unexplained metaphor, but based on the fact that the leather strap of a sandal that goes over the front of the foot (its *vamp¹*) is the simplest part, as a musical vamp is the simplest part of the show.]

vamp³ An enticer and destroyer of men. A *femme fatale.* [By back formation from *vampire,* of obscure Tartar origin into Central European legend, and into English primarily via Russian and German. The legendary vampire, akin to the werewolf, was a person who changed into a huge bat by night, sucking blood from the throats of its human victims. When the bite was not fatal, it was said to enslave the soul of the person bitten.

In epidemic use in the 1920's to label the slinky sirens of the silent screen. Now rare, and repeated questioning of the young persuades me that it has about passed from their recognition vocabulary.]

vandal One who destroys maliciously. Whence *vandalize* and *vandalism.* [< Vandal.]

HISTORIC. The Vandals were an East German tribe-nation that conquered and settled parts of Gaul and of Spain, migrating to North Africa in 429 A.D. Ever restless and ever ruthless, they captured Rome in 435 under King Genseric, and sacked it so ruthlessly that some of the scars remain visible today, perhaps most notably the holes they forced enslaved Romans to gouge in the walls of the Colosseum in order to strip it of the great vertical iron bars that originally bound the tiers of the stonework. (See ref. to Hebrew *cuz* under *john.*)

vane A flat piece *(weather vane)* sometimes set at an angle to the wind *(vanes of a windmill)* or for thrusting air or gases *(vanes of* *a turbine, of a supercharger),* or the guiding and stabilizing fins of a missile or rocket. A panel of metal or of stretched cloth, but also the feathers of an arrow. [Ult. < IE *pan-,* a woven fabric (as distinct from a hide, rawhide, or buckskin). And so Gk. *pēnos,* L. *pannus,* It. *panno,* all meaning cloth. The sense "flat thing" survives in Eng. *window pane.* The sense progression has been from "cloth" → "flat panel" → "flat panel (of various materials) that moves with the wind."]

vaseline   Petroleum jelly, a body lubricant once in common use as a vaginal lubricant.

> There once was a couple named Kelly
> Who went through life belly to belly
>   Because in their haste
>   They used library paste
> Instead of petroleum jelly.
>
> —Anon.

[A registered trade name, but like *kleenex* adopted into Am. as a generic term. The difference is that unless one writes Vaseline® and Kleenex®, there will come a foolish letter from someone in ® and ® setting forth the company's running fight with the American language, and the letter must then be thrown out with the trash. *Vaseline*® was painstakingly and effectively put together in 1872 by Robert A. Chesebrough, who took *vas-* from Ger. *Wasser,* water; *-el-* from Gk. *elaion,* oil; and *-ine* from L. *-inus,* having the characteristics of. Hence with the sense: "like water and oil together."]

Vatican   The Roman seat of the Pope, and therefore the center of Roman Catholicism. Once an independent state with large territories and a powerful army, it is now a few stone-walled acres permitted a symbolic autonomy by the Italian government. *Tourist tip:* If you stay long in Rome, and if you will fill out a form saying that you are there *per opere religiose,* and if you can persuade the head clerk to accept your assertion, the Vatican *cambio* (which functions as if in a separate country though its currency is Italian lire) will give you a slightly better exchange rate than is available in Rome proper. [After the Latin name of the slight elevation on which it stands, *mons Vaticanus,* Vatican Hill. The site was an ancient terraced Etruscan necropolis extending to the Tiber, but in the Middle Ages the retaining walls of the terraces were removed and the area smoothed in a slight slope in all directions.

The root sense of *Vatican* is not securely known, but L. *vaticanare,* to prophesy, and *vātēs,* prophet (VATIC), together with the ancient use of the *mons Vaticanus* as a city of the dead, suggest that the Etruscan root of L. *vaticanus* referred to the prophetic arts and to the hereafter.]

V-E Day   Victory in Europe Day, May 8, 1945. [After the obsessive acronymic habit of the U.S. armed forces. And by analogy:] *V-J Day,* Victory in Japan Day, Sept. 2, 1945 (though by then the war had been over for more than two weeks, as below).

HISTORIC. Gen. Eisenhower established his headquarters in a schoolhouse in Reims, France, and demanded an unconditional surrender.. Adm. Karl Dönitz, who had assumed control of Germany-in-ashes, sent as his representative Gen. Alfred Jodl. At 2:41 A.M., May 7, 1945, Jodl signed the unconditional surrender, to become effective at midnight.

On Aug. 14, 1945, a Japanese delegation at MacArthur's headquarters agreed to an unconditional surrender, stipulating only that the emperor remain as the Japanese head of state. MacArthur agreed but with the counter-stipulation that the emperor would be subject to supreme (MacArthur's) command. The war with Japan was over, but MacArthur insisted upon his ceremony and his chance to stage himself for posterity in front of the movie cameras. The articles of surrender were accordingly signed aboard the battleship *Missouri* in Tokyo Bay on Sept. 2, MacArthur's ego-trip day passing belatedly into forged history as the official V-J Day.

velvet   [IE *wel-,* wool. But at earliest stage, prob. "shaggy," as a pelt. → L. *villus,* hairy, shaggy; It. *velluto;* OF and ME *velvotte,* velvet.] 1. A soft fabric woven with a thick pile, originally of silk, now of various natural and synthetic yarns. It is woven with loops that may or may not be cut, whence *pile velvet* and *cut velvet.* 2. A symbol of sumptuous living. Whence: *rolling in velvet* Living sumptuously. *pure velvet* Pure profit. Easy money. *velvet trap* Enticement by soft luxurious means.

venom   [ME (and OF) *venim, venin* < L. *venenum,* love potion. See *Venus.* She could cause the soul to be seized (poisoned) by hopeless love. Her son, Cupid, could do the same by shooting a poisoned dart into a person's heart. And the same work was done since the days of primitive magic by love drafts and potions.] 1. Poison, esp. that secreted by certain snakes and by other biting and stinging creatures. 2. *Ext.* Spite. Malice.

ventriloquism The trick of projecting one's voice so that it seems to come from some source other than the speaker. The illusion of projection is achieved by slowing the escaping breath and squeezing the glottis, the mouth being held slightly open (and ideally motionless). Ventriloquism was early associated with speaking from the diaphragm, and actors commonly practice to speak so, but the use of the diaphragm is not essential to ventriloquism. [One Gk. term for a ventriloquist was *engastrimentes* < *gaster*, belly (stem *gastri-*: GASTRIC), *mantis*, prophet, soothsayer; at root: "belly prophet," with ref. to ventriloquism as practiced by temple priests. (See historic note, below.) In L. translation, *ventriloquus*, one who speaks from the belly < *venter*, belly, *loqui*, to speak.

HISTORIC. Early witch doctors must have mastered ventriloquism as an art of mystification, as still practiced by Eskimo, African, and Polynesian witch doctors, the geographical distribution indicating the antiquity of the practice. The priests of various oracles and idols used ventriloquism to make their voices sound as if from the sacred object. The true art, I suspect, lay not so much in the practice of this fraud, but in the priests' ability to believe the fraud was divinely directed.

Venus 1. The Roman goddess of love. She corresponds to Greek Aphrodite and to Teutonic Freia, or Friga, the obvious conclusion being that all three derive from a common prehistoric myth. 2. The second planet from the sun. Often called the morning or evening star. (Because, as seen from the earth, the planet often rises before the sun in the morning and follows it in the evening, as if it were the goddess of love forever seeking the beloved sun god.) 3. Any especially beautiful woman. [At root: "desired woman." < IE wen-, desire, to desire, thing desired. Via Gmnc. → OE *wine*, friend ("desired person"). Also *winnan*, to win ("to achieve a desired goal"): WIN. And via L. *ven-*, occurs in a wide range of Eng. words having to do with the pursuit of game or of sex.]

venery 1. *Obs.* The hunting of game. [< L. *venari*, to hunt game ("to pursue a desired thing").] 2. *Rare.* Skirt-chasing. [Same root sense but with lady meat substituted for game meat.]

venison Now specific to the flesh of deer as food. Earlier, any game meat. Or in a double sense that would have been amply clear in XVIII: *Charles II found Nell Gwyn to be a desirable venison, but his duchess, gamier.*

 mons veneris [L., the hill of love / of Venus.] The pubic swelling of the human female.

 venereal Having to do with physical sex. Of the sex organs. [L. *venereus*, of Venus. But these senses now inhibited by:] **venereal disease** An infection of the sex organs, most commonly gonorrhea or syphilis, or both.

 venerate To hold in awe. [To desire ardently.] And so, to: **venerable** Worthy of reverence. [To be desired.] And see *venom*, once "love potion."

vermouth A probably poisonous fortified dry white wine which, in combination with lye-soaked olives, and the venomous tincture of juniper berries in gin, blends into the ambrosial martini. There is also a sweet vermouth, but no one I am willing to know drinks it. [At root: "wormwood," the oil of *Artemisia absinthium*, used in making absinthe, and as a vermifuge. The cup swallowed by Socrates was a lethal concentration of this oil. OE *wermod*, cognate to Ger. *Wermut*, and ME *wormwode*, signified only the bitter oil, said to taste like wormy wood. Fr. variant *vermouth*, originally the oil, by late XVIII the wine. Into Eng. as the name of the wine in XIX.]

verse 1. Poetry in general. (But now commonly implying a light or slight composition, as *versifier* has become a slighting name for *poet.* 2. A poem. 3. A line of poetry. 4. A stanza of poetry. 5. A numbered subpassage of the Bible. **chapter and verse** A Scriptural reference to a specific verse of a specific chapter. **by chapter and verse** Exactly and authoritatively. In precise detail. [At root: "turning (of a plow at the end of a furrow)." Because poetry is written in straight lines (like furrows) across the field of the page, and requires a turning at the end of each line. L. *versare*, to turn.]

 NOTE. Many words and idioms, as one might expect, are metaphors based on plowing. *With furrowed brow* is a simple example. *Delirious* (Vol. I) is from L. *de-*, out of; *lira*, furrow; at root: "out of one's furrow," i.e., not in straight sequential order but as if plowing loopingly all over the field. *Verse* is based on an inexact metaphor, for the plow is not lifted out of the ground at the end of a furrow and set down again at the start of the next one. The accurate rendering of this turn occurs in *boustrophedon*, at Gk. root, "ox-turn," and used to label an ancient form of writing in which one reads alternately from left to right and from right to left, exactly as an ox plows.

vest   *n.* A sleeveless garment for the torso. Worn by men, usu., under a suit coat; by women, usu., as an exterior garment. [IE *wes-*, clothing, to clothe. (But not Brit. *weskit*, which is a corruption of *waistcoat*.) → L. *vestis*, garment, robe of office. Whence:] —*v.* 1. To don the robes of church or state office (INVESTITURE). 2. To commit to the authority of another. *by virtue of the powers vested in me.*

vested Established and empowered. *vested interests*

vestibule A small room to one side of a main door. [At root: "cloakroom."]

vestry [L. *vestiarum*, wardrobe.] The room, to one side of the altar, in which clergy and lay attendants don their robes. *vestments* The robes so donned. *vestryman* 1. A lay attendant who dons vestments for assisting in church services. Whence: 2. One of a lay group who assist in managing the temporal affairs of a church.

investment 1. *At root.* An investiture of church authority as symbolized by the robes of office thereupon donned. 2. *But in the now primary financial sense.* A stake in a venture. *money invested.* But also *an investment of time. divest* 1. *At root.* To strip of the robes of office; hence, to remove from power and authority. 2. *Financial.* To liquidate an investment ("remove it from one's portfolio"). *The courts ordered Du Pont to divest itself of all General Motors stock. divestiture* 1. *Originally.* The act of removing from office. 2. The act of giving up one's interest in a financial property.

vest pocket 1. *Lit.* Any one of usu. four small pockets in a vest. 2. *Hence.* Small. Esp. in *vest-pocket battleship Post WWI.* A German battleship of restricted tonnage as specified in the arms limitations of the Treaty of Versailles. But German ingenuity, while keeping these ships ostensibly within the specified limitations of tonnage, made them as battle-effective as larger battleships.

vestige   A remaining trace of a thing gone by. *Her time-ruined face retained vestiges of a former beauty.* [And this sense first emerged in XVIII. Earlier, a trail. Root sense: "footprint." < L. **vestigium:* 1. Footprint. 2. Soul of the foot. And so:] *investigate* At root: To follow a trail. (Not to be confused with words based on L. *vestire*, to dress; *vestis*, clothing, e.g., *invest, investiture, divest, divestiture.*)

vials of wrath   A symbol of terrible but just vengeance. *pour out the vials of one's wrath upon* 1. To take such a vengeance upon (though vengeance is mine, saith the Lord, and such vengeance, except in fantasies of reforming the U.S. Congress, are properly left to Heaven). *And so in softened ext.* 2. To rage at. To denounce/berate in raging anger. [Revelation 16:1: "And I heard a great voice out of the temple saying to the seven angels, Go your ways, and pour out the vials of the wrath of God upon the earth." Each of the vials contained a plague to punish humanity for its iniquity.]

NOTE. Today we think of a vial as a small, usu. glass, container, on the order of a common test tube or smaller. The word was earlier *phial* (still in Am. use, though rare) < Gk. **phialē,* a broad vessel, a capacious container. Only a brazen upstart would quarrel with the King James translation of the Bible, yet in this case, I will trepidate (a lovely verb I have borrowed from Partridge) that *vessels of wrath* might have better conveyed the intent of this passage.

vibes   *Beat Generation psychobabble, and surviving.* Psychic aura. Psychic emanation. [< *Vibrations,* in the language of psychics and spiritual readers. As if the soul / psyche / essential folderol of each person were a metaphysical wave transmitter to which self-styled sensitives can tune in.]

vicinity   1. The nearby neighborhood. *in the vicinity of the police station.* 2. *Ext.* Approximate range. *sports cars with price tags in the vicinity of $35,000.* [IE *wiek-,* house → Gk. *oikos,* house (ECONOMY). L. *vicus,* with widened sense: "group of houses."

Via Gmnc. → ON *vic,* OE *wic.* 1. place of residence. 2. Village. ("community of houses.") Whence *bailiwick* (see *bail,* Vol. I). Also a common element in British place names, as *Moorwick, Fenwick, Berwick.*]

Viking   A Scandinavian coastal raider. [Most standard Am. dicts. gloss as "origin unknown," but though the dating is uncertain, there are ponderable etymological traces. ODEE's first attestation is in the Icelandic form *vikingr,* and that not until c. 1800! Prob. based on ON *vik,* creek, fiord, sea inlet; with *-ingr,* here, one associated with → *vikingr,* person of the sea inlet(s). And Vikings not only came from sea inlets, but made their piratical descents upon communities along such inlets; for though late Vikings made dramatic pelagic crossings, there was nothing to raid far out to sea, and not enough coastal shipping to make piracy profitable. Vikings were pirates from the fiords (sea inlets) who raided settled communities built on sea inlets, thus "of the sea inlets" in a double sense.]

-ville   *Slang.* A fad suffix of the 1960's and early 1970's (now passé) in which condition of being is rendered as if it were a place. *Dullsville* for condition of being dull; *Nowheresville* for condition of being "out of it." "He went home for Christmas," could be rendered, *He's making Sleighbellsville.* But the same substitution of physical area for mental attitude is now current in Psychobabblesville (the seat of Marin County, Cal.) as *space* for "mental area one occupies / where one is coming from." Thus "don't crowd my space" might earlier have been rendered: "Stay out of Meville and I'll stay out of Youville."

violate   [IE *wei-*, pertaining to forces that sustain life (VITAL, VIO-LENCE, VIM) → L. *vis*, force, life force; *violare*, to act forcefully. ME *violaten*, to use force, to be forceful.] 1. To break a law. 2. To profane a holy place. 3. To break into another's privacy. 4. To offend principle, custom. *It violates my moral sense.* 5. To have illegal sex with a woman. To rape. But also (archaic) to seduce. (Felonious entry?)

And in recent police usage: *you violated.* A clipped form of "you violated the law." Used almost exclusively in minor infractions of traffic laws. Akin to "traffic violation."

Vitus: St. Vitus' dance   [Medically, *chorea* < Gk. *khorus*, dance (CHO-RUS). The root ref. is to the dances performed in the theater by Greek choruses.] A rheumatic infection of the nervous system. It causes irregular muscle spasms, esp. of the extremities, esp. in the young. The epidemics of manic dancing that broke out in Germany in XIV–XVI may have been the result of an untraced viral infection, but were more likely a sustained mass hysteria.

HISTORIC. St. Vitus (feast day, June 15) was martyred under Diocletian in 303. His age at death is uncertain, but that he was a pious boy of a substantial family is indicated by the fact that he was put to death along with his tutor and his nanny, whose creature he must have been.

He had no particular association with dancing. Word magic, however, is at the base of many pious legends. His name is < L. *vita*, life. By association, then, the legend grew, esp. in Germany, that those who danced before his statue on his feast day (i.e., showed their vitality) would remain vital and healthy all year. By dedicating one's vitality to his patronage, one could assure the preservation of one's life and health. And besides, any reason for dancing is good enough.

By a later increment of his legend, St. Vitus was said to be able to cure chorea in those who danced before his statue.

volume   [IE *wel-*, to turn, to roll up (as a hide). With the sense unchanged → L. *volvere* (REVOLVE, REVOLT, CONVOLUTE). Whence L. *volūmen*, lit. "rolled-up thing," but with effective senses: *(a)* Parchment scroll. *(b)* Wreath. *(c)* Eddy, whirlpool. And by association with lengthy scroll: "bulky object."] 1. A bound book. 2. One of a set of books. 3. All the numbers of a periodical published during a given period, usu. a year. [In late XVIII it began to be customary to save the twelve numbers of a monthly magazine and to have them bound as a single volume.] 4. *Ext. from the sense "bulky object."* *(a)* Cubic dimension. *(b) Further ext.* Amount. *(c) Still further ext.* Intensity, as of sound. *at full volume, turn down the volume.*

Also *voluminous* 1. Containing much. 2. Wound about, as the folds and drapes of a dress. *Isadora Duncan was given to voluminous flowing gowns.*

speak volumes To imply a great deal (enough to fill a book) without actually speaking. *She gave him a look that spoke volumes.*

$\mathcal{W}$

wainscot/(wainscot(t)ing/wainscot(t)ed [At root: "wagon siding." <
MLG *wagenschot*, < *wagen*, wagon; *schot*, wooden siding. Eng.
wain for "open farm wagon" was in common use into early XX. It
is now rare in Am., if not obs., but capitalized *Wain* is still in some
limited use for the Big Dipper conceived as an open farm wagon
and its shaft. Wains were built of oak. In Sicilian custom they were
elaborately carved and painted. The Nordic wain was less elaborate, tending to respond to the Pennsylvania Dutch formula: "She
ain't much for pretty, but she be all hell for strong."] *Architecture.*
In rich interiors, a facing for the lower part of a wall, usu. up to four
or five feet, the upper wall being finished in another material. The
usu. wainscoting is of wood paneling, once commonly ornately
carved, but marble or other stone is also used.

HISTORIC. The sense was once severely restricted, the one material being what the English called *wainscot oak,* which is not
native to England. It was imported from or through Holland, and
was prized because it could be carved more intricately than English oak, which has a tendency to split when fine-carved. The most
elegant and most expensive wainscoting of the stately homes of
England was of this oak, wainscoting of other material being so
called only by association.

walking encyclopedia 1. A person who knows everything. 2. One
who knows everything about a specific subject. [Dating uncertain.
Prob. early XX. Akin to, but not derived from, *he wrote the book
on it,* he knows all about it. An apt figure, based on *encyclopedia*
as a compilation of all knowledge, and personfied by giving it legs.
*Meredith L. Granger is a walking encyclopedia on the history of
radio broadcasting in the United States.*

walking papers Dismissal. *After going together nowhere for five
years, Mary gave John his walking papers.* [Perhaps based on dis-

292

charge papers from the armed services ("permission to walk away"), but not attested until late XIX Am., by which time it had become custom to fire employees by putting a slip ("pink slip") in the pay envelope or in the slot for one's punch card. In late XVIII Brit. *to give the sack,* because mechanics supplied their own tools, and the sack was notice to collect them and clear out. *To give someone his walking papers* and *to get the pink slip* became idiom at about the same time in late XIX. Had the ref. been to armed services discharge papers, the idiom would likely have an earlier date.]

wall [At root, a palisade of vertical logs as in the walls of early U.S. western forts. In Roman times such field fortifications were constructed with two such palisades, whence INTERVAL, lit. "the space between two walls." Ult. < IE *uel-, u'l-,* a stake → L. *vallus,* post, stake; *vallum,* a wall made of posts, tree trunks. L. *vallum* (after field fortifications and stockades constructed in Britain during the Roman occupation) → OE *weall,* ME *wal(le),* wall. At root, specific to an exterior wall.] 1. Any of the vertical sides of a building. [In Am. *wall* is commonly used for "inside wall." Strictly speaking, such a wall is a *partition,* but in loose usage *partition* is commonly applied to a vertical divider enclosing an interior space, often without extending to the ceiling, hence a screen around an interior space. In It. *muro* is specific to an exterior wall, implicitly of stone (and so *muratore,* a stonemason), with interior walls designated *pareti,* partitions.] 2. An enclosure along a boundary line, or to divide a tract into separate fields/areas. [In Am. usage called a *fence* if made of wire or wooden slats, a wall if made of piled stones.] 3. An inflexible barrier. *You look as if you had run into a wall.* (But note also *stone fence,* a drink made of applejack and cider, the applejack in about the proportions of the Scotch in a Scotch and soda.)

 wall in To enclose. *wall out* To exclude. *stonewall* To resist adamantly. To join forces in presenting an unbreachable front. [Common in federalese since c. 1950.]

 walleye 1. *Medicine.* An eye with a milky, opaque cornea. 2. [With the sense: "large eye."] Applied to various fish, esp. to the *walleye* or *walleyed pike. walleyed Slang. Now rare.* Inebriated. [Cf. the common *blind drunk.*]

 wallflower A girl who is something less than the belle of the ball. [Until recently, and still surviving in some areas, girls at dances and balls dressed in their best and sat along the wall of the ballroom or dance floor, waiting for the men to come up and ask for a dance. Those girls who were not asked spent the evening "blooming" along the wall, hence "wallflower."]

Wall Street 1. The main street in the NYC financial district, located in southernmost Manhattan. 2. *By synecdoche. (a)* The entire financial district of NYC. *(b)* The central, controlling structure of U.S. investment and financing.

the walls have ears Implies that everything one says will be overheard. [And eavesdropping or otherwise listening in to the conversations of others was once the prime sport of the courtier. Palaces were commonly built with convenient listening posts. Today walls have not only electronic bugs, but tape recorders and video cameras.]

wall-to-wall 1. Said originally of carpeting cut to fit against all walls without a border of bare floor. 2. *By ext.* Any complete coverage. *Advance men had arranged for wall-to-wall reporters.* 3. Without stint. *He lives on wall-to-wall money.*

be driven to the wall See *wall*, Vol. I.

four walls With a ceiling, the minimum house. *He drudged all his life just to keep four walls around himself.*

off the wall Recent slang. In a lunatic frenzy. [The root image is of a frenzied madman in a padded cell, hurling himself at the walls in his rage. Similarly:] *climb the wall(s)* To be in a frenzy. *drive (be driven) up a wall* To drive (be driven) into a frenzy.

Wailing Wall In Jerusalem, a wall said to be a survival of the temple of Solomon. It is known to be of much later construction, but faith is ever prepared to ignore the facts, and pious Jews make pilgrimages to say their prayers facing the wall, and to weep and wail in seeking atonement for their sins. *wailing wall* Any place or person to which/whom soggy souls bring tearful accounts of their guilt. *"Hey, Mac," said the bartender, "for three beers you get no license to turn my bar into a wailing wall."*

walnut   The tree, the edible nut, the prized, distinctively grained hard wood, of several species of the genus *Juglans.* [At root: "Welsh nut." OE *wealh-hnutu, walh-hnutu,* the second element being "nut" and the first "Welsh" < L. *Volcae.* The prob. progression has been *Volcae → Wolcae → Wolshae → Welsh. Volc-* is cognate with Ger. *Volk,* the people.]

HISTORIC. Etymology offers many hints to facts that lie beyond the reach of history. Here, the origin of the word might mistakenly suggest that the English walnut is indigenous to Wales. So to conclude, however, is to assume that the Welsh have always lived in Wales. Up to the Roman withdrawal in the third century, the Welsh occupied most of what is now England. They were driven to the south and west by invading Angles and Saxons, who came with bloody swords once the Romans had withdrawn. At ultimate root, *walnut* could be taken to mean "folk nut/nut of the people."

Walpurgis Night   And as commonly, in the German form *Walpurgis-nacht.* 1. The eve of May Day (May 1), which is the Feast of St. Walpurga or Walburga. 2. The principal annual witches' sabbath. 2. *Ext.* Any witches' sabbath. 4. Any weird orgiastic revel. *It was always Walpurgis Night in the Puritan imagination.* [Sense 1 is the original, but rarely functions in modern usage. The remaining, and surviving, senses arise from perversions of the saint's legend.]

HISTORIC. St. Walpurga, an English nun, died c. 780, after thirty years as a missionary in Germany, her last years as the revered abbess of the convent of Heidenheim. She was buried in a cave, above which a church was later built. Her cave, a popular shrine, exuded a black "oil of bitumin," as it was called in English. She became the special patroness to whom the pious prayed for protection against evil spells, and for the removal of hexes. May 1, moreover (sense 2, above), was the day of an ancient heathen witches' festival. It is still observed as the great annual witches' coven. All these associations have come together to fix this pious lady's name in the arcana of witchcraft.

want   *n. & v.* A lack. To lack. [The sense basically unchanged since IE *(e)wa-*, which suffixed *-n-* → L. *vanus,* lacking, empty (IN VAIN); and with a similar alteration in Gmnc. → ON *vanta,* to lack, to be lacking; and under IX–X Dane Law to ME *wanten,* to lack. A simple evolution slightly perturbed by the partial sense shift in Am. to "wish." *Live in want* retains the root sense in Am., but *what do you want?* = what do you wish? in Am.; what do you lack? in Brit.]

want ad A newspaper classified notice seeking employees, employment, services, goods for sale or purchase.

wanted Labels a person sought by the police. *wanted dead or alive* Labels a felon urgently wanted by the police, delivery of the corpus in one condition or the other, usu. with a reward for delivery or for information leading to an arrest. *wanted poster* The notice, now with photo, description, and vital information, announcing that the police seek the stated felon.

ten most wanted Purportedly a list of the ten most dangerous criminals in the U.S. at a given time, but in effect a self-promoting gimmick from the dank mind of J. Edgar Hoover. The FBI regularly has many criminals under surveillance. Hoover, at regular intervals, chose ten, from punks to desperadoes, who were already staked out, then proceeded to round them up, giving the impression that he was ridding society of its worst criminals, ten at a clip; all this publicity playacting at a time when syndicate crime was flourishing with something like the force of a subgovernment.

wanton   *adj.* Of undisciplined impulse. —*v.* To act on uncontrolled impulse, as lewdly, playfully, pettishly, overfamiliarly. —*n. Archaic.* A person of uncontrolled impulses. [At root: "not well-reared." (An exact translation would be It. *maleducato,* which is not "ill-educated" but "ill-bred.") OE *wan-,* neg. prefix; *tēon,* reared; p.p. of *to(g)en,* to rear. Ult. IE *deuk-,* to lead (DUKE, EDUCATE). With d/t and k/g in Gmnc. → OE stem *tog-.*]

WASP   A descendant of the first British emigrants to the American colonies. Hence the first-established and dominant power structure of the United States, esp. as distinct from the Roman Catholics and Jews of the XIX immigrant hordes. [Am. Dating uncertain. Perhaps no earlier than c. 1930, but I am unable to attest. The term is an acronym, and acronymic word formations, except in the armed services, were uncommon before the Roosevelt administrations made them pandemic. From White *A*nglo-*S*axon *P*rotestant.

Frances FitzGerald, *America Revised,* documents persuasively the view of XIX native Americans of colonial stock, who saw them themselves as transplanted British yeomen with a destiny to dominate the United States, and a duty to resist mongrelization by the immigrant hordes. *WASP,* though of later origin, is an attempt to label this yeomanry and its complacent assumptions.

The term, however, is a bit ridiculous. By the time the Norman Conquest had Frenchified Britain beginning in XI, there was nothing identifiable as an Anglo-Saxon to colonize America beginning in XVII. Some have even suggested WERSP (White Erse Protestant) as a historically sounder term.

To complicate matters, the usually estimable AHD (here in need of revision) defines WASP as "a white U.S. citizen of non-specific ethnic or religious origin"—as if *Anglo-Saxon,* though a fuzzy designation in this case, were not an ethnic assertion; and *Protestant,* not a religious one.]

wassail   A festive drinking with many toasts. Also any of the toasts proposed in such a revel. [Archaic, but known to any reader of our literature. Bars no longer call them wassails, but go boisterously about the same thing, esp. at stag parties at which everyone toasts and roasts the old pal about to commit matrimony. Though one could hardly recognize the relationship at a glance, the first element, *was-*, is akin to *astute*, which see. [Ult. (like astute) < IE *wes-*, being, to be (WAS). Via Gmnc. → ON *wesa*, to be; the imperative of which is *ves*, (you) be. So with *heill*, health ("good condition of being") → to the ON toast *ves heill*, be healthy (in Eng. idiom "to your health"), obviously cognate with OE *waes heill* → ME *wassail*.]

HISTORIC. The Germanic and early English tradition made much of festive drinking and ceremonial drunkenness. Dante scorns such revelry in his reference to "the guzzling Germans." In *Hamlet*, the king holds late wassail, and on the battlements his cannoneers fire a salute to re-sound and resound the king's toasts to heaven. Boys (of all ages) drink noisily. Men drink meditatively.

weasel   1. The ferret-like predator. One of the few animals that kill (chickens, for instance) out of sheer blood lust, long after their appetite is satisfied. 2. A sly, sneaky, dangerous person. [IE *weis-*, to seep, to exude. The ref. is to the powerful musk secreted by weasels. Via Gmnc. with dim. suffix *-l-* → OE *wesle*, ME *wesel*. Root sense: "little stinker."]

weasel (out of)   To elude slyly.

weasel words   Deliberately evasive and misleading words, seemingly honest, but in fact deceitful. (Nixon's claim to the support of the "silent majority" may be the most effective weasel wording in U.S. history, claiming, in effect, the wholehearted support of everyone who had had nothing to say.) [Am. Prob. latter XIX. A revised edition of Brewer's *Phrase and Fable* attributes the term to TR, but he may have popularized rather than coined it. There was a folk belief that weasels sucked eggs. So Jaques in Shakespeare's *As You Like It*: "I can suck melancholy out of a song as a weasel sucks eggs." And various dictionaries have explained this term by ref. to a sucked-out egg, seemingly whole and fair, but empty and worthless.

Our farming ancestors were commonly accurate natural observers, but egg suction is beyond the arts of the weasel, which simply cracks the shell and slurps the contents. In egg suction one makes small holes in both ends of an egg, then neatly sucks out the contents through one of the holes. I have no doubt that some stupid farmer found such sucked-out eggs at times and was led to believe a weasel had been at work, though it was certainly the work of a weasel-faced farm hand called Sneaky Ned. *Weasel words* are so called because they are as slyly elusive as a weasel.]

pop goes the weasel 1. A popular Am. country dance tune with a fine stomp cadence and a natural rhetorical flair, the expression meaning at root: "Now you see it, now you don't."

> That's the way my money went.
> *Pop* goes the weasel!

2. *In colloq. Am.* That's it. It's all over. [After the weasel's natural talent for popping up from a burrow or through a crevice, and then being instantly gone.]

wed To marry. [Root sense: "to pledge." (See *wedlock.*) Also: "to gamble, to place a bet, to pay off a gambling loss." Note that one still marries "for better or worse." The emergent effective sense of OE *weddian* was "to pledge oneself contractually," but the root sense was "to place a bet." So cognate Ger. *wetten,* to gamble. And *wager,* via L., is also ult. cognate. Ult. < IE *wadh-,* to pledge, to wager, to redeem a pledge, to pay off a bet.]

HISTORIC. The IE root must be understood in the context of an age before there was money. The root *peku-* (PECUNIARY, FEE) meant "wealth expressed in heads of livestock," primarily of cattle. (The Masai of Africa still reckon wealth by livestock.) When metal bars first appeared as a medium of exchange, they were commonly stamped with the head of bull, as an image of what the metal bar might convert into as its "real" value.)

Aryan man was certainly a gambler. (There are tales of early Teutons who gambled away their freedom, becoming slaves when they lost.) Such a man could not place his bets in cash. Nor could he conveniently go to a crap game bringing along a herd of cattle. After a battle he could dice his loot against that of a comrade. But in betting at dice, or on a horse race, or on a wrestling match, he would pledge a certain number of heads of cattle, or perhaps his land. (In the frontier West, ranches changed hands in poker games.) Such a pledge, and the loser's delivery of the cattle he had lost, were both expressed by IE *wadh-,* which also did for a contractual pledge, not a bet.

wedding ring finger The finger next to the little finger of the left hand. [The choice is not arbitrary. Many early anatomists, basing their teaching on God knows what, asserted that a supersensitive nerve ran from this finger directly to the heart. Swinburne, in his curious "Treatise of Spousals," called it the *"Vena amoris"* (vein of love) "which passeth from that finger to the heart."]

wedlock Marriage. The condition of being man and wife. [The suffix *-lock* is not as in "lock and key," though often so understood. It is a survival in modified form of OE *-lāc,* which may be rendered as "condition of being committed to." So *fechtlāc,* warfare (condition of being committed to war), and *rēaflāc,* theft (condition of being committed to thievery). And so *wedlāc,* originally not marriage but a troth plighting.

The suffix is akin to various Gmnc. forms expressing ritual dancing, athletic contests, and other commitments to action. Northumbrian dialect *laik,* to play, to engage in sports, to dance, is an evident survival of these Gmnc. forms, prob. by way of OE *lācan,* to swing, to caper, to dance. Etymologically, *wedlock* may be conceived not as an incarceration but as a frolic. Good luck.]

weird 1. Unaccountably strange. Beyond all common measure. Eerie. 2. Eccentric. Bizarre. Fantastic. [So in Am. use, but in earlier Brit., "fated (as one's decreed lot)"/ "of the mysteries of one's fortune." So Sc. *dree one's weird,* to endure one's fate. So, too, the *Weird Sisters* The Three Fates: Clotho, who spins the mysterious thread of life; Lachesis, who draws it out to its mysteriously assigned length; and Atropos, who cuts it off. Shakespeare, in *Macbeth,* calls the witches, in lower case, the *weird sisters,* his usage being intermediate to the earlier sense, "mysterious power of fate," and the later senses, "queer, eccentric, eerie." Ult. < IE *wert-,* to turn, which, with w/v, via L., is the base of INVERSION, ANIMADVERSION, ANNIVERSARY, VERSUS. Via Gmnc. with t/d and with sense accretion from "to turn" to "inscrutable turn of fate" → OE *wyrd,* fate.]

weird-o/ weirdo In Brit. (borrowed from Am.) the common form is *weirdie* 1. *Brit. & Am. slang.* An eccentric person. One beyond all normal bounds in dress and behavior. 2. *In Am. (a)* One who is eccentric to the point of being repugnant. A kinky creep. *(b)* A queer, bizarre, and therefore admirable person. [Cf. Black English *outrageous* for *admirable.*]

HISTORICAL. There is a tendency among American Negroes to equate "shocking, notably bad," with "assertive and therefore admirable" (at least not an Uncle Tom). This pattern has carried over into the slang of young whites (as in *bad,* or *big and bad,* for *good*). Young whites have long based their slang, music, manners, and recreational patterns on black modes.

welcome wagon   [*Wagon* for *station wagon* (and for alliteration), though any automobile will serve.] A suburban ritual conceived in neighborliness and dedicated to local commercialism. The welcome wagon is usu. driven by an ingratiating local woman who makes a "neighborly" call on new residents, bringing trivial free samples from local merchants, along with calendars, brochures, shopping bags, town maps, and the like, all of which are prominently emblazoned with the names of local merchants who want the family's patronage. "Ballyhoo," as the London *Times* once explained, "is rhetoric aimed at the pocketbook."

wench   [OE *wencel,* a child (of either sex). ME *wenchel,* a girl child, a young maiden. Ult. < IE *weng-,* bent, not straight → Gmnc. stem *wank-,* unreliable, inconstant ("not straight and firm"), with original ref. to a child ("person whose character has not yet firmed and grown straight"). Then, between ME and XVI the sense "inconstant" led to the sense "wanton," but always accompanied by the sense "minor, subordinate, and hence inferior person."] *n. Within the pat assumptions of the rigid British caste system.* A female of low degree. A "not-lady." A female servant or farm worker. ***wench/go wenching.*** To patronize whores. ***wencher*** A whorechaser. A womanizer.

HISTORIC. In feudal England female servants and farm workers were the property of the lord, and his to tumble at will. Having forced his pleasure upon such a wench, the lordling proved his aristocracy by labeling her a wanton. Nor did such views pass with the passing of feudalism. In the crushing poverty of XIX London, any roué with an income could have his pick of child whores. In between, gentility developed as an XVIII form of defense against these old aristocratic assumptions. Richardson's XVIII epistolary novels *Pamela* and *Clarissa Harlowe* portray such overly genteel servant girls defending themselves from backstairs rape by the master. And even a Briton might have some trouble tumbling a moral suffragette who is forever sermonizing on virtue, with one finger of a raised arm pointing to heaven.

west   270° on the 360° compass. With variations north and south because of the path of the ecliptic, the direction in which the sun sets. [At root: "where the sun sets." < IE *wes-*, night (VESPERS). Suffixed *-t-* in Gmnc. → OE *west*, direction of the setting sun.]

western (omelet) An omelet made with chopped or sliced ham, sometimes with sliced peppers, and always with chopped onions. *Eastern omelet*, the same without onions.

western A novel (and later a movie) set in the American West. [In pure form, the western is the closest (and crudest) we have come to achieving an epic form. The hero drifts in from nowhere. Against impossible odds, he guns down local evildoers, bringing law and order to the town. The formula calls for a heroine who yearns for his stolid magnificence, but once evil has been overthrown, the hero (despite the violence done by the movies to the pure form of this primitive epic) rides off alone, like a knight errant, always into the setting sun.]

wild and woolly West The untamed frontier West. [The reason for *wild* is as obvious as the alliteration. *Woolly* < 1. Uncurried range horses; 2. Sheepskin chaps; 3. The Saturday night paint-the-town-red boast of the carousing cowboy.

> I'm a woolly wolf and full of fleas.
> I never been curried below the knees.
> And this is my night to howl.]

law west of the Pecos Vigilante law, thinly disguised as a fair trial before a quick hanging. Roy Bean (c. 1825–1903), saloon keeper and self-styled judge of Langtry, Texas, billed himself as the "Law West of the Pecos." [The Pecos River rises in the Sangre de Cristo Mountains of New Mexico and flows about 700 miles south to the Rio Grande through eastern New Mexico and western Texas. "Judge" Bean was more given to lynching than to justice, but in his prime there was no other law in those parts, and he was willing to argue, with some justification, that most of the men he sentenced to hang were guilty as charged, and if not, that they were certainly guilty of something else, since no one would have fled to that country except to escape hanging.]

go west To die. [Amerind into Am. and in RAF usage in WWII. At root: "to go into the sunset," i.e., to God, whose immemorial symbol is the sun. So Wordsworth of God: "whose dwelling is the place of setting suns." Our earliest ancestors, as etymology demonstrates, were sun worshippers. To them each day's sun was the visible God.]

And see *go west, young man.*

wetware   *Computer jargon.* The human brain. [*Hardware* was established early as the computer itself; and with it, *software,* tapes and other supplies for the computer. Once these terms were fixed, *wetware,* the programmer's input, was all but inevitable, at least in hindsight.

Quarrel, a British journal of neologisms, was reviewed in the Manchester *Guardian* and the review was cited by *Logophile,* the *Cambridge Journal of Words and Language. Logophile* cited *wetware* but omitted an explanation of its origin. That's how it is with wetware; things get bogged down in it.]

NOTE. As some help in dating the word's formation, *wetware* could not have made even joking sense until *hardware* and *software* were established. *Hay burner,* for horse, is a similar case. It could only make joke sense after *wood burner* and *coal burner* had become established for a locomotive. Conversely, of course, the early locomotive was commonly an "iron horse."

wheedle   To cajole. To coax. [At root: "to wag one's tail (like a dog)." Echoic IE stem *we-, uee-,* to blow ("to cause the air to move"). → Ger. *wedeln,* to wag, as the tail of a dog (which is also a way of "causing the air to move").]

wheel: big wheel   One who operates on a large scale. The man who makes things happen. [I cannot date this common idiom, but it could hardly have arisen in Am. before early XIX and the establishment in the U.S. of large mills, especially of steam-driven factories, for the ref. could not be to wagon wheels, they being all of the same size, but must be to more or less elaborate machinery in which smaller cogwheels turn the big wheel that produces the output. And so, too:] ***wheeler-dealer*** A more or less flashy financial operator who invests large sums as if recklessly. Some wheeler-dealers have been swindlers, but most have specialized in seemingly brash plunging, though only after checking with a silent and methodical back-room comptroller. [Early XX. Esp. popular in Texas, and prob. of Texan origin. A redupl. based on *wheeler,* as in big wheel, rhyme-echoed by *dealer,* a professional gambler.]

which [< IE *kwi-*, which is the base of many relative and interrogative pronouns. Almost unaltered, via Italic → L. *qui*, who. Via Gmnc. with k/h, and suffixed → OE *hwilc, hwelc,* which.] 1. Asks "what thing, person, or event of a given set under consideration is the one?" (Identification is established by pointing to or otherwise identifying "that one." 2. *In common colloq.* Whatever. *every (any) which way.*

    every which way but loose Colloq. To turn (work over, punish, put through the paces) every way whatever, except toward freedom.

Whig An extinct political party opposed to the now also extinct Tories. In various shifting contexts over several centuries, Whigs have been opposed to what would now be called the establishment. [Root sense: "One who urges on/incites." < Sc. *whig!* a cry to urge on a horse. Roughly equivalent to *giddiup* (< get thee up). In XVII Sc. *whiggamaire* (< *whig,* as above; with *maire,* horse: MARE) labeled a hard, reckless rider. As Brit. *Whiggamore:* 1. A mid XVII Scottish insurgent. 2. In late XVII, a Scottish Presbyterian viewed as a dissenter. Whig (XVIII) began as a pejorative term, soon proudly accepted by those it meant to belittle.] 1. In Am. colonies, an anti-monarchist; later, a supporter of the Revolution; still later, one opposed to the Democratic or Locofoco Party. In 1856 succeeded by the newly founded Republican Party. 2. In Brit. *(a) XVII.* A derisive label for a Scottish Presbyterian dissenter. *(b) After the Restoration (1660).* An anti-monarchist who still sympathized with Oliver Cromwell and his Roundheads. *(c) XVIII–XIX.* The party opposed to the Tories. Succeeded in XIX by the Liberal Party.

whistle for it/go whistle for it *Common colloq.* To hope for more or less hopelessly. In the second form, as a command of curt dismissal, the effective sense is: "You won't get it from me; go whistle for it and see if it comes." [Unattested, but almost certainly of old nautical origin. Among sailors' superstitions, it was bad luck to whistle aboard ship, but when becalmed, it was also tradition to whistle (to make a sound like the wind) in order to attract a wind; a survival of the principle of primitive magic that like begets or attracts like. In the Latin medical formula (once taken in full earnest) *similia similibus curantur,* like cures like. (See *hair of the dog,* under *hair,* Vol. I.)]

whitewash *n.* 1. A solution of slaked lime in water, sometimes with glue added. Since colonial times, it was used to brighten walls and fences, and to conceal defects in weathered wood. Inferior to paint and seldom lasting for more than a season, it was cheaper and easily reapplied, esp. in the days of cheap labor. So the standard southern description of an aristocrat impoverished by the Civil War as *too poor to paint and too proud to whitewash.* 2. *Esp. in Am. politics.* An exoneration by covering up one's failings. —*v.* To cover up as if by a coating of innocence. *The newspaper treatment of the tyrannies and abuses of Robert Moses was always a whitewash.*

whole hog, to go (the) To spend or bet all one has. To commit oneself without reservation. [In XVII Brit. slang a shilling was called a hog. P. *Slang* guesses there may have been a XVII shilling minted with the figure of a pig on the obverse. He does not, however, identify the minting. In XVIII–XIX a *hog* was a sixpence, and I have seen a sixpence stamped with a pig, though I seem to recall that it was Irish. To go the whole hog at a XVII pub would do for an ample night's drinking. Into Am. in early XIX with the sense "to go all out."]

wide place in the road The smallest of small towns. (As if there were not even houses and shops there, but only a slight widening of the road surface.) [Am. In western usage by late XIX. Common among truckdrivers by 1930. But not popularized until 1956, when *Look* magazine ran a feature article on small towns, under the title "A Wide Place in the Road."]

win one's spurs To win recognition of one's ability. [Now generalized. Originally with specific ref. to the dubbing of a knight, it having once been custom for a king, on knighting a bachelor candidate, to give him golden spurs along with the title "Sir Knight."]

HISTORIC. Warrior knights were created on the field of battle in recognition of heroic feats. Carpet knights were courtiers created on the carpet surrounding the king's throne, in recognition of court services. I have been unable to determine whether or not carpet knights got gold spurs. Perhaps some better scholar than I can point me to a reference explaining the dubbing of carpet knights. Pending firm information, I conjecture that carpet knights did get the spurs. I base my conjecture on the fact that the chairborne marauders at headquarters have always picked off promotion, medals, and the other goodies before the combat units were served.

wing: take under one's wing   To shelter and protect. [As a mother hen spreads her wings to cover her chicks when danger threatens. In Am. usage the singular *wing* is firmly established (presupposing a hen with only one wing?). In general usage implies to shelter and nurture—a metaphorical license in that hens do not feed their young, who can in any case scratch for themselves.

The idiom, in its various corruptions, is based on an ancient natural observation. It is implicit in Psalms 63:7: "Because thou hast been my help, therefore in the shadow of thy wings will I rejoice"; and it becomes explicit in Matthew 23:37: ". . . how often would I have gathered thy children together, even as a hen gathereth her chickens under her wings."]

wolf   1. The dog-like, commonly pack-hunting predator. [IE *wlp-*, *ulp-*, and metathesized variant *lup-* → L. *lupus*, wolf. Same IE stem, via Gmnc. with p/f → IE *wulf*.

Aryan, before its abuse in Nazi racial assertions, meant simply "a speaker of Proto-Indo European" and later "of Indo-European." The early Aryan (c. 6000 B.C.) was nomadic, beginning to settle into fixed communities c. 4500 B.C. He must have been acutely aware of the wolf as a danger howling round the campfire, as a marauder of his first herds, and as a man-eater when compelled by hunger. It is also likely that northern European man's first dogs were wolf cubs to begin with. For millennia the wolf was a close companion of man. As late as XII wolves were reported to roam the streets of Paris during severe winters. The wolf was part of Aryan man's environment and legend, and all idioms based on *wolf* derive from this ancient association. Romulus and Remus, for example, the legendary founders of Rome, were said to have been adopted and suckled by a she-wolf when they were infants.] 2. A cruel and gluttonous person.

wolf down To eat ravenously. 3. *Slang.* A human male who is sexually predatory. [In Fr. idiom, attested in XVIII but probably earlier, *elle a vu le loup*, lit. "she has seen the wolf," has the effective sense: "she has lost her maidenhead." Or as it might have occurred in Boy Scout idiom (but has not), "Today's Cub is tomorrow's wolf," a change that occurs at about the time today's Brownie becomes tomorrow's cookie.]

wolf in sheep's clothing An enemy disguised as a friend. [There must have been some dawn age folk tale of a wolf that crept up on the flock wearing the hide of the last sheep it had eaten, but to my knowledge the earliest attestation is in Matthew 7:15 (in which it is used as a long-established idiom): "Beware of false prophets, which come to you in sheep's clothing, but inwardly they are ravening wolves."

cry wolf To give an alarm signal. *cry wolf once too often* To give a false alarm signal so often that one is ignored when real danger looms. [From the ancient but still familiar legend of the new shepherd boy who kept crying wolf when there was no wolf present. The older shepherds, tired of his false alarms, did not respond when a wolf did, in fact, attack the boy's sheep.]

keep the wolf from the door To manage to survive by great effort with no margin of subsistence. [To fight off all the ravages of nature, including its worst predators.]

throw to the wolves To throw a person to his creditors, to the lawyers, and to other predators, and esp. to do so in order to gain time for oneself. [As if to eject one person from a house beset by a hunger-crazed wolf pack with the thought that one kill might appease the pack's hunger, so lessening the danger to others. The standard Russian folklore version is of a family sleigh pursued by wolves, whereupon a baby is thrown to the pack at intervals. Each time the pack stops to devour the latest offering, the sleigh gains a little more time in its race for the safety of the farm house.]

woofer *In early hi-fi technology.* A large speaker designed for the faithful reproduction of low-frequency bass tones. It was paired, or arranged in various combinations, with a *tweeter,* a smaller speaker designed for high-frequency treble sounds. [*Woofer* equated to a dog (woof-woof); *tweeter,* to a bird (tweet-tweet). The nomenclature testifies to a natural touch of folk poetry among the technicians. But technology, alas, has won, for *woofer* and *tweeter* have all but disappeared, replaced in the catalogues and shop talk by the accurate but dull *bass* and *treble.*]

wool [Via Gmnc. < IE *wel-*, wool, the form unchanged except for a vowel modification.] 1. The hair of sheep, goats, and various other animals. 2. The thread spun from such hair. 3. The fabric woven of such thread. 4. Anything resembling a clump of wool. *steel wool.* (Some of the many idioms based on *wool* are treated in Vol. I, but I repeat those here for a single, fuller treatment.)

woolgathering Daydreaming. The act (nonact?) of allowing

one's mind to roam at random. [On British medieval estates children and the aged were granted the right to gather from the bushes any tuft of wool that had been snagged from passing sheep. For most of the poor, such tufts were the only available source of homespun. Such gathering did not proceed in a straight line, but from tuft to tuft as one happened to spot one; a natural metaphor for the randomness of free association.]

woolly-headed 1. Having snarled and kinky hair. 2. Stupid. [As if having wool for brains.]

all wool and a yard wide An expression of approval when referring to a person. [*All wool,* unadulterated; *and a yard wide,* and full measure.]

dyed in the wool Steadfast. The same all the way through. [Originally "color-fast." The ref. is to yarn or woolen thread that is deep-dyed before weaving. Because the thread, in offering the maximum absorbent surface to the yarn, is more securely dyed than a woven fabric would be.]

pull the wool over one's eyes To hoodwink. [And "to hoodwink" was the literal sense, with ref. to pulling the capacious woolen hood of a monk over his eyes. But also to pull a woolen stocking cap over one's eyes, blinding the wearer. And variantly ***pull the wool over one's ears*** With specific ref. to a stocking cap, and meaning the same thing, for if the cap is pulled over the ears it will also, in all likelihood, be pulled over the eyes.]

The Woolsack Brit. The seat of the Lord Chancellor in his office as Speaker of the House of Lords. As such, he is technically outside the House and has to move to his bench if he chooses to speak as a peer. [The seat, a sort of hassock, was once one of four sacks stuffed with wool and placed prominently in the House of Lords, a custom established by Edward II (reigned 1327–1377) to signalize the importance of wool to the British economy. Acts of 1666 and 1678 made it illegal to use anything but wool for burial shrouds or coffin linings, thus making even the dead into customers for British wool.]

word to the wise   In essence, an "or else." Effective sense: "(No advice will serve the stupid, but) be wise enough to heed what I say, or suffer the consequences." [Translation of L. *verbum sapienti.* In British university usage, commonly *verb. sap.* Cf. common *infra dig.* for *infra dignitātem,* below one's dignity. *In federal prose nothing digs more infra than a verb. sap.*]

works, the   All of it. Everything. *What'll ya have on your hot dog?—*
The works. (I.e., all the relishes, condiments, and garnishes available.) **shoot the works** In gambling. To bet everything one has on
the board. To go for broke. [These are relatively late forms. In Am.
early XX slang *give one the works* meant to thrash a man
thoroughly, or to gun him down, as in a gangland execution. P.
Slang notes that the idiom, with these senses, was Anglicized c.
1939, and still so functions in Brit. In Am., however, it has lost the
sense "deadly assault" and now means "all there is."]

world   [A much condensed form, its elements visible in OE *werold,*
the world of mankind. At root: "the ancient place of man's sustenance." The first element < IE *wir-,* man. (So L. *vir,* man: VIRILE.
And so Gmnc. *wera-,* man: WEREWOLF.) The second element is ult.
< IE *al-,* to nurture. (So L. *alere,* to nourish: ALIMENTATION. And
so Ger. *alt,* earlier *alth,* old, the root sense of which is "nourished
to old age.") *World* therefore is at root: "the ancient place of our
nurture." *World* and *earth* are commonly interchangeable, but the
root distinction is between the "populated planet" and the "physical planet." To speak precisely, dinosaurs roamed the earth but not
the world.] 1. The planet as man's *mis en scène.* [The common ref.
is to this planet, but loosely to any planet with an intelligent population. So *worlds in space,* a common science fiction theme, but not
a new one. Giordano Bruno, the Italian Renaissance scholar, argued
the existence of many worlds in space, one of the heresies for which
he was burned at the stake in Rome's Campo dei Fiori, Feb. 2,
1600. Bruno conceived man-like worlds. But the likelihood of a
parallel evolution is near zero, and since *world* is specifically "place
of man," some other term would be more appropriate for a planet
populated by intelligent creatures of other evolutionary origins.] 1.
This planet as man's home place. 2. Social existence in various
subdivisions. *the ancient world, the world of ideas, the underworld.*
3. A vast plenty. *He has a world of tricks.*

worms: can of worms   An unpleasant surprise. [As if opening a can
labeled *pâté* and having maggots spill out: it cannot happen because of the hermetic sealing, but were it to happen, it would not
improve the picnic. Dating uncertain. I believe, but cannot attest,
that the idiom arose in ad-agency jargon just after WWII, and then
passed into federal and corporate jargon, and then into general
use.] More recently the basic metaphor has become **open a can of
worms** 1. To run into trouble. 2. To cause trouble by posing embar-

rassing or unmanageable questions. *The investigating committee opened a large can of worms and has dumped it into the laps of the oil companies.*

NOTE. There is, in fact, such a thing as a can—or at least a jar —of worms. My late dear friend Fletcher Pratt used to raise marmoset monkeys, probably because of an endearing family resemblance. As their special treat, he bought for them in the pet department of one or another of the large NYC department stores jars of large mealy worms imported from Africa by air. I do not know how the packers kept the worms alive, but I can testify that I have seen them squirm in the jar, as I have watched the marmosets put a delicate and efficient end to their squirming.

worship   *v.* 1. To adore a god, idol, fetish. 2. To hold in reverent regard. *She worships the ground her husband's business stands on.* —*n.* The act of worship(p)ing. *Your Worship* Obs. in Am. since early colonial days. A British title of respect in addressing a magistrate, mayor, or other sub-noble figure of dignity and authority. [And *Your Worship* is closest to the root sense: "condition of (great) worth," as if "worthy" plus "ship," condition of being. So ME *worshipe,* OE *weorthscipe,* worth, dignity, honor, reverence. Ult. < IE *wer-,* to bend, to turn toward. So L. *vertere,* to turn; Ger. *Wurst,* sausage ("thing turned into itself"); OE *weard,* turned (TOWARD), and variant *wyrd,* fate ("what one is turned toward / headed for") (WEIRD). At root, therefore, the religious sense of *worship* is: "the act (or state) of turning to a deity in recognition of great worth."]

wrote the book on   Knows all about. *Ronald Reagan wrote the book on economic ignorance.* [Am. Dating uncertain. Prob. early XX. Perh. earlier. Perh. a slant reference to Hoyle, who "wrote the book" on card games (and other indoor games) in mid XVIII. With later revisions, *Hoyle's Rules* remains the authoritative text. If Hoyle is the original ref., *wrote the book on* could have evolved in early XIX, but I cannot find an attestation before early XX.]

X Y Z

X   Also **ex/aix/aix'l**   An axle. [New England dialect from at least XVIII. James Russell Lowell, *Bigelow Papers,* notes that the Yankee has clung to Anglo-Saxon usage in *aix* for *axle.* I do not know what he meant. *Axil* is first attested in ME, prob. into Eng. under Dane Law, from ON *öxull.* But his ref., along with various others, makes it clear that all four of the given forms were in common New England use.]

Yarborough   *Now.* A bridge hand with no face cards or aces. [After Charles Anderson Warsley, second earl of Yarborough, died 1897. He liked to bet, giving 1,000–1 odds, that such a hand would not be dealt at whist. By his rules the hand must contain no card higher than a nine. Unsupported rumor has it that he once lost his bet and paid out his thousand pounds. But Yarborough was no fool. I am told by my mathematical betters that the odds against such a hand are a bit better than 1,825 to 1. If he could place his bet often enough, his chances of coming out ahead were better than those of a casino. (But how often can one find a taker for such a bet?)]

year   [Root sense: "what passes." < IE *ei-*, to go. → L. *ire,* to go. Variant *ye-ro-*, modified in Gmnc. → OE *gear.* (Cognate with Ger. *Jahr,* year.) The OE form with regular g/y → ME *yere,* year.] The period of a planet's orbit around its sun; earth's being approx. 365¼ days.

yeoman   *Naval.* A ship's clerk. [ME *yemen* was a slurred contraction of *yengman,* young man, a specific ref. to a younger son. In feudal England estates were traditionally entailed to the firstborn son. Being landless, younger sons had little to choose but military service, clerical orders, or roguery.

I cannot trace securely the derivation of *yeoman* as ship's clerk

310

from *yemen*, younger son. Perhaps in preparation for religious orders and a church benefice, younger sons were tutored, the clergy being the one literate class. Perhaps then the boy chose arms rather than the cloth, so entering the services able to read and write.

It was once custom for the king, after a great victory, to give grants of unentailed land to soldiers who had distinguished themselves. Thus the soldiering yemen became the British yeomen, freeholders who ranked below the gentry but above the landless. *Yeoman* became the title of a freeman with his own land, and continued so as a proud label of U.S. freeholders (see historic note, below) in XIX, but has fallen out of use except as above and in the idiom: *do yeoman's service* 1. To fight bravely, as befits a freeman. 2. To eat and drink heartily, as befits a strapping man of arms. (Members of the lower house of New Jersey are still officially designated freeholders.)

HISTORIC. In the American colonies, and in the U.S. up to c. 1900, the American farmer thought of himself proudly as a yeoman, a freeman on his own land, and with the added egalitarian assurance that there was no social caste superior to his. Noah Webster (1758–1843) was a thumping advocate of the American yeoman:

> Let Englishmen take notice that when I speak of the American yeomanry, the latter are not to be compared to the illiterate peasantry of their own country. The yeomanry of this country consist of substantial, independent freeholders, masters of their own persons and lords of their own soil. These men have considerable education. . . . In the Eastern states, there are public schools sufficient to instruct everyman's children, and most children are actually benefited by these institutions.

The self-styled yeoman's pride of these "native" Americans, implicit in their British orientation and fanned by Webster's widely read opinions, became in late XIX (following the arrival of immigrant hordes in mid XIX) a national dread of mongrelization by the new arrivals, as in the once common "Workers Wanted" sign, regularly followed by "No Irish Need Apply."

yokel A country bumpkin. The country cousin conceived as a gullible boob. [Echoic. From the call of the English green woodpecker rendered as *yo-KEL*. Hence, person from out where the green woodpeckers call. And see *podunk*.]

yore   Time long past. [Archaic, but survives in tale telling, esp. in the formula *days of yore.* < OE *gēar,* genitive plu. *gēara,* of years (gone by). OE *g* → Eng. *y* is a standard shift; and with vowel modification → *yore.*]

Young Turk   Also, but now rare *Young Ottoman* 1. In late XIX and early XX Ottoman Empire, a member of the Secret Society of Union and Progress, consisting primarily of students and young professionals dedicated about equally to fiery oratory and to the overthrow of the autocratic rule of Abdul-Hamid II and the establishment of a constitutional democracy. 2. Any fervent young political reformer working within a party to seize control from entrenched conservatives. 3. Any fervent young political idealist. [In 1908, somewhat to their own surprise, the Young Turks stopped being a secret society and emerged as the party in power. *Young Turk* came into English soon thereafter as newspapers reported the embarrassment of these idealists upon being saddled with the responsibilities of practical government.]

you're another   A standard, though uninspired, formula for returning an insult. *You're a liar. —You're another.* [Common in verbal exchanges between children. Still very much alive, this form is attested in Brit. as early as 1534, in Udall's *Roister Doister:* "You are another your selfe, sir."]

you're telling me?   A formula of one-upmanship in street colloquial. In effect, I know all about it—and more. A variable term, but one-upmanship is the gist of it in all contexts. In answer to: "I tell you, business couldn't be worse," "You're telling me," asserts that the respondent's affairs are so much worse off than those of the speaker that the speaker could not begin to understand what true business worries are. In answer to: "Now that's what I call a beautiful woman," the formula is a put-down, asserting that the respondent knows more about beautiful women than the speaker could ever learn. And so in the old Yiddish joke in which one Jew expresses his sorrow by saying, "Oi!" and is answered by another, "You're telling me!"

   Note that the formula is often not a question but an exclamation of surprise that the speaker should be so presumptuous as to mention such a thing to the infinitely more experienced and more knowledgeable respondent.

z's *Slang.* Sleep. *catch (grab) some z's* To get some sleep. [Am. only. Of recent though uncertain date, perh. as late as 1960's. After the comic strip convention of indicating sleep by drawing a long string of Z's to indicate snoring.]

zenith The celestial point directly over one's head. [The word has been formed as a typographical error. (See *sneeze,* Vol. I., for a similar formation by typographical error.) < Arabic *semt-ar-ras,* lit. the way / road / path / course of the head. Shortened to *semt* in Arabic, and with the cursive *m* misread as *ni,* mistranslated into Medieval L. as *cenit,* whence OF *cenith,* ME *senyth.*]

zero hour The time set for an attack to begin, in WWI implying a charge out of the trenches and "over the top" to attack the entrenched enemy. Usu. preceded by an artillery barrage, but *zero hour* was specific to the moment at which men leaped up to slaughter and be slaughtered. The term had some currency in WWII, primarily in the vocabulary of WWI officers who had stayed in the reserve and went back into the fighting forces as retreads. It was early replaced by D-Day (debarkation day) for invasion day, the time before it designated D-Day minus 3, 2, 1, for example, with the progress of the invasion noted as D-Day plus 1,2,3, etc.

zest Relish. Gusto. Anything that increases one's relish. Originally with ref. to drink, then almost at once to food (both in XVII). And now further extended. *The chorus girls from the Roxy line added a little zest to the party.* [Origin in doubt. First attested in Fr. *zeste, zec,* which Cotgrave (XVII) translated as "the thicke skin . . . whereby the kernel of a wall-nut is divided." And this definition suggests a likely (but unattestable) derivation from L. *cesta,* basket, the meat of walnuts being contained in a fibrous integument crudely like a basket. In any case, the early XVII sense shift was to something like a slice of lemon peel used to add flavor to a drink, and soon thereafter to any spice for food. There is no Latin word for citrus (see *orange,* Vol. I), these fruits having been introduced into Europe only in XII–XIII, prob. as a result of the Crusades. Citrus must have been introduced into Palestine from the east, prob. no earlier than IX–X. It did not grow there in the era of the Roman conquerors.]

zoo A collection of live wild creatures on public display, usually for a fee. [A specimen of English back formation based on earlier *zoological garden,* only the first (and slightly altered) of the seven syllables surviving, and doing the work of all. *Zoological garden* does survive as a formal designation, but *zoo* is now fully established standard English. *Mob,* by back formation from L. *mobile vulgus,* the fickle multitude, was reviled as a vulgar neologism by Jonathan Swift in 1720, yet was accepted as standard English by the arch-Tory Dr. Samuel Johnson in 1755. Slang *rep,* by back formation from *reputation,* continues to be offensive to the literate, and I believe it will remain so. No rule can be made to cover all cases. As frequently noted in these glosses, language does what it does because it does it, and we concur or disapprove after the fact, because we are native to the convention of our own tongue.]

zounds   Mild exclam. of surprise, vexation. [Archaic, but surviving in affected speech, and within the recognition vocabulary of the literate. Now pronounced to rhyme with *sounds;* earlier, with *wounds.* A minced oath, but earlier an offensive blasphemy. (See note on *Shock Language,* Vol. I.) < *His (Christ's) wounds* → *'iswounds* → *zounds.*]

SUPPLEMENT

Since the publication of the first volume of *A Browser's Dictionary*, I have turned up additional information about a number of the terms there discussed. The entries in this small supplement expand, modify, and sometimes entirely supersede those in the first *Browser's*. They also attempt to deal with a number of distressing errors, typographical and moronogenic.

agnostic   T. H. Huxley was cited in error as the father of Julian and Aldous. He was their grandfather. Their father was Leonard Huxley, 1860–1933. Their mother was Julia Arnold, a niece of Matthew Arnold.

apple pie order   Some derive this form from *cap à pied order,* in order from *cap to foot / head to foot.* Perhaps. But the Fr. form would be *en ordre cap à pied.* If an illiterate Saxon servant of a French manor house managed to twist the Fr. form to *(c)ap a pie order,* no such form has ever been attested. In view of the extraordinary alteration such a derivation must presuppose, the derivation, as given in Vol. I, from Fr. *nape pliè en ordre* is in every way more persuasive.

Attic salt   (See under *salt.*) In the citation refering to Scipio, a typographical error resulted in *Scipio omnes sale superabit* (he will surpass all others in wit). It should have read *omnes sale superavit,* he did (continuing action in the past) surpass all others.

balls out   At high speed. [Nautical. Engine room. As an engine's speed of rotation increased, certain mechanical governors spread out hinged arms by centrifugal force, and heavy metal balls attached to their "elbows" projected farther and farther toward a set limit, the whole apparatus doing the work of a horizontal flywheel.

When the "balls" were farthest "out," the engine was turning at highest speed.

Balls has an obvious sexual connotation, and *be going at it balls out* means to be approaching a violent sexual climax, whence the associated sense, to be on an unrestrained spree.]

baseball   The legend persists that Abner Doubleday invented the game at Cooperstown, N.Y., in 1839. He did not, despite the fact that sportswriters and commentators assert his fathership, and despite the fact that there is in Cooperstown, as part of the Baseball Hall of Fame, an Abner Doubleday Memorial Stadium, whose plaques salute him in bronze as the father of baseball.

Doubleday, later a Union general at the Battle of Gettysburg, did teach at a military academy at Cooperstown in 1839, and did coach his boys in baseball or rounders, but some of them at least must already have known the game, nor is there a single rule of baseball traceable to Doubleday, nor did he ever claim to have invented the game. Nor is it certain that the stadium named for him in Cooperstown is the field on which his boys played the game. There had, of course, to be a field, but the likelihood is that the Hall of Fame directors simply picked a field conveniently near the hall.

Various English novels, beginning in early XVIII, refer to baseball as a country sport. Allowing for a reasonable lag between the first emergence of the sport and the first reference to it in print, the game was probably established by at least late XVII, and was probably played with a ball of crude India rubber (caoutchouc), probably with a stitched cloth or leather cover. There are similar references to the game played in the south of England and called there *rounders.*

Less securely dated, but probably by at least the end of XVIII, came *one old cat* or *one o' cat*, improvised when there were only 3 or 4 players to a side and using only one base (cat). *Two o' cat*, played with 5 or 6 players to a side, used two bases. There was no *three o' cat*, for if 7 to 9 players were available for each side, the three-base game went back to baseball or rounders.

Doubleday was cast in bronze and legend as the work of A. G. Spaulding, who played professional baseball in XIX, went on to found the well-known sporting goods firm, and was high in the inner circle of baseball officialdom circa 1900. In 1907 Spaulding appointed a commission of dignitaries to trace the origin of the game. This commission turned up the fact that Doubleday's cadets had played the game in 1839, and declared him to be the father of the game. Their findings were announced with a fanfare in the 1908 *Baseball Guide,* and that ill-informed report has since been widely accepted as the truth.

The fact is that the commission was not made up of researchers but of more or less distinguished poops whose names would give luster to their misinformation. Nor were they, nor was Spaulding, in pursuit of the truth. For jingo reasons, Spaulding was out to prove that "the great American pastime" was a native sport. If the commission did turn up any evidence to the contrary, the poops and Spaulding simply ignored it. Doubleday gave them what they wanted, and Doubleday it is. Except that it isn't. And see *rounders,* below.

beaver   A new sense (since c. 1965) is: pubic hair. Also **beaver shot** *News photography.* The ultimate cheesecake: a girlie photo that shows the pubic hair.

Thomas H. Middleton, among others, has commented on the more recent use of the word. *"Beard* for *beaver,"* he writes, "is definitely passé these days—[ed. note: not quite, though Middleton's points are sound—at least in the U.S.] Now it is a lot raunchier. It means, roughly, pussy. There's a bumper sticker that's quite popular out here [California]: *Save a tree—Eat a beaver.* I think this usage started as a photographer's term. . . . During the days of violent student protests, it was common for photographers to yell "Beaver!" when the cops hassled a girl who, it became apparent, was not wearing underthings; then all the photographers would fight for position to get a *beaver shot."*

Let me add that coeds of the 1960's showed their liberation by shedding underwear and by taking part in student protests. A common tactic of resisting the police who ordered the demonstrators to disperse was to sit or lie down and remain inert. The police who arrested demonstrators were required to remove dead weight. It was tiresome work. One method was for two cops to team up, each grasping one leg, and drag the protesters to the police vans. It did not take much dragging for the skirt of a liberated coed to ride up over her liberated pubic bush, thereby giving photographers their *beaver shot.*

blackberry winter   Whether or not there is a spell of cold days following the blossoming of the blackberries (and I can find no evidence of such a weather pattern in North America), this idiom, slightly modified, was imported from Britain. It is there called *blackthorn* *winter,* variously said to occur in late April, early May, or the second week of May (prob. the blooming spread of blackthorns from southern to northern Britain). The second week of May is favored by the British idiom *ice saints,* those saints whose feast days occur during that week. *Ice* is certainly hyperbolic, meaning not "frozen" but "unseasonably cold." Such a reverse "Indian summer" does seem to be a regular pattern of the British climate. The American language, on the other hand, seems to have imported the idiom, but not the weather pattern.

blunderbuss   The XVII modification of Du. *dunderbus* to Eng. *blunderbuss* was the more natural in that slightly earlier Eng. *blunderbuss* had had some currency with the sense: "clumsy loud-mouthed worker" (a box of blunders). "We could now wish we had a discreet and intelligent adversary, and not such a hare-brained blunderbuss as you to deal with."—John Milton, preface to *A Defense of the People of England.*

boot   To my note in Vol. I, I must add a note from *Dictionary of Obsolete English* by the estimable Richard C. Trench, Anglican Archbishop of Dublin in the latter XIX:

> Not the luggage, but the chief persons used once to ride in the boot, or rather the boots of a carriage, for there were two. Projecting from the sides of the carriage and open to the air, they derived, no doubt, their name from their shape.

I quote Trench without understanding him for I have been unable to find any illustration of a carriage with anything like boots projectiong from the side, and I am inclined to think that any such projections would make for sideswiping in tight traffic; but the ignorance is certainly mine, for Trench was not a man to be mistaken in such a matter.

In any case, by the end of the XVII, *boot* had become specific to the rear of the carriage or stage coach.

broadcast   George M. Carney of Hilton, N.Y. has made himself a scholar of the history of radio broadcasting in the U.S. I am grateful to him for correcting my comments on the first American political broadcast, which was much earlier than I had supposed. He tells me that according to an advertisement in the *National Geographic* of March 1940, station KDKA, Pittsburgh, broadcast the Harding-Cox election returns on Nov. 2, 1920, and Harding's inaugural address on March 4, 1921. The election returns probably reached Pittsburgh by telegraph; the inaugural, by leased telephone wires. *Broadcast*, in the now standard radio sense, may not have been in use in 1920, but it certainly was by 1924, when the emergent radio industry gave a much wider coverage of the Democratic National Convention of 1924, at which the deadlock between McAdoo and Smith threw the nomination to dark horse John W. Davis, who was defeated by Calvin Coolidge.

Caesar   To the long list of words derived from Caesar's name add *sherry*, after the Spanish city of *Xeres*, later *Jerez*, long famous for its production of sherry (in XVI Eng. *sherris, sherris wine*). Xeres/Jerez was a city built by the Romans in the first century A.D. and named by them *Caesarea*, City of Caesar, the name corrupted in Spanish in much the way the Channel Island called by the Romans *Caesarea* became *Jersey*.

carn-   Line 5: for *carni*, read *carnis*.

chippy/chippie   A whore. [Am. only. In Brit. slang *chip/chippy* refers to a carpenter (< wood chips), and more recently to a counterman who serves fish and chips.] *Chippy* as a label for a whore has nothing to do with the chipping sparrow, nor with girls lined up along the street and chipping or cheeping to attract a john. As earlier noted, MMM cites the first attested usage from a Colorado newspaper, 1890: "The leading dudes and chippies of Europe."

I am indebted to a correspondent who put me on the right track and whom, I am sorry to say, I treated badly. He wrote me that a chippy was a Mexican house whore who was paid with chips the customers bought from the madam, much as taxi dancers in earlier U.S. dance halls were paid with paper tickets (10¢ a dance) from ticket strips bought from the management. My correspondent explained that payment in chips was to prevent the customers from robbing the girls. Because no whorehouse can continue in business without a tough resident bouncer, at least in honky-tonk red-light districts, I replied briefly that I rejected the explanation, tossed out the man's letter, and do not know now how to address the writer to whom I owe both thanks and an apology. Mexican whorehouses *(chippy house* is cited in *American Thesaurus of Slang)* did use chips as American taxi dancers used paper tickets, turning their chips back to the management and receiving a percentage of the going rate for each chip. In Sp. a poker chip is called *una ficha*. I have been unable to attest but must suppose that a girl who worked for *fichas* was a *fichera*. The point does not ultimately matter. *Mexican whorehouse* can mean "house in Mexico" or "house in the western states staffed by Mexican girls." The 1890 first attestation in Colorado conforms neatly to these facts. *Chippy* may be a simple translation of *fichera*, or it may be a direct reference to the chips Anglo customers bought in such houses, and it probably is both.

cocksure   In citing John Fox's *Book of Martyrs*, I was mistaken in saying he was the "founder of the Society of Friends." The society was founded c. 1652 by George Fox, 1624–1691.

cold shoulder   A related Fr. form is *chasse-cousin*, lit. "chase-away cousin (poor relation)," said of a wine so bad that not even a poor relation will return to eat at one's table.

dead man's hand   My account of Wild Bill Hickok, Calamity Jane, and Jack McCall was derived from faulty sources. I am indebted to Richard Allen Pence of Fairfax, Virginia, who writes to put matters straight: "The poker game was not in Calamity Jane's saloon. It was in the No. 10 Saloon, owned by a man named Mann, who was playing in the game. . . . I have never heard that Jack McCall was Calamity Jane's lover. . . . There are stories that link Calamity and Wild Bill, but these, too, are probably apocryphal.

"Jack McCall was not 'hanged for interfering in a local poker game.' He was acquitted of murder by the citizens of Deadwood, but persisted in bragging about his deed until he was arrested, retried, convicted, and hanged at Yankton, the territorial capital. . . . He is not buried by Calamity Jane. Calamity and Wild Bill are buried in Deadwood's 'Boot Hill,' now the Mt. Moriah Cemetery."

dismal   Archbishop Trench (Richard Chevenix Trench), *Dictionary of Obsolete English*, without offering any explanation, denies the derivation from L. *diēs malī*. This derivation, he writes, "is exactly one of those plausible etymologies to which one learns after a while to give no credit. Yet there can be no doubt that our fathers so understood the word, and that this assumed etymology often over-rules their usage of it."

Trench was a monumental scholar of language, if sometimes an eccentric one, and he wrote more than a century ago, before an era of enormous advances in etymology. Those advances have securely demonstrated *diēs malī* to be the base of *dismal*, and have left

Trench in hot defense of an error, but let it be added as a fit tribute that it is a rare error.

forty acres and a mule   Typographical error. My note gave a quarter section as being 140 acres; it should have read *160 acres.*

funky   The derivation from Fr. *fumer,* to smoke (as a ham), into Creole *funkier,* whence *funky* acquired the senses "mildewed, earthy, back on the plantation, primitive," whence the later senses, discussed in Vol. I. *Fumer* to *funkier* is an unusual shift, however, and suggests the presence of a third influence.

Robert F. Thompson, master of Timothy Dwight College, Yale, is one of the few scholars who has commented knowledgeably on West African languages and their influence on Creole and Southern American idiom. He cites Ki-Konga *lu-fuki* as a powerfully operative term. Its root sense is "strong body odor," but it is accompanied by a native belief in the beneficial power exerted by the healthy sweat of a powerful man. Thompson cites Ki-Konga *Yati, nkwa, lu-fuki! Ve miela miami ikwenda baki,* which he translates into idiomatic Am. as: "Like, there is a real funky person! My soul advances toward him to receive his blessing." In Africa, he reports, boys snuggle up to such a man to inhale the blessing of his power.

The oral transmissions of a people kept in ignorance and degradation cannot be attested except by the chance report of a literate third party. I was partly brought up in a community of illiterate Italian immigrants and their partly Americanized children, and can attest to the violence the children did to the patois Italian they retained. For those who will entertain a speculation (that cannot be asserted), I suggest that Fr. *fumer* and Ki-Konga *fuki* blurred together in the plantation patois of the slaves, perhaps at first as *fumky* and then as *funky,* the Creolized form becoming a basic term of jazz musicians c. 1900. (And see, in the body of this book, *Congo Square.*)

funny bone   In Vol. I, I wrote: "I have never found an explanation for this idiom. What's funny about the so-called funny bone?"

It is too late for me to be surprised by my own stupidity. *Funny* is, of course, a pun on *humerus* rendered as if *humorous.* The *humerus* is the upper-arm bone between the shoulder and the elbow.

gas   *Halitum ilum,* line 3, should read *Halitum illum.*

gen-, gene-   Item 6, line 2: *nascire* should read *nasci,* to be born.

George   Add *by George!* Exclam. of surprise. Originally also of deter-
mination. *I say I will, by George!* And in this form has the effect
of a (now) mild oath. *By George, it's good to see you!* [In all cases
a short form of "I swear (it) by St. George." St. George is the
informal but effective patron saint of England. And so since c. 1350
the battle cry *St. George and the dragon for merry England!* (I do
not know why British enthusiasm included the dragon: St. George
had no use for it except to stick it with his lance.)]
    HISTORIC. St. George is a figure of legend rather than of history.
A warrior saint, he is usu. depicted on horseback, lancing the dragon of evil. St. Demetrios is so depicted in Greek Orthodox icons.
George and Demetrios must have a common, though now lost,
mythic ancestor.
    Though legends of St. George were known in Britain by VI, he
remained one of many pious myths until returning crusaders reported seeing a vision of him at the battle of Antioch in 1098,
attributing their victory to his patronage. Their reports added awe
to piety, but George did not emerge as the specific patron of England and of English arms until a bit more than 250 years later,
when Edward III (reigned 1327–1377) founded the Order of the
Garter, placing its chivalry under the warrior saint's fervently im-
plored but nebulous protection. All fact aside, 'tis thinking makes
it so.

G.I.   (This corrected and expanded note replaces the entry in Vol. I.)
In WWII and since. An enlisted man or woman. [Commonly, but
wrongly, derived from *G*overnment *I*ssue, but this term has never
been in standard service use. Douglas MacArthur (in *American
Caesar,* by William Manchester) is quoted as rejecting the use of
G.I. "G.I. means General Issue . . . call them soldiers." Yet G.I.s
called themselves G.I.s and generally took the initials to mean
Government Issue. They were, after all, citizen soldiers. The army
could bend them and dent them, but they reserved the right to
express themselves in their own way about the abysmal snafu of the
whole adjectival G.I. army.]
    Colonel Roman C. Grady, U.S. Army, writes: "I believe this
term G.I. evolved entirely during WWII. I certainly never heard
it applied to a soldier until after the time of the first draftees in early
1941 (although I was a plebe at West Point at the time and it may
have come into use in 1940). On the other hand, *G.I. can* is of

ancient (??) use in the army . . . listed in property books and receipts as, *Can, G.I. forty gallon, utility,* and the G.I. meant Galvanized Iron."

And see *gyrene,* below.

grass widow   Spook etymology commonly refers this idiom to Fr. *veuve de grace,* grace widow (whatever that may mean). I can find no such idiom in French, nor could the heads of several Romance language departments whom I consulted. OED notes *grace widow,* but only to dismiss it. The spooks, I have been forced to conclude, invented both French and English forms after the fact, by way of spooky explanation.

Gunpowder Plot   (See under *gun.*) The king who was to attend the sitting of Parliament on Nov. 5, 1605, and whom Guy Fawkes meant to blow up along with the Parliament, was not, as stated in Vol. I, Henry VII but James I of England, who was also James VI of Scotland.

gyrene   A United States Marine. (Applies to all ranks.) [I had earlier supposed the form was a telescoping of *G.I.* and *marine,* but I was wrong. Wilfred Granville, *Sea Slang of the Twentieth Century* (Philosophical Library), gives: "*Gerines,* An old Navy term for the Royal Marines." P. *Slang* defines the term in the same way, but dates it more accurately as arising in mid XIX and expiring in early XX. Neither P. nor G. explains the origin of the term, but Am. obviously picked up the obsolescent British term c. 1900 and altered it to still surviving *gyrene.*]

hat   (Some idioms not treated in Vol. I.)
Mexican hat dance A sex ritual. In the exuberance of the music at a fiesta, the man throws his broad-brimmed sombrero at the feet of a chosen lady as a courtship ritual. If she dances around the rim and then picks up the hat and puts it on, she has accepted him.

at the drop of a hat 1. Instantly. On signal. [A common Am. signal for starting a race was to hold an ample hat aloft and then to bring it down sharply at the end of the extended arm.] 2. *Ext.* Upon the slightest provocation.

eat one's hat To eat crow. To pay a forfeit as a loser. [From the common Am. formula: "I'll eat my hat if . . ." The verbal form is common, but has anyone ever actually eaten his hat? Can one?]

hat in hand Humbly. [In ancient custom one doffed one's hat in the presence of a superior. And related:] ***take one's hat off to*** To show respect and admiration. To acknowledge a superior accomplishment.

Also: ***old hat*** Passé. [Few things change as rapidly as hat styles.] ***pass the hat*** Take up a collection for a cause. ***keep under one's hat*** To keep secret. [In one's own head.] ***talk through one's hat*** To prattle at random. To talk wildly, foolishly. [As if not through the mouth (with considered words) but rantingly out of the top of one's skull. Cf. the common slang idiom *to flip one's lid.*] ***go shit in your hat (and pull it down over your ears)*** Derisive, vulgar rejection. [Implies that the person so commanded is stupid enough to do as he is told.]

hat trick Cricket is a British ritual prob. beyond the understanding of one not born to the faith. In my ignorance I said, in Vol. I, that the *hat trick* was so called because the star feat of knocking over three wickets in three successive bowls was signalized by passing the hat among the spectators. I was once so assured by a Cockney cabby, and I apologize for transmitting his error. The hat (cap) is roughly the equivalent of the Am. varsity letter and was bestowed upon the star athlete by his teammates. Such hats (caps) are now awarded to all members of the English team. They are somehow related as a mark of distinction to the light and dark "blues" worn by Oxford and Cambridge cricketers as badges of distinction.

As an American sports term, *hat trick* has been almost entirely restricted to hockey, originally a Canadian game, and therefore more closely phrased to Brit. idiom. In hockey it labels the act of a single player in scoring three goals in a single game. In Vol. I, I suggested that the Am. term would, in time, be applied to other sports. On Jan. 25, 1981, in Super Bowl XV, Rod Martin of the Oakland Raiders intercepted three Philadelphia Eagles passes, and one of the sportscasters labeled his feat "a hat trick." It was the first time I heard the term used in Am. with ref. to a sport other than hockey.

ice Add: *Am. theater.* A kickback paid by scalpers to the box office in token of blocks of choice seats it saves for them. It can amount to a substantial sum and is commonly, or was once, variously divided among the director, producer, stage manager. [Origin and dating unknown. Perh. (guess only) by association with *putting the frosting (icing) on the cake.*]

innuendo   Line 7: *innuare* should read *innuere.*

Irish bull   (See under *bull.*) I am indebted to John T. Edsall of Cambridge, Mass., for a saying he attributes to Joseph Barcroft, English physiologist: "The great virtue of the Irish bull is that it is always pregnant." A lovely mot, if only it were true. If the bull is pregnant, the result is always a miscarriage.

jazz   I was wrong in thinking that Creole *jass,* as in *jasshouse,* brothel, was from some lost Afro-Carib-pidgin root. It is from Fr. **jaser,* to exchange social banter, to give and take. Whence Creole *jass,* sex, sexual give and take. So *don't gimme none of your jazz* means: 1. Don't give me any of your lip. 2. Don't you try to fuck me. A correspondent writing to William Safire, N.Y. Sunday *Times,* attested a mid XIX Brit. use of *jazz* in the pure Fr. sense, and I meant to save the reference but the paper was thrown out before I got to my scissors.

johnnycake   I still resist the commonly offered derivation < *journey cake.* A johnnycake is something between a taco and a tamale, and unless somehow leavened and moistened (in which case it would no longer be johnnycake), it would crumple to crumbs in a saddlebag or in a hunter's pocket or backpack. The word is somehow connected with the unexplained New England *joniken,* to which I can find no clue, except to believe it may be of Dutch origin, though I cannot find it in Dutch.

Jolly Roger   (See under *roger.*) I described the pirate's flag as having: "a black field (signifies 'no quarter'), usu. with a white skull and crossbones superimposed (also meaning 'no quarter')." On further inquiry, I have been able to turn up no evidence that any pirate, anywhere, at any time, flew a skull and crossbones on his black flag. That insignia, I am beginning to believe, is a literary invention sustained most recently by Hollywood pirate films. I welcome any reliable evidence that the skull and crossbones was ever in actual use during the XVI–XVII era of piracy on the Spanish Main, but lacking such evidence, I must apologize for "usu. with a white skull and crossbones superimposed."

mass Line 3: *mittare* should read *mittere*.

meticulous Line 8: *metis* should read *metus*, fear.

minister Line 6. I lapsed partially into Italian in *servo servorum*. It should read *servus servorum*.

morganatic marriage The examples of morganatic marriages as given in the last five lines of the entry in *Browser's I* are frivolous and incorrect. I beg the reader to delete them.

mustard: cut the mustard Prof. Miller Williams of the University of Arkansas tells me that in local idiom *mustard* by association with *mustard greens* does for female pubic hair and that *he can't cut the mustard* = he cannot manage an erection sufficient to get through the pubic hair, i.e., he is no longer a joy-boy. As local idiom, I suspect this turns out to be a perversion of general idiom. He also tells me that in Arkansas one says *tight as Kelsey's hatband,* an obvious mongrelization of distinct idioms. (See *Kelsey* and *hat* in Vol. I. And how on earth did Kelsey Allen, the aged drama critic of NYC's *Women's Wear Daily* in the 1920's, get into Arkansas local idiom wearing a perverted hatband?)

obligation Line 2: *legare* should read *ligare,* to bind.

pontifex Line 3: *pontus* should read *pons.*

pot luck (See under *pot.*) Thomas H. Middleton has identified a changed sense in recent usage. He writes: "No one under forty knows what *pot luck* used to mean. These days, it means what I think we used to call 'community dinner'—those affairs to which all the ladies bring their individual specialties. Invite some youngster of thirty-nine to a *pot luck* dinner and I guarantee she'll ask what she should bring."

precocious Line 3: For *praecos* read *praecox.*

proves: the exception proves the rule Line 5: *regum* should read *regulam.*

roger *v.* To fuck. To bugger.
  Since I gave this sense of the word in Vol. I, attesting it in XVIII

from William Byrd's *Secret Diary,* many readers have written to resist or to pester the point. I offer three further attestations.

I forgot to check our old friend Francis Grose, *A Classical Dictionary of the Vulgar Tongue,* 1785. He gives the entry: *to Roger,* to copulate.

G. Legman, *The Limerick* (N.Y.: Bell Publishing Co., 1964), gives the following limerick, which he dates 1941:

> There once was a girl named McGoffin
> Who was diddled amazingly often.
> She was *rogered* by scores
> Who'd be turned down by whores
> And was finally screwed in her coffin.

Much more to my taste is an anecdote from C. M. Bowra's *Memories,* 1898–1939, pointed out to me by Norman L. Reynolds of Bridgeville, Delaware:

> Clark [A. C. Clark, professor of Latin at Oxford] was visiting a college farm, and the party witnessed a bull servicing a cow. Clark turned to Alan Blakeway and said, "Blakeway, *omne animal post coitum triste.* There was, Blakeway, a firm of solicitors in London called Mann, Rogers, and Greaves."

With this, I will assert that the sexual sense of *to roger* is conclusively attested, and that there remain better things to write letters about.

rounders   (See *baseball,* in this supplement.) I am afraid I left the impression that *baseball* and *rounders* were simply variant names of the same game in XVIII Britain. True, *baseball* was the more common name in central England, as *rounders* was in the south. Since no one has set down the rules of the XVIII game, a number of questions are left open, but as played in the United States well into XX (and still, though not commonly called *rounders* now), there are set and distinct rules for *rounders,* which is played with less than two full teams, though ideally with nine defensive players, one or more outfielders being eliminated (and sometimes one or two bases) if there are not enough players available.

The team at bat consists of two or three players, or more if they are available. When a batter is out, he goes into the defensive outfield, rotating through the various positions according to local option, then to the infield, then to the pitcher's mound, then to home plate as catcher. When the next batter is put out, the catcher becomes a batter. Minor details of this rotation may vary, but one rule remains constant: a fielder who catches a fly ball changes places with the batter. *Rounders,* it follows, refers not simply to rounding the bases, but—and primarily, I believe—to this rotation.

There is no score in rounders, but only the success of individual players in remaining at bat, and in the speed with which they are able to advance through the rotation. I am indebted to Frank A. Riddick, Jr., M.D., of New Orleans for reminding me of these things I had known and forgotten. He tells me he played rounders as late as 1940.

satire   Page 341. L. *satura* is the sing., not the plu. adj. form. *Lanx* is the nominative sing. *Satura lanx* should have been rendered "the heaped platter," not "the heaped platters."

say/cry Uncle!   (See under *uncle.*) In rendering the Roman boys' formula, I lapsed into Italian, and gave it as *patrue, mi patruissimo.* It should read *patrue, mi patruissime,* with all three words in the vocative. The nominative singular form is *patruus.*

shavetail   Add now obs. but colorful **shavetail cavalry** In the Civil War, the 2nd N.J. Cavalry Regiment, Colonel Joseph Karge commanding. Sent to Tennessee in 1863, the regiment was forced to cramp its mounts, nose to tail, into horse cars. So packed, underexercised, and inadequately fed on the long train trip, the horses took to nibbling the tails in front of their noses. I do not know how this situation could fail to start a horse riot in cramped quarters, nor is it easy to commend Colonel Karge on his organization of things, but once arrived in Tennessee, the 2nd rode into camp on notably bare-tailed mounts, to be dubbed on the spot the *Jersey Shavetails.* I hope Karge finally got his mounts properly fed and watered.

snake in the grass   (See under *snake.*) Line 7: The quotation from Virgil should read *latet anguis in herbis.*

stump   Add *stump-broken* Professor Miller Williams, a native Arkansan and now director of the University of Arkansas Press, but above all one of my favorite poets, tells me that in local idiom, *stump-broken* labels a cow that has been trained to back up to a stump on which a lusty and lonely farm boy can stand to sodomize her. Williams writes: "It is a fairly common expression in these parts."

And, by a simplest sense extension. A girl who will assume the position on command.

touch and go   Add: 3. *Pilot training.* The act of setting a plane down on a landing strip, rolling a short distance, and taking off again; a training exercise for practicing landings.

CULTURES OF THE WORLD

Argentina

Marshall Cavendish
Benchmark

New York

PICTURE CREDITS

Cover: © Imagebroker.net/Photolibrary
Corbis/Click Photos: 26, 27, 97, 112 • Getty Images: 37, 90, 107, 108 • Inmagine.com: 10, 11, 28, 30, 34, 50, 58, 62, 82, 85, 96, 99, 114, 115, 117, 124, 125, 127, 128 • Lonely Planet Images: 81, 83 • Marshall Cavendish International (Asia): 130, 131 • Northwind Picture Archives: 25 • Photolibrary: 1, 3, 5, 6, 7, 8, 9, 12, 15, 17, 18, 20, 22, 23, 32, 33, 38, 39, 40, 41, 42, 43, 45, 48, 49, 51, 52, 53, 55, 57, 60, 61, 63, 64, 65, 68, 70, 71, 72, 73, 75, 78, 84, 86, 89, 91, 92, 93, 94, 95, 98, 100, 101, 102, 104, 105, 106, 109, 110, 111, 116, 118, 122, 123, 126 • Topfoto: 24

PRECEDING PAGE
A stunning view of Lago Roca at Los Glaciares National Park in Patagonia.

Publisher (U.S.): Michelle Bisson
Writers: Ethel Caro Gofen, Leslie Jermyn, Yong Jui Lin
Editors: Deborah Grahame-Smith, Mindy Pang
Copyreader: Tara Tomczyk
Designers: Nancy Sabato, Benson Tan
Cover picture researcher: Tracey Engel
Picture researcher: Joshua Ang

Marshall Cavendish Benchmark
99 White Plains Road
Tarrytown, NY 10591
Website: www.marshallcavendish.us

© Times Media Private Limited 1990. First Edition.
© Times Media Private Limited 2002. Second Edition.
© Marshall Cavendish International (Asia) Private Limited 2012. Third Edition.
® "Cultures of the World" is a registered trademark of Times Publishing Limited.

Originated and designed by Times Media Private Limited
An imprint of Marshall Cavendish International (Asia) Private Limited
A member of Times Publishing Limited

Marshall Cavendish is a trademark of Times Publishing Limited.

Library of Congress Cataloging-in-Publication Data
Gofen, Ethel, 1937-
  Argentina / Ethel Caro Gofen, Leslie Jermyn, and Yong Jui Lin. — 3rd ed.
    p. cm. — (Cultures of the world)
  Includes bibliographical references and index.
  Summary: "Provides comprehensive information on the geography, history, wildlife, governmental structure, economy, cultural diversity, peoples, religion, and culture of Argentina"—Provided by publisher.
  ISBN 978-1-60870-797-3 (print) — ISBN 978-1-60870-805-5 (ebook)
 1. Argentina—Juvenile literature. I. Jermyn, Leslie. II. Yong, Jui Lin.
III. Title. IV. Series.

  F2808.2.G64 2012
  982—dc23   2011023035

Printed in Malaysia
7 6 5 4 3 2 1